Real Time

New technologies = new perceptions
Reality is a man-made process. Our images of the universe, of ourselves, are, in part, the models resulting from our perceptions of the technologies that we generate as products. Seventeenth-century clockworks inspired mechanistic metaphors ("the heart is a pump") just as twentieth-century developments in self-regulating engineering devices resulted in the cybernetic image ("the brain is a computer"). New metaphors constantly emerge and old ones fade. This is the "real" world, and it exists not in some fixed place or time but in the continuing process of describing the models that tells us who, what, and where we are.

Real Time is a sensing and monitoring device, presenting an interdisciplinary view of new models and metaphors of reality, as seen through our own perceptions and those of the individuals whose ideas and activities we include in this catalogue.

Among contributors to *Real Time* are:

Jay Bail	John Lilly	Alan Sondheim
Gerard Dombrowski	Michael Perkins	Gerd Stern
Abbie Hoffman	Edwin Schlossberg	Michele Stowell
Arie Kopelman	Bennett L. Shapiro	

Ordering books
As a convenience to our readers, books published in the U.S. may be ordered directly from *Real Time.* To order, send check or money order for the price of the books and an appropriate shipping charge to: *Real Time,* P.O. Box 488, Planetarium Station, New York, N.Y. 10024.

REAL TIME

John Brockman and Edward Rosenfeld

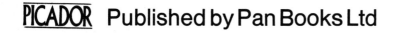 Published by Pan Books Ltd

First British edition published in Picador by Pan Books Ltd, Cavaye Place, London SW10 9PG
© John Brockman and Edward Rosenfeld 1973
ISBN 0 330 24255 5

Printed by Cripplegate Printing Co Ltd, London and Edenbridge

CONTENTS

Communications

Human Systems

Mind

Science and Technology

Trends

ACKNOWLEDGMENTS

Material from *The Hidden Dimension* by Edward T. Hall, © 1966 by Edward T. Hall, is used with permission of the publisher, The Bodley Head.

Material from *The Ghost Dance* by Weston La Barre, © 1970 by Weston La Barre, is used with permission of the publisher, George Allen & Unwin Ltd.

Material from *Asimov's Biographical Encyclopedia of Science and Technology* by Isaac Asimov, © 1972 by Isaac Asimov, is used with permission of the publisher, George Allen & Unwin Ltd.

Material from *Passion to Know* by Mitchell Wilson, © 1972 by Mitchell Wilson, is used with permission of the publisher, George Weidenfeld & Nicolson Ltd.

Material from *Self and Others* by R. D. Laing, © 1961 by R. D. Laing, is used with permission of the publisher, Tavistock Publishers.

Material from *The Case of the Midwife Toad* by Arthur Koestler, © 1972 by Arthur Koestler, is used with permission of the publisher, Hutchinson & Co. Ltd.

Material from *The Roots of Coincidence* by Arthur Koestler, © by Arthur Koestler, is used with permission of the publisher, Hutchinson & Co. Ltd.

Material from *Future Shock* by Alvin Toffler, © 1970 by Alvin Toffler, is used with permission of the publisher, The Bodley Head.

Material from *Biology and the Future of Man* by Philip Handler, © 1970 by Oxford University Press Inc., is used with permission of the publisher, Oxford University Press.

Material from *Innovations* by Dennis Gabor, © 1970 by Oxford University Press Inc., is used with permission of the publisher, Martin Secker & Warburg Ltd.

Material from *A Year from Monday* by John Cage, © 1963, 1964, 1965, 1966, 1967 by John Cage, is used with permission of the publisher, Calder & Boyars Ltd.

Material from *Changing Perspectives on Man* by Ben Rothblatt, © 1968 by Ben Rothblatt, is used with permission of the publisher, University of Chicago Press.

Material from *The Structure of Scientific Revolutions* by Thomas S. Kuhn, © 1962 by Thomas S. Kuhn, is used with permission of the publisher, University of Chicago Press.

Material from *Cosmic View* by Kees Boeke, © 1957 by Kees Boeke, is used with permission of the publisher, Faber & Faber Ltd.

Material from *Atlas of the Universe* by Patrick Moore, © by Mitchell Beazley Ltd., is used with permission of the publisher, Mitchell Beazley Ltd.

COMMUNICATIONS

1. The Bias of Communication

HAROLD A. INNIS. University of Toronto Press, Ely House, 37 Dover Street, London W1X 4AH; 1965; £1.30; 266 pp.

The seminal work of Marshall McLuhan's teacher and mentor. Innis used the analysis of information-communication systems to provide a unique perspective of history. Rather than a chronology of people, places, and events, his history is one of insightful pattern recognitions dealing mostly with the dominant communication technologies of an era. Although written prior to "the electronic age," this book is a beginning for anyone interested in the cybernetic image. McLuhan provides a valuable introduction. JB

The effect of the discovery of printing was evident in the savage religious wars of the sixteenth and seventeenth centuries. Application of power to communication industries hastened the consolidation of vernaculars, the rise of nationalism, revolution, and new outbreaks of savagery in the twentieth century. Previous to the invention of printing the importance of Latin and the drain on intellectual energies of a dual language had been evident in the problems of scholastic philosophy. After the invention of printing, interest in the classics in Italy and France and in the Bible in Protestant countries divided the Western world. Hebraism and Hellenism proved difficult to reconcile as did Aristotle and Plato. Roman law and the classics in Italy and the cathedrals in France checked the influence of the Bible and in France emphasized an interest in literature. In Germany the influence of the Bible strengthened the power of the state and favoured the growth of music and letters independent of political life. In England division between the crown, parliament, law, the universities, and trade checked the dominance of single interests, but favoured mediocrity except in finance and trade. In England monasticism contributed to the delay in education and printing which strengthened the position of the vernacular to the point that violence broke out in destruction of the monasteries in the sixteenth century, civil war in the seventeenth century, and the American Revolution in the eighteenth century.

The Industrial Revolution and mechanized knowledge have all but destroyed the scholar's influence. Force is no longer concerned with his protection and is actively engaged in schemes for his destruction. Enormous improvements in communication have made understanding more difficult. Even science, mathematics, and music as the last refuge of the Western mind have come under the spell of the mechanized vernacular. Commercialism has required the creation of new monopolies in language and new difficulties in understanding. Even the class struggle, the struggle between language groups, has been made a monopoly of language. When the Communist Manifesto proclaimed, "Workers of the world unite, you have nothing to lose but your chains!" in those words it forged new chains.

Paper production spread from Baghdad to the West. After the capture of Baghdad by the Mongols in 1258, manufacturing was confined to western centres. With its development in Italy in the latter part of the thirteenth century new processes were introduced and a much better quality of paper produced. The art of paper making spread to France in the fourteenth century. Since linen rags were the chief raw material and the large cities provided the chief market for paper, production was determined to an important extent by proximity to cities with access to supplies of water and power. The commercial revolution beginning about 1275 paralleled increasing production of paper. The activity of the commercial cities of Italy weakened the Byzantine Empire. Religious prejudice against a product of Arabic origin was broken down and the monopoly of knowledge held by the monasteries of rural districts was weakened by the growth of cities, cathedrals, and universities.

I have attempted to show elsewhere that in Western civilization a stable society is dependent on an appreciation of a proper balance between the concepts of space and time. We are concerned with control not only over vast areas of space but also over vast stretches of time. We must appraise civilization in relation to its territory and in relation to its duration. The character of the medium of communication tends to create a bias in civilization favourable to an over-emphasis on the time concept or on the space concept and only at rare intervals are the biases offset by the influence of another medium and stability achieved. Dependence on clay in Sumerian civilization was offset by dependence on stone in Babylon and a long period of relative stability followed in the reign of the Kassites. The power of the oral tradition in Greece which checked the bias of a written medium supported a brief period of cultural activity such as has never been equalled. Dependence on the papyrus roll and use of the alphabet in the bureaucracy of the Roman Empire was offset by dependence on parchment codex in the church and a balance was maintained in the Byzantine Empire until 1453.

2. Understanding Media: The Extensions of Man

MARSHALL McLUHAN. Routledge & Kegan Paul Ltd., 68–74 Carter Lane, London EC4V 5EL; (H) 1964; £3.50; or Sphere Books (Abacus) Ltd., 30–32 Gray's Inn Road, London WC1X 8JL; (P) 1973; £0.70; 364 pp.

McLuhan in this now famous book systematically and alogically unbuilds the reassuring world we inhabit, creating an existence in which everything happens at once, including the past and the future. One geared to looking for "meaning" and "value judgments" will have to look elsewhere as McLuhan leads the reader through the experiencing of both curiosity and awareness in his attempt to give the world a new definition of itself. JB

After three thousand years of explosion, by means of fragmentary and mechanical technologies, the Western world is imploding. During the mechanical ages we had extended our bodies in space. Today, after more than a century of electric technology, we have extended our central nervous system itself in a global embrace, abolishing both space and time as far as our planet is concerned. Rapidly, we approach the final phase of the extensions of man—the technological simulation of consciousness, when the creative process of knowing will be collectively and corporately extended to the whole of human society, much as we have already extended our senses and our nerves by the various media.

In the mechanical age now receding, many actions could be taken without too much concern. Slow movement insured that the reactions were delayed for considerable periods of time. Today the action and the reaction occur almost at the same time. We actually live mythically and integrally, as it were, but we continue to think in the old, fragmented space and time patterns of the pre-electric age.

Submerging natives with floods of concepts for which nothing has prepared them is the normal action of all of our technology. But with electric media Western man himself experiences exactly the same inundation as the remote native. We are no more prepared to encounter radio and TV in our literate milieu than the native of Ghana is able to cope with the literacy that takes him out of his collective tribal world and beaches him in individual isolation. We are as numb in our new electric world as the native involved in our literate and mechanical culture.

The new electric structuring and configuring of life more and more encounters the old lineal and fragmentary procedures and tools of analysis from the mechanical age. More and more we turn from the content of messages to study total effect. Kenneth Boulding put this matter in *The Image* by saying, "The meaning of a message is the change which it produces in the image." Concern with *effect* rather than *meaning* is a basic change of our electric time, for effect involves the total situation, and not a single level of information movement.

The message of the electric light is total change. It is pure information without any content to restrict its transforming and informing power.

If the student of media will but meditate on the power of this medium of electric light to transform every structure of time and space and work and society that it penetrates or contacts, he will have the key to the form of the power that is in all media to reshape any lives that they touch.

Except for light, all other media come in pairs, with one acting as the "content" of the other, obscuring the operation of both.

Clothing as an extension of our skin helps to store and to channel energy, so that if the Westerner needs less food, he may also demand more sex. Yet neither clothing nor sex can be understood as separate isolated factors, and many sociologists have noted that sex can become a compensation for crowded living. Privacy, like individualism, is unknown in tribal societies, a fact that Westerners need to keep in mind when estimating the attractions of our way of life to nonliterate peoples.

For most people, their own ego image seems to have been typographically conditioned, so that the electric age with its return to inclusive experience threatens their idea of self. These are the fragmented ones, for whom specialist toil renders the mere prospect of leisure or jobless security a nightmare. Electric simultaneity ends specialist learning and activity, and demands interrelation in depth, even of the personality.

3. The Universals of Language

Edited by JOSEPH H. GREENBERG. The M.I.T. Press, 126 Buckingham Palace Road, London SW1W 9SD; 1966; (H) £4.50; (P) £1.65; 337 pp.

About ten years ago a group of linguists, anthropologists, and psychologists gathered together to examine the possibility of studying generalizations about language. The result has been termed " a bloodless revolution. Quietly and without polemics, we have seen linguistics taking a giant step from being merely a method for describing language to being a full-fledged science of language. " Studies have shifted from differences in languages to formularization of similarities, of universals, and this book, edited by Joseph Greenberg, serves as an introductory reader in this field. JB

Underlying the endless and fascinating idiosyncrasies of the world's languages there are uniformities of universal scope. Amid infinite diversity, all languages are, as it were, cut from the same pattern. Some interlinguistic similarities and identities have been formalized, others not, but working linguists are in many cases aware of them in some sense and use them as guides in their analyses of new languages. This is an important but limited and incomplete use of these consistencies. Language universals are by their very nature summary statements about characteristics or tendencies shared by all human speakers. As such they constitute the most general laws of a science of linguistics (as contrasted with a method and a set of specific descriptive results). Further, since language is at once both an aspect of individual behavior and an aspect of human culture, its universals provide both the major point of contact with underlying psychological principles (psycholinguistics) and the major source of implications for human culture in general (ethnolinguistics).

These are characteristics possessed by all languages which are not merely definitional; that is, they are such that if a symbolic system did not possess them, we would still call it a language. Under this heading would be included not only such obvious universals as, for example, that all languages have vowels, but also those involving numerical limits, for example, that for all languages the number of phonemes is not fewer than 10 or more than 70, or that every language has at least two vowels. Also included are universally valid statements about the relative text or lexicon frequency of linguistic elements.

A language universal is a feature or property shared by all languages, or by all language. The assertion of a (putative) language universal is a generalization about language. "The only useful generalizations about language are inductive generalizations ". This admonition is clearly important, in the sense that we do not want to invent language universals, but to discover them. How to discover them is not so obvious. It would be fair to claim that the search is coterminous with the whole enterprise of linguistics in at least two ways. The first way in which this claim is true is heuristic: we can never be sure, in any sort of linguistic study, that it will not reveal something of importance for the search. The second way in which the claim is plausible, if not automatically true, appears when we entertain one of the various possible definitions of linguistics as a branch of science: that branch devoted to the discovery of the place of human language in the universe. This definition leaves the field vague to the extent that the problem of linguistics remains unsolved. Only if, as is highly improbable, the problem were completely answered should we know exactly what linguistics is—and at that same millennial moment there would cease to be any justification for the field. It is hard to discern any clear difference between "the search for language universals" and "the discovery of the place of human language in the universe." They seem rather to be, respectively, a new-fangled and old-fashioned way of describing the same thing.

One last thought: There is no reason to include only rules of dependency in a statement of language universals. It is just as interesting to point out factors which are independent. We will not be surprised to find that questions of phonemic inventory have no relation to the presence or absence of certain grammatical categories, say, that the presence of a voiced/voiceless distinction in stops is independent of the presence of a category of person in verbs. This is merely a trivial example of the general rule of the arbitrariness of the linguistic sign, that is, the independence of sound and sense. However, it might be of some interest to find that there is no relation between, say, the number of vowels and the number of consonants, either in the inventory, or in permissible sequences. This would, of course, be a peculiar use of the term *universal,* but such statements result from exactly the same procedures which yield statements about the other-than-chance cooccurrence of features.

The following lines of inquiry, it seems to me, might be profitable:

c. From the semiotic point of view, language is not a homogeneous mechanism. What are the semiotic submechanisms utilized in language? Are the several mechanisms analyzed by Wittgenstein as "language games" uniformly distributed throughout the languages of the world? What formal features of languages are correlated with their semiotic strata?

d. What are the effects of sign combination on the meanings of signs? In particular, how do the grammatical and phraseological limitations on the freedom of combination affect the functioning of linguistic signs?

e. Despite the basically arbitrary quality of semantic "mapping" displayed by languages, there are nevertheless remarkable parallelisms between both related and unrelated languages. How are these parallelisms to be formulated and quantified?

f. What generalizations can be made about any vocabulary as a structured set, imperfect as the structuring may be? Can any over-all structural characteristics of a particular vocabulary be formulated, and if so, can the distribution of such characteristics in the languages of the world be studied?

4. Language, Thought and Reality: Selected Writings of Benjamin Lee Whorf

Edited and with an introduction by JOHN B. CARROLL. The M.I.T. Press, 126 Buckingham Palace Road, London SW1W 9SD; 1956; (H) £3.75; (P) £1.40; 278 pp.

The Whorfian hypothesis deals with the relationship between language and thinking, and how language creates as well as describes the world. It is a linguistic relativity principle which maintains that all observers are not led by the same physical evidence to the same picture of the universe, unless their linguistic backgrounds are similar or can in some way be correlated. In other words, the cosmos is a creature of the language which describes it, and nature is not something created but something said.

Benjamin Lee Whorf, an engineer by training, spent his working career as a fire inspector-engineer for the Hartford Fire Insurance Company. His linguistic work, as well as his self-education in the area, was conducted in his spare time. JB

In the Hopi view, time disappears and space is altered, so that it is no longer the homogeneous and instantaneous timeless space of our supposed intuition or of classical Newtonian mechanics. At the same time, new concepts and abstractions flow into the picture, taking up the task of describing the universe without reference to such time or space—abstractions for which our language lacks adequate terms. These abstractions, by approximations of which we attempt to reconstruct for ourselves the metaphysics of the Hopi, will undoubtedly appear to us as psychological or even mystical in character. They are ideas which we are accustomed to consider as part and parcel either of so-called animistic or vitalistic beliefs, or of those transcendental unifications of experience and intuitions of things unseen that are felt by the consciousness of the mystic, or which are given out in mystical and (or) so-called occult systems of thought. These abstractions are definitely given either explicitly in words—psychological or metaphysical terms—in the Hopi language, or, even more, are implicit in the very structure and grammar of that language, as well as being observable in Hopi culture and behavior.

The possibilities open to thinking are the possibilities of recognizing relationships and the discovery of techniques of operating with relationships on the mental or intellectual plane, such as will in turn lead to ever wider and more penetratingly significant systems of relationships. These possibilities are inescapably bound up with systems of linguistic expression. The story of their evolution in man is the story of man's linguistic development—of the long evolution of thousands of very different systems of discerning, selecting, organizing, and operating with relationships.

Does the Hopi language show here a higher plane of thinking, a more rational analysis of situations, than our vaunted English? Of course it does. In this field and in various others, English compared to Hopi is like a bludgeon compared to a rapier.

Formulation of ideas is not an independent process, strictly rational in the old sense, but is part of a particular grammar, and differs, from slightly to greatly, between different grammars. We dissect nature along lines laid down by our native languages. The categories and types that we isolate from the world of phenomena we do not find there because they stare every observer in the face; on the contrary, the world is presented

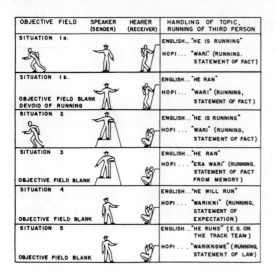

Figure 11. Contrast between a "temporal" language (English) and a "timeless" language (Hopi). What are to English differences of time are to Hopi differences in the kind of validity.

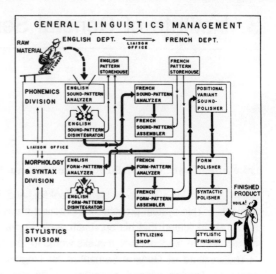

Figure 14. Flow sheet of improved process for learning French without tears. Guaranteed: no bottlenecks in production.

Figure 16. The English sentences "I push his head back" and "I drop it in water and it floats" are unlike. But in Shawnee the corresponding statements are closely similar, emphasizing the fact that analysis of nature and classification of events as like or in the same category (logic) are governed by grammar.

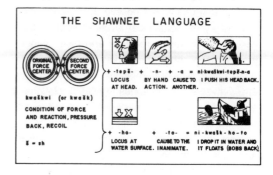

in a kaleidoscopic flux of impressions which has to be organized by our minds—and this means largely by the linguistic systems in our minds. We cut nature up, organize it into concepts, and ascribe significances as we do, largely because we are parties to an agreement to organize it in this way—an agreement that holds throughout our speech community and is codified in the patterns of our language. The agreement is, of course, an implicit and unstated one, BUT ITS TERMS ARE ABSOLUTELY OBLIGATORY; we cannot talk at all except by subscribing to the organization and classification of data which the agreement decrees.

What surprises most is to find that various grand generalizations of the Western world, such as time, velocity, and matter, are not essential to the construction of a consistent picture of the universe. The psychic experiences that we class under these headings are, of course, not destroyed; rather, categories derived from other kinds of experiences take over the rulership of the cosmology and seem to function just as well.

5. Institute of General Semantics

Lakeville, Conn. 06039; Bulletin, semi-annual, $4 per issue.

Alfred Korzybski, a Polish nobleman, soldier, and inventor, was the founder and originator of general semantics. This system provides a theoretical framework for the investigation of words as maps of reality. Korzybski indicated that his approach was "non-aristotelian" and the errors his philosophy attempts to correct are the tendencies to mistake words for the things they symbolize.

The Institute of General Semantics for Linguistic, Epistemologic, Scientific Research and Education seeks to develop general semantics as an interfield discipline. The Institute's *Bulletin,* in addition to publishing articles related to the treatment of general semantics, also publishes the texts of the annual Korzybski Memorial Lectures. Recent speakers in this series have included Henry Margenau, L. L. Whyte, Gregory Bateson, R. Buckminster Fuller, F. S. C. Northrop, Abraham Maslow, Alvin Weinberg, and Warren McCulloch. ER

1. In Einstein's Special and General Theories of Relativity, it is assumed that in a fundamental analysis temporal relations cannot be separated from spatial relations. I believe this cannot apply in a theory of hierarchical levels of spatial structure, in which spatial relations and their changes in course of time must play a primary role, quantitative temporal relations being secondary and derivable from changes in spatial relations. If so, a radical change is necessary, but fortunately one towards the immediacy of 3-D space, as against the abstract higher spaces of relativity and quantum theory.

2. Since 1890 many scientific theories and philosophical concepts, expressing a reaction from the extreme analytic-atomic ideas of the late XIXth Century, have stressed the importance of global properties and parameters, i.e. those associated with the totality of a system. The most important of these are: Gestalt Theory (psychology); Emergent Evolution, Organicism, and Integrative Levels (biology); Symmetry Theory (crystallography, quantum theory); cooperative processes (physics), field effects (embryology), and unitization (information theory). Lying behind these ideas and common to them all, lies one basic principle: *the quantitative laws which some systems obey are best expressed, not in localizable atomic or field parameters associated with*

particles or points, but in global system variables (such as deformations from symmetry).

———————

A theory of organic structural levels treats a highly coordinated sequence of types of ordering. An organism is a system which, when not pathological, tends to promote characteristic orderings at several correlated levels. Organic ordering has internal and adaptive value for organisms. This means that the separation of fact and value in recent academic philosophy vanishes in a hierarchical theory of organisms. Organic value is present in the objective representation of organic facts. Value plays an inescapable part in any theory of organism, and organic coordination necessarily possesses value for reflective organisms. Thereby the supposed 'objective' in the sense of neutral 'science of man' does not exist. The movement towards this supposed science transforms science into something more than science.

———————

I expect that by 1979 a major advance in fundamental physical theory, in the *quantum theory of electromagnetism,* will have been made which:

(i) Explicitly treats the relations of *hierarchically paired levels of structure* in physical theory.

(ii) Identifies one such pair as follows:

(a) A spatially more extended level covering *electrons and photons*.

(b) A more stably localized level covering *protons*.

(iii) Uses 3-dimensional *geometrical relations* as primary in the theory of hierarchical systems, and treats temporal relations as secondary.

Verbal and Nonverbal "Thinking."—It will be noticed that I have put quotation marks around the word "thinking." This term usually implies a more "cortical" activity, indicating verbally some sort of a split between the functioning of the cortical and thalamic *regions* of our nervous system where there is actually no such split, but an interaction and integration on different levels.

"Is all thinking verbal?" Some say "yes," some say "no." If, however, we limit ourselves to verbal "thinking," we are caught in our old linguistic ruts of bygone generations, socio-culturally trained and neurologically canalized in the inherited forms of representation.

THE CIRCULARITY OF HUMAN KNOWLEDGE

The electronic or electro-colloidal processes are operating on submicroscopic levels. From the indefinitely many characteristics of these processes, our nervous system abstracts and integrates a comparatively few, which we may call the gross or macroscopic levels, or the "objective" levels, all of them not verbal. The microscopic levels must be considered as instrumentally aided "sense data" and I will not deal with them here. Then, abstracting further, first on the labeling or descriptive levels, we pass to the inferential levels, and we can try to convey to the other fellow our "feeling about feeling," "thinking about thinking," etc., which actually happen on the silent levels. Finally, we come to the point where we need to speak about speaking.

Scientifically it is known that the submicroscopic levels are not "perceptible" or "perceptual." We do not and cannot "perceive" the "electron," but we observe actually the results of the eventual "electronic processes." That is, we observe the "effects" and assume the "causes." In other words, as explained before, our submicroscopic knowledge is hypothetical in character. The world behaves *as if* its mechanisms were such as our highest abstractions lead us to believe, and we will continue to invent theories *with their appropriate terminologies* to account for the intrinsic mechanisms of the world we live in, ourselves included. We read into nature our own latest highest abstractions, thus completing the inherent circularity of human knowledge, without which our understanding of nature is impossible.

6. Aspects of the Theory of Syntax

NOAM CHOMSKY. The M.I.T. Press, 126 Buckingham Palace Road, London SW1W 9SD; (H) 1965; £3.50; (P) 1969; £1.40; 251 pp.

Are the basic elements of life to be found in subatomic, microscopic phenomena? Or are "they" perhaps really creatures of syntax—"minimally syntactically functioning units (formatives)"? Chomsky studies generative grammars in an attempt to determine from the data of performance the underlying system of rules that have been mastered by the speaker-hearer and that are put to use in actual performance. His "linguistic theory is mentalistic, since it is concerned with discovering a mental activity underlying actual behavior." JB

Linguistic theory is concerned primarily with an ideal speaker-listener, in a completely homogeneous speech-community, who knows its language perfectly and is unaffected by such grammatically irrelevant conditions as memory limitations, distractions, shifts of attention and interest, and errors (random or characteristic) in applying his knowledge of the language in actual performance. This seems to me to have been the position of the founders of modern general linguistics, and no cogent reason for modifying it has been offered. To study actual linguistic performance, we must consider the interaction of a variety of factors, of which the underlying competence of the speaker-hearer is only one. In this respect, study of language is no different from empirical investigation of other complex phenomena.

A grammar of a language purports to be a description of the ideal speaker-hearer's intrinsic competence. If the grammar is furthermore, perfectly explicit—in other words, if it does not rely on the intelligence of the understanding reader but rather provides an explicit analysis of his contribution—we may (somewhat redundantly) call it a *generative grammar.*

Modern linguistics, however, has not explicitly recognized the necessity for supplementing a "particular grammer" of a language by a universal grammar if it is to achieve descriptive adequacy. It has, in fact, characteristically rejected the study of universal grammar as misguided; and, as noted before, it has not attempted to deal with the creative aspect of language use. It thus suggests no way to overcome the fundamental descriptive inadequacy of structuralist grammars.

In brief, it is clear that no present-day theory of language can hope to attain explanatory adequacy beyond very restricted domains. In other words, we are very far from being able to present a system of formal and substantive linguistic universals that will be sufficiently rich and detailed to account for the facts of language learning. To advance linguistic theory in the direction of explanatory adequacy, we can attempt to refine the evaluation measure for grammars or to tighten the formal constraints on grammars so that it becomes more difficult to find a highly valued hypothesis compatible with primary linguistic data. There can be no doubt that present theories of grammar require modification in both of these ways. the latter, in general, being the more promising. Thus the most crucial problem for linguistic theory seems to be to abstract statements and generalizations from particular descriptively adequate grammars and, wherever possible, to attribute them to the general theory of linguistic structure, thus enriching this theory and imposing more structure on the schema for grammatical description. Whenever this is done, an assertion about a particular language is replaced by a corresponding assertion, from which the first follows, about language in general. If this formulation of a deeper hypothesis is incorrect, this fact should become evident when its effect on the description of other aspects of the language or the description of other languages is ascertained. In short, I am making the obvious comment that, wherever possible, general assumptions about the nature of language should be formulated from which particular features of the grammars of individual languages can be deduced. In this way, linguistic theory may move toward explanatory adequacy and contribute to the study of human mental processes and intellectual capacity—more specifically, to the determination of the abilities that make language learning possible under the empirically given limitations of time and data.

7. Language and Mind (Enlarged Edition)

NOAM CHOMSKY. Harcourt Brace Jovanovich, Ltd., 24–28 Oval Road, London NW1; 1972; (H) £2.75; (P) £2.05; 194 pp.

This book is an excellent introduction to Chomsky's thinking. Six chapters fall into two groups: the first three constitute the monograph *Language and Mind,* published in 1968, and the last three were presentations prepared for students and teachers (ch. 4), psycholinguists (ch. 5), and professional philosophers (ch. 6). Chomsky presents his theories of "deep structure" and "generative grammar," as well as continuing his attack on behavioral scientists, pointing out that investigation of direct relations between experience and action, between stimuli and responses, will be vain pursuit. "In all but the most elementary cases, what a person does depends in large measure on what he knows, believes, and anticipates." Thus studies of behavior must relate to the formulation of knowledge and systems of belief: language. JB

The technological advances of the 1940's simply reinforced the general euphoria. Computers were on the horizon, and their imminent availability reinforced the belief that it would suffice to gain a theoretical understanding of only the simplest and most superficially obvious of phenomena—everything else would merely prove to be "more of the same," an apparent complexity that would be disentangled by the electronic marvels. The sound spectrograph, developed during the war, offered similar promise for the physical analysis of speech sounds. The interdisciplinary conferences on speech analysis of the early 1950's make interesting reading today. There were few so benighted as to question the possibility, in fact the immediacy, of a final solution to the problem of converting speech into writing by available engineering technique. And just a few years later, it was jubilantly discovered that machine translation and automatic abstracting were also just around the corner. For those who sought a more mathematical formulation of the basic processes, there was the newly developed mathematical theory of communication, which, it was widely believed in the early 1950's, had provided a fundamental concept—the concept of "information"—that would unify the social and behavioral sciences and permit the development of a solid and satisfactory mathematical theory of human behavior on a probabilistic base.

The person who has acquired knowledge of a language has internalized a system of rules that relate sound and meaning in a particular way. The linguist constructing a grammar of a language is in effect proposing a hypothesis concerning this internalized system. The linguist's hypothesis, if presented with sufficient explicitness and precision, will have certain empirical consequences with regard to the form of utterances and their interpretations by the native speaker.

The principles that determine the form of grammar and that select a grammar of the appropriate form on the basis of certain data constitute a subject that might, following a traditional usage, be termed "universal grammar." The study of universal grammar, so understood, is a study of the nature of human intellectual capacities. It tries to formulate the necessary and sufficient conditions that a system must meet to qualify as a potential human language, conditions that are not accidentally true of the existing human languages, but that are rather rooted in the human "language capacity," and thus constitute the innate organization that determines what counts as linguistic experience and what knowledge of language arises on the basis of this experience. Universal grammar, then, constitutes an explanatory theory of a much deeper sort than particular grammar, although the particular grammar of a language can also be regarded as an explanatory theory.

It is quite natural to expect that a concern for language will remain central to the study of human nature, as it has been in the past. Anyone concerned with the study of human nature and human capacities must somehow come to grips with the fact that all normal humans acquire language, whereas acquisition of even its barest rudiments is quite beyond the capacities of an otherwise intelligent ape—a fact that was emphasized, quite correctly, in Cartesian philosophy. It is widely thought that the extensive modern studies of animal communication challenge this classical view; and it is almost universally taken for granted that there exists a problem of explaining the "evolution" of human language from systems of animal communication. However, a careful look at recent studies of animal communication seems to me to provide little support for these assumptions. Rather, these studies simply bring out even more clearly the extent to which human language appears to be a unique phenomenon, without significant analogue in the animal world.

It is an interesting question whether the functioning and evolution of human mentality can be accommodated within the framework of physical explanation, as presently conceived, or whether there are new principles, now unknown, that must be invoked, perhaps principles that emerge only at higher levels of organization than can now be submitted to physical investigation. We can, however, be fairly sure that there will be a physical explanation for the phenomena in question, if they can be explained at all, for an uninteresting terminological reason, namely that the concept of "physical explanation" will no doubt be extended to incorporate whatever is discovered in this domain, exactly as it was extended to accommodate gravitational and electromagnetic force, massless particles, and numerous other entities and processes that would have offended the common sense of earlier generations.

To summarize: The generative grammar of a language specifies an infinite set of structural descriptions, each of which contains a deep structure, a surface structure, a phonetic representation, a semantic representation, and other formal structures. The rules relating deep and surface structure—the so-called "grammatical transformations"—have been investigated in some detail, and are fairly well understood. The rules that relate surface structure and phonetic representation are also reasonably well understood (though I do not want to imply that the matter is beyond dispute; far from it). It seems that both deep and surface structure enter into the determination of meaning. Deep structure provides the grammatical relations of predication, modification, and so on, that enter into the determination of meaning. On the other hand, it appears that matters of focus and presupposition, topic and comment, the scope of logical elements, and pronominal reference are determined, in part at least, by surface structure. The rules that relate syntactic structures to representations of meaning are not at all well understood. In fact, the notion "representation of meaning" or "semantic representation" is itself highly controversial. It is not clear at all that it is possible to distinguish sharply between the contribution of grammar to the determination of meaning, and the contribution of so-called "pragmatic considerations," questions of fact and belief and context of utterance. It is perhaps worth mentioning that rather similar questions can be raised about the notion "phonetic representation." Although the latter is one of the best established and least controversial notions of linguistic theory, we can, nevertheless, raise the question whether or not it is a legitimate abstraction, whether a deeper understanding of the use of language might not show that factors that go beyond grammatical structure enter into the determination of perceptual representations and physical form in an inextricable fashion, and cannot be separated, without distortion, from the formal rules that interpret surface structure as phonetic form.

8. Symbol Sourcebook: An Authoritative Guide to International Graphic Symbols

HENRY DREYFUSS. McGraw-Hill Book Company (UK) Ltd., McGraw-Hill House, Shoppenhangers Road, Maidenhead SL6 2QL; 1972; £13.70; 292 pp.

The late Henry Dreyfuss was a leading industrial designer—a creator of product, environmental, and packaging designs. He also created something much more important: this dictionary of the contemporary language of graphic symbols and signs. JB

REVIEW BY GERD STERN. A product and part of a process, the *Symbol Sourcebook* is an ongoing assemblage of a data bank under the "authoritative guidance" of Henry Dreyfuss, best known as the principal pioneer of American industrial design. The product is a first interconnect of international usage in multiple fields and disciplines. The process of establishing a resource center for such work will hopefully be supported by the many national and international organizations whose endorsements and praises appear in and on this book. (One wonders whether the project will indeed continue, since as I write this review a newspaper head alleges the self-destruct of Mr. and Mrs. Dreyfuss.)

The *Symbol Sourcebook* contents are cross-referenced in English, Arabic, Chinese, Danish, Dutch, Finnish, French, German, Hebrew, Hindi, Italian, Japanese, Norwegian, Portugese, Russian, Spanish, Swahili, and Swedish. The categories of discipline listed and graphically exploded in consistently excellent line drawings are accompanied by a Bucky Fuller foreword, essays on C. K. Bliss's Semantography and Neurath's Isotypes and other explanatory and ancillary materials. The work is a necessary reference tool.

No book related to symbols would be complete without a bow to C. K. Bliss. In "Semantography," a word conceived by his fertile imagination, he has developed a complete system which crosses all language barriers. The lines and curves of his symbols, reminiscent of actual objects and actions, are translatable into all tongues. Mr. Bliss is an intrepid pioneer; his words and ideas are proudly included in this book. HD

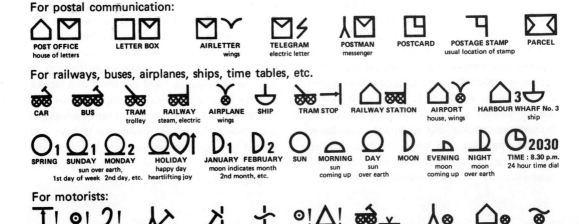

There now looms into silent recognition a new exclusively visible language, that of roadside and street intersection signs, airport signs, and supermarket signs, etc., which accommodate the worldaround motorist, air traveller and telephoner. The travellers' high speed needs of swiftly integrating solutions to traffic problem solving has induced the invention of a wide variety of new symbolic language forms. At the same time TV animation also tends to return to generalized conceptual modeling.

The fundamentally visual language which Ezra Pound esteemed in early peoples' ideography now trends to bringing communication tools back into universal use and comprehension.

BIOLOGY

MALE (OR)	FEMALE (OR)	NEUTER	NEUTER HERMAPHRODITE
SEX UNKNOWN or UNSPECIFIED	DEATH, MALE	MATING	CONSANGUINEOUS MATING	MATING, MALE PROGENY	DIZYGOTIC TWINS, MALE
MONOZYGOTIC TWINS, MALE	PROPOSITUS (Proband)	MALE with TRAIT UNDER STUDY	AUTOSOMAL INHERITANCE	SEX-LINKED INHERITANCE	ABORTION of UNKNOWN SEX
P — PARENTAL	F_1 — FIRST GENERATION OFFSPRING	X — MATED WITH	Papilio philenor / Papilio asterias — HYBRID	‖ — PRIMARY HOMONYM	# — SECONDARY HOMONYM
= IDENTICAL WITH	+ LONGER THAN	− SHORTER THAN	HEAD	THORAX	ABDOMEN
EGG	LARVA	PUPA	ADULT (Imago)	INCORRECT CITATION	DOUBTFUL CITATION
§ TYPICAL SPECIMEN	! SPECIMEN VERIFIED		

▲ A number indicating quantity may be placed within the figure.
● Female indicated when circle (○) is used instead of square (□).
★ Heterozygous recessive.
■ Number in subscript indicates generation. **Example:** F_2 would be second generation.

In the beginning, man created the symbol—and pictures on cave walls were sufficient for a time to express his ideas about the relatively simple processes of procuring food and shelter. It was when man began to feel a need to express abstractions—differences in degree, nuances in definition, philosophical concepts—that symbols proved inflexible and inadequate. Then languages began to proliferate. It now appears that in some increasingly important areas we need an adjunct to our sophisticated speech and need to work our way back to the simple universality of an under-

RELIGION

BUDDHISM Buddha	**BUDDHISM** Buddha's Footprint	**BUDDHISM** Lotus
BUDDHISM Wheel of Law	**BUDDHISM, Tibetan** The Path of Universality	**BUDDHISM, Zen** Eternal State of Buddha
CHRISTIANITY Latin Cross	**CHRISTIANITY** Celtic Cross	**CHRISTIANITY** Orthodox Cross
CHRISTIANITY Christ Victorious	**CHRISTIANITY** Chi Rho	**CHRISTIANITY** Triquetra
CHRISTIANITY The Fish	**CHRISTIANITY** Agnus Dei	**CHRISTIANITY** Descending Dove; Holy Spirit
CHRISTIANITY Anchor; St. Clement	**CHRISTIANITY** Ten Commandments	**CHRISTIANITY,** **Church of Christ, Scientist** Cross and Crown
CONFUCIANISM Confucius	**CONFUCIANISM** Conjugal Bliss	**HINDUISM** Mandala

▲ The design of the Cross and Crown seal is a trademark of the Trustees under the Will of Mary Baker G. Eddy, registered in the United States and other countries. Used by permission.

standable, albeit limited, symbology. Symbols have multiplied to an alarming degree along much the same lines of divergence as languages. Today it is this very diversity and multiplicity of symbols in our international life that is a matter of such immediate concern. As the world grows steadily smaller, the need for easy communication becomes increasingly acute, and man has apparently come full circle—from prehistoric symbols, to sophisticated verbal communication, and now back to symbols, to help us all live together in today's Tower of Babel.

HINDUISM Shiva	**HINDUISM** Vishnu	**HINDUISM** Aum; Brahman-Atman
ISLAM Star and Crescent	**ISLAM** Holy Qur-an	**JAINISM** Brush and Bowl
JUDAISM Star of David	**JUDAISM** Menorah	**JUDAISM** Ten Commandments
SHINTO Torii	**SIKHISM** Kirpan	**TAOISM** Water; Life-giving Source
TAOISM Yin-Yang	**ZOROASTRIANISM** Sacred Fire	

PALM SUNDAY

In Jerusalem, where the palm tree flourishes, Christ's triumphal entry was celebrated by the waving of palm fronds. Hence the Western world's traditional symbol for the Sunday before Easter. But in Russia where palms are scarce, the substitute symbol is *pussy-willow*!

9. Nonverbal Communication: Notes on the Visual Perception of Human Relations

JURGEN RUESCH and WELDON KEES. University of California Press, 2–4 Brook Street, London W1Y 1AA; 1972; £2.25; 205 pp.

Before people spoke with one another they communicated. It is probable that it was easier to describe a bird by nonverbal imitation (using human arms to mimic flapping wings) when the word for " bird " had not yet been devised. *Nonverbal Communication* provides new vantage points for understanding the many varieties of nonverbal language.

The authors provide three basic forms of nonverbal communication: sign language, action language, and object language. How these " other " languages operate in the everyday world are described through a series of pictures and essays. The emphasis is on seeing what is visible. A cartography of nonverbal effects is provided. ER

When communicating with each other, people not only exchange messages containing information that refers to outside events, but they also exchange messages referring to the communication process itself. These *metacommunicative messages* include:

> The specific instructions given by a sender about the way messages ought to be interpreted and the respective interpretations made by the receiver
>
> Implicit instructions contained in what is commonly referred to as role
>
> Institutionalized instructions, either explicit or implicit, that are inherent in the structure of social situations and the rules governing the flow of messages

When a person has expressed an idea in words to others, a reaction is necessarily expected. And this reaction contributes to clarify, extend, or alter the original idea. *Feedback, therefore,* refers to the process of correction through incorporation of information about effects achieved. When a person perceives the results produced by his own actions, the information so derived will influence subsequent actions. Feedback of information thus becomes a steering device upon which learning and the correction of errors and misunderstandings are based.

It should be added that the photographic assessment of visual cues is not aimed at elucidating the psychophysiological problems of perception. We have tried to illustrate how such factors as redundancy in language, the familiarity or strangeness of stimuli, the relationship of things to words, the placement of an object within a framework, the relationship of the state of an organism to a perceived cue, and many other complexly determined total conditions affect communication. In daily life both object and action codifications are not commonly or clearly regarded as a means of communication, and it is precisely for this reason that they are of a particular effectiveness. Occasionally their use makes possible a disguise of intention; at other times, those who use actions and material objects as a medium of communication are, paradoxically, often unaware that they are revealing themselves. Be that as it may, to logicians, linguists, and philosophers our approach may seem insufficiently academic. Even such an objection does not contradict the principal argument we wish to advance: that *in practice, nonverbal communication must necessarily be dealt with analogically, and this without delay.* Although verbal communication permits a long interval between statements, certain action sequences and gestures necessitate an immediate reply. Then the reaction must be quick and reflexlike, with no time to ponder or to talk. And whenever such a situation occurs, the slower and exhaustive verbal codifications are out of the question for both the actual reply and the scientific method of study.

THE IDENTIFICATION OF SOCIAL SITUATIONS

SERVICE STATION
Cues derived from background,
equipment, costume, and posture

PLAY SITUATION
Cues derived from prop, age, and activity

CONVERSATIONAL SITUATION
Cues derived from grouping
and gestures

FAMILY SITUATION
Cues derived from age, sex, grouping,
and the ways in which the participants
face each other

10. Kinesics and Context: Essays on Body Motion Communication

RAY L. BIRDWHISTELL. Allen Lane, 74 Grosvenor Street, London W1X 0AS; 1971; £3.75; 338 pp.

This is a study of the author's work, which he calls "kinesics"—a systematic method of anthropological investigation based on the theory "that human communication needs and uses all the senses, that the information conveyed by human gestures and movements is coded and patterned differently in various cultures, and that these codes can be discovered by skilled scrutiny of particular movements within a social context." Birdwhistell teaches at the University of Pennsylvania. JB

REVIEW BY GERD STERN. This is a collection of previously published and unpublished essays, "based on the conviction that body motion is a learned form of communication." The author defines the book as an introduction to the investigation of human communication by linguistic and kinesic techniques. He states that the work is neither a text nor a manual. However, the structure is an academic compendium of data in sequenced parts: Learning to Be a Human Body, Isolating Behavior, Approaching Behavior, Collecting Data, Observing, Filming, Interviewing, and Research on an Interview. A series of appendixes are devoted to kinesic orthography, notation and recording.

Among the basic assumptions of kinesics are that "no body movement or expression is without meaning in the context in which it appears," and that "like other aspects of human behavior, body posture, movement and facial expression are patterned and, thus, subject to systematic analysis." Exhaustive analysis of multi-channel behavior of the body employs media techniques: film and video, slow-motion and motion-analysis projection. The description of such work and observations has caught the interest of artists, designers and architects, who find in Birdwhistell's Kinesics and Edward T. Hall's Proxemics, analyses and measurements of processes which lend themselves to the evaluation and configuration of environment.

Who knows how any human internalizes the conventional understandings of his social group to the extent that his social behavior becomes by and large predictable to other members of his group? Even the sketchiest survey of human societies reveals that he does this. There is little solace in a so-called "learning theory," although one is impressed with the brilliance of the learning experimentalist who can create a training situation in which human beings can be persuaded to deal with new information in a manner analogous to that apparently employed by white rats or Grey Walter's machines. The fact remains that infants from every society in the world can and *do* internalize the communicational system of that society in approximately the same amount of time, so that the "normal" 6-year-old is able to move smoothly within the communication system of his society. There is no need to become involved in arguments for gestalt versus associational or any other model of learning. Years of carefully ordered observation and analysis of children in the learning situation are necessary before the mechanisms of this incorporation can be known, and the traditional learning experiment apparatus does seem inapplicable for this study. But one thing is clear. We cannot study the social behavior of a fish by taking him out of water. The child is a child in his world—the pieces he displays in a laboratory represent a very small and, perhaps, unrepresentative sample of his repertoire.

Early in my research on human body motion, influenced by Darwin's *Expression of the Emotions in Man and Animals,* and by my own preoccupation with human universals, I attempted to study the human "smile." Without recognizing my own preconceptions, I had been attracted to a simplistic theory which saw "verbal" communication as subject to (and responsible for) human diversification while "nonverbal" communication provided a primitive and underlying base for (and was the resultant of) human unity. Smiling, it seemed to me, provided the perfect example of a behavior bit which in every culture expressed pleasure (in the jargon which I was using then, "positive response") on the part of the actor. Almost as soon as I started to study "smiling" I found myself in a mass of contradictions. From the outset, the *signal* value of the smile proved debatable. Even the most preliminary procedures provided data which were difficult to rationalize. For example, not only did I find that a number of my subjects "smiled" when they were subjected to what seemed to be a positive environment, but some "smiled" in an aversive one. My psychiatric friends provided me with a variety of psychological explanations for this apparent contradiction, but I was determined to develop social data without recourse to such explanations. Yet, inevitably, these ideas shaped my early research.

It is well to remember that physiology as we know it is less than a century old. The discovery of electricity led to the development of information about neural processes; the emergence of modern biochemistry laid the groundwork for endocrinology; clinical and, particularly, military medicine established a basis for the comprehension of the circulatory system. However, until the living system as a whole was examined, modern physiology with its complex considerations of homeostasis, balance and organization of its subsystems, could not be conceived.

As long as the investigation of communication was limited to the dissection of the cadaver of speech, writing—by anatomists who used imperfectly understood Latin rules of grammar to describe its parts—and relied on introspectively derived dictionaries to determine its meanings, the communication process could not be detected, much less understood. This operation, like the researches, psychological or sociological, that depend on its products, can do no more than prescriptive or deceptively elaborate but clearly inconclusive correlation studies.

This is not a book about telecommunication. However, insofar as telecommunicative devices are necessary for either kinesic or linguistic teaching and research and thus for education about communication research, it seems advisable to stress the instrumentation problem a bit further. A movie film or a tape ties together a string of behavior—and can include in its record more people and behavior than can other telecommunicative devices: still pictures, blackboards, or books—or, by the way—all of the conventions of lecture and recitation. At the same time, in a sense, in its record of the unidirectional stream, the movie and television screens give a more primitive record. To the extent that the stream of behavior which we apprehend seems "realistic" it lacks the explicit warning about selection more manifest in other devices. This leaves us defenseless against our conventional habits of observation which seem so natural because they are customary.

Not only does the movie and television screen reinforce, by the very velocity of its image and sound presentation, our preconception of past, present, and future in a single line, but only the most sophisticated are aware of the coercion of the technology which prepares the record. It is not difficult for the thoughtful viewer or producer to be aware of the exigencies of conscious censorship in the preparation of a script. It is extraordinarily difficult to be constantly alert to the extent of control exerted by the focus and the selection of the cameraman and his recording team. Close-ups feel right to experienced viewers, the shift of camera from speaker to auditor, or from speaker to speaker seems natural, too. They influence all of us trained by Western and, particularly, American dramaturgical conventions which see communication, the interpersonal situation, and interaction itself, as action-reaction sequences.

We must recognize the inherent difficulties in body motion research. How are we to identify the "whats" of body motion? How do we isolate, differentiate, and measure a body motion? What are the initiation and end points of a particular motion or motion sequence? Until we can find devices whereby we can isolate units for quantification, it is evident that we are going to have great difficulty in determining particles of motion which serve as symbols and have meaning. I believe that this is not an impossible limitation. However, research in this area will be exceedingly expensive. A sound camera, observation laboratory, and specially designed electromechanical recording devices will probably be necessary for any definitive research in the "grammar" or "syntax" of body motion.

11. Relations in Public

ERVING GOFFMAN. Allen Lane, 74 Grosvenor Street, London W1X 0AS; (H) 1971; £3.50; or Penguin Books Ltd., Harmondsworth, Middx; (P) 1972; £0.60; 396 pp.

Communication as assessment. Goffman creates gamelike behavioral models isolated from other communication forms to render visible the human interaction on a social/public scale. JB

REVIEW BY GERD STERN. Despite the jacket lauds of Goffman as a precise and perceptive "people watcher," this is not a voyeuristic volume. The acuteness of the observations and examples is grammatical rather than anecdotal. This grammar is that of public order as seen in social relationships and public life (that is, life in public).

Relations is made up of six chapters and an appendix, each unit a paper unto itself, yielding to a common definition of terms and sights. The first chapter deals with individuals as vehicular units—describing routing practices, scanning range, and other such traffic acts—and as participation units—describing singles and together units termed "withs" in their daily rounds. "The Territories of Self" (second chapter) concerns claims to preserve made visible by markers of various kinds and violations in offense of possessions including territorial intrusions and exposures. Interpersonal rituals such as greetings are covered in "Supportive Interchanges," and "Remedial Interchanges" considers norms that regulate public life, notions of offense and rule-breaking, and the nature of the ritual moves termed remedial.

Relationships are described as "anonymous" or "anchored" and the objects, acts and expressions evidential of these relationships are identified as ritual idiom in "Tie-Signs." The sixth chapter, "Normal Appearances," takes natural, nothing-out-of-the-ordinary, routine experiences as "normal" and counterpoises to these—"alarm" and the *Umwelt*—that sphere or surround of potential alarm. Vulnerability in public life (space), exposure, acting natural, and other constraints practiced in maintaining normal appearances are delineated. In his appendix, "The Insanity of Place," Goffman attempts to "sketch some of the meanings of mental symptoms for the organizations in which they occur, with special reference to the family." He deals with "illness," with the collusive conspiracies involving "patient," "doctor," and "family," and with forms of social control, personal, informal and formal. In the end the "troublemaker" turns out to belong to a category of people "who do not keep their place."

Goffman's subtitle identifies these incisive observings and analyses as "Microstudies of the Public Order." They are highly technical and responsible modelings of familiar social interactions.

Concepts are devised on the run in order to get on with setting things up so that trials can be performed and the effects of controlled variation of some kind or other measured, the science of which is assured by the use of lab coats and government money. The work begins with the sentence, "We hypothesize that...," goes on from there to a full discussion of the biases and limits of the proposed design, reasons why these aren't nullifying, and culminates in an appreciable number of satisfyingly significant correlations tending to confirm some of the hypotheses: as though the uncovering of pattern in social life were that simple. A sort of sympathetic magic seems to be involved, the assumption being that if you go through the motions attributable to science then science will result. But it hasn't. (Five years after publication, many of these efforts remind one of the experiments children perform with Gilbert sets: "Follow instructions and you can be a real chemist, just like the picture on the box.") Fields of naturalistic study have not been uncovered through these methods. Concepts have not emerged that reorder our view of social activity. Frameworks have not been established into which a continuously larger number of facts can be placed. Understanding of ordinary behavior has not accumulated; distance has. /

What is needed now is description. Take, for example, techniques that pedestrians employ in order to avoid bumping into one another. These seem of little significance. However, there are an appreciable number of such devices; they are *constantly* in use and they cast a pattern on street behavior. Street traffic would be a shambles without them. Yet until very recently no student anywhere gave them a thought, most being involved in studies not subject to modest, naturalistic observation.

A vehicular unit is a shell of some kind controlled (usually from within) by a human pilot or navigator. A traffic code is a set of rules whose maintenance allows vehicular units independent use of a set of thoroughfares for the purpose of moving from one point to another. The arrangement is that collision and mutual obstruction are systematically avoided by means of certain self-accepted restrictions on movement. When adhered to, a traffic code provides a safe passage pattern.

At the center of social organization is the concept of claims, and around this center, properly, the student must consider the vicissitudes of maintaining them.

To speak closely of these matters, a set of related terms is needed. There is the "good," the desired object or state that is in question; the "claim," namely, entitlement to possess, control, use, or dispose of the good; the "claimant," that is, the party on whose behalf the claim is made; the "impediment," meaning here the act, substance, means, or agency through which the claim is threatened; the "author" (or "counter-claimant"), namely, the party—when there is one—on whose behalf the threat to claims is intended; and finally, the "agents," these being the individuals who act for and represent the claimant and counter-claimant in these matters involving claims.

When we restrict our attention to activity that can only occur during face-to-face interaction, the claimant tends to be an individual (or a small set of individuals) and to function as his own agent. The same can be said of the counter-claimant, but in addition the impediment that occurs in his name is likely to involve his own activity or body. Therefore, conventional terms such as "victim" and "offender" will often be adequate. And one type of claim becomes crucial: it is a claim exerted in regard to "territory." This concept from ethology seems apt, because the claim is not so much to a discrete and particular matter but rather to a field of things—to a preserve—and because the boundaries of the field are ordinarily patrolled and defended by the claimant.

Individuals, whether in human or animal form, exhibit two basic modes of activity. They go about their business grazing, gazing, mothering, digesting, building, resting, playing, placidly attending to easily managed matters at hand. Or, fully mobilized, a fury of intent, alarmed, they get ready to attack or to stalk or to flee. Physiology itself is patterned to coincide with this duality.

The individual mediates between these two tendencies with a very pretty capacity for dissociated vigilance. Smells, sounds, sights, touches, pressures—in various combinations, depending on the species—provide a running reading of the situation, a constant monitoring of what surrounds. But by a wonder of adaptation these readings can be done out of the furthest corner of whatever is serving for an eye, leaving the individual himself free to focus his main attention on the non-emergencies around him. Matters that the actor has become accustomed to will receive a flick or a shadow of concern, one that decays as soon as he obtains a microsecond of confirmation that everything is in order; should something really prove to be "up," prior activity can be dropped and full orientation mobilized, followed by coping behavior. Note, the central thesis here is Darwinian. If individuals were not highly responsive to hints of danger or opportunity, they would not be responsive enough; if they carried this response far on every occasion of its occurrence, they would spend all their time in a dither and have no time for all the other things required for survival.

12. Speaking and Language: Defense of Poetry

PAUL GOODMAN. Wildwood House, 3rd Floor, 1 Wardour Street, London W1Y 3HE; 1973; £3.00; 242 pp.

Paul Goodman was a spirited and provocative social critic whose books included *Growing Up Absurd* and *New Reformation: Notes of a Neolithic Conservative*. In this volume he applies his thinking to the media-mix of the latter sixties (McLuhan in particular) and finds strong grounds for criticism. JB

REVIEW BY MICHELE STOWELL. The late Paul Goodman, writer and social critic, has written a very personal book in praise and defense of, language. As a writer, he praises the power of language: it *is* communication, not just a means of communicating information. As a humanistic social critic, he defends language against the rigid codification imposed on it by scientific linguists, cultural anthropologists, and communication theorists. Colloquial language, speech as it is spoken, transcends any system for describing it. Although based on a common, conservative linguistic system, speech is personal, active, creating meaning as it flows. Goodman criticizes those systems that ignore these crucial functions of language.

Literature springs from colloquial speech, but is both more conscious of the tradition of the language, and more innovative than most speech. Goodman discusses the process of literary creation. He sees style as creating a hypothesis about the nature of reality, using Hemingway as an example. In his role as social critic, he discusses the attempts of social or technical systems to reduce language to format, but he has faith that our spontaneous speech will not be colonized by the collective styles of television or the schools. The book ends with a personal "defense of poetry," of literary language as a vital force, and as Goodman's own way of being in the world.

Thus, there is a silence that is preverbal, not yet interpersonal or even personal. There is speaking, which recognizes persons. And there is a silence beyond speech, an accord closer than verbal communication and where the situation is unproblematic. In one of the scriptural lives of Buddha there is a remarkable sentence, at the conversion of Anathapindika: "The Lord consented by becoming silent." I take it that this means that the silence of the Lord creates accord, *is* accord; and from the human point of view, if the *Lord* consents, what further is to be said?

When speaking intervenes in the world and shapes experience, it often is, or is taken as, a direct action in the environment, an energy or even a physical thing, rather than the use of the common code for communication. We can show a wide range of important cases where this is so; one cannot understand what language is without taking it into account.

The method of constructing a positivist grammar is to find or postulate the fewest possible grammatical forms and spin out from them, by rule, the forms of the rest of the sentences. As with the Basic vocabulary, this was not, of course, the historical development of the language; nor is it how children learn to speak. Chomsky, the best known of the structuralist grammarians, specifically advises against using such a method in pedagogy, rather than letting the child do his own grammar-forming. But the structural model would be capital for making programs for translation-and other language-machines—e.g. Chomsky's *Syntactic Structures* was paid for by technological corporations. My own humanistic caution about the method is, again, that this is not how grammar *is;* it does not show its vital impulse which is, as with the rest of language, to say what needs to be said.

Deliberate literature, oral or written, is not spontaneous speech, but it has compensating advantages in providing samples for exploring language. In the process of making literature, an author finds his structure in handling the words, and he does not exclude any aspect or use of language—at any turn he may resort to precise denotation or metaphor or syllogism or a dramatic colloquial scene, or say his feelings. And he has to make the words fill out what the ordinary speaker relies on non-verbal means to do. There is no active respondent, so a literary work has to incorporate both sides of the dialogue. This inevitably produces a certain amount of idiolect— the writer's whim or delusion of what English is or should be—yet writers are also more than average respectful of the tradition and genius of the language: They are its keepers. An artist organizes a whole work, with beginning, middle, and end, so it is usually possible to figure out what the various parts are accomplishing—whether the choice of words, the syntax, the metaphor, the connotations, the tone and rhythm, the narrative or dramatic manner. And of course a literary work is a concrete whole of speech that stands fixed, is repeatable, lets itself be examined closely.

I have a scientific disposition, in a naturalistic vein. I get a continual satisfaction from seeing, objectively, how things are and work—it makes me smile, sometimes ruefully—and I like to write it down. But I do not exclude how I am and work as one of the things, unfortunately an omnipresent one in my experience. (I can occasionally smile at this, too, but I am happier when I am not there.) God is history—how events actually turn out—but history includes also the history of me. God creates the world and I am only a creature, but I *am* a creature and He takes me into account, though He doesn't always know what's good for me and I complain a lot. Thus, my objective naturalistic sentences are inevitably colored by, and likely distorted by, my own story and feelings. They turn into literature.

This brings me to a question. Why am I so polemical about recent language theory, as in this chapter? Why don't I let those scholars do their thing, while I, as a man of letters, do mine? Frankly, I am made politically uneasy by it, by the thrust of cultural anthropology, Basic languages, scientific linguistics, communications engineering,

and the Theory of Communications. They usually treat human communication as far more mechanical than it is; they are technological in an anti-humanistic sense. They suit State and corporate policy too well and have crashingly pre-empted too many research grants and university appointments. My own bias, to be equally frank, is to play up the animal, spontaneous, artistic, and populist forces in speech. These forces are both agitational and deeply conservative—as I think good politics is. And as a writer, I want to defend literature and poetry as the indispensable renovators of desiccated and corrupt language.

———————————

Besides, taken uncritically, as people take them, words do work physical magic: The nature of things is amenable to being manipulated by words, spectacularly in science and technology. Powerful sentences like the inverse square law of gravity and $E = mc^2$ are sentences. Critical philosophies like pragmatism and operationalism have tried to de-verbalize science and reduce its explanations to efficient causes, non-verbal behavior, and the manipulation of things. But people ask what the laboratory operations or the behaviors "mean"; they want a fuller kind of explanation and they are not satisfied with the answer "Nothing," which is obviously a hoax, for nothing comes from nothing. Another critical approach tries to take the metaphysics out of language by devising methodical languages which are just "postulated." But, unfortunately, directions for the use of a tight methodical language have to be said in everyday language, and ambiguity and magic seep back. And even more important, that a formal language can be applied to real things seems to most people (and to me, too) to be exactly magic. If mathematics is just an agreed-on procedure, it is sheer magic that it works so well. Meantime, scientists themselves, not to speak of the rest of us, persist in using the language that suits them. To de-mystify words is not a novel idea; it goes from Socrates and Hsün-tze to Rudolf Carnap and Otto Neurath. The only methodical language that seems to catch on internationally and across the boundaries of disciplines is computer language, and this has been for technological and commercial reasons, not prophylaxis.

13. The Image: Knowledge in Life and Society

KENNETH BOULDING. The University of Michigan Press, 615 East University, Ann Arbor, Mich. 48106; 1956; (H) $4.40; (P) $1.95; 175 pp.

Our experience is the experiencing of images: of ourselves, our world, people, things, etc. Boulding proposes a new science—"eiconics"—as a unifying element in the study of the message-image relationship. In his world, the image is the reality, and the ultimate question—"what, who determines the image?"—is not to be answered. It can't be answered, because it's already here, it's us . . . as we ask the question. JB

We must distinguish carefully between the image and the messages that reach it. The messages consist of *information* in the sense that they are structured experiences. *The meaning of a message is the change which it produces in the image.*

———————

One of the most important propositions of this theory is that the value scales of any individual or organization are perhaps the most important single element determining the effect of the messages it receives on its image of the world. If a message is perceived that is neither good nor bad it may have little or no effect on the image. If it is perceived as bad or hostile to the image which is held, there will be resistance to accepting it. This resistance is not usually infinite. An often repeated message or a message which comes with unusual force or authority is able to penetrate the resistance and will be able to alter the image. A devout Moslem, for instance, whose whole life has been built around the observance of the precepts of the Koran will resist vigorously any message which tends to throw doubt on the authority of his sacred work. The resistance may take the form of simply ignoring the message, or it may take the form of emotive response: anger, hostility, indignation. In the same way, a "devout" psychologist will resist strongly any evidence presented in favor of extrasensory perception, because to accept it would overthrow his whole image of the universe. If the resistances are very strong, it may take very strong, or often repeated messages to penetrate them, and when they are penetrated, the effect is a realignment or reorganization of the whole knowledge structure.

———————

With all the gaps in our theoretical structure, one thing is clear. It is that as we proceed from lower to higher levels of organization, the concept of the image becomes an increasingly important part of any theoretical model, and the image itself becomes increasingly complex. At the first and second levels we can get along almost without any concept of the image at all, although there are analogues of the image in the idea of the limitations of static structures and of dynamic processes. The valency of an element in chemistry, for instance, is a concept which has some relationship to the image insofar as it is a kind of "know how." A rudimentary image is exhibited in simple control mechanisms. It is clearly present even at the very earliest stage of life. It grows in importance and complexity as we ascend the biological ladder. It is of overwhelming importance in the interpretation of human behavior and of the dynamics of society.

———————

We have first the spatial image, the picture of the individual's location in the space around him. We have next the temporal image, his picture of the stream of time and his place in it. Third, we have the relational image, the picture of the universe around him as a system of regularities. Perhaps as a part of this we have, fourth, the personal image, the picture of the individual in the midst of the universe of persons, roles, and organizations around him. Fifth, we have the value image which consists of the ordering on the scale of better or worse of the various parts of the whole image. Sixth, we have the affectional image, or emotional image, by which various items in the rest of the image are imbued with feeling or affect. Seventh, we have the division of the image into conscious, unconscious, and subconscious areas. Eighth, we have a dimension of certainty or uncertainty, clarity or vagueness. Ninth, we have a dimension of reality or unreality, that is, an image of the correspondence of the image itself with some " outside " reality. Tenth, closely related to this but not identical with it, we have a public, private scale according to whether the image is shared by others or is peculiar to the individual.

14. The Human Use of Human Beings: Cybernetics and Society

NORBERT WIENER. Sphere Books Ltd., 30–32 Gray's Inn Road, London WC1X 8JL; 1969; £0.30; 288 pp.

In his work in founding cybernetics, Wiener set up a communications model: man and society could be properly understood only through a study of the messages and communication facilities that belong to them. He believed that "the physical functioning of the living individual and the operation of some of the newer communication machines are precisely analogous in their attempts to control entropy through feedback." Wiener used as his model the human brain. He extended the central nervous system into the environment and used it as a model/mirror.JB

One interesting change that has taken place is that in a probabilistic world we no longer deal with quantities and statements which concern a specific, real universe as a whole but ask instead questions which may find their answers in a large number of similar universes. Thus chance has been admitted, not merely as a mathematical tool for physics, but as part of its warp and weft.

It is the thesis of this book that society can only be understood through a study of the messages and the communication facilities which belong to it; and that in the future development of these messages (and communication facilities), messages between man and machines, between machines and man, and between machine and machine, are destined to play an ever-increasing part.

When I give an order to a machine, the situation is not essentially different from that which arises when I give an order to a person. In other words, as far as my consciousness goes I am aware of the order that has gone out and of the signal of compliance that has come back. To me, personally, the fact that the signal in its intermediate stages has gone through a machine rather than through a person is irrelevant and does not in any case greatly change my relation to the signal. Thus the theory of control in engineering, whether human or animal or mechanical, is a chapter in the theory of messages.

Information is a name for the content of what is exchanged with the outer world as we adjust to it, and make our adjustment felt upon it. The process of receiving and of using information is the process of our adjusting to the contingencies of the outer environment, and of our living effectively within that environment.

We have modified our environment so radically that we must now modify ourselves in order to exist in this new environment. We can no longer live in the old one. Progress imposes not only new possibilities for the future but new restrictions.

The behavior of an ant is much more a matter of instinct than of intelligence. *The physical straight jacket in which an insect grows up is directly responsible for the mental strait jacket which regulates its pattern of behavior.*

Here the reader may say: "Well, we already know that the ant as an individual is not very intelligent, so why all this fuss about explaining why it cannot be intelligent?" The answer is that *Cybernetics takes the view that the structure of the machine or of the organism is an index of the performance that may be expected from it.*

One thing at any rate is clear. The physical identity of an individual does not consist in the matter of which it is made. Modern methods of tagging the elements participating in metabolism have shown a much higher turnover than was long thought possible, not only of the body as a whole, but of each and every component part of it. The biological individuality of an organism seems to lie in a certain continuity of process, and in the memory by the organism of the effects of its past development. This appears to hold also of its mental development. In terms of the computing machine, the individuality of a mind lies in the retention of its earlier tapings and memories, and in its continued development along lines already laid out.

———————————

Information is more a matter of process than of storage. That country will have the greatest security whose informational and scientific situation is adequate to meet the demands that may be put on it—the country in which it is fully realized that information is important as a stage in the continuous process by which we observe the outer world, and act effectively upon it. In other words, no amount of scientific research, carefully recorded in books and papers, and then put into our libraries with labels of secrecy, will be adequate to protect us for any length of time in a world where the effective level of information is perpetually advancing. There is no Maginot Line of the brain.

I repeat, to be alive is to participate in a continuous stream of influences from the outer world and acts on the outer world, in which we are merely the transitional stage. In the figurative sense, to be alive to what is happening in the world, means to participate in a continual development of knowledge and its unhampered exchange.

15. Purposive Systems: Proceedings of the First Annual Symposium of the American Society for Cybernetics

Edited by HEINZ VON FOERSTER, et al. Spartan Books, 432 Park Avenue South, New York, N.Y. 10016; 1968; $10; 179 pp.

During World War II, The Josiah Macy Foundation sponsored a small " Conference on Cerebral Inhibition. " This eventually resulted in the Macy Conferences on Cybernetics, a gathering of many diverse intelligences toward the formation of this new science and perspective. Some twenty-odd years later, the " American Society for Cybernetics " held its first annual symposium. The results are recorded in this volume. The subtitle of the meeting, " The Edge of Knowledge, " conveys the latest developments of the cybernetic overview as it applies in a wide range of fields including philosophy, anthropology, psychiatry, electronics, and microbiology. ER

We are dealing with new kinds of partial organization among areas of much higher and much lower organization which none of our theories take into account. In the past, it was possible to view opposing and organized systems in some degree of isolation. Today we are dealing with a sort of social metastasis in which there are fragments of formerly highly organized behavior which are unsystematically related to each other. We have no way of thinking about this.

If we think of the steps through the early interdisciplinary development of cybernetic models, through general systems theory and our growing willingness to include more and more complex systems, I think that now we have to take another step and develop ways of thinking about systems that are still bounded but within which there are loci of very contrasting degrees of organization and disorganization. If we approach them with our former methods, if we treat some of these organized pieces in isolation, we may get something that can be treated as a system, but we learn nothing about the way in which it is embedded in intractable ways in some larger and less organized context, and we may also do a great deal of harm. I believe that finding ways of meeting this dilemma is the next step that this society should take.

The simplest genetic system is one in which the genetic vectors have only a single element which may have two values, e.g., 0 and 1. If one of these elements has a higher probability of survival than the other, then the probability of the population acquiring increased survival follows fairly simple algebraic statements. However, the genetic system of any organism does not involve just a single pair of alleles; instead, a population will be genetically variable at many, if not all, of its hundreds of genetic loci. The problem is to devise methods of describing and analyzing the changes that will occur in such systems of extensive variability, in which many different genetic vectors have effectively the same survival value. Evolution becomes a question of whether a meaningful genetic change is possible from a basis of almost infinite genetic diversity.

———

Let me begin with some general statements. Any system is composed of a number of different elements, united by connections and functioning as a whole. Complex systems differ from simple ones in that they not only transform energy, but process information as well (Fig. 1).

The information which is processed by a system we consider as a certain knowledge about an object, usually presented in the form of a model.

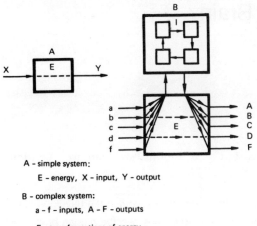

A - simple system:

    E - energy, X - input, Y - output

B - complex system:

    a - f - inputs, A - F - outputs

    E - transformations of energy

    I - selections and processing of information

Figure 1. Systems.

The model reflects—with some simplifications and distortions—the structure and functions of the object. Model and information are inseparable. The model is often described by a human language, creating a "model of a model" within which any sequence of actions of the system is designated by the word "program."

Simulation or modeling of the object called human thinking is necessary for the sake of studying human cognition, for creation of an artificial intelligence, and for development of sociological or economic models of human inter-

actions. The most general model of a human being is that represented by an automaton with three types of programs: "for himself"—the instinct of self-preservation; "for stock" (family)—instinct of reproduction; and "for species" or "for society"—the programs of social behavior.

Each of these three programs functions in the human on several layers: a rigid congenital part, laid in the subcortex and endocrine system; another, implanted by learning, in the lower area of the cortex; and a third one, generated during the process of creative work, in the highest areas of the cortex.

When change becomes that pervasive in the world, it must color the ways in which we understand, organize, and evaluate the world. The sheer fact of change will have an impact on our sensibilities and ideas, our institutions and practices, our politics and values. Most of these have to date developed on the assumption that stability was more characteristic of the world than change, i.e., that change was but a temporary perturbation of stability or a transition to a new (and presumed better or higher) stable state. When that fundamental metaphysical assumption is undermined, our whole attitude toward and approach to the world and society undergo fundamental and far-reaching alterations. We are forced to a posture of *systematic expectation of change,* which has intellectual, social, and political implications.

16. The Computer and the Brain

JOHN VON NEUMANN. Yale University Press Ltd., 20 Bloomsbury Square, London WC1A 2NP; 1958; £2.25; 82 pp.

John von Neumann was one of the great mathematicians of this century. His work in the development of the computer led to an interest in the analogies between computing machines and the human brain. This book—a brief, preliminary work—presents an understanding of the nervous system from a mathematician's point of view. JB

The organization of large digital machines is more complex. They are made up of "active" organs and of organs serving "memory" functions—I will include among the latter the "input" and "output" organs, although this is not common practice.

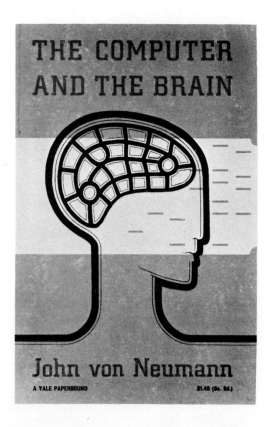

THE COMPUTER AND THE BRAIN

John von Neumann

A YALE PAPERBOUND $1.45 (9s. 6d.)

The active organs are the following. First, organs which perform the basic logical actions: sense coincidences, combine stimuli, and possibly sense anticoincidences (no more than this is necessary, although sometimes organs for more complex logical operations are also provided). Second, organs which regenerate pulses: restore their gradually attrited energy, or simply lift them from the energy level prevailing in one part of the machine to another (higher) energy level prevailing in another part (these two functions are called amplification)—which restore the desired (i.e. within certain tolerances, standardized) pulse-shape and timing. Note that the first-mentioned logical operations are the elements from which the arithmetical ones are built up (cf. above).

I have described, in some detail, the nature of modern computing machines and the broad alternative principles around which they can be organized. It is now possible to pass on to the other term of the comparison, the human nervous system. I will discuss the points of similarity and dissimilarity between these two kinds of "automata." Bringing out the elements of similarity leads over well-known territory. There are elements of dissimilarity, too, not only in rather obvious respects of size and speed but also in certain much deeper-lying areas: These involve the principles of functioning and control, of overall organization, etc. My primary aim is to develop some of these. However, in order to appreciate them properly, a juxtaposition and combination with the points of similarity, as well as with those of more superficial dissimilarity (size, speed; cf. above) are also required.

As I mentioned before, the fully developed nerve impulses are comparable, no matter how induced. Because their character is not an unambiguously defined one (it may be viewed electrically as well as chemically, cf. above), its induction, too, can be alternatively attributed to electrical or to chemical causes. Within the nervous system, however, it is mostly due to one or more other nerve impulses. Under such conditions, the process of its induction—the *stimulation* of a nerve impulse—may or may not succeed. If it fails, a passing disturbance arises at first, but after a few milliseconds, this dies out. Then no disturbances propagate along the axon. If it succeeds, the disturbance very soon assumes a (nearly) standard form, and in this form it spreads along the axon. That is to say, as mentioned above, a standard nerve impulse will then move along the axon, and its appearance will be reasonably independent of the details of the process that induced it.

We have now accumulated sufficient evidence to see that whatever language the central nervous system is using, it is characterized by less logical and arithmetical depth than what we are normally used to. The following is an obvious example of this: the retina of the human eye performs a considerable reorganization of the visual image as perceived by the eye. Now this reorganization is effected on the retina, or to be more precise, at the point of entry of the optic nerve by means of three successive synapses only, i.e. in terms of three consecutive logical steps. The statistical character of the message system used in the arithmetics of the central nervous system and its low precision also indicate that the degeneration of precision, described earlier, cannot proceed very far in the message systems involved. Consequently, there exist here different logical structures from the ones we are ordinarily used to in logics and mathematics. They are, as pointed out before, characterized by less logical and arithmetical depth than we are used to under otherwise similar circumstances. Thus logics and mathematics in the central nervous system, when viewed as languages, must structurally be essentially different from those languages to which our common experience refers.

17. Principles of Holography

HOWARD M. SMITH. Wiley-Interscience, Div. of John Wiley & Sons, Inc., 605 Third Avenue, New York, N.Y. 10016; 1969; $10.95; 239 pp.

Holography is lensless photography. In normal, lens photography, a picture is formed of the image of an object. In lensless holography, the wave (formed from the points of light of any object) rather than the image is recorded. This creates the possibility of recording more than two dimensions of an object.

Howard Smith is a research physicist at Eastman Kodak. His monograph provides basic introductory material on holography as well as the theoretical aspects necessary for technical comprehension of holographic processes. FR

The holographic method differs significantly from the conventional photographic process in several basic respects and has distinct advantages in many areas. The most obvious advantage of holography is the ability to store enough information about the object in the hologram to produce a true three-dimensional image, complete with parallax and large depth of focus. There has been a great deal of work done in the attempt to produce three-dimensional images using conventional photographic techniques. These methods have been only partially successful because of the limited depth of field and restricted viewing conditions. An observer viewing a stereo pair, for example, cannot move his head from side to side and look behind foreground objects as he can with a hologram. The lenticular-type three-dimensional photograph allows limited parallax but has a rather severe depth limitation. The hologram, on the other hand, has a field of view that is limited in general only by the resolution of the recording medium. The depth of field recorded in a hologram is limited only by source bandwidth. Thus if a hologram is made of a three-dimensional object, it is equivalent to many conventional photographs, each taken from a different point of view and each focused at a different depth. Subsequent viewing of the hologram image at different depths requires only a refocusing of the viewing system. Hence it is fair to say that one hologram is worth a thousand pictures!

The quality of a holographic image is less sensitive to the characteristics of the recording medium than is the quality of a photograph. Holograms made on high-contrast material reproduce tonal variations of the object over a wide range. Nonlinear recording has only a small effect on the final image. Also, imperfections in the emulsion, such as scratches, have very little effect on the final image. Indeed a modern hologram is so redundant that only a small fraction of the holographic record is necessary to form a complete image.

Because of these basic differences between holography and conventional photography, many interesting and novel applications have been proposed. Few of these have been put to commercial use as yet, but the field is still young.

HOLOGRAPHIC MICROSCOPY

As mentioned in Chapter 1, holography was originally invented as an improvement of microscopy—specifically, electron microscopy. In the early years workers extended Gabor's ideas to include x-ray microscopy. Although neither of these could be made to come up to expectations, there is still a great deal of promise for holographic microscopy.

There are three main features that make the wavefront reconstruction method potentially more suitable for microscopy than conventional imaging techniques. The first of these is that, theoretically at least, many of the wave aberrations present in the recording process can be corrected by means of a suitable recording and readout arrangement. Thus the final image wave will be nearly free of aberrations, leading to almost a diffraction-limited image. The second feature is that in holography, the field of view is a function of the recording medium resolution and size. We can therefore expect, again theoretically, good imagery over much larger fields than are attainable with conventional microscopy. The third feature is, of course, that magnification is possible by employing a change in wavelength between recording and reconstructing the wavefront. Thus, as was originally proposed, we can record the wavefront in a very short wavelength and subsequently reconstruct it with a much longer one.

THREE-DIMENSIONAL OBSERVATION

One of the most striking aspects of the modern hologram is the three-dimensional image which it is capable of producing. This three-dimensional image indicates that there is a large amount of information contained in a single hologram, certainly much more than is contained in a conventional photograph of the same size. This is especially true when the object in question is many times the depth of field in depth. Because of the many perspectives which are available, the hologram is well suited to display purposes. With a hologram, one can present all of the observable characteristics of a three-dimensional object in a clear and concise manner. Complicated molecular or anatomical structure can be simply presented with a single holographic image, with little chance of error or misinterpretation on the part of the viewer. Such a hologram would take the place of several conventional drawings or photographs. The use of holograms in textbooks would be a great aid to the student in many areas. Holograms made so that they are viewable with a small pen light and a colored filter have already been produced in large quantities and distributed in magazines and books.

The use of holographic images for simulation systems has some drawbacks, such as magnification and/or power for illumination, but these are difficulties easily overcome if the need and usefulness outweigh the costs. Their use as training devices may well prove to be quite advantageous.

The use of holograms as information-storage devices has been one of the most promising right from the start. Intially, we tend to think that a hologram is capable of storing much more information on a two-dimensional medium than a photograph can. This is certainly true if the photograph is merely an image of the information. But there are more suitable ways to photographically store information which make the contest between holography and photography about even. The question of whether or not holography is the best means for storing information has tantalized scientists and engineers. The question has not yet been resolved, but there is still significant effort being applied in this area.

Further, when the third dimension is added—the depth of the holographic recording medium—it becomes clear that holography looks very promising indeed. The gain in storage capacity by utilizing the depth of a photographic emulsion is very real but not nearly as significant as the gains which may be realized with the use of the very thick (of the order of 1 mm or more) photochromic materials.

The proven information capacity of a two-dimensional photographic emulsion is of the order of 10^8 bits/cm^2, whether the information is in the form of a binary code or microimage. This is for a signal-to-noise (S/N) ratio of about 10. This is the number holography must surpass. On a commercial basis, conventional imaging techniques are used for storage capacities of the order of 10^3 bits/cm^2 with a S/N of the order of 10^3. For holographic data storage, in two dimensions, we shall see that the capacities are about the same. Holographic data-storage techniques do offer two possible advantages: (a) the possibility of the utilization of a three-dimensional recording medium, and (b) a large redundancy because of the way in which the data are stored.

Ever since 1900 man has been able to record and retain as a permanent record almost any scene that his eyes perceived—through the process of photography. The optical lens had been invented and used several centuries before, and the formation of optical images with lenses was well understood by 1900. With the invention of the photographic process the importance of the lens in scientific investigation was greatly enhanced. The fortunate combination of lens and photographic emulsion made possible the charting of stars, planets, and galaxies; the recording of optical spectra; the picturing of minute microscopic specimens; the storage of large amounts of data in the form of small recorded images; and myriad other uses. Because of the vast scope of its scientific importance, the science of photography has advanced steadily over the past 70 or more years; even today new and important uses are being found.

Now science has at its disposal a new method of forming optical images: holography.

Holography is a relatively new process which is similar to photography in some respects but is nonetheless fundamentally different. Because of this fundamental difference, holography and photography will not be competing in the same areas. There are several applications for which holography is more suitable than photography, whereas most of the more important uses for photography remain unchallenged. Further, there are several tasks which can be performed with holography but not at all with conventional photography.

In order to point out the fundamental differences between holography and photography, we should understand in a general way how each works.

Photography basically provides a method of recording the two-dimensional irradiance distribution of an image. Generally speaking, each "scene" consists of a large number of reflecting or radiating points of light. The waves from each of these elementary points all contribute to a complete wave, which we will call the "object" wave. This complex wave is transformed by the optical lens in such a way that it collapses into an image of the radiating object. It is this image which is recorded on the photographic emulsion.

Holography is quite different. With holography, one records not the optically formed image of the object but the *object wave itself.* This wave is recorded in such a way that a subsequent illumination of this record serves to *reconstruct* the original object wave, even in the absence of the original object. A visual observation of this reconstructed wavefront then yields a view of the object or scene which is practically *indiscernible from the original.* It is thus the recording of the object wave itself, rather than an image of the object, which constitutes the basic difference between conventional photography and holography.

18. Fax: The Principles and Practice of Facsimile Communication

DANIEL M. COSTIGAN. Chilton Book Company, 401 Walnut Street, Philadelphia, Pa. 19106; 1971; $10; 270 pp.

In 1970 about 95 per cent of the material delivered by the U. S. Post Office within the United States of America need never have been mailed. It could just as easily have been ' delivered ' by means of FAX, or facsimile communication.

Daniel Costigan, an information-systems planner with Bell Telephone Labs, defines FAX as " any system by which printed or pictorial matter (graphics material, in general) is transmitted electrically from one place to another and a reasonably faithful copy [is] permanently recorded at the receiving end in any one of several forms. " Costigan reviews the history and the technical and economic considerations of facsimile communications, and speculates on the future of FAX and its prospective new applications. ER

FAX

CURRENT APPLICATIONS

Newspictures
Weather Forecasting
Commercial Communications relating to:
   shipping goods
   expediting customer orders,
   expediting monetary transactions.
Publishing:
   to expedite graphic communication between editorial offices and printing facilities,
   to dispatch news copy from satellite offices or bureaus to a paper's main newsroom,
   to eliminate duplication of typesetting effort between separate printing facilities.
Engineering and Manufacturing
   Law Enforcement
   Messages
   Libraries

Two significant events in the field of telecommunications took place within the first four months of 1926. One was the first public demonstration of television—by John Baird, in a little laboratory in London's Soho district in January. The other was the inauguration of commercial transatlantic radio facsimile service—for the transmission of news photos—by the Radio Corporation of America three months later.

That the two events occurred within a few months of each other is perhaps not in itself significant. What is interesting is the relative state of development of these two loosely related picture transmission media at that time. They were technologically similar, both employing essentially the same electromechanical techniques of dissecting and reconstructing pictures. But while TV remained confined to the laboratory bench, its static counterpart (static in the sense that it was concerned with still, as opposed to moving, images) already had several decades of practical application behind it, in the course of which it had steadily progressed to a high state of refinement.

Although TV was to enjoy a somewhat more rapid technological growth than facsimile in the ensuing years, it was not for another two decades that it finally caught up in the sense of having become a full-fledged commercial reality. And it was not until the advent of communications satellites in the 1960s that it was able to span the seas on even a limited commercial basis.

As late as 1949 it was still believed in some quarters that facsimile could compete actively with TV as a home news and entertainment medium. Although that dream has not material-ized, facsimile has nevertheless managed to maintain—and, in fact, gradually reinforce—its position as an indispensable telecommunications medium.

At this point it might be well to clarify exactly what the word facsimile means as a telecom-munications term. There are conflicting definitions. To some, the word is confined to describing what is essentially a "message" medium through which written or printed messages and sketches are exchanged via wire or radio and are visibly recorded by *non*photographic means—i.e., by electrochemical or electromechanical means not requiring further processing. By this definition, the systems customarily used for transmission of news photographs are excluded.

To others, facsimile refers to any system by which printed *or* pictorial matter (graphics material, in general) is transmitted electrically from one place to another and a reasonably faithful copy permanently recorded at the receiving end in any one of several forms.

This book takes the latter view, lumping together the news photo and so-called "mes-sage" or "document" facsimile systems simply as variations in facsimile recording technique, which is, in fact, the only genuine distinction existing between them.

19. The Video Publisher

Knowledge Industry Publications, Inc., Tiffany Towers, White Plains, N.Y. 10602; $75 year, published semi-monthly.

As industrial development becomes increasingly specialized, the information resources that serve industries tend to break down data into more discrete and separate units. When new technologies are involved, industry lines often overlap. Hence *The Video Publisher,* "a newsletter for executives who produce, distribute, advertise in or broadcast programming for cable, cartridge, closed circuit, subscription or local television." The newsletter's information is slanted toward the profit incentive but accurately assesses the transformation of culture by a new technology. ER

3M CASSETTE PROGRAMMING REVEALED

3M/Wollensak, St. Paul, Minn., which signed a cross licensing hardware agreement with Sony (see VP, Oct. 28, '71) has revealed that they had developed video cassette programming plans before settling on a hardware system. 3M has announced that test marketing of the Sony U-Matic video cassette units with the Wollensak label will begin this spring in Los Angeles, Chicago, New York, Washington, D.C. and Minneapolis-St. Paul, with national distribution scheduled for this fall. It is reasonable to suppose that software will be marketed at the same time.

In an interview, W.F. Jensen, marketing manager for Wollensak educational products, outlined the 3M strategy. According to Jensen, 3M decided against a catalog of products previously made for other media; discounted the entertainment market for the near future and insisted that programs be produced specifically for video cassettes. 3M is interested in distributing programming developed by others which fits this description but as yet they haven't found anything suitable.

In further defining their market, 3M focused on education and within education on vocational education. Jensen gave five reasons for this decision: 1) Vocational education is well administered at federal, state and local levels; 2) It is well funded; 3) vocational education has a well defined curriculum; 4) the field in general is

responsive to change; and 5) It offers good secondary markets in industrial training.

Following this strategy, 3M is well along in the development of 30-40 programs in paramedical training with eight already in the can. 3M has also developed series in graphic arts, shop arithmetic and other vocational/industrial training areas. The company is also funding the work of young, experimental filmmakers and the pilots may become cassette series.

Jensen also pointed out that each series in production also provides market assets to other 3M divisions. Examples include the Medical Products and Graphic Arts divisions. Thus, 3M is combining most of the elements of successful video publishing. They have chosen a narrow, well-funded market area in which they have an existing franchise and they propose to supply it with specifically defined video cassette programming. Furthermore, 3M is supplying hardware and service as well as software—an ideal combination in the birth of a market. To hedge its bet, however, 3M will also offer its programming in 8mm and reel-to-reel helical formats.

HOPE REPORT MEASURES CASSETTE INTEREST AND AREAS OF AGREEMENT

The "Hope Report: Motion Pictures and Video Cassettes 1971," published by Thomas W. Hope,

Rochester, N.Y., contains a survey of potential video cassette customers and an analysis of areas of agreement in the available literature. The survey reveals that 45% of the institutions responding are considering going into a test program using video cassette systems, and the literature is unanimous in asserting that magnetic tape will be the preferred system in the institutional/educational market.

There were 82 responses, representing a 41% return on the survey but the respondents from industry, school systems and universities represented a $60-70 million annual audio-visual equipment and materials budget. Four out of five of the respondents had seen at least one video cassette unit or witnessed a demonstration and only one third of the respondents have formed an opinion as to the general type of video cassette system or the specific make they might prefer.

Although almost half of the schools, businesses and universities surveyed indicated an intention to start an experimental program utilizing video cassettes, only 17% of the respondents indicated a willingness to buy equipment when it becomes available. This hesitation about video cassettes is underlined by the fact that 78 of the 82 respondents plan to continue or expand their current 16mm, 8mm, reel-to-reel, and filmstrip programs. In the final analysis, therefore, the Hope Report is far from optimistic about the future of video cassettes.

The available literature surveyed by Hope Reports revealed total agreement on a rather wide range of issues confronting the industry. Besides seeing tape as the preferred system for the institutional market, the literature agrees that the video disc has the best potential in the consumer market and that programming should appeal to specialized markets, particularly youth and those not interested in commercial TV programs. Incompatibility between systems will retard market growth and in the long run there is a place for one low-cost playback-only, and one record/playback system. Mass production is absolutely essential to reduce costs and equipment prices must be in the $300 range for the consumer market and $500 range for the industrial market.

If one puts the two Hope Report surveys together, the future actually looks bleaker for video cassettes. Institutions are not ready to leap on the cassette bandwagon, but without mass production costs will remain too high to attract many customers. It looks like a vicious circle. The complete Hope Report can be obtained from the publisher at 58 Carverdale Drive, Rochester, N.Y. 14618.

Time-Life Video Launches Video Cassette Marketing to Business . . . . page 1-2; FCC Finally Acts on CATV Regulation But Suggests Nothing New . . . . page 4; RCA Exploring Broad-Band Communications Involvement . . . . page 5; Telebeam To Demonstrate Laser Pay-TV Distribution System . . . . page 6; November Sweep Shows "Hee Haw" Most Successful Early Access Program . . . . page 7-8.

CASSETTES BRIEF . . .

Visual Information Systems, NYC, will shortly announce the availability of its AVENS cassettes developed in conjunction with the Markle Foundation and the Society of Neurological Surgeons. First program is on "Intracranial Operations on the Pituitary ". . . *TelePrompTer has concluded* that Sony video cassettes offer the best programming distribution system for CATV and is phasing players into all their systems. . .

A.C. Nielsen Co. is doing a survey on tape vs. film utilization for 3M . . . *Zenith* will announce the licensing of the Teldec cassette disc system in the next month . . . . *Magnavox* may also license Teldec but has only announced the showing of Cartrivision players to its dealers . . . *Ampex claims* to be moving ahead with Instavideo system development . . . *Watch for announcement* that major labor union and major insurance company are into cassette field . . . . *New Hope Report* on "Motion Pictures and Video Cassettes 1971 " is now available from Hope Communications, Rochester, N.Y. . . . . *Matsushita* is showing facsimile and "snap-shot" TV systems in Japan . . . *Japan Victor* will enter U.S. market with cassettes in early '73 . . . *Visual Sounds,* N.Y., which is now doing audio cassettes for Sports Illustrated is seeking capitalization for video cassette development.

CABLE BRIEFS . . .

TelePrompTer has announced that it plans to spend about $55-million to expand its domestic CATV operations and begin development of the

European market . . . *Tele-Communications, Inc.* Denver, has completed acquisitions of Com-West, Inc., with 10,000 subscribers in Oklahoma and Minnesota . . . *American Television & Communications Corp.* has obtained franchises for Maitland and Casselberry suburbs of Orlando, Florida . . . *Sterling Manhattan has completed wiring of Bellevue Hospital . . . Television Communications Corp.* shareholders have approved acquisition by Kinney Services . . . *Westerly Cable TV* is offering credit courses from the University of Rhode Island extension division.

TELEBEAM TO DEMONSTRATE LASER
SYSTEM IN MARCH

Telebeam Corp., N.Y. will demonstrate a system which uses laser beams, a computer and a television set to provide subscription entertainment, information, reservation and security system services to hotels in the Americana and City Squire Hotels in New York this March. First system installations are targeted for October.

Telebeam describes its system as a multi-channel TV laser transmission system. From a central location in a tall building Telebeam will multiplex ten program channel transmissions on a laser beam aimed at an optical receiving station at each hotel. Through a computer in each hotel, programs will be switched to each guest subscriber on an unused TV channel. Because it is a two-way system linked to a computer, Telebeam proposes offering a data bank of useful shopping information, restaurant guides and airline reservations which can be interrogated by the hotel guest. Furthermore, Telebeam proposes that a hotel install a security system which will detect any attempt to enter a room without authorization.

It is estimated that installation will be about $100 to $200 per hotel room depending on the number of services involved. Essentially Telebeam services could be available through most two-way cable systems and it is envisioned that Telebeam will work with cable operators, linking one cable system to another.

The laser transmission from a central location provides economies which a wired system might not be able to offer. But the real significance is not in any marginal economies but in the fact that another subscription and interrogation system is available which could have an impact on the video environment and quicken the race to introduce hardware.

20. The Information Machines: Their Impact on Men and the Media

BEN H. BAGDIKIAN. Harper & Row, Publishers, 49 East 33rd Street, New York, N.Y. 10016; 1971; (H) $8.95; (P) $2.95; 359 pp.

Ben Bagdikian, assistant managing national news editor for the Washington *Post*, was the director of the Rand Corporation study of the impact of future technology on the news. This book is an outgrowth of that two-year project and of his own personal researches.

Bagdikian examines computers, cable television, communications satellites, conglomerates, and the future development of video as an information transmission medium. Two appendixes present a typical twenty-four-hour broadcast day in Grand Rapids-Kalamazoo, Michigan, and predictions for the appearance of new devices on the technological scene. ER

In 1927 a young Mormon, Philo T. Farnsworth, working in a darkened San Francisco apartment, transmitted television images without wires. Perhaps it was symbolic that Farnsworth used the dollar sign as a test pattern and that police raided his apartment under the impression that he was distilling intoxicants. Forty years later, television was still being used primarily as a collector of advertising dollars by selling parlor entertainment.

It has taken forty years to see even dimly that this machine transformed American culture and politics, to realize that its ultimate impact is not going to be idle relaxation but active social transactions like education, community development, politics, commerce, and the direct observance of public affairs.

As the mass media become more pervasive, versatile, and vivid, these conflicts will become even more heated. So, before new technological systems become fixed, it may be useful to consider the choice of characteristics that lie before us, and what difference our decisions will make.

If daily news were just another household commodity, like potatoes, thinking about its future would not lead so quickly to a concern with the evolution of American society.

News as a commodity is economically interesting. Like other mass-consumption goods it is produced and disseminated through networks of men and machines, but, unlike most, each item is a handcrafted intellectual effort, making it an intriguing product of personal judgment, technology, and bureaucracy.

But the ultimate significance of the news system is not economic, technological, or organizational. It is social. News is the peripheral nervous system of the body politic, sensing the total environment and selecting which sights and sounds shall be transmitted to the public. More than any other single mechanism, it decides which of the countless billions of events in the world shall be known to the generality of men. Having done so, it alters men's perceptions of the world and of themselves: the more rapid and vivid the communication, the greater this alteration.

Inventions that increase speed and immediacy of information have always changed the nature of their world. The introduction in Europe of printing by movable type in the fifteenth century helped to produce the Renaissance and Reformation. Telegraph, railroads, and high-speed presses in the nineteenth century led to the overthrow of oligarchies and launched mass politics. Television in the 1950s crystallized the civil-rights revolution, rebellion on the campuses, and a dislocation between those who were shaped by the new machine and those who were not.

Electrons have no morals. They serve free men and dictators with equal fervor. Their use in transmitting human ideas depends on those who design the machines and control their use, and in the United States this ultimately will depend on the general public. If the designers of the new machines and the policy makers who enunciate the rules for their use commit them to narrow and restrictive goals, it will be because this is what the public accepts. The public in every country, including the United States, desperately needs to know the nature of the information machines and how much they will influence lives. It needs to know more clearly than it now learns in schools, the reason why individual freedom of expression on the new machines as well as in person is central to the survival of a creative democracy.

The information machines will do what they are instructed by their human masters. But from then on the roles will be reversed and the machines in their impersonal efficiency will thenceforth become the teachers of a generation of human beings.

21. International Broadcast Institute

Tavistock House East, Tavistock Square, London WC1H 9LG; Newsletter, quarterly.

While members of the alternative cultures sort out the differences between broadcast television and video, members of the non-alternative cultures bring together series of experts and attempt to generate international research, policy, symposia, and other information-exchange facilities.

Such an international organization is the International Broadcast Institute (IBI), "an international, cross-disciplinary forum for independent analysis of social, economic, political, cultural and legal issues related to the effects of communications, particularly broadcast media, on societies and individuals."

Recent IBI-initiated research has involved TV production in Ireland, Nigeria, and Sweden; a study of tariff structures on international satellite usage; and a study of the right to privacy in relation to the freedom of information. ER

The International Broadcast Institute (IBI) is a non-profit, non-governmental, foundation-supported organization concerned with the contemporary revolution in communications. Its founders believe that advances in the technology of the mass media have far outraced man's understanding of their utilization in the service of society. The IBI, therefore, seeks to stimulate social and institutional arrangements which will encourage wider international use of this technology for informational, cultural and educational purposes in both developed and newly-developing countries.

As one of a number of activities to hasten this process, the IBI sponsored a Symposium of *The New Communications Technology and its Social Implications* at Ditchley Park, Oxfordshire, England, November 2 - 6, 1970.

This publication constitutes the Report of that Symposium. As participants were assured of independence and privacy in their discussions, their individual views are expressed but not identified. These should not be considered as representing the policy of the International Broadcast Institute or its Members.

This Report was prepared by the Conference Rapporteur, Dr. Roger P. Morgan, Assistant Director of Studies, The Royal Institute of International Affairs.

NEW APPLICATIONS
CANADA - THE VIDEOGRAPH

The Videograph is an interesting system developed by the National Film Board of Canada as a part of its "Challenge for Change" programme, financed in equal parts by the Board and a number of Government Agencies. The total budget for the year 1971/72 is $1,000,000. It exists in order to train technicians and provide qualifications in audio-visual production also for research on various television systems.

Although such groups might have success at the local level, the real beneficiaries of the new technology would be the large industrial firms. One experienced speaker said that the reality of "the industrialization of communications" must be faced—and that governments themselves would not easily relinquish control of communications media. It was even argued that McLuhan was quite wrong in saying that the communications revolution had turned the world into a "global village." In the eighteenth century, when national frontiers were less impermeable, said a participant, communications between people were relatively better than today, considered in relation to the means available, since it was an age of nationalism, censorship, and restrictive behavior by governments in general. Governments appeared to agree that the new media were potentially as dangerous as the atomic bomb, which the major powers possessed but had no intention of using. Neither the United Nations and its Agencies nor the regional broadcasting unions could be used effectively against the power of governments since governments have a strong interest in keeping traditional broadcasting alive.

VIDEOCASSETTES

There are now definite signs that the videocassette market has settled for evolution instead of for the much-vaunted revolution. Progress of various kinds is reported within the major technical groups: new film methods (EVR, SelectaVision), videotape-recorders (Sony, Phillips, Cartrivision, etc.), super-8 films and the videodisc.

It is interesting to note that there have been suggestions for compulsory standardisation of videocassettes by the US Government. Standardization could, of course, only take place between systems using the same basic techniques (e.g. videotape recorders) but, even so, discussions between the industry and government led to the view that standards cannot be imposed but only achieved through technological competition.

Progress is reported on RCA's holographic, laser-based SelectaVision system (sometimes now called HoloTape). At a recent technical convention in New York, a laboratory prototype showed colour pictures for the first time in public. RCA has added stereo sound recorded on a groove on the tape (of inexpensive vinyl-plastic) and read by a stylus like a grammophone record. The picture quality is said to be extremely good. Furthermore, one of the advantages of the holographic method is to provide good images despite dust, scratches and cuts. Fast, slow, stop-frame and reverse playback are all possible. The holographic tapes can be played on any TV set in the world regardless of the standard used (which is not the case with the videotape-based systems). The growth potential of the RCA device is considerable since hologrammes can be superimposed by changing the angle of recording without interfering with one another. It is said in theory to be possible to record 180 hours of programming on a half-hour length of tape. RCA has also envisaged the possibility of projecting the image directly on to a screen rather than through a television set. Finally, it seems that the holographic technique might provide the basis for three-dimensional television on which work is proceeding in a number of countries and new methods are reported particularly from Japan.

A system which has not appeared but which is nevertheless arousing considerable attention is the videodisc which has been demonstrated in West Germany, the United Kingdom, Canada and the United States. It is manufactured by the Teldec Company which is a subsidiary of Telefunken (Germany) and Decca (United Kingdom). At present, the videodiscs have a running time of only five minutes but this drawback has been overcome by the use of an auto-changer holding twelve discs which will enable 60 minutes continuous running time. Development work is also proceeding to achieve 12-minute discs.

BOOKS

Brian Groombridge:
TELEVISION AND THE PEOPLE PENGUIN PRESS, LONDON, 1972

Brian Groombridge who works for Britain's Independent Broadcasting Authority looks at television's potential to contribute to a healthy democracy in the future. He is aware of the many disappointments brought about by the mass medium, but after looking at experiments in participatory democracy in Europe and America, he argues that TV can perform a unique role.

Brenda Maddox:
" BEYOND BABEL " ANDRE DEUTSCH. LONDON, 1972.
Mrs. Brenda Maddox, who writes for " The Economist " has produced an account of the growth and potential of the telecommunications industry with particular reference to satellites, cable television and the telephone industry. Her book looks particularly at the political problems of Intelsat and the interrelationship between various national and international agencies such as the ITU, Intelsat, the PTT's, broadcasting authorities and international corporations. Everybody might not agree with Mrs. Maddox's views but her book is highly readable.

22. Video Tools

Edited by CYRIL GRIFFIN and PAULA JAFFE; CTL Electronics, Inc., 86 West Broadway, New York, N.Y. 10007; 1972; Vol. 1, No. 1, 25 pp.

As new technologies proliferate, the hardware systems thus generated grow with exponential speed. Video, a new tool system, has its own esoteric enclaves, including gurus, garbage men, advance scouts, and service stations.

CTL Electronics, run by C.T. Lui, is just such a service station and Video Tools is their catalogue-plus. It attempts to establish the boundaries between television and video, while bringing to the surface needed wisdom on the hardware capabilities and propensities of a variety of commercial systems. Cy Griffin and Paula Jaffe have packed this first issue with information and ideas on tape systems, lighting, portable and closed-circuit systems, as well as an introduction and wrap-up of video as a way of being. ER

Survival

VIDEO MOVEMENTS

The $1500 video system allowed large numbers of people to produce video that never had access to such a system before. A number of groups formed in the New York State area, and they have been funded primarily by the New York State Council on the Arts. These groups are the People's Video Theatre, Raindance, Videofreex, and Global Village.

New York State Council on the Arts (NYSCA)

The State Council on the Arts should be credited with having had the imagination to fund these groups two years ago. Not only did it fund them, but it left them pretty much alone. No government agency has gotten more energy and real information for its money than the State Council has from the video community.

1971-72 NYSCA Grants for TV/Media:

WCNY-TV, Syracuse $26,350
to cover costs of one or more 1/2-hour or one-hour color programs for the New York Network Art series, to be aired by all 7 member networks.

WLIW-TV, Garden City, with (each) $21,350
WMHT-TV, Schenectady; WNED-TV, Buffalo; WSKG-TV, Binghamton; and WXXI-TV, Rochester -- same as above.

WNET-TV, New York City (Ch. 13) $69,200
same as above, and to support the Artists' TV Workshop as a unit of the Experimental TV Center (artist-in-residence Nam June Paik).

American Crafts Council $ 2,800
to further the use of video feedback in the context of crafts exhibits.

The Block of 7th Street $19,986
Media Project, Inc. -- to support media workshops and work with teenagers; to produce fund-raising & publicity programs.

Broadway Local $ 2,000
to buy video equipment to record & play back community events.

Brooklyn Museum $ 5,000
to explore the potential of Museum arts programs for use on TV.

Collaborations In Art, $20,000
Science & Technology -- for continuation of collaborative art & technology program including "Multi-Media Poetry Tour."

Electronic Arts Intermix, Inc. $35,300
to support three existing programs: Perception; Avant Garde Festival; Open Circuit.

Experimental TV Center, Ltd. $12,248
toward design and construction of Paik-Abe video synthesizer.

People's Video Theatre $18,000
toward continuation & expansion of community television programming.

Port Washington Public $14,000
Library -- to continue an experimental media project in the community.

Priority One of Greater $ 3,000
Syracuse, Inc. -- to continue multi-media productions dealing with community issues.

Raindance Foundation $19,500
to continue Radical Software and community program origination for cable TV.

Rochester Museum & $15,000
Science Center -- to continue video equipment pool.

Space for Innovative $38,400
Development -- salaries for directors of Space VideoArts, general costs of administration of the Space; for an independent non-urban cable TV pilot project conducted by Paul Ryan.

Sonic Arts $ 5,000
to continue and develop multi-media concerts.

Elaine Summers Experimental $14,000
Intermedia Foundation -- to continue experiments in intermedia production, including the relation of video to dance & theatre.

Supernova of the Arts, Inc. $14,000
to continue existing programs.

Unit Productions, Ltd. $ 3,000
for six in-studio interviews with Long Island artists for broadcast. to video tape multi-media workshops organized by the Museum of the City of New York.

United Presbyterian Church $ 6,750
for trainees in cable TV workshops.

Western New York Educational $65,000
Television Association, Inc. -- to produce and tape three or four concerts and to produce a 1/2-hour program on artist Charles Burchfield.

Creative Artists Public Service Program (CAPS)

A spin-off of the State Council is the Creative Artists Public Service Program. This program was specifically designed to aid individual artists who had no support of a university, foundation, or other bureaucracy.

The individuals who got commissions in 1971 and 1972 are:

THE PYRAMID AND THE CIRCLE

It was man's presumption to use tools to harness the earth. Agriculture created cities and "civilization," where status is measured in proportion to one's distance from the earth.

Men grew distant from one another as they went further and further from their natural environment. In early Greece, the annual rebirth of spring was celebrated with songs to the ram in which all members of the community participated. As the Greeks became more sophisticated and their civilization grew, the collective songs were changed into a contest in which only a few competed to see who was "best." Eventually what started out as a collective hymn to life became a contest between dramatists to see who could write the best play about individual conflict. The participation of all had been abandoned. Now the many were passive spectators; few were the active participants.

It would seem that civilization is based on pyramidal structures, in which the few actively participate in the flow of information. Tribal man's culture, on the other hand, is based upon the circle, in which all participate equally, all have access to all the information. "In the democratic society of the Plains," Richard Erdoes writes in his book, The Sun Dance People, "every member of the tribe had his say. In a tribal council he would be listened to respectfully and without interruption." The tribal council was circular. There was no filtering down of information from the top. There were only participants, no spectators.

Until portable video, all media was in the hands of the few. Starting with writing or any other recording system, the use of the communications media was always limited to those at the top of the pyramid. What is exciting about hand-held portable video is that any person who can afford a new car can afford his own recording, storage, and playback system. Short video tapes on 1/2" equipment produced for less than $15.00 can be as moving as films or TV documentaries costing $150,000.

Video raises the consciousness of those who use it because it verifies what they see. People are frequently inarticulate about a meaningful experience; with video there is a document which communicates that experience.

In television time is money and therefore time is scarce. Real people are seldom seen on network television. Instead the time is given to stars and politicians. With video, time is abundant, and real people are its content. Stars and politicians look out of place on video -- their aura of importance is lost in the midst of honesty.

Video is not the television experience, nor the reading experience, nor any other communications experience where the many are passive receivers of information. Video may be the tool to help people get back to the circle, natural communication, and the earth.

Griffin

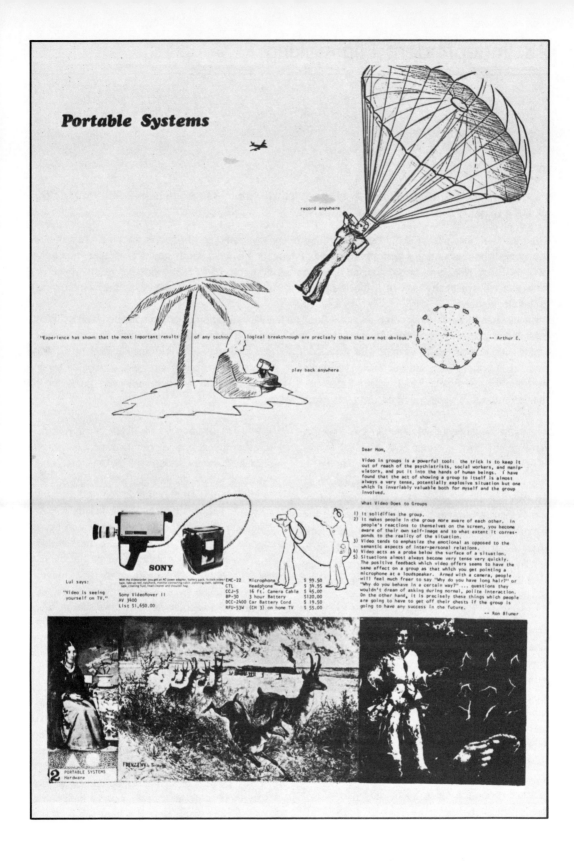

Portable Systems

record anywhere

"Experience has shown that the most important results of any technological breakthrough are precisely those that are not obvious." — Arthur C.

play back anywhere

Dear Mom,

Video in groups is a powerful tool: the trick is to keep it out of reach of the psychiatrists, social workers, and manipulators, and put it into the hands of human beings. I have found that the act of showing a group to itself is almost always a very tense, potentially explosive situation but one which is invariably valuable both for myself and the group involved.

What Video Does to Groups

1) It solidifies the group.
2) It makes people in the group more aware of each other. In people's reactions to themselves on the screen, you become aware of their own self-image and to what extent it corresponds to the reality of the situation.
3) Video tends to emphasize the emotional as opposed to the semantic aspects of inter-personal relations.
4) Video acts as a probe below the surface of a situation.
5) Situations almost always become very tense very quickly. The positive feedback which video offers seems to have the same effect on a group as that which you get pointing a microphone at a loudspeaker. Armed with a camera, people will feel much freer to say "Why do you have long hair?" or "Why do you behave in a certain way?" ... questions they wouldn't dream of asking during normal, polite interaction. On the other hand, it is precisely these things which people are going to have to get off their chests if the group is going to have any success in the future.

— Ron Blumer

Lui says:

"Video is seeing yourself on TV."

Sony VideoRover II
AV 3400
List $1,650.00

With the Videorecorder, you get an AC power adaptor, battery pack, ½-inch video tape, take-up reel, earphone, monitor connecting cable, polishing cloth, splicing tape, cleaning fluid, lined cleaner and shoulder bag.

EMC-22	Microphone	$ 99.50
CTL	Headphone	$ 34.95
CCJ-5	16 ft. Camera Cable	$ 45.00
BP-30	3 hour Battery	$120.00
DCC-2400	Car Battery Cord	$ 19.50
RFU-53W	(CH 3) on home TV	$ 55.00

2 PORTABLE SYSTEMS Hardware

FRENZENVL

23. Independent Filmmaking

LENNY LIPTON. Straight Arrow Books, 625 Third Street, San Francisco, Calif. 94107; 1972; $5.95; 431 pp.

There's lots of talk around about decentralization of society, power to the people, etc., but, unfortunately, the idealization obscures the performance. And performance is what it's all about. Somebody has got to do it if CBS or NBC is to be sidetracked as shaper of the public mind. Somebody has got to spend real time with his eye at the lens of a movie camera if Hollywood is to be usurped as the creator of our corporate imagery.

Lenny Lipton has written a comprehensive book on the filmmaking process. It's a masterful presentation, a book that was created by both Lipton and the 1960s, a period of frenetic, independent film activity when Lipton was at once both an important participant and a spokesman-critic. He knows what he's talking about. The book is filled with technical information on equipment, film, processing, etc., as well as serving as a manual on shooting and editing. It can be used as a complete and comprehensive guide for the filmmaker through all stages of his or her development. JB

The traditional concept of judging image quality in terms of fine grain, accurate color rendition (whatever that is), sharpness, gradation and so on, is hopelessly outmoded. A creative filmmaker must be aware of all of these factors which do contribute to the appearance of the final image. But the filmmaker is cheating himself if he fails to realize that the traditional concept of best or good quality, while it may be suitable for commercial filmmakers, is of no value and may in fact restrict creative expression.

One of the constructs (or models) that scientists use to explain the nature of light, is that light is propagated in the form of a wave, traveling in a straight line from the source or origin. For our purposes this statement is essentially correct for light traveling through a medium like space or air. But when light travels from one medium to another, from air to glass or to water, its rate of propagation through that medium changes. Light travels through air or space at about 186,000 miles a second; it loses about one third of that velocity through glass.

The fact that light is a wave phenomenon and that it travels at different speeds through different media accounts for the fact that light is bent as it moves from one medium to another.

When light travels from air to glass, it is bent towards the normal. The normal is a line drawn perpendicular to the surface at the point where the light enters or leaves. Light is always bent toward the normal when it enters a denser medium. This process of light bending is called *refraction*. Each transparent medium can be assigned a number, determined experimentally, which serves to indicate how much that medium will bend light. This number is called the *index of refraction*. The index of refraction of air, with respect to a vacuum, is 1.0003, so that its value may be taken as unity, for most purposes. Water has an index of refraction of 1.334, diamond 2.419 and crown glass, sometimes used for lenses, has an index of 1.517.

A lot of mystery surrounds the *A and B editing* technique. It is a tedious, time-consuming technique and, when used to match camera footage with a workprint, not any more creative than simple preparation of one printer roll, or *A rolling*. However, the A and B technique can be used as a method of filmic composition, and although previously confined to 16mm, there are a growing number of labs offering this service for the super 8 format.

Here we are concerned with conforming camera film with workprint. When you A and B your camera film, you can expect to achieve invisible splices, fades and dissolves (fades, by the way, are available for A rolled reversal film, but not negative—if you want fades for negative-positive printing you must A and B roll), multiple images, toned sections and burnt-in titles. The list may not be complete, and there is some overlapping in the classifications: for example, burnt-in titles are a special case of multiple images.

Now what is A and B rolling anyway? It involves the preparation of two picture rolls, an A roll and a B roll, each of which consists of a series of images alternated with black leader. When there is an image on the B roll there is usually complementary black leader on the A roll. Black leader is simply processed film with an opaque black emulsion. The best leader sold for this purpose is offered by the lab you use.

The first print made from the edited footage and mag track is called the *answer print*. The answer print is a trial print which may be used as a basis for making further prints. If more than one answer print has to be made (this might be required because of additional editing, for example), the first print made becomes known as the first answer print, the second will be the second answer print and so on. Hopefully, the first answer print will match your intention closely enough so that you can use it for projection purposes. Prints made after this stage are called *release prints*.

You present your *master material,* whatever is used to print your film, to the lab. It could be camera original, or an intermediate copy made for protecting the original and the sound track material. From this the lab makes a *married* or *composite answer print* that combines both picture and sound track. If you want to have a mag track recorded on a stripe, instruct the lab to go ahead and do just that. When you get your answer print back, watch the image, listen to the track and decide if things are as they should be. You may decide that the sound, our concern here, is just fine—no alterations are necessary. If you don't like what the lab has done, you can have the lab rerecord it. This is much cheaper than having to pay for a whole new print, as you'd have to if your film had an optical track. As a matter of fact, at any time during the life of a mag striped print, you can have it rerecorded: a print with an optical track can be mag striped over the optical track.

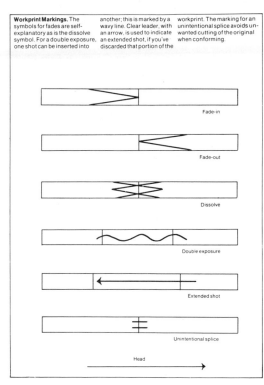

Workprint Markings. The symbols for fades are self-explanatory as is the dissolve symbol. For a double exposure, one shot can be inserted into another; this is marked by a wavy line. Clear leader, with an arrow, is used to indicate an extended shot, if you've discarded that portion of the workprint. The marking for an unintentional splice avoids unwanted cutting of the original when conforming.

Fade-in

Fade-out

Dissolve

Double exposure

Extended shot

Unintentional splice

Head

Independent Filmmaking

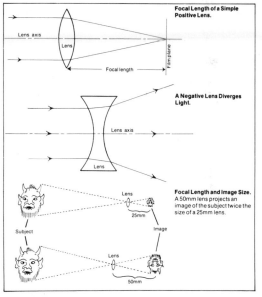

Focal Length of a Simple Positive Lens.

Lens axis

Lens

Focal length

Film plane

A Negative Lens Diverges Light.

Lens axis

Lens

Focal Length and Image Size. A 50mm lens projects an image of the subject twice the size of a 25mm lens.

Lens

25mm

Image

Subject

Lens

50mm

The Lens

24. The Last Whole Earth Catalog

Whole Earth Catalog. **Penguin Books Ltd., Harmondsworth, Middx; £1.75; 448 pp.**

The Last Whole Earth Catalog is a large record of an experiment in information processing. The experiment was a communications and monetary success, and this last catalog (there were five previous editions of the *Whole Earth Catalog*) is a testament to that success as well as a manual for others to do something similar on their own.

The *Catalog* provides "access to tools"—tools that are useful, relevant to independent education, high-quality or low-cost, and easily available by mail. The *Catalog's* purpose: "We *are* as gods and might as well get good at it. So far remotely done power and glory—as via government, big business, formal education, church—has succeeded to the point where gross defects obscure actual gains. In response to this dilemma and to these gains a realm of intimate, personal power is developing—power of the individual to conduct his own education, find his own inspiration, shape his own environment, and share his adventure with whoever is interested. Tools that aid this process are sought and promoted by the *Whole Earth Catalog.*" ER

HOW TO DO A WHOLE EARTH CATALOG

The masked man left behind a silver bullet.
The people said, "We'd rather have a scribbled diagram," and they shot him with his silver bullet. Here's our scribbled diagram.

RESEARCHING

For us this consisted of three big jobs. 1. Encouraging an incoming flow of information—spontaneous research by the readership. 2. Scanning "the literature" for promising stuff. 3. Sorting the good from the bad.

1. The incentives we laid out for spontaneous suggestions were: reward of money ($10 for published review, later $10 for any used suggestion); reward of recognition (we published the name of the reviewer and suggestor, spelled as correctly as possible); reward of honor-by-association (to the extent that we kept valid high standards, and honored the famous suggestor no more than the teenage one); reward of doing a good deed (to be a noble conduit we had to stay clean); reward of return (to the extent that we gave good, people returned it).

2. "The literature" for us consisted of *Publisher's Weekly, Forthcoming Books in Print* (both from R. R. Bowker, source of all the basic cataloging information on books in the U.S.—I consider R. R. Bowker a major pillar of Western Civilization; they labor endlessly, invaluably, without bias and of course unheralded). *Science* (who list all the books sent to them for review), *Scientific American* (the first national publication to notice us, by the way), *Popular Science* (for tools), and later our cooperative competition such as *Mother Earth News, Big Rock Candy Mountain, Canadian Whole Earth Almanac, Natural Life Styles.*

Other major sources: catalogs from the publishers, bibliographies in good books (especially when annotated), big book stores, especially Kepler's, friends' bookshelves, the Stanford and Menlo Park libraries, and our own bookshelves revisited.

At the beginning of the *Catalog* I ordered copies of promising titles from the publishers at 40% discount on ABA's Single Copy Order Plan. After about a year of this MIT said we didn't really have to pay for review copies from them. After that we requested free review copies from all the publishers and usually got them, at least on new books. It took some self-policing to keep from requesting "review copies" that we just wanted to have. There are some built-in conflicts-of-interest in the reviewing business.

Sorting. Fuller calls it "tuning out everything that's irrelevant", and considers it the core activity of thinking. It is utterly unglamorous; it is shovelling shit by the mountainload. I never spent my time reading the good stuff—whose quality was usually evident in 2-3 minutes. I spent the yellow-brown hours reading the lousy books, digging past their promising facades to the hollow within. Some of these wound up in the stove, where their publishers belonged.

———————

At the beginning of the *Catalog* I imagined us becoming primarily a research organization, with nifty projects everywhere, earnest folk climbing around on new dome designs, solar generators, manure converters; comparing various sound systems, horse breeds, teaching methods . . . the only product-project we ever did was build a BD-4 airplane, and I felt guilty about that because of the big expense for low yield of information.

In fact we didn't do enough research. Not the studious kind. Of our staff of about 26, only 2 or 3 were ever engaged in active search for *Catalog* material. It could have been much more and better, but it never got organized, probably because of prima donna failings on my part.

———————

REVIEWING

Usually I review a book before I read it. These are almost always shorter, pithier, more positive and useful reviews. You're approaching the book from the same perspective as the reader—unfamiliarity—and you're not apt to fall into imitation of the author's style or petty argument with his views, as critics do.

So, I review the book, enthusiastically, on what I know from its title, its subject, the author, my own experience, and a hasty glance at the pages. Then I look a little more deeply to see if the review is fulfilled. If not, I either rewrite the review or discard the book.

The quickest clues to the authority of a book are its illustrations and its back pages. Cheap shit editor's-idea books puff up their illustrations. If a book has a whole page devoted to a photograph of nothing, with a nothing caption and credit to some manufacturer for the photo, throw the book.

Look for photographs that contain real information related to the text, and captions that multiply the use of the picture; or diagrams that deliver complex understanding simply. In the back of the book look at the bibliography. If it's absent, or inflated endlessly, or unannotated, or oddly limited, be suspicious. The bibliography is an easy way to compare the author's judgment with your own.

The *Catalog* format for reviews includes excerpts from the book (or magazine or catalog). The excerpts should expose the book—convey quickly what's in it, and deliver a few complete ideas independently useful to the reader. I always attempt to gut the book with the excerpts, extract its central value. Really good books like *On Growth and Form,* or *Stick and Rudder,* or *Natural Way to Draw* will not be gutted; practically any line or picture in them can be used.

An ideal review gives the reader: a quick idea of what the item is, what it's useful for, how it compares to others like it, and how competent the reviewer is to judge. (This last is why I stopped having unsigned reviews—the reader gradually grows familiar with the weaknesses and strengths of the various reviewers.)

The horrible temptation in reviews is to show off rather than simply introduce the item and the reader to each other and get out of the way.

25. A Year from Monday: New Lectures and Writings

JOHN CAGE. Calder & Boyars Ltd., 18 Brewer Street, London W1R 4AS; (H) 1968; £3.50; (P) 1972; £1.25; 167 pp.

John Cage started out as a composer. One could say his major interest has gone from music to "everything." For Cage, there's only one mind, the one we all share. Mind's socialized. We can't change our minds without changing the world. As an extension of our central nervous system, our mind is everywhere we look, everything we see, everything we hear. JB

The question is: Is my thought changing? It is and it isn't. One evening after dinner I was telling friends that I was now concerned with improving the world. One of them said: I thought you always were. I then explained that I believe—and am acting upon—Marshall McLuhan's statement that we have through electronic technology produced an extension of our brains to the world formerly outside of us. To me that means that the disciplines, gradual and sudden (principally Oriental), formerly practiced by individuals to pacify their minds, bringing them into accord with ultimate reality, must now be practiced socially—that is, not just inside our heads, but outside of them, in the world, where our central nervous system effectively now is.

Why this palaver about structure? Particularly since he doesn't need to have any, involved as he is with process, knowing that the frame that will be put around the all that he makes will not make the environment invisible? Simply in order to make clear that these flags-numbers-letters-targets are not subjects? (That he has nothing to say about them proves that they are not subjects rather than that he as a human being is absent from them. He is present as a person who has noticed that *At every point in nature there is something to see.* And so: *My work contains similar possibilities for the changing focus of the eye.)* Structures, not subjects—if only that that will make us pause long enough in our headstrong passage through history to realize that Pop

Art, if deducted from his work, represents a misunderstanding, if embarked upon as the next step after his, represents a non-sequitur. He is engaged with the endlessly changing ancient task: the imitation of nature in her manner of operation. The structures he uses give the dates and places (some less confined historically and geographically than others). They are the signature of anonymity. When, dealing with operative nature he does so without structure, he sometimes introduces signs of humanity to intimate that we, not birds for instance, are part of the dialogue. Someone, that is, must have said Yes *(No)*, but since we are not now informed we answer the painting affirmatively. Finally, with nothing in it to grasp, the work is weather, an atmosphere that is heavy rather than light (something he knows and regrets); in oscillation with it we tend toward our ultimate place: zero, gray disinterest.

The question is not: How much are you going to get out of it? Nor is it How much are you going to put into it? But rather: How immediately are you going to say Yes to no matter what unpredictability, even when what happens seems to have no relation to what one thought was one's commitment?

Kwang-tse points out that a beautiful woman who gives pleasure to men serves only to frighten the fish when she jumps in the water.

**LOOKING IN ALL DIRECTIONS
NOT JUST ONE DIRECTION.** Housing
(Fuller) will be, like telephoning, a
service. Only circumstance to stop your
living there: someone's there already
(it's busy). Thus we'll learn to
desire emptiness. Not being able to say,
"This is mine," we'll want when we
inquire to get no response at all. 4:00
P. M. throughout the world. Whether
we like it or not (is what he said)
it's happening to us. **Advertisements are
all good; the news is all bad (McLuhan).
But how we receive bad news can change:
we're glad to hear unemployment's
increasing. Soon, all that will be
required of us will be one hour's
work per year (Fuller).** *X. They ask what
the purpose of art is. Is that how
things are? Say there were a thousand
artists and one purpose, would one
artist be having it and all the nine
hundred and ninety-nine others be
missing the point?* **Arcata Bottom sign
said: Experiment endlessly and keep
humble.** "Write to Center for the Study
of Democratic Institutions; they'll
know about the global services." I
did. They answered they knew nothing,
˗ suggested writing to State Department.
Books one formerly needed were hard to
˗ locate. Now they're all out in
paperback. Society's changing.
Relevant information's hard to come
by. Soon it'll be everywhere, unnoticed.

XXII. Heaven's no
longer paved with gold (changes in
church architecture). Heaven's a motel.
She changed part of the loft: wall-to-wall
carpeting, mobile TV. No conflicts.
Twenty-two telephone calls were made
by Betty Zeiger "disrupting efficiency
of federal agencies . . . dedicated to
pursuit of peace." State Department
said Hawaii speaker was a woman.
Fifty-five (now sixty-one) global services
are in area of humanities "beyond
mere provision of food/shelter." Not
technological services. *State Department:
Global village developed from
"Literary Villages" (plan for the
betterment of life in India).* "We are
packages of leaking water." "The next
water you drink may be your own."
XXIII. **LET'S CALL IT THE
COLLECTIVE CONSCIOUSNESS (WE'VE GOT
THE COLLECTIVE UNCONSCIOUS). THE
QUESTION IS: WHAT ARE THE THINGS
EVERYONE NEEDS REGARDLESS OF LIKES
AND DISLIKES? BEGINNING OF ANSWER:
WATER, FOOD, SHELTER, CLOTHING,
ELECTRICITY, AUDIO-VISUAL
COMMUNICATION, TRANSPORTATION. FORM
OF ANSWER: GLOBAL UTILITIES NETWORK.**

At any point in time, there is a tendency when one "thinks" about world society to "think" that things are fixed, cannot change. This non-changeability is imaginary, invented by 'thought' to simplify the process of 'thinking.' But thinking is nowadays complex: it assumes, to begin with, the work of Einstein. Our minds are changing from the use of simple, critical faculties to the use of design, problem-solving, creative faculties, from an unrealistic concern with a non-existent status quo to a courageous seeing of things in movement, life as revolution. History is one revolution after another.

26. The Shape of Time:
Remarks on the History of Things

GEORGE KUBLER. Yale University Press Ltd., 20 Bloomsbury Square, London WC1A 2NP; (H) 1962; £2.25; (P) 1965; £0.65; 136 pp.

The remarkable thing about the world is the fact that it simply " is " (as opposed to how or why it is). Yet, in this century, the creation of symbols and the study of meanings have dominated the intellectual and artistic climate. The mere isness of things, of the world, of you and me, is also an exciting area for exploration. Kubler, an art historian, points out that "what a thing means is not more important than what it is" and presents the basis for this approach to the realignment of events. JB

Let us suppose that the idea of art can be expanded to embrace the whole range of man-made things, including all tools and writing in addition to the useless, beautiful, and poetic things of the world. By this view the universe of man-made things simply coincides with the history of art. It then becomes an urgent requirement to devise better ways of considering everything men have made. This we may achieve sooner by proceeding from art rather than from use, for if we depart from use alone, all useless things are overlooked, but if we take the desirableness of things as our point of departure, then useful objects are properly seen as things we value more or less dearly.

In effect, the only tokens of history continually available to our senses are the desirable things made by men. Of course, to say that man-made things are desirable is redundant, because man's native inertia is overcome only by desire, and nothing gets made unless it is desirable.

Such things mark the passage of time with far greater accuracy than we know, and they fill time with shapes of a limited variety.

The narrative historian always has the privilege of deciding that continuity cuts better into certain lengths than into others. He never is required to defend his cut, because history cuts anywhere with equal ease, and a good story can begin anywhere the teller chooses.

For others who aim beyond narration the question is to find cleavages in history where a cut will separate different types of happening. Many have thought that to make the inventory would lead toward such an enlarged understanding. The archaeologists and anthropologists classify things by their uses, having first separated material and mental culture, or things and ideas. The historians of art, who separate useful and aesthetic products, classify these latter by types, by schools, and by styles.

Schools and styles are the products of the long stock-taking of the nineteenth-century historians of art. This stock-taking, however, cannot go on endlessly; in theory it comes to an end with irreproachable and irrefutable lists and tables.

For the shapes of time, we need a criterion that is not a mere transfer by analogy from biological science. Biological time consists of uninterrupted durations of statistically predictable lengths: each organism exists from birth to death upon an " expected " life-span. Historical time, however, is intermittent and variable. Every action is more intermittent than it is continuous, and the intervals between actions are infinitely variable in duration and content. The end of an action and its beginning are indeterminate. Clusters of actions here and there thin out or thicken sufficiently to allow us with some objectivity to mark beginnings and endings. Events and the intervals between them are the elements of the patterning of historical time. Biological time contains the unbroken events called lives; it also contains social organizations by species and groups of species, but in biology the intervals of time between events are disregarded, while in historical time the web of happening that laces throughout the intervals between existences attracts our interest.

Time, like mind, is not knowable as such. We know time only indirectly by what happens in it: by observing change and permanence; by marking the succession of events among stable settings; and by noting the contrast of varying rates of change. Written documents give us a thin recent record for only a few parts of the world. In the main our knowledge of older times is based upon visual evidence of physical and biological duration. Technological seriations of all sorts and sequences of works of art in every grade of distinction yield a finer time scale overlapping with the written record.

As it is, our perception of things is a circuit unable to admit a great variety of new sensations all at once. Human perception is best suited to slow modifications of routine behavior. Hence invention has always had to halt at the gate of perception where the narrowing of the way allows much less to pass than the importance of the messages or the need of the recipients would justify. How can we increase the inbound traffic at the gate?

The task of the present generation is to construct a history of things that will do justice both to meaning and being, both to the plan and to the fullness of existence, both to the scheme and to the thing. This purpose raises the familiar existential dilemma between meaning and being. We are discovering little by little all over again that what a thing means is not more important than what it is; that expression and form are equivalent challenges to the historian; and that to neglect either meaning or being, either essence or existence, deforms our comprehension of both.

HUMAN SYSTEMS

27. An Introduction to the Study of Man

J.Z. YOUNG. Oxford University Press, Ely House, 37 Dover Street, London W1X 4AH; 1971; £6.00; 719 pp.

In his previous books John Zachary Young has explored different models and systems encompassing the octopus, vertebrates and mammals, memory, belief structures in science, and the brain. In essence, Young is a biologist and he now brings his biological framework to the study of man.

In *An Introduction to the Study of Man* Young presents what biology and a variety of other disciplines know about the life of human beings. But it is always the biologist speaking, whether about cultural anthropology, population ecology or epistemology. An enormous wealth of data is presented dealing with heredity, aging, growth, reproduction, intelligence, race, war, aggression, philosophy, sociology, and the development of the individual.

What is discovered in the *Introduction* is that the background, the brain, is predominant. The brain shapes our language and so our thinking according to pre-programs that have their source in the very organization of the brain. ER

Our theme then is that living things act as they do because they are so organized as to take actions that prevent their dissolution into the surroundings. They maintain this organization by virtue of a system that may be called the transfer of information from the past. Human living organization is maintained and transmitted by its own special operations, among which the most characteristic are the use of language and of tools or artefacts to assist with bodily functions. We shall try to reach an understanding of the significance of the events of human life by examining how they contribute to this process of maintenance of continuity or homeostasis. We shall find that a surprising range of actions can be understood in this way. Many simpler ones such as breathing and eating or the healing of wounds are necessary to preserve the individual, other obvious ones perpetuate the species. But man's particular genius is for the transfer of information between individuals and many subtle features are involved in his homeostasis. Communication by symbols is improved by all the agencies that we include as art, literature, and aesthetics, and these, far from being "impractical", *are major contributors to human homeostasis* (Chapters 36 and 37). So are, of course, all the actions that contribute to social organization, religion, politics, law, and education.

Human homeostasis therefore depends upon an infinitely complex set of factors, which no one author or book could possibly cover. Our attempt is only to make an introduction to the study of man.

---

10. Development of consciousness

One line of investigation that is open to us is to study so far as we are able the growth of awareness in the child. There is abundant evidence that even up to about the age of 7 the child does not make the distinction between itself and the world that is so characteristic of the adult. We shall see something of the study by Piaget of the growth of concepts by which the child learns to operate (Chapter 21). It is relatively late before he has ideas of space, size, and direction that are adequate to describe the relationship of objects in the world to each other and of himself to them. Inded at first the child is in the stage characterized as 'absolute realism', where it confuses itself with the world. When it comes to use words and names, these are considered, as it were, to be resident in the things they describe.

Clearly all this shows once again that what we call awareness has more to do with communication and indeed with social situations than naïve adult analysis implies. There is a story told by Edmund Gosse that he only began to think of himself as a person when he lied to his father and was not found out. Thus he learned that there was a secret belonging to Edmund Gosse and to someone who lived in the same body with him. 'There were two of us and we could talk together . . . the sense of my individuality now suddenly descended upon me ' (Gosse 1907).

Here the weakness of our concepts becomes glaring, and they will no doubt seem childishly ridiculous to our successors. Even today to look for God among the stars will seem as impious and old-fashioned to some people as it may seem imaginative to others. 'The kingdom of God is within you', might be the response of the religious. And the biologist might not greatly disagree with him. For instead of beginning our account as we did, with the elements and molecules that men are made of, we might better have begun by emphasizing our knowledge of the brain, by which all knowledge comes to us, including that of atoms, astronomy, and Final Cause. To discuss brain function adequately we must consider operations commonly called 'mental' (Harre 1970). Yet we do begin to see how each brain is the centre of a very special type of deductive/inductive forecasting system (Chapter 42). Here again, our concepts remain primitive and incomplete, but what we know about the brain already gives us understanding far beyond anything our predecessors had. We do not fully understand the dilemma of our awareness of self and otherness, but there are enough facts known about aberrations of consciousness to make us very suspicious of the apparently self-evident dualist propositions of ordinary language on this subject. The categories of mind and body are not, as they seem at first, simple or easy to contrast (Chapter 10).

Again, it is not known in detail how the cerebral system forms representations of the world and uses them for forecasting. We have used the concept of a 'model in the brain', but it is little more than a general metaphor (Craik 1943). It is a useful way of referring to an entity whose existence we can recognize but whose properties we cannot yet define. To use such a phrase at all may seem not merely irritating but specious and even unscrupulous to those psychologists and others who appreciate the complexities of the operating system that is involved. The neurologist is the first to agree with these doubts, for he knows only too well how complicated the brain is. No one who has tried to discover the connection patterns and operations of even a small part of it can fail to appreciate that we do not know how to describe what is involved in such a multichannel system. These very difficulties may have led neurologists to be overcautious in their attempts to understand the mechanisms responsible for animal and human actions. Yet in some respects we can begin to give real meaning to the concept of a model in the brain (Chapter 42).

It is certainly a further large step to our suggestion that the model in its early stages in each of us is built around the use of symbolic representations of persons and their communications (Chapter 19). Knowledge about this may, however, provide light on the reasons why we cannot help thinking 'anthropomorphically' about all sorts of matters, from personal ones such as our own references to ourselves, our egos, ids, and superegos, to searches for ultimates in physics, metaphysics, or religion. It is certain that attitudes to all these great questions will be fundamentally changed as we come to know how it is that our brains deal with them as they do. We can only reap the meagre first fruits of such knowledge in practical matters yet. The facts of its existence and yet feebleness warn us not to be 'simpleminded' and yet to be humble in our ignorance. We may be encouraged by the thought that perhaps we are of a generation that first *begins* to understand the cerebral basis of thinking.

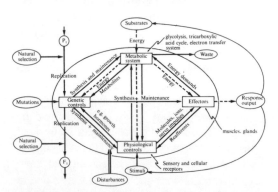

Diagram to show the flow of information and energy by which homeostatis is achieved (After Waterman 1968)

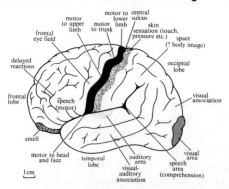

Left side of the human brain showing the main sensory and motor areas heavily shaded or stippled. Some of the functions that can be referred to other areas are also indicated.

28. Man Adapting

RENÉ DUBOS. Yale University Press, Ltd., 20 Bloomsbury Square, London WC1A 2NP; 1967; (H) £5.65; (P) £1.75; 527 pp.

Dubos is a Nobel laureate microbiologist recently retired from Rockefeller University. The dominant theme of his written work is the exploration of biological and social implications of man's responses to his total environment. In studying microbial diseases he discovered that prevalence and severity are conditioned to a great extent by the ways of life of the person afflicted. Man, as organism, responds uniquely to stimuli: ". . . his responses are determined less by the direct effects of the stimuli on his body fabric than by the symbolic interpretation he attaches to the stimuli." JB

The problems of human adaptation could be presented as a dialectic between permanency and change. To a surprising extent, modern man has retained unaltered the bodily constitution, physiological responses, and emotional drives which he has inherited from his Paleolithic ancestors. Yet he lives in a mechanized, air-conditioned, and regimented world radically different from the one in which he evolved. Thus, persistence of ancient traits does not mean that human history is a mere extension of the past; nor do changes in the ways of life imply a loss of the biological heritage.

The components of the body machine *react with* the environment, in the same way as do similar components in any other living or inanimate system. But living man *responds* to his environment. I have intentionally differentiated between *reaction* and *response* to emphasize that human adaptation can seldom be regarded as merely the result of man's body reacting with environmental forces. In fact, man's responses are not even necessarily aimed at coping with the environment. They often correspond rather to an expressive behavior and involve the use of the environment for self-actualization.

Physicians and experimenters interested in the forces which determine the physical and mental state of man find it useful to differentiate between genetic, historical, and environmental factors, or between conscious and unconscious responses. In reality, however, man is an integrated entity and all these forces operate simultaneously in every event of his life. The body and the mind are the living records of countless influences which have shaped each individual person from the most distant past to the present instant. Man is indeed the product of his history, but this history is far more complex than Ortega's statement would suggest. The history of each human being includes his private experiences and personal decisions; it encompasses also the evolutionary as well as the social past. Man's physical and mental state, in health and in disease, is always conditioned by all the multiple determinants of his nature.

Most forms of sensory deprivation, especially during the early phases of life, thus seem to prevent the organism from developing essential mechanisms and patterns of responses without which adaptability is severely handicapped throughout the rest of life. In other words, complete psychological development depends on a multiplicity of environmental stimuli. In their absence or if they are inadequate, intelligence does not develop normally and the personality becomes grossly atypical.

Another illustration of the fact that modern man retains essential traits of his evolutionary past is the persistence in him of hormonal and metabolic responses which were developed to meet threatening situations during his animal ancestry, but which no longer fit the needs of life in civilized societies. In a normal person as well as in animals, the physiologic and metabolic changes required for the successful performance of a physical effort begin before the actual effort is set in motion, indeed as soon as the need for them is anticipated by the body. This power to mobilize in an anticipatory manner and almost instantaneously the various bodily resources required for flight or for fight has been certainly of great advantage throughout evolution; it increased the chance of success in dealing with the harsh forces of the external environment, and in particular with predators and enemies of all sorts. But what was once an advantage is increasingly becoming a handicap under the conditions of modern human life.

While so essential in everyday discourse, the word adaptation is treacherous because it can mean so many different things to different persons. The layman, the biologist, the physician, and the sociologist use the word, each in his own way, to denote a multiplicity of genetic, physiologic, psychic, and social phenomena, completely unrelated in their fundamental mechanisms. These phenomena set in motion a great variety of totally different processes, the effects of which may be initially favorable to the individual organism or social group involved, and yet have ultimate consequences that are dangerous in the long run. Furthermore, an adaptive process may be successful biologically while undesirable socially.

29. Mankind Evolving

THEODOSIUS DOBZHANSKY. Yale University Press Ltd., 20 Bloomsbury Square, London WC1A 2NP; 1962; (H) £4.50; (P) £1.50; 381 pp.

Human evolution has been described in terms of all kinds of things, of constructs, the most predominant of which are (a) a purely biological process, and (b) history of culture. But the truth, if there is such an animal, probably lies not in pat explanations, but in the capacity of the human mind to exercise itself with new patterns of subtlety and complexity, with new shadings.

Dobzhansky, a leading geneticist, develops a "superorganic view"—an interaction between the two presupposed components, both of which serve the same function: the adaptation to, and control of, man's environment. JB

Infinity is a notion which most people find hard to conceive of. Creation myths were accordingly constructed to show that man and the universe did have a beginning. Once created, they thought, things were established forever. Before the idea of universal change was thrust upon people by evolutionary science, whether they liked it or not, change was regarded with misgiving, as something more apt to result in deterioration than improvement. Deterioration was, indeed, the only kind of "evolution" people could imagine readily: the Age of Gold is far in the past, the Iron Age is our lot. Hindu sages combined this with the idea of eternal recurrence—the ages of benevolent gods are succeeded by ages of less benevolent ones; ours is the age of the terrible goddess Kali; this will end in a cataclysm; whereupon everything will be repeated from the beginning. Even the ancient Greeks, whose wisdom we find so congenial, did not think of evolution. Yes, the world had a start, they thought, but it was not growing progressively better. Although man can aspire to see the beauty of eternal ideas, these ideas are distorted, and only dimly reflected in the things met in the world.

Indeed, man lives not by bread alone. Play and aesthetics, two "hungers" which have at first glance baffling biological meanings, may be considered briefly. There exists a voluminous literature on play in humans and animals, but the concept of play is hard to define with precision. By and large, play is a self-rewarding activity, i.e., the performance of the action constitutes its own recompense. Play occurs chiefly, if not exclusively, in vertebrate animals, and particularly among the higher ones, mammals and birds. The behavior of invertebrates is too stereotyped to permit play. In other words, their "appetitive behavior" (such as courtship) is too rigidly tied to its satisfaction in the consummatory act (copulation). Man has been described as the most playful of all animals (Homo ludens, Huizinga 1955). At any rate, playing and games are among the cultural universals in all mankind.

Far-reaching cultural transformations have manifestly taken and are taking place. Do genetic changes accompany the cultural ones? White (1949) believes that "in the man-culture equation over a period of a million years, we may assume some absolute increase in magnitude of the biological factor. But during the last hundred, or even the last fifty thousand years, we have no evidence of an appreciable increase in mental ability." The assumption of the psychic unity, or uniformity, of mankind is probably pivotal in the working philosophy of a majority of anthropologists, psychologists, sociologists, and of not a few biologists. They maintain that biological evolution has achieved the genetic basis of culture and run its course; it is now a matter of the past. The genetic basis of culture is uniform everywhere; cultural evolution has long since taken over.

Although all men now living are members of a single biological species, no two persons, except identical twins, have the same genetic endowment. Every individual is biologically unique and nonrecurrent. It would be naive to claim that the discovery of this biological uniqueness constitutes a scientific proof of every person's existential singularity, but this view is at least consistent with the fact of biological singularity.

Anyway, genetic individuality is not the whole story. Superimposed on the individual variability there is a group variability. Very few biological species are panmictic, i.e., consist of a single Mendelian population in which the chances of mating of any two adult individuals of opposite sex are equal. Such panmictic species are shrunken relics of formerly more differentiated species now on the verge of extinction. Man is certainly not such a species.

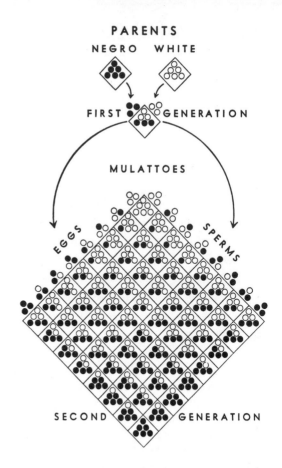

Figure 4. A scheme of the inheritance of the skin color difference between Negroes and whites, on the assumption that this difference is due to three pairs of genes. Black—genes producing more pigment; white—producing less pigment.

Figure 10. The geographic occurrence of a majority of the thirty-four races of man.

1. Northwest European
2. Northeast European
3. Alpine
4. Mediterranean
5. Hindu
6. Turkic
7. Tibetan
8. North Chinese
9. Classic Mongoloid
10. Eskimo
11. Southeast Asiatic
12. Ainu
13. Lapp
14. North American Indian
15. Central American Indian
16. South American Indian
17. Fuegian
18. East African
19. Sudanese
20. Forest Negro
21. Bantu
22. Bushman and Hottentot
23. African Pygmy
24. Dravidian
25. Negrito
26. Melanesian-Papuan
27. Murrayian
28. Carpentarian
29. Micronesian
30. Polynesian
31. Neo Hawaiian
32. Ladino
33. North American Colored
34. South African Colored

30. Changing Perspectives on Man

Edited by BEN ROTHBLATT. University of Chicago Press Ltd., 126 Buckingham Palace Road, London SW1W 9SD; 1969; £3.80; 298 pp.

What is a man? Plato defined him as a featherless biped. Diogenes handed Plato a plucked rooster and said: "Here's your man. " This book offers a few more ideas on the subject from a group brought together in 1966-67 as part of the "Monday Lectures " at the University of Chicago. JB

. . . If we investigate the form and meaning of sentences and if we pay careful attention to the characteristic creative aspect of language use, we are led to the conclusion that a person's knowledge of his language is representable as a generative grammar that is organized in the following way: it contains a set of *base rules* that define deep structures and a set of *transformational rules* that convert a deep structure into a surface structure. The grammar will then contain rules of semantic interpretation, which determine the meaning of a sentence on the basis of the intrinsic semantic content of its lexical items and the grammatical relations represented in the deep structure, and it will contain rules of phonetic interpretation, which determine the phonetic form on the basis of the intrinsic phonological content of its minimal elements and the grammatical organization represented in the surface structure. The rules that form and manipulate these structures are highly abstract and, furthermore, meet certain formal conditions and satisfy certain principles of organization of a quite specific sort. One would certainly suppose that much of this structure is universal, and what information is presently available from detailed investigation of language structure seems consistent with this supposition.

I regard the great epochs in evolutionary advance as the development of (1) the gene, which gave continuity; (2) of sex, which allowed gene shuffling and speeded change; (3) of multicellularity, which allowed specialization of function and the allocation of pliability or malleability to a particular group of cells, (4) of the nervous system which—first in the attributes of the individual unit, then in the richness and intricacy in the patterns of the connections, and finally in the sheer aggregation of larger and larger numbers of units and patterns—rapidly took on greater capacity for being modified, thus increasing the malleability of organisms. Thereafter, the environment could act on the race, by selection, *and* on the maturing human being so that individual experience could be passed on.

In social evolution, I see three sub-epochs, each of immense importance. The first great achievement was the use of a symbol to represent some thing: this is *prelanguage.* Many higher animals besides man clearly can use symbols; to some extent, they have also made a second step, the use of organized symbols: this is *language.* None except man has taken the third step, the use of tested organized symbols: this is *science.*

Speculation is rife concerning the possibility that there may be life of some sort on other planets, on other planetary systems, and in other galaxies. Some authorities go so far as to proclaim it a certainty that life not merely could, but must have arisen in many places in the universe. More than that, sentient and rational beings must have evolved on many planets where there is life. In other words, "We are not alone. " The name "exobiology " has been invented for the study of the assumed extraterrestrial life. The problems of exobiology cannot be adequately discussed here;

I realize that the following remarks may do injustice to the ingenious speculations advanced in the field. I cannot, however, help wondering if the exobiologists may not turn out to be high-powered specialists on a nonexistent subject.

The relation of the brain to the problem of ground living may be illustrated in a different way. Man's use of the ground, his perception of space, is very different from that of the nonhuman primates. Most monkeys and apes spend their lives within a few square miles, perhaps as much as 15 square miles for gorilla and chimpanzees, but much less for the vast majority of primates. Here are animals with senses like our own, which can see food, water, and other animals beyond their range, but which make no use of this information. Both in gathering and in hunting, man utilizes vastly larger areas, and in the larger area there is a far greater diversity of plant and animal life. The knowledge necessary for human gathering and hunting is of a different order from the comparable activities of the nonhuman primates, and learning the resources, possibilities, and dangers of 300 square miles is utterly different from the knowledge necessary for the kind of adaptation seen in apes and monkeys. Learning to utilize the diversity of a large area requires a brain capable of that learning, and only in man, among the primates, has such a brain evolved.

Within our own lifetime we are experimenting with the change of these ancient forms. The house may be no longer cubical, but cylindrical, suspended from a central column. That column may be a bank of elevators, which have replaced the stairs. Architects are experimenting with rooms whose walls may be moved easily. Most important, the holes in the box, the windows, have become walls, so that the entire side of a building may be open to view. This has had important psychological consequences. It is difficult to sit in a living room with a huge picture window and insist that a man's home is his castle. The defenses of the castle are coming down.

31. The Roots of Civilization: The Cognitive Beginnings of Man's First Art, Symbol and Notation.

ALEXANDER MARSHACK. Weidenfeld & Nicolson Ltd., 11 St. John's Hill, London SW11 1XA; 1972; £5.50; 413 pp.

Where does thought begin? Where does language first begin to be used among men? Alexander Marshack, of the Peabody Museum of Archeology and Ethnology, Harvard, has some answers, some postulations and some thoughts, based on his examinations of the habits and movements of Ice Age man. By examining the artifacts and cave drawings of the Ice Age, Marshack develops a view of the cognitive and symbolic systems of the hunters of that period.

It now appears that estimates of when man began complex thinking have been shortsighted. Long before the beginnings of agriculture, and before the appearance of towns, hunters roamed across Europe, just below the great ice sheets of the North. These men sought horses, mammoth, bison, reindeer, and even rhinoceros. The drawings and implements that survive this era, a time between 35,000 and 10,000 B.C., indicate that these men and women were capable of complex thought, notation, and certainly art. ER

The cord is of vast importance, telling us much about man, his cognition, and the nature of his early culture. There is, first, a cognitive difference between a recognition of plant forms and varieties, which to a degree can be done by all animals, and the use of a plant as an image or symbol. There is also a difference between these visual recognitions and the practical recognition required to cut the proper plant in the correct season to obtain the right fiber, a complex recognition that implies a series of skills for preparation of the fibers, twining them into string, and using the cord. It is not agriculture, but it is in a cognitive relation to it.

There are different levels of cognition implied in these diverse recognitions and uses. Each extends the plant to more complex usage *in time*. How much these increasingly complex uses are due to evolved capacities of the brain and how much to the specialized culture man developed in the Paleolithic is a difficult question. Plant images and twined cord are equally parts of human "culture," contemporaneous products of the brain and society. They cannot, therefore, be functionally separated, though they can be separated for study by students of the evolution of intelligence or the evolution of culture.

It would seem that the levels of cognition required for the two forms of plant usage, in one case as a sign and symbol of process and story, and in the other as a product for direct use, are different. The ape, for instance, can use a stick, branch, or leaf for specialized purposes such as probing an ant hole, chasing a leopard or sopping up water.

Clearly, the *Homo sapiens* potential for symbol-making represents a genetic advance over the more generalized mammalian potential for a recognition of forms. But what is the nature of that advance? Is it a factor of brain size with a greater capacity for memory storage, cross-reference and feedback? In what way is it evolved from the ancient capacity for toolmaking, which already contains these cognitive, kinesthetic, time-factored elements in simpler form?

Neanderthal man, with a larger brain than *Homo sapiens*, was an exquisite toolmaker and also a *user* of varied symbols. He used bear skulls ritually, structured his sanctuaries, buried ceremonially, used red ocher, and he may have made crude notational marks. Nevertheless, he was not apparently a large maker of "art," that is, a maker of secondary images, though a sanctuary circle or a burial structure is a kind of image. He was more often a *user* of existing images or objects. Was the difference in the brain or in the culture, or, as seems likely, in some aspect of both? What was the nature of the fine, cognitive, kinesthetic, cultural, and time-factored difference?

The cognitive processes were not the same as the cultural data that were being offered to the *Homo sapiens* brain for cognition. The processes refer to evolved capacities and potentials. The data refer to cultural structures and the physical, ecological reality which supply inputs to the brain.

The brain is a constant within evolutionary species limits in a period of 100,000 to 200,000 years. The data are inherently variable, though within any one area and culture the pace of that variability is itself a variable. In general, one might say that culture varied more slowly as one goes back in prehistory, though the *Homo sapiens* cultural revolution of about 35,000 B.C. seems to have been relatively rapid and widespread, compared with what had occurred before. Because of differences in the cultural data and the way of life, a man of today would not have understood the man of the Ice Age, since languages, stories, knowledge, and skills were different. The Ice Age hunter had not the range of comparisons that even a poorly educated man has today.

Increasingly, as we understand more of what it means to be an evolved human, particularly in a formative period such as the Ice Age, we are beginning to understand some of the relevant processes though we may be perplexed by the details. Born into Upper Paleolithic society and surviving to adulthood, each of us could be either a paleolithic hunter or his wife. There is danger in such simple generalizations. They do not present us with the enormity of the differences that did, in fact, exist between the life and thoughts of the Upper Paleolithic hunter and those of a modern man in an industrial culture.

For example, because of the relatively sparse human population, man was, and he could see that he was, a minority creature in the world of nature. Today he lives in an almost totally man-made, man-regulated world. Partly for this reason, the time-factored structures and regulations were of a different sort and order in the Upper Paleolithic.

Where art and notation exist, therefore, we must recognize the play of these time-space factors and recognize a separation and differentiation among groups, though the cultures may have been generally uniform. These are deductions based on the cognitive levels implied in the symbol and art; they cannot always be made from the technology or industry of a culture or period.

Line rendition of both faces of broken, engraved bone disc or plaque from Mas d'Azil (Ariège) depicting on one face a masked dancer before the paw of a bear and on the other a naked dancer with a pole on his shoulder, apparently baiting a bear. On face one, the subsidiary, associated figure is the head of a horse in reverse at right below. On face two, there is a plantlike figure, perhaps a flower.

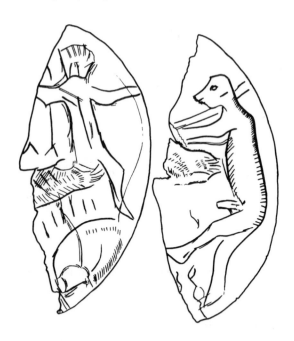

32. The Evolution of Man and Society

C.D. DARLINGTON. Allen & Unwin Ltd., 40 Museum Street, London WC1A 1LU; 1969; £4.75; 753 pp.

A single technological advance, the method of exact archaeological dating by the radioactive isotope of carbon (C14) opened the way for this intriguing study of history. Darlington seizes upon this advance, combined with new developments in the field of genetics, to attempt—on a massive scale—a unified historical study of man and society, a recording of human history through the connectedness between man's history and his biology. The book is epic in scope, well documented through the use of tables, maps, diagrams, and good writing. This book illustrates how technical advances of the present (carbon dating) allow for the continual recreation of the past.

C.D. Darlington, a Darwinian and a geneticist, is Professor of Biology at the University of Oxford. JB

In the evolution of animals and plants change often proceeds in one direction for a long time. It was in the brain that change followed this course in certain apes and consequently took the lead in their evolution. By its changed character it came to govern the whole development of that group of species which included man's ancestors. Its predominance in turn demanded a number of other radical changes in sexual and social behaviour. These determined the character of modern human societies and prepared for the upheaval which brought the paleolithic world to an end.

But all this is not our main interest today. What we are concerned with is not to show where man came from. That we no longer doubt. But to show how he came; to show the processes by which some ape-like animals became men; processes of breeding, of variation and of selection which can be explained to us in terms of what we can see and, if need be, test by experiment. To help us here we have two new instruments out of Darwin's reach but arising from his work: the science of genetics and the fossil record of our ancestors.

The fifteenth century saw, with the revival of learning in Italy, also the most rapid development of those practices and ideas in Europe generally which were to give rise to the Scientific and Industrial Revolutions. As in all historical interpretation there has been a desire to represent these developments in terms of the paramount effects of particular discoveries, like the invention of printing, or of particular discoverers, like the great Florentine Leonardo da Vinci (1452-1519). Recently more elaborate and more convincing interactions have come to be understood and explained.

The most obvious of these interactions is that between the mechanic and the philosopher. The mechanic is faced with the practical problems of spinning and weaving, mining and smelting, stoneworking and shipbuilding, using the power of wind and water for pumping or milling, and above all of constructing the engines of war. He works with his hands. He turns his mind to the things he handles. His problems were those already faced by his paleolithic ancestors, who devised the first implements for fashioning wood and for killing animals and men. Like them his numbers were great; his rewards were poor; and his position in society was humble.

The philosopher on the other hand is able to generalize events, to imagine rules, to construct hypotheses and to handle numbers. He is not paleolithic. He sprang from roots in Sumeria and Egypt and also later independently in China. In Europe, so far as the future of science was concerned, he was represented in Ionia and in Alexandria. Later his kind had been concentrated in the Mediterranean, but he had risen in society and was obviously among the educated classes.

The Evolution of the Breeding System in Man

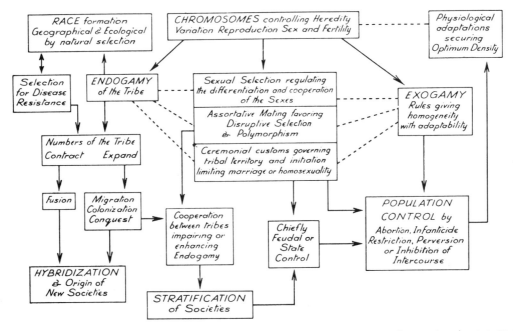

Diagram showing the connections between the variable factors shaping the breeding system in man on the assumption that all human behavior has genetic effects which are subject to natural selection.

This great population of Mongolian peoples was restricted in its variation by its restricted origin from one arctic section of Old World peoples. It has never produced in its five hundred generations any mutations which could give curly hair (or even fair hair apart from the albino mutants of Panama), a heavy beard or a black skin colour. Natives of the Venezuela coast have, like Arabs in the Hadhramaut, to paint their faces to protect themselves from the sun. Nevertheless the American people became greatly diversified in other respects. Why? Because as they expanded in numbers the pressure of natural selection was removed. Resistance to the Old World diseases disappeared or failed to develop; even some of the Old World blood groups were lost in the rapid expansion, an easy circumstance for which their posterity would pay dearly. But new adaptations appeared, notably to life in the high Andes, in the tropical forest and in the great deserts of north and south. But the important region for diversification we can hardly doubt was the complex area on either side of the central isthmus through which all populations entering South America had to pass.

From the new development of genetics even more far-reaching consequences ensue. For the evolution of man and society arises from what individual men and women do, and from the purposes they have in doing it; in other words from their character, which in the long run is conditioned by genetic processes. What we have now come to understand is that these genetic processes are entirely at the mercy of the system of breeding.

Breeding varies, as we have seen, between the opposite poles of inbreeding and outbreeding. With inbreeding heredity is all-powerful; determination is absolute: the group, the population, the caste or the race are invariable; they can be destroyed or removed but if they remain nothing can change them. With outbreeding heredity disintegrates; recombination produces unpredictable variability, endless innovation. Uncertainty, organized uncertainty, dominates not the organism but the population; determination in controlling evolution is transferred to the selective power of the environment. Between these two extremes, it now appears, every species of animal and plant is adapted to preserve some kind of balance. In man, since the neolithic revolution, the balance has fluctuated between extremes owing to the social vicissitudes we have seen. But where it has failed to be preserved we have also seen the results in the great crises of history.

33. Biological Rhythms in Psychiatry and Medicine

GAY GAER LUCE. Public Health Service Publication No. 2088, Superintendent of Documents, U. S. Government Printing Office, Washington, D.C. 20402; 1970; $1.75; 183 pp.

(Under the title of *Biological Rhythms in Human and Animal Psychology*), Dover Publications Inc., Tiptree Book Services, Tiptree CO5 OSR; 1972; £1.25.

This report, a monograph appearing under the auspices of the National Clearinghouse for Mental Health Information, is an example of government reports, available at reasonable prices, providing great amounts of information on current research.

The biological rhythms of the title refer to the daily changes from light to darkness, the twenty-eight-day lunar cycles, the changing of the seasons throughout the year, and other regular environmental cycles that affect behavior beyond our awareness. More births and deaths occur at night and in the early morning; give a rodent non-lethal medicine at the wrong time and he dies; people with ulcers and allergic reactions have extra trouble in the spring; and the body temperature of human beings fluctuates by as much as two degrees each and every day. ER

In concert with the turning earth, plants and animals exhibit a very pronounced daily rhythm. Often external cues synchronize living organisms into an exact tempo. However, when men or animals are isolated from their usual time cues, they do not keep to a precise solar day (24 hours) nor even a precise lunar cycle (24.8 hours). Nonetheless, isolated creatures do show rhythms that do not deviate very much from the 24 hours. This daily rhythm is denoted by the popular term "circadian." It means "about a day," from the Latin, *circa dies*.

Mollusks, fish, cats, marigolds, baboons, men—indeed, most living organisms show a circadian rhythm of activity and rest. Time-lapse photography has captured the circadian dance of plant life, showing how leaves lift and drop, open and close every 24 hours. Man, no exception to this daily ebb and flow, may be unaware that his body temperature, blood pressure, and pulse, respiration, blood sugar, hemoglobin levels, and amino acid levels are changing in a circadian rhythm.

In health we have an appearance of stability that cloaks a host of rhythms, hormonal tides, intermeshed with surges of enzyme activity, production of blood cells, and other multitudinous necessities for life. Our smoothness of function seems to rest upon a high degree of integration among these circadian production lines, and they in turn may act as timekeepers for us, guiding us in our periods of energetic endeavor, or rest, acting as distrubutors of our dreams and the tidal motions underlying our ever-shifting moods. Although we appear constant from the outside, we can feel inside that we are not really the same from one hour of the day to the next.

If human beings and animals change as they follow multitudinous cycles each day and night, subtle diagnostic tests (psychiatric, endocrine, etc.) will evoke different responses at different points on the person's daily cycle. As psychiatric experiments now demonstrate, the relation between rhythmicity and mental health is not coincidental. Experiments at the Institute of Living indicate that biological time influences learning, memory, and the rate at which an animal can unlearn fear. Stress has been followed by psychotic and neurotic behavioral reactions, accompanied by characteristic changes in circadian physiological rhythms.

———————————

Each day, as we know, a person's body temperature rises and falls about 1 1/2-2 degrees, reaching its peak around afternoon or evening, a time of peak performance on tasks requiring close attention or muscle coordination. The hormones of the adrenal cortex (17-hydroxycorticosteroids), which so influence our nervous apparatus, are dropping at this time. They fall to their nadir at night, and reach their peak levels in blood sometime before a person arises in the morning or shortly after.

At this time, levels of the male hormone, testosterone, are at their daily high point in a man, and he tends to show peak excretion of elements such as sodium and potassium. Hormones, such as insulin, follow a daily rhythm as do blood glucose and levels of amino acids. The body utilizes protein differently, depending upon time of day. Protein eaten at 8 a.m. rapidly raises the amino acid levels in the blood, but the same meal at 8 p.m. does not. Some researchers conjecture that foods may be more efficiently utilized early in the day, indicating that a dieter may be well advised to have a hearty breakfast as his main meal of the day.

There are 24-hour rhythms in liver enzymes, in the biochemicals of the brain and the spinal chord, in the division of cells, and throughout the nervous and endocrine system. These multitudes of cyclic functions are in different phases at any given hour, lending an overall appearance of steadiness. ———————————

This summary of human susceptibility rhythms was prepared by the Chronobiology Laboratory at the University of Minnesota. *H = Healthy; M = Morbid; A = Allergic; B = Asthmatic, bronchitic, or emphysematous. **VC = Vital Capacity; FEV = 1-second forced expiratory volume. Acrophase (the peak represented by the dot) indicates the circadian phase of maximum response.

Human Circadian System
Birth, Death, Morbidity, Susceptibility And Reactivity

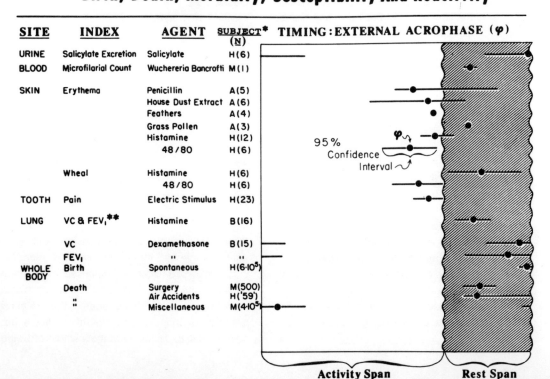

SUBJECTIVE TIME

Despite the fact that we live on a globe dominated by the solar rhythm of day and night, by lunar tidal rhythms and cycles of seasonal change, we exclude these rhythms from much of our social planning. Technologically advanced people tend to ignore cycles of day and night with rapid east-west travel and night life. In fact, we may need to know even more about our time-structure because we are no longer in tune with the slow tempo of the natural environment. We may need to learn about the effects of the electric daylight in which we live, as well as the effects of irregular schedules and phase shifts. Individuals may need a sense of the oscillations within, the rising and falling of energy, undulations of attention, mood, weight, activity, sexuality, and productiveness. Because the clocks and calendars of social activity are designed for economic efficiency or convenience, an individual may have to learn to detect his own cycles, and become aware of scheduling to protect his health.

34. The Hidden Dimension

EDWARD T. HALL. The Bodley Head Ltd., 9 Bow Street, London WC2E 7AL; 1969; £2.10; 201 pp.

Hall is an anthropologist based in Chicago whose work deals with the structure of experience as it is molded by culture. An earlier book, *The Silent Language,* deals with the "language of time "; in this more recent work, the "language of space. " Language, that is, in the sense of being more than a *transmitter* of thought, but, in fact, a major element in the *formation* of thought. Hall extends this hypothesis to the cultural experience of man. JB

Man is an organism with a wonderful and extraordinary past. He is distinguished from the other animals by virtue of the fact that he has elaborated what I have termed *extensions* of his organism. By developing his extensions, man has been able to improve or specialize various functions. The computer is an extension of part of the brain, the telephone extends the voice, the wheel extends the legs and feet. Language extends experience in time and space while writing extends language. Man has elaborated his extensions to such a degree that we are apt to forget that his humanness is rooted in his animal nature. The anthropologist Weston La Barre has pointed out that man has shifted evolution from his body to his extensions and in so doing has tremendously accelerated the evolutionary process.

In light of what is known of ethology, it may be profitable in the long run if man is viewed as an organism that has elaborated and specialized his extensions to such a degree that they have taken over, and are rapidly replacing, nature. In other words, man has created a new dimension,, the cultural dimension, of which proxemics is only a part. The relationship between man and the cultural dimension is one in which both *man and his environment participate in molding each other.* Man is now in the position of actually creating the total world in which he lives, what the ethologists refer to as his biotope. In creating this world he is actually determining *what kind of an organism* he will be.

Personal distance is the term applied by Hediger to the normal spacing that non-contact anaimals maintain between themselves and their fellows. This distance acts as an invisible bubble that surrounds the organism. Outside the bubble two organisms are not as intimately involved with each other as when the bubbles overlap. Social organization is a factor in personal distance. Dominant animals tend to have larger personal distances than those which occupy lower positions in the social hierarchy, while subordinate animals have been observed to yield room to dominant ones. Glen McBride, an Australian professor of animal husbandry, has made detailed observations of the spacing of domestic fowl as a function of dominance. His theory of "social organization and behavior" has as a main element the handling of space. This correlation of personal distance and status in one form or another seems to occur throughout the vertebrate kingdom. It has been reported for birds and many mammals, including the colony of ground-living Old World monkeys at the Japanese Monkey Center near Nagoya.

Probably there is nothing pathological in crowding per se that produces the symptoms that we have seen. Crowding, however, disrupts important social functions and so leads to disorganization

CHART SHOWING INTERPLAY OF THE DISTANT AND IMMEDIATE RECEPTORS
IN PROXEMIC PERCEPTION

FEET	0	1	2	3	4	5	6	7	8	10	12	14	16	18	20	22	30

INFORMAL DISTANCE CLASSIFICATION

INTIMATE | PERSONAL | SOCIAL – CONSULTIVE | PUBLIC

CLOSE | NOT CLOSE | CLOSE | NOT CLOSE | CLOSE | NOT CLOSE | ← MANDATORY RECOGNITION DISTANCE BEGINS HERE | NOT CLOSE BEGINS AT 30' – 40'

KINESTHESIA

HEAD, PELVIS, THIGHS, TRUNK CAN BE BROUGHT INTO CONTACT OR MEMBERS CAN ACCIDENTALLY TOUCH. HANDS CAN REACH & MANIPULATE ANY PART OF TRUNK EASILY.

HANDS CAN REACH AND HOLD EXTREMITIES EASILY BUT WITH MUCH LESS FACILITY THAN ABOVE. SEATED CAN REACH AROUND & TOUCH OTHER SIDE OF TRUNK. NOT SO CLOSE AS TO RESULT IN ACCIDENTAL TOUCHING.

ONE PERSON HAS ELBOW ROOM.

2 PEOPLE BARELY HAVE ELBOW ROOM. ONE CAN REACH OUT AND GRASP AN EXTREMITY.

JUST OUTSIDE TOUCHING DISTANCE.

2 PEOPLE WHOSE HEADS ARE 8'–9' APART CAN PASS AN OBJECT BACK & FORTH BY BOTH STRETCHING.

OUT OF INTERFERENCE DISTANCE. BY REACHING ONE CAN JUST TOUCH THE OTHER.

THERMAL RECEPTORS

CONDUCTION (CONTACT)

RADIATION — NORMALLY OUT OF AWARENESS | ANIMAL HEAT AND MOISTURE DISSIPATE (THOREAU)

OLFACTION — CULTURAL ATTITUDE

WASHED SKIN & HAIR	– – – – – – OK
SHAVING LOTION-PERFUME	– – – – OK – – TABOO –
SEXUAL ODORS	VARIABLE – – – – – TABOO –
BREATH	ANTISEPTIC OK, OTHERWISE TABOO
BODY ODOR	TABOO
FOOT ODOR	TABOO – – – – – – – – –

FEET	0	1	2	3	4	5	6	7	8	10	12	14	16	18	20	22	30

VISION

DETAIL VISION (VIS ∠ OF FOVEA 1°)

VISION BLURRED DISTORTED | ENLARGED DETAILS OF IRIS, EYEBALL, PORES OF FACE, FINEST HAIRS | DETAIL OF FACE SEEN AT NORMAL SIZE. EYES, NOSE, SKIN, TEETH CONDITION, EYELASHES, HAIR ON BACK OF NECK | SMALLEST BLOOD VESSELS IN EYE · LOST. SEE WEAR ON CLOTHING. HEAD HAIR SEEN CLEARLY. | FINE LINES OF FACE FADE. DEEP LINES STAND OUT. SLIGHT EYE WINK. LIP MOVEMENT SEEN CLEARLY | ENTIRE CENTRAL FACE INCLUDED | SHARP FEATURES DISSOLVE, EYE COLOR NOT DISCERNIBLE, SMILE-SCOWL VISIBLE, HEAD BOBBING MORE PRONOUNCED | SNELLEN'S STANDARD FOR DISTANT VISION EMPLOYING ANGLE OF 1 MIN. GUILD OPTICIANS OF AMERICA EYE CHART. A PERSON WITH 20-40 VISION HAS TROUBLE SEEING EYES & EXPRESSION AROUND EYES THOUGH EYE BLINK IS VISIBLE.

CLEAR VISION (VIS ∠ AT MACULA 12° HOR, 3° VERT)

25" x 3" ON EYE NOSTRILS OR MOUTH | 3.75" x .9° UPPER OR LOWER FACE | 6.25" x 1.60" UPPER OR LOWER FACE | 10" x 2.5" UPPER OR LOWER FACE OR SHOULDERS | 20" x 5' 1 OR 2 FACES | 31" x 7.5 FACES OF TWO PEOPLE | 4'2" x 1'6" TORSOS OF TWO PEOPLE | 6' 3" x 1' 7" TORSOS OF 4 OR 5 PEOPLE

60° SCANNING

1/3 OF FACE EYE EAR OR MOUTH AREA FACE DISTORTED | NOSE PROJECTS WHOLE FACE SEEN UNDISTORTED | UPPER BODY CAN'T COUNT FINGERS | UPPER BODY & GESTURES | WHOLE SEATED BODY VISIBLE. PEOPLE OFTEN KEEP FEET WITHIN OTHER PERSON'S 60° ANGLE OF VIEW | WHOLE BODY HAS SPACE AROUND IT, POSTURAL COMMUNICATION BEGINS TO ASSUME IMPORTANCE

PERIPHERAL VISION

HEAD AGAINST BACKGROUND | HEAD & SHOULDERS | WHOLE BODY MOVEMENT IN "HANDS-FINGERS" VISIBLE | WHOLE BODY | OTHER PEOPLE SEEN IF PRESENT | OTHER PEOPLE BECOME IMPORTANT IN PERIPHERAL VISION

HEAD SIZE

FILLS VISUAL FIELD FAR OVER LIFE SIZE | OVER NORMAL | NORMAL SIZE | NORMAL TO BEGINNING TO SHRINK | VERY SMALL

NOTE: PERCEIVED HEAD SIZE VARIES EVEN WITH SAME SUBJECTS AND DISTANCE

ADDITIONAL NOTES

SENSATION OF BEING CROSS-EYED | PEOPLE & OBJECTS SEEN AS ROUND UP TO 12'–15' | ACCOMMODATIVE CONVERGENCE ENDS AFTER 15' PEOPLE & OBJECTS BEGIN TO FLATTEN OUT

TASKS IN SUBMARINES

67% OF TASKS IN THIS RANGE | 23% FALL IN THIS RANGE | DIMMICH, F. L. & FARNSWORTH, D. VISUAL ACUITY TASKS IN A SUBMARINE, NEW LONDON, 1951

ARTISTS' OBSERVATIONS CF GROSSER

VERY PERSONAL DISTANCE | ARTIST OR MODEL HAS TO DOMINATE | A PORTRAIT. A PICTURE PAINTED AT 4'–8' OF A PERSON WHO IS NOT PAID TO "SIT" | TOO FAR FOR A CONVERSATION | BODY IS 1/3 SIZE | FULL LENGTH STATE PORTRAITS. HUMAN BODY SEEN AS A WHOLE, COMPREHENDED AT A GLANCE, WARMTH AND IDENTIFICATION CEASE

ORAL AURAL

GRUNTS GROANS WHISPER | SOFT VOICE INTIMATE STYLE | CONVENTIONAL MODIFIED VOICE CASUAL OR CONSULTIVE STYLE | LOUD VOICE WHEN TALKING TO A GROUP, MUST RAISE VOICE TO GET ATTENTION FORMAL STYLE | FULL PUBLIC SPEAKING VOICE FROZEN STYLE

NOTE: THE BOUNDARIES ASSOCIATED WITH THE TRANSITION FROM ONE VOICE LEVEL TO THE NEXT HAVE NOT BEEN PRECISELY DETERMINED

and ultimately to population collapse or large-scale die-off.

The sex mores of the rats in the sink were disrupted, and pansexuality and sadism were endemic. Rearing the young became almost totally disorganized. Social behavior of the males deteriorated, so that tail biting broke out. Social hierarchies were unstable, and territorial taboos were disregarded unless backed by force. The extremely high mortality rates of females unbalanced the sex ratio and thus exacerbated the situation of surviving females, who were even more harassed by males during the time they came in heat.

In the briefest possible sense, the message of this book is that no matter how hard man tries it is impossible for him to divest himself of his own culture, for it has penetrated to the roots of his nervous system and determines how he perceives the world. Most of culture lies hidden and is outside voluntary control, making up the warp and weft of human existence. Even when small fragments of culture are elevated to awareness, they are difficult to change, not only because they are so personally experienced but *because people cannot act or interact at all in any meaningful way except through the medium of culture.*

35. On Aggression

KONRAD LORENZ (tr. by Marjorie K. Wilson). Methuen & Co. Ltd., 11 New Fetter Lane, London EC4P 4EE; 1966; (H) £2.25; (P) £0.90.

There are valuable lessons to be learned from comparative ethology. We can learn about our flocking **instincts** by looking at birds. We can get data on effects of crowding by looking at rat communities. We can **study** spontaneous aggression in mammals and perhaps learn something about ourselves. There is, **however,** a limit to these comparisons: there is really no comparison to man, man who has all the words, **all** the terminology that informs our comparing minds. "Evolution," "natural selection," "aggression," "life," "death" . . . words, only words. JB

It is almost impossible to portray in words the functioning of a system in which every part is related to every other in such a way that each has a causal influence on the others. Even if one is only trying to explain a gasoline engine it is hard to know where to begin, because the person to whom one seeks to explain it can only understand the nature of the crankshaft if he has first grasped that of the connecting rods, the pistons, the valves, the camshaft, and so on. Unless one understands the elements of a complete system as a whole, one cannot understand them at all. The more complex the structure of a system is, the greater this difficulty becomes—and it must be surmounted both in one's research and in one's teaching.

Generally, other conditions being equal, mere acquaintanceship with a fellow member of the species exerts a remarkably strong inhibitory effect on aggressive behavior. In human beings, this phenomenon can regularly be observed in railway carriages, incidentally an excellent place in which to study the function of aggression in the spacing out of territories. All the rude behavior patterns serving for the repulsion of seat competitors and intruders, such as covering empty places with coats or bags, putting up one's feet, or pretending to be asleep, are brought into action against the unknown individual only. As soon as the newcomer turns out to be even the merest acquaintance, they disappear and are replaced by rather shamefaced politeness.

A third great obstacle to human self-knowledge is—at least in our Western cultures—a heritage of idealistic philosophy. It stems from the dichotomy of the world into the external world of things, which to idealistic thought is devoid of values, and the inner world of human thought and reason to which alone values are attributed. This division appeals to man's spiritual pride. It supports him in his reluctance to accept the determination of his own behavior by natural laws.

None of our Western languages has an intransitive verb to do justice to the increase of values produced by very nearly every step in evolution. One cannot possibly call it development when something new and higher arises from an earlier stage which does not contain the constituent properties for the new and higher being. Fundamentally this applies to every bigger step in the genesis of the world of organisms, including the first step, the origin of life, and the most recent one—the origin of man from the anthropoid.

36. The Ghost Dance: The Origins of Religion

WESTON LA BARRE. Allen & Unwin Ltd., 40 Museum Street, London WC1A 1LU; 1972; £6.95; 677 pp.

The study of religion as a strictly human phenomenon relies on descriptive fact as opposed to the search for metaphysical truth. Anthropologist La Barre points out that the real mystery isn't religion, but "what religion purports to be about." He proceeds to examine the anthropology and psychology of religion in societal contexts. JB

Cultural relativity, with its existentialist view of culture, has now destroyed the final prop of fundamentalist tribal man—that inveterate absolutist whose very animal nature it is to embody experiments in value-paradigms. This latest threat to human narcissism seems shattering, for it means that the culture heroes and charismatic ancestors of the sacred past are no longer gods, but only men like ourselves. Still, the struggle with each successively dethroned vanity has always heretofore been edifying; and from each discovered limitation we can learn. But it means the scrutiny of a most sacred belief—that our culture is the distilled essence of a cumulative and historic evolution toward an ultimate new Eden of knowledge and truth, as embodied especially in that seemingly truest of geometries, our basic religion, be that Science or some traditional faith. It means that we must examine both culture and religion, not in the context of "truth" at all, but rather as animal phenomena that *do something for us adaptively*—leaving aside for the moment the question *which* reality, inside or outside our human skins, they may be in turn adaptive to—but which may often be irrelevant to a serenely indifferent universe. Culture and its most comforting component, religion, may be only adaptive mechanisms peculiar to this kind of animal, whose unique biology we must therefore scrutinize.

But to be free in the pursuit of ethnographic and psychological fact, we must give up the search for theological truth. The gain may be greater than we anticipate. In fact, in our value-disoriented world, *the understanding of religion may be the key to an understanding of the nature and function of culture at large and hence the survival of our species*—and for this we have some continuing appetite and need.

Hominid neo-carnivorousness is the major ecological event in the early formative history of mankind. Because meat is a far more concentrated food than vegetable materials, and hence more easily transported and more worth sharing, active animal-hunting meant that *for the first time among primates,* these early humans became habitual food sharers—an event of major biological significance. From physical evidence to be presented shortly it is evident that hominids had all-male hunting groups that left females behind during this activity. That males separated from females of the horde during the hunt was critically important not only for all subsequent human evolution but also for man's peculiar social nature, species-specific psychology and cultural institutions—in particular his religion.

Science is not religion, because it tries not to see the world in man's image, and not to worship man's image projected into the unknown. The scientist knows that he is a man, and would serve

90

men; but even humanism, become a religion, can slip into worshipful arrogance. Is it necessary to impute one's having been created, and ultimate death, to the whole uncreated and undying universe? Is it possible that the nature of Being is simply to be, without beginning or end? Does my loved father yet live? What anthropomorphic arrogance is it that steals the essence of cosmic eternity and absurdly imputes it to our immortal selves! Must we always confuse the attributes of man and of the universe! To be a man means to suffer vicissitudes, and also to contemplate with equanimity the ultimate horror and humiliation of animal "omnipotence," death—one's own death and the death of all lovers and friends, perhaps the death of our feisty and admirable species, even the death of this planet at the death of its central star. Small matter: for at one place in this cold cosmos there once lived values, and mind.

———————————

Exorbitant attention has been paid to the nature of gods, whose nature it is to be inaccessible to examination. Comparatively little attention has been paid to the impresarios of gods, their prophets, shamans and priests. These persons are the *de facto* source of all our religious information and, in contrast to the gods, they are themselves available for study. The nature of deities, in default of any other empirical data, might therefore be sought in the psychic disposition of their exponents. More than this, curiously, the ancestor of the god is the shaman himself, both historically and psychologically.

37. The Forest People:
A Study of the Pygmies in the Congo

COLIN M. TURNBULL. Jonathan Cape Ltd., 30 Bedford Square, London WC1B 3EL; (H) 1974; £3.50; 296 pp.

The Forest People are the BaMbuti Pygmies of the Congo. Anthropologist Turnbull lyrically records their behavioral code and its relationship to the forest environment. The result is a unifying structure, summed up by the attitude of one of the Pygmies: "The forest is our home; when we leave the forest, or when the forest dies, we shall die: we are the people of the forest." JB

They speak of the world beyond the plantations as being a fearful place, full of malevolent spirits and not fit to be lived in except by animals and BaMbuti, which is what the village people call the Pygmies. The villagers, some Bantu and some Sudanic, keep to their plantations and seldom go into the forest unless it is absolutely necessary. For them it is a place of evil. They are outsiders.

This, in fact, is the opinion of the villagers. For them the ritual act is the important thing. In their religious rites it is the correct performance of the ceremonial that counts most. If correctly performed it is bound to bring the desired results, regardless of the accompanying thought, if indeed there is any. All attention is focused on the act itself. And it must not only be performed correctly, but with a solemnity that betrays fear.

Our stay among the BoMbo and BaBali was not much more fruitful than that with Kachui from the point of view of meeting or learning anything about the local Pygmies. The chiefs, Isiaka and Lukamba, both had the same complaints to make—they simply could not control their Pygmies.

"How can we control them?" Isiaka said. "It is their forest, and they can hide from us whenever they want to. They are worthless people. They only come to the village when they want to steal."

But above all, his entire code of behavior and thought is geared to his nomadic forest life: to bring him to a settled life in a village is to ask him overnight to abandon one way of life, a way he has lived for thousands of years, and adopt another. Where the Pygmies did make the attempt there was complete moral as well as physical disintegration. Not long ago a Belgian friend from the Congo told me that the day before he had left, on one small "model plantation" where the Pygmies were being liberated, twenty-nine had died in one day from sunstroke.

92

38. The Mountain People

COLIN M. TURNBULL. Jonathan Cape Ltd., 30 Bedford Square, London WC1B 3EL; (H) 1973; £3.50; or Picador, Cavaye Place, London SW10 9PG; (P) 1974; £0.75; 309 pp.

The Ik are a tribe of hunters who have been forced to give up hunting and become farmers. Uganda set up a National Game Reserve on the hunting grounds where the Ik previously prospered. Unwilling to leave the mountains, they have been forced to farm a land with no rain to speak of, and without the necessary technical skills to make their farming successful.

The result of these conditions is that these people are starving to death and have deteriorated from proud hunters into loveless, hostile people. The young are cared for until the age of three and are then cast out into the world to fend for themselves. When the sick and the elderly (over thirty is old) do manage to find food, they must guard carefully as they eat to make sure younger and stronger tribesmen do not steal the food from their mouths. ER

In so far as ritual survived at all, it could hardly be said to be religious, for it did little or nothing to bind Icien society together. But the question still remained, only greatly sharpened: Did this lack of social behavior and of communal ritual or religious expression mean that there was no community of belief? In larger-scale societies we are accustomed to diversity of belief, we even applaud ourselves for our tolerance, not recognizing that a society not bound together by a single powerful belief is not a society at all, but a political association of individuals held together only by the presence of law and force, the very existence of which is a violence. But we have already seen that the Ik had no such law, let alone the means for enforcing conformity to any code of behavior. Such coercion as there was came simply from the circumstances in which they lived and their own will, as individuals, to survive. Their belief, if one existed, was not manifest in any communal practice, ritual or otherwise, and only in a very peculiar sense could one say it was manifest in any common sentiment. Such sentiment at best could hardly be said to be social.

The Ik teach us that our much vaunted human values are not inherent in humanity at all, but are associated only with a particular form of survival called society, and that all, even society itself, are luxuries that can be dispensed with. That does not make them any the less wonderful or desirable, and if man has any greatness it is surely in his ability to maintain these values, clinging to them to an often very bitter end, even shortening an already pitifully short life rather than sacrificing his humanity. But that too involves choice, and the Ik teach us that man can lose the will to make it. That is the point at which there is an end to truth, to goodness and to beauty; an end to the struggle for their achievement, which gives life to the individual while at the same time giving strength and meaning to society. The Ik have relinquished all luxury in the name of individual survival, and the result is that they live on as a people without life, without passion, beyond humanity. We pursue those trivial idiotic technological encumbrances, and imagine *them* to be the luxuries that make life worth living, and all the time we are losing our potential for social rather than individual survival, for hating as well as loving, losing perhaps our last chance to enjoy life with all the passion that is our nature and being.

Amuarkuar, where he lay down to die, after pleading for some water to drink. His wife was off trying to gather enough food to keep herself alive; he was not strong enough to make the trip. But he was old enough to remember to love, and he died while collecting grass to keep a home for when his wife would return.

Below left: Kokoi regarded her body as her greatest asset in the game of survival and used it wisely if not well. It helped fill her stomach with *ngag,* or food, which made her a good person. Eighteen months after this picture Kokoi fell ill and was unwanted. She lost her assets and died.

Below right: After eighteen years of age Icien women lose their ability to charm the cattle herders, and their fellow Ik have neither the energy nor the affection to spare. At eighteen a woman begins to enter the loneliness and isolation of old age.

39. Social Indicators

Edited by RAYMOND A. BAUER. The M.I.T. Press, 126 Buckingham Palace Road, London SW1W 9SD; (H) 1966; £4.65; (P) 1967; £1.65; 357 pp.

This volume was prepared by the American Academy of the Arts and Sciences for NASA and deals with the impact of the space program on American society. The contributors attempt to establish a quantum set of social indicators that will provide information on the state of society. The precedent for this project is in the kind of quantitative indicators developed by economists thirty years ago. The emphasis here is on yardsticks for human values. JB

As I have indicated, technical changes have proved historically to be particularly explosive sources of second-order social, economic, and political changes that were never envisioned. This arises largely because at the beginning technical developments tend to be viewed in a rather restricted context. They are seen as an answer to an agreed problem, and tend to be judged in terms of their adequacy in solving that problem. Probably the most dramatic example of this in modern times has been the development of potent insecticides, which were only later found to have profound effects on the ecological cycles of man and beast. Similarly, there is the instance of the innocuous substitution of detergents for soap. It was scarcely anticipated that detergents would disrupt the plumbing systems of tall apartment buildings, causing waste to back up into sinks, tubs, and toilet bowls; or that streams would be contaminated to the point of destroying their fish life.

Social statistics also manifest cultural lags. Three kinds of lags affecting the appropriateness of indicators occupy our attention here:

1. Indicators fail to keep abreast of the techniques of statistical measurement.

2. New indicators are not developed to meet new needs for information.

3. Indicators fail to change in the manner needed to reflect alterations in the nature of the phenomena for which they are an index.

Many of the indicators most frequently used for important judgments concerning the state and trends of the society are certainly misleading. This is true not only where the best indicators provide inexact or ambiguous measures of the magnitude of change, but also where they leave doubt about the direction of change.

A social system is rarely a taut system. A change at any one point does not necessarily mean a significant change at some other point. There is usually considerable slack in the system.

A social system is only partially knowable. There are not merely "black boxes" but "black regions" with amorphous boundaries. There are always unforeseeable (not merely unforeseen) consequences for good and evil (and usually both together). Although myths of perfect knowledge, wisdom, or infallibility may be cultivated by some governors, central omniscience by them or anyone else is impossible.

A social system is never fully controllable. The myths of central omnipotence always hide imperfections; internal disunity lurks behind the façade. Perfect coordination can be achieved by neither hierarchy, bargaining, nor any combination of the two. There are always uncontrollable aspects of the biological and physical environments in which social systems are imbedded. Tight control of some elements may usually be achieved only at the cost of diminished control over others.

In sum, social systems are so loose that one

may well ask skeptically, "Is this a system?" Perhaps the best answer is, "An unsystematic one."

Four requirements must be met to better the situation:

1. We must endeavor systematically to anticipate the occurrence of events that may constitute important objects of research.

2. Research plans must be developed, using to the fullest extent our ability to anticipate the demands that will confront research on the occurrence of the event.

3. Where a study of change caused by the anticipated event is indicated, base-line measures should be made before the event. Such measures should be aimed at both relevant publics and variables.

4. A ready capability must exist for carrying out research observations *where* and *when* events significant for study occur.

———————————

The survival of an organization indicates a feedback process of at least minimal effectiveness. The feedback associated with bare survival has, however, a limited quality, involving as it does information gathering in relation to only the most essential of the organization's linkages to its environment.

Feedback for survival ordinarily reflects the reactions of only the organized and politically significant interests. Unorganized or politically insignificant interests are not represented, or else they are ignored. In addition, the organization tends to act on the immediate and apparent (nonrationalized and nonintegrated) responses of these interests to current organizational actions.

Thus it appears that the less obvious, more subtle, and far-reaching second-order effects are not incorporated in the survival feedback process, because they are neither "real" nor urgent. The survival process therefore gives an opportunistic quality to an organization. It also makes the organization appear as though it is easily intimidated by any strong outside force.

40. Take Today: The Executive as Dropout

MARSHALL McLUHAN and BARRINGTON NEVITT. Harcourt Brace Jovanovich, Inc., 757 Third Avenue, New York, N.Y. 10017; 1972; or *Real Time.* $9.95; 304 pp.

Marshal McLuhan's seminal work is *Understanding Media,* a profound book that synthesized a lifetime of insights and information. Since *Understanding Media,* McLuhan has co-authored a number of books with experts in art, poetry, culture, and now, business management. Having devised a systemization of reality, McLuhan takes chunks and segments of the socio-cultural context and runs them through new system-analyzers (books). This work, with management consultant Barrington Nevitt, is a solid study on mid-twentieth century management, filled with insights and perceptions that will be valuable to anyone interested in the organization of social systems. JB

Point of view is failure to achieve structural awareness. No static viewpoint is possible in the vortex of process. Nor can the effects of human organization be understood in terms of single isolated causes. All processes whatever involve clusters of interacting effects with causes. As a *figure,* every manager creates a service environment or *ground* that is an extension of himself. He puts on his organization like "The Emperor's New Clothes." The managing process is both a creation and an extension of man. As such, it is a *medium* that processes its users, who are its *content.* Whereas the *meaning* of management is the set of relationships engendered by the user, the *message* of management is the totality of its effects. IN THE WORLD OF ELECTRIC INFORMATION, ALL CENTERS OF POWER BECOME MARGINAL.

———————————

Today the cultural historian can reveal the hidden factors in the cultures of the past, just as the programmers of innovational processes have the means of seeing the effects of any action before it begins. The approach is that of the instantaneous testing of processes under controlled conditions. *When we push our paradigms back, we get "history": when we push them forward, we get "science."* The historian, such as Eric Havelock in his *Preface to Plato,* has now the same power to recall ancient events. History offers the controlled conditions of a laboratory for observing patterns of change, much as primitive societies living in prehistory (preliteracy) give postliterate man the

means of observing the action of the latest technologies.

———————————

Accountants themselves are increasingly perplexed about procedures and assumptions underlying accounting practice. What constitutes suitable yardsticks for private business "performance"? With the shift from manufacturing to service industries, the market value of people's knowledge in a "going concern" more and more exceeds the value of its plant. The resale value of past-perfect or a "gone concern" tends to vanish completely. Business profit is no longer *counted* as cash, either in the till or in the bank. It has become an *estimate* of "potential cash": the difference between what you might sell your operation for now and this time last year. It also assumes buyers. The selling price of a business depends on its *promise* of continuing profits, which are also *promises* of cash, that is, of "legal tender" or government I O U's.

———————————

To include in a single capsulated space the totality of planetary ecology is characteristic of electronic man in every phase of his activity. What Peter Drucker calls the "world shopping center" is identical with the scope of Apollo 11. The world shopping center does not have to be big enough to include the world population or all the "hardware" packages in the world. On the contrary, it has to be a capsule *structurally* inclusive of all possible forms. The amount of any one component that is present is unimportant. If Apollo 11 had been a half mile in diameter it would have had no more ecological features than it had. That is, it had to be a complete model of space capsule Earth. In the same way, the world shopping center has to be viable in a planetary, *structural* sense, not in the sense of *moreness*. It is an inclusive service environment of information and images that is indicated by the phrase and concept "world shopping center."

New uses of the words "hardware" and "software" have come in with computer technology. It is a typical case of using the old media and terminology in new specialist ways. "Interface" is another instance of inept appropriation of an ordinary word to express "the connexion between any two units" of computer systems (see Anthony Chandor. *Dictionary of Computers).* There are, in fact, no connections in the material universe. Einstein, Heisenberg, and Linus Pauling have baffled the old mechanical and visual culture of the nineteenth century by reminding scientists in general that the only physical bond in Nature is the resonating interval or "interface." Our language, as much as our mental set forbids us to regard the world in this way. It is hard for the conventional and uncritical mind to grasp the fact that *"the meaning of meaning" is a relationship: a* figureground *process of perpetual change.* The input of data must enter a *ground* or field or surround of relations that are transformed by the intruder, even as the input is also transformed. Knowledge, old or new, is always a figure that is undergoing perpetual change by "interface" with new environments. Thus it is never easy to divorce knowledge and experience. In the same way that knowledge and experience are continuously modifying each other, the relation between

"hardware" and "software" is not fixed but is in a perpetual state of metamorphosis.

Since our concern is with human organization, it is necessary to ask what kind of organization will suffice under these new conditions. Bigness will not serve, since it alienates the individual. The human scale adds new effectiveness in the age of speed-up. As "hardware" yields to miniaturization and etherealization, the giant organizational structures become helpless dinosaurs incapable of maneuvering in the new environment. Specialism and inadaptability are the fate of all large structures. They have no meaning relative to a fast-changing environment. The dinosaur had no option whether to drop in or drop out. He died hard in his tracks. The piranha can swallow the whale.

Time was when the big structure created its own environment and dictated the ground rules to many other organizations. The new electric rim spin ends that. Electric information movement means that you are here and we are there simultaneously. Under these conditions everybody is dropin and dropout impartially. There is no part of the world in which we do not participate, whether we know it or not. And there is no part of us which is not equally invaded by everything in the world. "Nipping in" and "nipping out" anywhere in the world now involves responsibilities for having altered that part of the world. The dropin and dropout alter the situation totally.

Private individual man is a "civilization freak" made possible by the power of the phonetic alphabet to impose visual criteria on the whole of social life and communication. Paradoxically, Western man with his highly specialized and precarious individual ego (or private psyche) has resisted all efforts to study the *effects* of technologies, old or new, upon his own psychic life.

41. The Stress of Life

HANS SELYE, M.D. McGraw-Hill Book Company, 1221 Avenue of the Americas, New York, N.Y. 10020; 1956; or *Real Time*. $2.75; 324 pp.

Stress is neutral, except to organisms. When someone experiences the death of a parent he undergoes stress. When the same person experiences a promotion that changes work habits he also undergoes stress.

Hans Selye defines stress as "the state manifested by a specific syndrome which consists of all the nonspecifically induced changes within a biologic system." By analyzing stress within the body's tendency toward homeostasis and adaptation, Selye develops a theory whereby knowledge about stress and its effects can be pragmatically integrated toward new concepts of health and health maintenance. ER

Book I:
The Discovery—evolution of the stress concept.

STRESSOR

Book II:
The Dissection—an analysis of the mechanism through which our bodies are attacked by, and can defend themselves against stress.

Book III:
The Diseases of Adaptation—maladies which result largely from failures in the stress-fighting mechanism.

Book IV:
Sketch for a Unified Theory—how the knowledge of stress can further an understanding of the theory of life.

Book V:
Implications and Applications—how the knowledge of stress can be applied medically, psychosomatically and philosophically to insure a better and happier life.

No one can live without experiencing some degree of stress all the time. You may think that only serious disease or intensive physical or mental injury can cause stress. This is false. Crossing a busy intersection, exposure to a draft, or even sheer joy are enough to activate the body's stress-mechanism to some extent. Stress is not even necessarily bad for you; it is also the spice of life, for any emotion, any activity causes stress. But, of course, your system must be prepared to take it. The same stress which makes one person sick can be an invigorating experience for another.

It is through the *general adaptation syndrome,* or G.A.S. (the main subject of this book), that our various internal organs—especially the endocrine glands and the nervous system—help to adjust us to the constant changes which occur in and around us.

Life is largely a process of adaptation to the circumstances in which we exist. A perennial give-and-take has been going on between living matter and its inanimate surroundings, between one living thing and another, ever since the dawn of life in the prehistoric oceans. The secret of health and happiness lies in successful adjustment to the ever-changing conditions on this globe; the penalties for failure in this great process of adaptation are disease and unhappiness. The evolution through endless centuries from the simplest forms of life to complex human beings was the greatest adaptive adventure on earth.

———————

All these diverse adaptive reactions are, in the final analysis, due to exposing different combinations of tissue-elements to stress. There emerges the impression of some fundamental unifying law. But this is still only an impression. As the picture stands at this point, perhaps its most disturbing feature is the difficulty of correlating the " morbid " phenomena of transformative or redevelopmental adaptation (for instance, of a regular muscle cell into an irregular structure which engulfs foreign particles) with the " physiologic " type of simple tissue development (growth and maturation). The evolution of our tissues from infancy to adulthood appears to be directed by the laws of heredity, without any manifest dependence upon stress.

———————

What makes me so certain that the natural human life-span is far in excess of the actual one is this:

Among all my autopsies (and I have performed quite a few), I have never seen a man who died of old age. In fact, *I do not think anyone has ever died of old age yet.* To permit this would be the ideal accomplishment of medical research (if we disregard the unlikely event of someone discovering how to regenerate adaptation energy). To die of old age would mean that all the organs of the body would be worn out proportionately, merely having been used too long. This is never the case. We invariably die because one vital part has worn out too early in proportion to the rest of the body. Life, the biologic chain that holds our parts together, is only as strong as its weakest vital link. When this breaks—no matter which vital link it be—our parts can no longer be held together as a single living being.

42. The Myth of the Machine (I): Technics and Human Development

LEWIS MUMFORD. Secker & Warburg Ltd., 14 Carlisle Street, London W1V 6NN; 1967; £3.15; 342 pp.

Mumford rejects the supremacy of the view of "man the tool-maker," and shows how tools themselves did not and could not develop without a much more significant series of inventions in ritual, language, and social organization. The key to his analysis is the idea that the so-called machine age originated not with the Industrial Revolution of the eighteenth century, but at the very outset in the organization of an archetypal machine composed of human parts—the "megamachine"—consisting of thousands of humans toiling on pyramids, palaces, and military campaigns.

From the beginning man's brain was more important than his hands. The most important artifacts transmitted through history are ritual language and social organization. Mumford traces the archetypal machine through history to the threshold of the modern world: the sixteenth century in Western Europe. He shows that rather than being primarily motivated to conquer nature, man's overactive nervous system dealt mainly with the creation of a human self, developed by fabrication of symbols—the only tools that could be constructed out of the resources of his own body; dreams, images, sounds.

Mumford has spent a lifetime of serious scholarship and creative thinking on the subject of man and technology. Although his thinking today may not seem as "electric" as some of the ideas floating around, it is still imperative to read and study him for a grounding in the subject. JB

In terms of the currently accepted picture of the relation of man to technics, our age is passing from the primeval state of man, marked by his invention of tools and weapons for the purpose of achieving mastery over the forces of nature, to a radically different condition, in which he will have not only conquered nature, but detached himself as far as possible from the organic habitat.

With this new 'megatechnics' the dominant minority will create a uniform, all-enveloping, super-planetary structure, designed for automatic operation. Instead of functioning actively as an autonomous personality, man will become a passive, purposeless, machine-conditioned animal whose proper functions, as technicians now interpret man's role, will either be fed into the machine or strictly limited and controlled for the benefit of de-personalized collective organizations.

The misleading notion that man is primarily a tool-making animal, who owes his inordinate mental development largely to his long apprenticeship in making tools, will not be easy to displace. Like other plausible conceits, it evades rational criticism, especially since it flatters the vanity of modern 'Technological Man,' that ghost clad in iron.

During the last half century, this short period has been described as the Machine Age, the Power Age, the Steel Age, the Concrete Age, the Air Age, the Electronic Age, the Nuclear Age, the Rocket Age, the Computer Age, the Space Age, and the Age of Automation. One would hardly guess from such characterizations that these recent technological triumphs constitute but a fraction of the immense number of highly diversified components that enter into present-day technology, and make up but an infinitesimal part of the entire heritage of human culture. If only one phase of the remote human past was blotted out—the cumulative inventions of paleolithic man, beginning with language—all these new achievements would be worthless. So much for our boasted one-generation culture.

What all this seems to add up to is that primitive man's first attack upon his 'environment' was probably an 'attack' upon his own body; and that his first efforts at magical control were visited upon himself. As if life were not hard enough under these rude conditions, he toughened himself further in such grotesque ordeals of beautification. Whether decoration or surgery was involved, none of these practices had any direct contribution to make to physical survival. They count rather as the earliest evidence of an even deeper tendency in man: to impose his own conditions, however ill-conceived, upon nature. Yet what they point to even more significantly is a conscious effort toward self-mastery and self-actualization; and even—though often exhibited in perverse, irrational ways—at self-perfection.

———————————

Here a new kind of science, different from the close observation and intimate association that fostered domestication, came into existence: now based on an abstract impersonal order: counting, measurement, exact notation—attributes without whose early development no such consummate monuments as the pyramids could have been built. The counting of the days, the observations of the lunar months and the solar year, the determination of the rise and the flood stage of the Nile—all this was the task of the priestly caste. This new power and order were effectively symbolized, as I have already noted, by the establishment of the first Egyptian solar calendar.

Though heavily overlaid by dramatic legend, sensuous metaphor, and infantile magic, astronomical order spread into every department. The emerging institutions of civilization were power-minded, cosmos-centered, mechanically regulated and regimented. Space and time, power and order, became the main categories of a divinely regulated existence: the recurrent movements of the moon and the sun, or great expressions of natural power, such as flood and storm and earthquake, left a profound impression on the mind and awakened, it would appear, at least in the dominant minority, an interest in exerting their own physical power in imitation of the gods themselves.

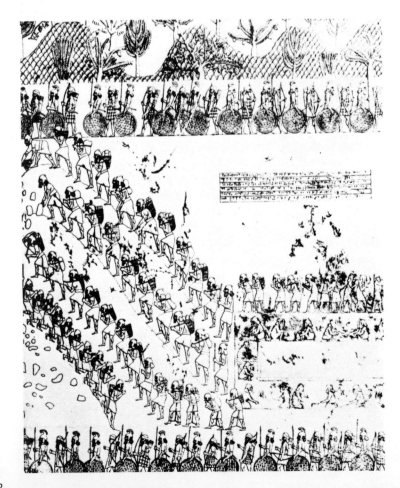

Megamachines in Operation

Assyrians building a mound for the erection of a palace. Note the frieze of soldiers. Both taskmasters and soldiers were essential parts of the megamachine.

Achievements of the Megamachine

The first exhibition of megatechnics comes from the Step Pyramid at Sakkara, constructed under the architect, engineer, scientist, and physician, Imhotep, who well earned his later deification. This pyramid of King Zoser, the dominant feature of a whole city dedicated to the dead, surpassed all contemporary works and has defied time almost as well as the colossal later pyramids of Chephren and Cheops. The megamachine was reassembled repeatedly for military purposes under the institution of divine kingship. But it displayed its best form and highest efficiency in large-scale engineering activities. The Great Wall of China, built in the third century B.C., to keep Mongol invaders at bay, pushing across a difficult terrain for 1,500 miles, gives evidence of the megamachine's massive constructive powers. *(Photographs from Ewing Galloway, New York.*

Because the components of the machine, even when it functioned as a completely integrated whole, were necessarily separate in space, I shall for certain purposes call it the 'invisible machine': when utilized to perform work on highly organized collective enterprises, I shall call it the 'labor machine': when applied to acts of collective coercion and destruction, it deserves the title, used even today, the 'military machine.' But when all the components, political and economic, military, bureaucratic and royal, must be included, I shall usually refer to the 'megamachine': in plain words, the Big Machine. And the technical equipment derived from such a megamachine thence becomes 'megatechnics' as distinguished from the more modest and diversified modes of technology, which until our own century continued to perform the larger part of the daily work in the workshop and on the farm, sometimes with the help of power machinery.

Men of ordinary capacity, relying on muscle power and traditional skills alone, were capable of performing a wide variety of tasks, including pottery manufacture and weaving, without any external direction or scientific guidance, beyond that available in the tradition of the local community. Not so with the megamachine. Only kings, aided by the discipline of astronomical science and supported by the sanctions of religion, had the capability of assembling and directing the megamachine. This was an invisible structure composed of living, but rigid, human parts, each assigned to his special office, role, and task, to make possible the immense work-output and grand designs of this great collective organization.

———————————

The rituals of sacrifice and the rituals of compulsion were accordingly unified through the operation of the military machine. And if anxiety was the original motive that brought about the subjective response of sacrifice, war, in the act of widening the area of sacrifice, also restricted the area where normal human choices, based on

respect for all the organism's creative potentials, could operate. In a word, *a compulsive pattern of orderliness was the central achievement of the negative megamachine.* At the same time, the gain in power that the organization of the megamachine brought was further offset by the marked symptoms of deterioration in the minds of those who customarily exercised this power: they not merely became dehumanized but they chronically lost all sense of reality, like the Sumerian king who extended his conquests so far that when he returned to his own capital he found it in the hands of an enemy.

———————————

The machine, 'advanced' thinkers began to hold, not merely served as the ideal model for explaining and eventually controlling all organic activities, but its wholesale fabrication and its continued improvement were what alone could give meaning to human existence. Within a century or two, the ideological fabric that supported the ancient megamachine had been reconstructed on a new and improved model. Power, speed, motion, standardization, mass production, quantification, regimentation, precision, uniformity, astronomical regularity, control, above all control—these became the passwords of modern society in the new Western style.

Only one thing was needed to assemble and polarize all the new components of the megamachine: the birth of the Sun God. And in the sixteenth century, with Kepler, Tycho Brahe, and Copernicus officiating as accoucheurs, the new Sun God was born.

43. The Myth of the Machine (II): The Pentagon of Power

LEWIS MUMFORD. Secker & Warburg Ltd., 14 Carlisle Street, London W1V 6NN; 1967; £3.15; 496 pp.

The mistake is in substituting the part for the whole, in identifying tools and machines with technology. Mumford continues his study of *The Myth of the Machine* in this second volume, in which he looks at technology not as a tool, but as part of the psychobiological construct we call humanity. As we all know, the last century has witnessed a radical transformation in the entire human environment, largely as a result of the impact of mathematical and physical sciences upon technology. New advances in nuclear energy, supersonic transportation, cybernetic intelligence, and instantaneous distant communication have come so dramatically and so quickly that the image of man has qualitatively changed and will continue to change. Mumford takes a look at the idea of technological progress as man's highest good, noting that it is not the result of mechanical inventions by themselves but of the new Mechanical World Picture. The problem is that this " new " picture is now hopelessly outmoded, and based on erroneous conceptions in the first place.

Mumford has written a few dozen books leading up these recent volumes. The erudition and research, the comprehensive annotated bibliographies, the scope and range of the subject matter and thinking, all add up to a highly charged reading experience. JB

Between the fifteenth and nineteenth centuries, the New World opened by terrestrial explorers, adventurers, soldiers, and administrators joined forces with the scientific and technical new world that the scientists, the inventors, and the engineers explored and cultivated: they were part and parcel of the same movement. One mode of exploration was concerned with abstract symbols, rational systems, universal laws, repeatable and predictable events, objective mathematical measurements: it sought to understand, utilize, and control the forces that derive ultimately from the cosmos and the solar system. The other mode dwelt on the concrete and the organic, the adventurous, the tangible: to sail uncharted oceans, to conquer new lands, to subdue and overawe strange peoples, to discover new foods and medicines, perhaps to find the fountain of youth, or if not, to seize by shameless force of arms the wealth of the Indies. In both modes of exploration, there was from the beginning a touch of defiant pride and demonic frenzy.

Unfortunately, in seeking to read the book of nature more faithfully, the new thinkers repeated the error made by Thales and Aristarchus: unthinkingly, they banished the thinker himself from the picture as peremptorily and arbitrarily as Socrates, and after him the Christian theologians, had turned their backs on nature. Not until astronomers discovered that a source of error in their observations was the length of time it took the nervous system to transmit a message from the eye to the brain did they realize that no part of the external world was wholly extraneous to man, or could be investigated except by utilizing man's physiological aptitudes and cumulative cultural inventions—that the very notion of a universe independent of man was itself a peculiarly human achievement, dependent upon human history and human consciousness.

Comenius' work makes plain the interweaving of inventions, mechanical experiences, regimented institutions, and, underlying them all, exorbitant magical expectations, which produced the new industrial and political fabric. The combination of astronomical regularity, absolute political authority, and lifelike automatism proved increasingly

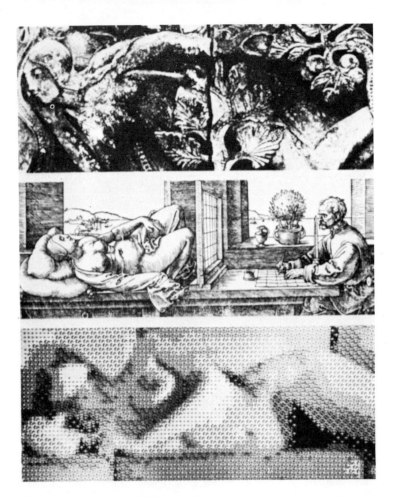

Mechanization of the World Picture

(Top) Woman is seen and felt by a twelfth-century craftsmen (Saint-Lazare d'Autun, France). (Center) Woman as mapped by a Renaissance painter, using Cartesian co-ordinates before Descartes. (Bottom) Woman as translated into fashionable computer language as a pseudo-photograph.

irresistible. We need hardly be surprised, then, that when Comenius finally reaches the clock in his enumerations his words become nothing less than ecstatic: "Is it not a truly marvelous thing that a machine, a soulless thing, can move in such a life-like, continuous, and regular manner? Before clocks were invented would not the existence of such things have seemed as impossible as that trees could walk or stones speak?"

But one unfortunate feature of the pecuniary power complex has still to be noted; for it sets off recent manifestations from the earlier myth of the machine, and makes them even more obstructive to further development. Whereas in the past the power-pleasure nucleus was under the exclusive control of the dominant minority, and so could seduce only this extremely limited group, with the growth of megatechnics all its major features have been distributed, under the canons of mass society (democratic participation) to a far larger population.

To discuss the proliferation of inventions during the last two centuries, the mass production of commodities, and the spread of all the technological factors that are polluting and destroying the living environment, without reference to this immense pecuniary pressure constantly exerted in every technological area, is to ignore the most essential clue to the seemingly automatic and uncontrollable dynamism of the whole system. In order to 'turn on' this insensate pleasure center 'technological man' now threatens to 'turn off' his life. Money has proved the most dangerous of modern man's hallucinogens.

There is a simple way of establishing the downright absurdity—or more accurately the menacing irrationality—of accepting such technological compulsiveness; and that is to carry von Neumann's dictum to its logical conclusion: *If man has the power to exterminate all life on earth, he will.* Since we know that the governments of the United States and Soviet Russia have already created nuclear, chemical, and bacterial agents in the massive quantities needed to wipe out the human race, what prospects are there of human survival, if this practice of submitting to extrav-

Encapsulated Man

Behold the astronaut, fully equipped for duty: a scaly creature, more like an oversized ant than a primate—certainly not a naked god. To survive on the moon he must be encased in an even more heavily insulated garment and become a kind of faceless ambulatory mummy. While he is hurtling through space, the astronaut's physical existence is purely a function of mass and motion, narrowed down to a pinpoint of acute sentient intelligence demanded by the necessity of co-ordinating his reactions with the mechanical and electronic apparatus upon which his survival depends. Here is the archetypal proto-model of Post-Historic Man, whose existence from birth to death would be conditioned by the megamachine, and made to conform, as in the space capsule, to the minimal functional requirements by an equally minimal environment—all under remote control.

agant and dehumanized technological imperatives is 'irresistibly' carried to its final stage? In the light of these facts, the central problem of technics must be restated: *It is that of creating human beings capable of understanding their own nature sufficiently to control, and when necessary to suppress, the forces and mechanisms that they have brought into existence.* No automatic warning system can solve this problem for us.

————————————

At least one thing should soon become clear: once the majority of any nation opts for megatechnics, or passively accepts the system without further question, no other choices will remain. But if the people are willing to surrender their life completely at source, this authoritarian system promises generously to give back as much of it as can be mechanically graded, quantitatively multiplied, scientifically sorted, technically conditioned, manipulated, directed, and socially distributed under supervision of centralized bureaucracy. What held at first only for increasing the quantity of goods, now applies to every aspect of life. The willing member of megatechnic society can have everything the system produces—provided he and his group have no private wishes of their own, and will make no attempt personally to alter its quality or reduce its quantity or question the competence of its 'decision-makers.' In such a society the two unforgivable sins, or rather punishable vices, would be continence and selectivity.

————————————

One final aspect of materialization remains to be noted: a paradox. And this is that subjective expressions remain alive in the mind far longer than the corporate organizations and physical buildings that seem to the outward eye so solid and durable. Even when a culture disintegrates, the loss is never quite complete or final. From the total achievement much will remain and leave its imprint on later minds in the form of sport, play, language, art, customs. Though few Westerners have seen a Hindu temple, the Sanskrit root for mother and father still remains on their tongue in addressing their parents, more durable than any monument; and this symbolic debris of past cultures forms a rich compost for the mind, without which the cultural environment would be as sterile as that of the moon.

44. The Entropy Law and the Economic Process

NICHOLAS GEORGESCU-ROEGEN. Harvard University Press, Kittridge Hall, 79 Gordon Street, Cambridge, Mass. 02138; or *Real Time*. $16.00; 457 pp.

The entropy law is based on the intricate physical facts of the Second Law of Thermodynamics. The entropy of the universe (or of an isolated structure) increases constantly and irrevocably. In the universe there is a continuous and irrevocable qualitative degradation of free into bound energy. A modern interpretation of this pattern is the notion of a continuous turning of order into disorder. Sir Arthur Eddington maintained that the position of the entropy law is "supreme." This law is a refutation of classical Newtonian mechanics, which holds that everything which happens in any phenomenal domain consists of locomotion alone. According to this dogma there is no irrevocable change in nature. But the key to the entropy law is that there is a change undergone by matter and energy, a qualitative and irrevocable change. This alters the entire epistemology of the phenomenal world inherited from classical mechanics.

The manner in which such a new concept can creep into the perceptions of related and/or distant fields is evidenced by this book of twelve papers, plus a five-chapter essay which deals with the nature of scientific and economic explanation. The author maintains that economic activity is in fact a biological extension and a complement of man's biological evolution, and that the economic process, instead of being a mathematical analogue as traditionally represented in economics, is an entropic process.

In a way, Georgescu-Roegen is applying the entropy law to economics in much the same spirit as it was applied to information theory by physicist Leon Brilluoin in his two books *Science and Information Theory,* and *Scientific Uncertainty and Information* (Academic Press). In each case, a brilliant synthesis points out how the interpretation of new physical facts has a creeping and devastating effect on the way in which we view the world.

Nicholas Georgescu-Roegen is Professor of Economics at Vanderbilt University. JB

Revolution is a fairly recurrent state in physics. The revolution that interests us here began with the physicists; acknowledging the elementary fact that heat always moves by itself in one direction only, from the hotter to the colder body. This led to the recognition that there are phenomena which cannot be reduced to locomotion and hence explained by mechanics. A new branch of physics, thermodynamics, then came into being and a new law, the Entropy Law, took its place alongside—rather opposite to—the laws of Newtonian mechanics.

From the viewpoint of economic science, however, the importance of this revolution exceeds the fact that it ended the supremacy of the mechanistic epistemology in physics. The significant fact for the economist is that the new science of thermodynamics began as a physics of economic value and, basically, can still be regarded as such. The Entropy Law itself emerges as the most economic in nature of all natural laws. It is in the perspective of these developments in the primary science of matter that the fundamentally nonmechanistic nature of the economic process fully reveals itself.

As we shall gradually come to realize in the course of this volume, the position occupied by the Entropy Law among all other laws of nature is unique from numerous viewpoints. And this fact accounts for the wealth of questions and issues that overwhelm any student interested in assessing the importance of the Entropy Law beyond the strictly physical domain.

No one would deny that entropy, together with its associated concepts of free and bound energies, is a much more mysterious notion than locomotion. The only way man can consciously act on the material environment is by pushing or pulling, even when he starts a fire. But this limitation is no reason for clinging to the idea that the entropic process must be reducible to locomotion. Monism has long since ceased to be the password in science. Even the argument that science must be free of any contradiction is no longer commanding. Physics itself now teaches us that we must not insist on molding actuality into a noncontradictory framework. Just as we are advised by Niels Bohr's Principle of Complementarity that we must accept as a brute fact that the electron behaves both as a wave and as a particle—concepts irreducible to one another—so must we at present reconcile ourselves to the existence of thermodynamic and mechanical phenomena side by side, albeit in opposition.

From the epistemological viewpoint, the Entropy Law may be regarded as the greatest transformation ever suffered by physics. It marks the recognition by that science—the most trusted of all sciences of nature—that there is qualitative change in the universe. Still more important is the fact that the irrevocability proclaimed by that law sets on a solid footing the commonsense distinction between locomotion and true happening.

Like all inventions, that of the arithmomorphic concept too has its good and its bad features. On the one hand, it has speeded the advance of knowledge in the domain of inert matter; it has also helped us detect numerous errors in our thinking, even in our mathematical thinking. Thanks to Logic and mathematics in the ultimate instance, man has been able to free himself of most animistic superstitions in interpreting the wonders of nature. On the other hand, because an arithmomorphic concept has absolutely no relation to life, to *anima,* we have been led to regard it as the only sound expression of knowledge. As a result, for the last two hundred years we have bent all our efforts to enthrone a superstition as dangerous as the animism of old: that of the Almighty Arithmomorphic Concept. Nowadays, one would risk being quietly excommunicated from the modern *Akademia* if he denounced this modern superstition too strongly.

To illustrate now the difference between blueprint and simile, let me observe that one does not need to know electronics in order to assemble a radio apparatus he has purchased in kit form. All he needs to do is follow automatically the accompanying blueprint, which constitutes an *operational* representation by symbols of the corresponding mechanism. The fact that no economic model proper can serve as a guide to *automatic action* for the uninitiated, or even for a consummate economist, necessitates no special demonstration. Everyone is familiar with the dissatisfaction the average board member voices after each conference where some economic consultant has presented this "silly theory." Many graduate students too feel greatly frustrated to discover that, in spite of all they have heard, economics cannot supply them with a manual of banking, planning, taxation, and so forth. An economic model, being only a simile, can be a guide only for the initiated who has acquired an analytical insight through some laborious training.

And as I have argued in many places of this book, no electrode, no microscope, indeed no physical contraption can reveal to us how men's minds work. Only one man's mind can find out how another man's mind works by using the bridge provided by the familiar mental categories and propensities that are common to both. Man may not be as accurate an instrument as a microscope, but he is the only one who can observe what all the physical instruments together cannot. For if it were not so, we should send some politoscopes to reveal what other people think, feel, and might do next—not ambassadors, counselors, journalists, and other kinds of observers; and as we have yet no politoscopes, we should then send nothing.

But perhaps one day we will all come to realize that man too is an instrument, the only one to study man's propensities. That day there will be no more forgotten men, forgotten because today we allegedly do not know how to study them and report on what they think, feel, and want. A "peace army," not only a "peace corps," is what we need. This, I admit, may be an utopian thought, reminiscent of the *Narodniki's* slogan, "To the people." But I prefer to be utopian on this point than on the New Jerusalem that uncritical scientism of one kind or another holds out as a promise to man.

45. Two-Factor Theory: The Economics of Reality

LOUIS O. KELSO and PATRICIA HETTER. Vintage Books, 201 East 50th Street, New York, N.Y. 10022; 1967; or *Real Time*. (H) $4.95; (P) $1.95; 202 pp.

The increasing pattern of automation has created a situation whereby the productive factor of human work is no longer the key measure for productive wealth. The economy is based on income outtake directly related to non-human productive input: i.e., capital. Capital, new innovations, and new organizational patterns are the keys to new wealth. Where does this leave most of the people? Kelso and Hetter (a lawyer and a political scientist) make a stab at some answers. JB

Never a precise term, "capitalism" today provides no descriptive information about any economic system, either existing or theoretical. Future generations may well wonder how ideological stances for nearly two centuries could have been fixed by a concept so functionally useless. The one true, fruitful inference that might have been drawn from the primitive industrial system that gave us the word was not drawn. The idea that inanimate things produce wealth in the same sense that animate things do, and thus can be productive surrogates for personal toil in the economic world, never dawned. Nor could it, as long as economic speculation was dominated, as it has been throughout the history of political economy, by pre-industrial mores and modes of thought that interpret all industrial reality in terms of only one of the two factors of production: man's labor. One-factor economic thought is incapable of explainig a physical world in which major productive instruments are nonhuman.

In addition to its main premise that capital and not labor is the source of affluence in an industrial society—indeed the only possible source of affluence in any free industrial society—the theory of universal capitalism is based upon certain other assumptions.

ECONOMIC ASSUMPTIONS

1. Mass production implies mass consumption; it is illogical to build the industrial power to produce goods and services without building at the same time the commensurate economic power of families and individuals to consume the output.

2. Where millions of families are downright poor and the vast majority of the rest live well below the standard that is physically feasible, the realization of general affluence, even in such advanced industrial economies as the United States and Canada, will require an economic growth rate of several times the three and a half or four percent that is currently achieved in the U.S. and in most Western economies. That growth must represent real increases in the economy's power to produce consumer-useful goods and services, not make-work ones such as excessive munitions, space hardware, supersonic transports (when over 90% of the population is too poor to use our present subsonic jet airplanes), etc. Measures that do not increase the output of consumer-useful goods and services, but which create additional purchasing power or redistribute the purchasing power arising from production in the existing economy, have no possibility of bringing about the vast new capital formation, the "second economy", necessary to produce genuine affluence for everyone.

3. Production and consumption in a market economy form a natural equation. That is implicit in Say's Law, which holds that in a market economy the aggregate market value of the

wealth produced is equal to the aggregate purchasing power created by the process of production. The problem is one of structuring production in such a way that every household has an opportunity to make a viable productive input into the economy, thereby automatically entitling it to receive purchasing power equivalent to its productive contribution.

Discourse on "tools," "investment," the "investment function" of the owner of concentrated financial savings, the "job-creating magic" of financial capital, or the sacrificial beneficence of the owner of concentrated savings for "risking his savings," belongs to the pre-industrial age of one-factor thinking. It is no substitute for recognizing that the nonhuman factor produces wealth for its owners in precisely the same physical, economic, political and moral sense as the human factor. Nor is it a substitute for recognizing that if there is indeed a right to life and liberty in an industrial society, then it is the heritage of every man to own a viable share of the factor of production that is the chief source of life and the chief bulwark of liberty in that society.

As public and private debt (owned entirely by the top 10% of wealth holders) mounts upward from the one and a half trillion-dollar level to support this grotesque arrangement, the claims of the few upon the future productive power of the many and the future productive power of the nonhuman factor threaten the legal foundations of the economy. Viewed in the light of the concept of universal capitalism, the debt structure of the United States has a vastly different significance than that popularly attributed to it: power gap. They only make the gap bigger to the extent of the interest charged on the loans.

46. The Russell Sage Foundation

230 Park Avenue, New York, N.Y. 10017; 1971.

The Russell Sage Foundation is engaged in the support of new research in the development of the social sciences. In addition to funding researchers, whose work is published in book form under their imprint, the Foundation also occasionally publishes papers reviewing new fields for social science development. The first of these papers, published in 1969 and now out of print, was Diana Crane's "Social Aspects of the Prolongation of Life." The second paper was Otis Duncan's "Towards Social Reporting: Next Steps."

The current paper in the Social Science Frontiers series is James R. Sorenson's "Social Aspects of Applied Human Genetics," which explores "the social adaptation of man to technological change in medicine and innovation in medical practice." Social Science Frontiers papers are published in very limited quantities. ER

Recent advances in science and medicine are increasing man's control of the quantity and quality of human populations. The development of highly effective and relatively efficient birth control techniques permits expanded regulation of population size and growth. In addition, advances in medical genetics are making possible growing intervention and manipulation of the genetic quality of human populations.

Progress in medical genetics can alter man's role in evolution. Man is no longer limited to passive acceptance of all inherited characteristics but is rapidly expanding his technological capacity to include the active treatment, selection, and elimination of many individual genetic attributes. These developments pose complex questions of a moral, ethical, political, psychological, or economic nature. For instance, what genetic attributes or constitutions are desirable? Who is to decide? Should genetic anomalies be reduced in a population? Who shall say how or when? As with most technological developments, knowledge that permits increasing intervention and control of the genetic quality of life is accumulating more rapdily than is man's ability to apply this knowledge wisely.

Some of the technological developments that permit control of the quality of human life have not precipitated serious problems. In most Western societies medical research and practice have achieved near complete control of many of the major infectious diseases that have plagued mankind for centuries; such control has met little resistance. A case in point is the development of polio vaccine and the subsequent virtual elimination of poliomyelitis.

The success of such medical advances was dependent on several things, especially prevailing values. For example, the implementation of programs to control infectious disease required a value system in which disease was interpreted as a natural event. If parents felt shame or guilt for the infectious diseases suffered by their children, attempts to treat the disorders and to develop curative methods would have been obstructed. Also, such a value system had to provide for the approval of man's active intervention to control disease. The doctor in Western society has not only received approval for his intervention in disease control but also has achieved a great deal of esteem and prestige from the society he has served.

The idea of treatment and intervention in man's genetic health is not universally accepted today, by either the general public or the medical profession. This is due in part to existing values and beliefs. Parents often experience guilt and shame for genetic disorders in their offspring. More important perhaps, many people including some medical personnel, believe that medical procedures are not capable of correcting or treating any genetic disorders, or that doctors and parents should not attempt genetic intervention.

Through the ages man has interpreted the significance of genetic anomalies in many ways. Sometimes, anomalies were interpreted as the favor of the gods, and at other times they were considered to be portents of divine wrath. Today where these beliefs still linger, they limit the use of genetic knowledge by the public and by medical practitioners. Counterbalancing these beliefs and values is a rapidly increasing technological capacity to treat and to select certain genetic conditions. The eventual role of applied human genetics in medical practice and society will reflect the complex intertwining of existing values and beliefs with increasing technical capacity. Neither factor alone will predict man's orientation toward an intervention in his genetic future.

The increasing intervention in and control of genetic disease and the selection or avoidance of certain genetic constitutions have fostered debates within and between many different groups in society. Medical professionals, life scientists, lawyers, ministers, biologists, and philosophers are engaged in discussions concerning the proper use of such knowledge. A prerequisite for intelligent discussion of these issues is information about how genetic knowledge is used today. Which doctors give genetic counseling? Which parents seek counseling? What types of reproductive decisions do people make when faced with genetic disorders? Very little information is available on these topics. If man is to understand and to employ the potential good inherent in medical genetic advances, he must begin by determining by whom and how these advances are used. The social sciences, by providing such information, can make significant contributions to discussions on the use of genetic knowledge.

Because psychological and sociological research on applied human genetics has been very limited, extensive studies are needed in at least five major areas: (1) the social organization of medical genetics; (2) the training, practices, and attitudes of genetic counselors; (3) the clients of genetic counseling, their problems, atttiudes, and decisions; (4) the legal implications and social consequences of applied human genetics; and (5) the economic aspects of the delivery and utilization of medical genetics.

47. The Aspen Institute for Humanistic Studies

P.O. Box 219, Aspen, Colo. 81611.

The core program of the Aspen Institute for Humanistic Studies is called the Executive Seminar Program. Initially designed to involve business leaders in major streams of basic humanistic thought, the program has now been broadened to include representatives of labor, science, the arts, minority groups, and youth.

In addition, the Institute has special programs in five areas: 1. environment and the quality of life; 2. communications and society; 3. educational reform; 4. science, technology, and humanism; and 5. justice and the individual. ER

We can predict ecological disaster by statistically extrapolating trends or we can recall that unpleasant phenomena, like pollution and genetic defects, have been taken for granted as facts of life for millenia. Or we can take another tack and note that the one sure thing about the future is that it will not be a straight-line projection of the past.

The uncertainties derive from a simple lack of adequate knowledge about the ecology and how it works. To characterize the present state of ignorance, it is enough to quote a single sentence of a report prepared within recent months by a study group for the National Academy of Sciences. "To control the environment effectively, we need to know what it is, what it has been, and what it could be. "

There is a tendency these days to foster the notion that Nature is in perpetual peace and in perfect balance at all times and everywhere—gentle, friendly and inherently benign in its relations with living species. As though a tornado could not level Lubbock as the A-bomb leveled Hiroshima; as if there were no tidal waves or floods or droughts or hailstorms or volcanic eruptions to threaten the survival of early man and still kill and destroy in the twentieth century. Man had to survive the violent side of Nature and still suffers from environmental events to which he is an innocent party.

Neither environmental pollution nor addiction to growth is, as it turns out, an American or a Western phenomenon. Search for the Holy Grail of rising per capita gross national product is near-universal. And in that pursuit the newly industrializing countries are making most of the mistakes made by those who brought off the industrial revolution in the first place. This may lay a special burden on the shoulders of the highly industrialized, but hardly justifies self-flagellation about the sins of " materialism. "

Faced with finite resources and unable to turn back the clock, a radical solution of the resources problem must be identified before long.

One place to start might be with the proposition that Man can alter Matter but he cannot destroy it. In this sense, nothing is " consumed " and " non-renewable " resources like minerals are used but not " depleted. "

This makes an urgent case for a massive R&D program on the technological possibilities for recycling and reusing resources now effectively " consumed " in industrial processes.

For the short term, a wide variety of new measures may be needed: a requirement on biodegradable materials; an end to planned obsolescence; inclusion of disposal costs in price calculations; new methods of using or recovering wastes; a moratorium on the launching of some types of new products; power rationing, etc.—all of which will have pervasive effects on traditional thoughts about economics, social policy, relations with government and other matters difficult to identify at this point.

But unless finite resources ultimately can be reused more or less infinitely, there is a traumatic barrier somewhere down the road which the world is currently traveling. Whether the "fusion torch" holds a large part of the answer remains to be seen. Meanwhile, it is not unreasonable to demand, as *Science* magazine did recently, that "the next industrial revolution" must take place in the area of new technology for reusing and recycling the materials we extract or divert from Nature.

In gearing up for such an effort, it might be useful to think of the whole process as one of converting the economy from a "dirty" to a "clean" production-consumption-disposal system. This may turn out to be more difficult and prolonged than the conversion of the economy from a peace-time to a war-time footing in the early 1940's. But the analogy may not be wholly useless; we learned how to allocate resources to priority tasks very efficiently indeed. The catch is that the war-time system was highly authoritarian—which brings up something close to the ultimate question: how to devise democratic participation in decision-making on the use of limited resources.

- A revolution in medical technology greatly increased life expectancy—and largely created the population explosion.
- Successive industrial revolutions relieved whole populations of arduous physical labor and provided them with undreamed-of material standards of living; they also led to a prodigal exploitation of natural resources and a sinister fouling of the natural environment.
- A revolution in agricultural technology permitted less than 10 percent of the U.S. population to raise enough food for itself and the other 90 percent, to export large quantities and give away more; it also sparked a mass migration of people from land to city which became a major cause of urban crowding and decay.
- A revolution in international communications and transport technology—coming at a time when over 100 million people were being released from colonial status—increased the inter-dependence of nation-states; they also helped stimulate leaders in a hundred or more countries to want to "develop" essentially along the lines of the industrialized West.
- A revolution in the science of physics converted matter to energy, opened up vast new sources of power—and led to a mutual capacity for mutual destruction on the part of the two most powerful nations in the world.

These paradoxes and ambiguities all arise from man's historical struggle against disease, hunger, poverty, war, and ignorance; they are by-products of the classical pursuit of "security" and "progress." What is new is the speed with which each of those trends has come to the point of crisis in the twentieth century. And in a fundamental sense, it is all the same crisis: in its population dimension—in its urban dimension—in its nuclear weapons dimension—in its environmental dimension, the overall crisis represents the social fallout of modern science.

In this perspective the question of whether the greatest danger to human health comes from the tires, brake linings or exhaust pipes of an automobile is a technical quibble: even "the Environment" is too narrow a framework for thinking about the total impact of science upon society.

48. A.D. (Architectural Design)

The Standard Catalogue Company Limited, 26 Bloomsbury Way, London WC1A 2SS, England. Monthly, £6.40 per year (£4.30 for students).

There is an old Zen story about three monks sitting in a temple garden one evening. The moon is high in the sky, and one of the monks points to a pail filled with water and exclaims: "The clear water reflects the image of the moon." The second monk is quick to chastise the first: "There is no water, no moon." The third monk rises and kicks over the bucket of water.

A.D. is consistently kicking over buckets and exposing illusions as mere containers, lined with applications. Ostensibly this periodical's field of interest is architecture and design. But what it presents each month is a compendium of products, services, developments, philosophies, tools, systems, approaches, and details. ER

Architectural Design Vol XLII 10 1972

ROYSTON LANDAU
COMPLEXITY
(OR HOW TO SEE THE WOOD IN SPITE OF THE TREES)

Contents

This month

AD and guest editor, Roy Landau, are once again considering the basic contextural philosophies of architecture and planning; looking as depth at the complexities of Complexity (in a sequel to the September 1969 issue entitled 'Despite popular demand, AD is thinking about architecture and planning.')

The need for an understanding of complexity is all too evident.

Few current social and political pre-occupations can be understood or solved without an acceptance of an 'holistic' view of systems — a look at the whole picture as against the 'atomistic' view-point of the specialist, who sees the world as a conglomeration of separate items that make up the whole but are not interactive.

Complexity is reflected in many facets of contemporary life — with a shift in such attitudes as the moves from beach cleaning to ecology, from bureaucracy to parti-cipation, from centralisation to frag-mentation, and from closed systems to open systems.

These articles are important for under-standing total systems the potential they imply and their application to real problems the problems of societies, of cities, of resourses and of individuals.

Next month

New work and projects by Norman Foster Associates

Publication date First day of each month

Editor Monica Pidgeon
Technical editor Peter Murray
Editorial assistants Shirley Wilson (Information)
  Mike Gough (artwork)
Subscriptions Dawn Giboire

Consultant editors Roy Landau, Robin Middleton, Colin Moorcraft, Alexander Pike, Martin Pawley, Robin Thompson

Publishers The Standard Catalogue Co. Ltd, 26 Bloomsbury Way, London WC1A 2SS. Telephone: 01-405 6325. Telex: 261244 Whitstan London. Telegrams: Brittsanex. Typesetters Specialised Printing Services Ltd. Printers W.W.Web Offset Ltd and Whitefriars Press Ltd.

Subscription rates/annual
UK/Eire: £4.80 plus £1.00 postage and packing.
  Special student rate £3.00 plus £1.00 p. and p.
North America: $17.00 plus $2.40 p. and p.
  Special student rate $10.80 plus $2.40 p. and p.

Other countries: £7.70 plus £1.00 p. and p.
  Special student rate £4.50 plus £1.00 p. and p.

Single and back copies
Each copy at ,50p/$1.20 including p. and p.
Orders will not be accepted unless accompanied by cheque/postal order/money order.

Index Free on request.

Binder for 12 copies
£1.00 including p. and p.

THE SELF-EXCITING SYSTEM
GEOFFREY VICKERS

One thing is clear from a study of systems of all kinds—no trend, literally no trend, can be expected to continue in the same direction indefinitely, least of all one that increases at an exponential rate, however slow. So anyone who makes proposals based on the assumption that any such trend will continue should be asked to show reasonable grounds for thinking that it will do so at least last long enough to support whatever proposal or argument he is basing on it.

Nearly all scenarios of the future make two of these assumptions. One is that, at least in Western societies, everyone will go on getting richer and so will have more abundant personal choices. The other is that the present institutions of society will go on dealing with the society's collective choices without any change in their character so radical as to deserve attention. These forecasters do their best to startle us out of our old-fashioned assumptions about the nature of work, the scope for enjoyment, the place of authority, even the meaning of life. But they accept these linear assumptions of their own, that the system will be able to deal with the economic and the political results of its own activities.

These assumptions need to be questioned, like any other linear assumptions; first on general grounds, secondly because several conspicuous trends suggest that they cannot be true. There is already evidence of incipient breakdown, both economic and political; and an examination of the system suggests why it should be less able to deal with the problem it is generating now than with those of the past.

It is convenient to begin by asking how it is that the System has become, in the West, so powerfully exciting.

This is a shortened and modified version of a chapter in the author's Freedom in a Rocking Boat (1970. Allen Lane, The Penguin Press: 1972. Penguin Books) and is published with the kind permission of the publishers.

Sir Geoffrey Vickers: *b.1894 Now retired—was Head of Economic Intelligence at Ministry of Economic Warfare in World War II, member of National Coal Board responsible for manpower, training, education, health and welfare. Author of " Freedom in a rocking boat."*

To view society as a dynamic system can reveal components and directions which may cause surprise. An analysis of the elements and characteristics of such a societal system can make clear the underlying nature of current troubles.

Kaleidozoom II
Claimed to be one of the most exciting liquid effects projectors, the Kaleidozoom II produces an ever changing picture of vibrating and pulsating colours that is always symmetrical. The projector employs a 250 watt low voltage quartz iodine projector with turbo fan cooling.
Lightomation Ltd,
South Hill Lodge, South Hill Avenue, Harrow, Middlesex HA1 3NZ.

Poster stand
Marler Haley's free-standing poster holder takes A1 or double-crown (20 x 30 ins) in landscape or portrait positions. The steel support tube with satin chrome finish comes in 3 ft or 4 ft lengths. With a 3 ft stand, the double crown size costs £9.50, and A1 costs £10.
Marler Haley (Barnet) Ltd,
7 High St, Barnet, Herts.

Domes

Domeletter
Domeletter is an information sharing news letter which is intended to serve as a means of communicating new ideas among those interested in domes and other experimental structures. In its few (10) duplicated pages, Domeletter 2 describes how to build a very cheap dome and give lists of names, contacts and publications concerned with dome building. Single copies are 25c. Overseas readers send extra for postage.

John Prenis, 161 Penn St., Phila. Pa. 19144, USA.

Blow-up form
Basic Products have developed a system they call 'The Building Method' for building large open span structures using foam and gunnite sprayed onto a pneumatic form. Initially, polyurethane foam is sprayed onto the permanent hypalon coated nylon in flated form; then reinforcing steel is hung from the underside of the structure before the gunnite is sprayed on in successive thin layers.
Basic Products Development Co,
PO Box 955, Oakland, Calif. 94604.

Domecrete
Domecrete is a dome building system, developed by Haim Heifetz at the Haifa Technion, which utilises re-usable inflatable forms as shuttering for a permanent sprayed concrete finish. Using the system a contractor can build one dome per day complete with interior plaster, stucco, doors, windows, water pipes and electric conduits.

The Domecrete service includes: consultation to architects and designers, know-how to licensed contractors, training and supervision of construction crews.

The most recent project to be undertaken using the Domecrete system is a synagogue in Tel-Aviv.
Haim Heifetz, 34 Soederot, Haifa, Israel.

Grass

Europe's first full-size synthetic turf soccer pitch — made from Monsanto's AstroTurf — has been installed at Caledonian Park, North London.

The 110 yards by 70 yards pitch has a capital cost, exclusive of base, of approximately £121,000.

The London Borough of Islington has one of the highest populations per acre of any London borough and very little open space for sport. The new pitch will be available for normal hiring, with priority given to local borough teams. It will be floodlit and can be used seven days a week. The full-size pitch, which can be used for hockey as well as soccer, can be divided into two junior size pitches during weekdays for local schools.

The surface at Islington consists of 3/8 inch long, nylon blades on a nylon and polyester backing. This is bonded to a 3/4 inch shock absorbing pad, which, in turn, is bonded to an asphalt base.

The completed surface is usable under all ground conditions and has good impact absorption.

Whilst the Islington project is the first full-size, synthetic turf, soccer pitch in Europe, a major indoor installation and smaller outdoor scheme have been completed at Hennef, West Germany, and work has recently started on an AstroTurf hockey pitch, also in West Germany.
Monsanto Chemicals Ltd, Monsanto House, 10-18 Victoria St, London SW1.

Foam backed turf
A new type of turf — called Tana turf — which will grow from seed in less than 6 weeks has recently been developed. The process works hydroponically by floating the seeds on a plastic foam slurry which is itself floated on a shallow lagoon of water. The sponge effect of the foam ensures a constant level of moisture for the seeds.

In less than six weeks the seeds grow to form a firm, hardwearing carpet of turf which is particularly suitable for applications such as golf greens, bowling greens and cricket squares as well as sports grounds and lawns.
BASF Agricultural Division, Greyfriars, Ipswich IP1 1LE
Financial Times

52

49. Arts of the Environment

Edited by GYORGY KEPES. Aidan Ellis Publishing Ltd., Cobb House, Nuffield, Henley-On-Thames, RG9 5RU; 1972; £5.50; 244 pp.

Without the world of nature, the world of the senses, man loses the basis for most of his abilities, achievements, and aspirations. The destruction of the natural environment radically alters the potential for attaining higher forms of life. Language, both verbal and visual, provides the connection needed between perception of the natural world and expression and evocation of that world. It is with these connections in mind that Gyorgy Kepes, founder and director of the Center for Advanced Visual Studies at MIT, has collected a series of essays on communications, technology, systems planning, anthropology, and art to establish a new model for ecological consciousness.

Contributions by Kepes, Edward T. Hall, Rene Dubos, Jay Forrester, Erik Erikson, Dennis Gabor, and several others present a new understanding of the artist as a "sensor" of the ecological context. Artist is used synonomously with painter, architect, designer, and planner, and is meant to designate the person most capable of experiencing what is happening to the environment and bringing that experience into fruitful communication. ER

Every physical form, every living form, every pattern of feeling or thought has its own unique identity, its boundaries, its extension and its wider context; it contains or is contained by another pattern; it follows or is followed by another pattern. The unique identity, discrete shape, and nature of a space-occupying substance are shaped by the boundary that separates it from and connects it to the space outside. An organic form lives and grows only through its intricate transactions with its environment. An optical event becomes a visually perceived figure only when seen against its ground. The quality, feeling, and meaning of a sound is cast in the matrix of the physical processes that generated it; it is not independent of its surrounding silence or the other sounds that frame it. In the same way the physical, biological, or moral individuality of man is the function of his active relationship with the physical and social environment.

But the world is not made of discrete fixed entities. The boundaries that separate and connect them are fluid. The world's infinitely complex fabric is in a process of never-ending transformation; biological forms, social groups, human feelings and understandings undergo continuous changes. They may merge into larger, more encompassing, more complex configurations or fall apart into smaller, simpler constituents.

Perception psychologists, investigating the dynamics of visual figure-ground relationships, discerned a dynamic hierarchy of gestalts—perceptual patterns moving toward larger, more inclusive patterns. Our present relationship to our environment is at the threshold of such a process of reorientation. New circumstances have now forced us to see that we can no longer think of ourselves as separate and independent from our environment: rather, together they form a new, higher gestalt.

Quite simply, *man does not see the way he thinks he sees.* Instead of a passive-receptive act in which scenes in the outside world are simply recorded like a camera with film in it, the act of perceiving visually is one in which man is totally involved and in which he participates actively, screening and structuring very much in the same way that one selects and constructs when talking or writing. The visual process is therefore *active and creative;* learned early in life, it is cast in cultural molds and can be as stereotyped or as creative as the viewer.

These remarks are at variance with much of

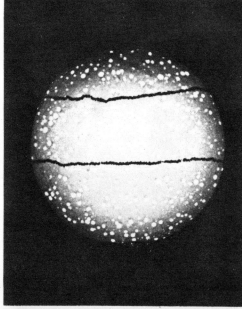

Figs. 2-4. Nuclear fireball. High-speed photographs taken in the mid-1950's. Photographed for the U.S. Atomic Energy Commission by EG&G, Incorporated.

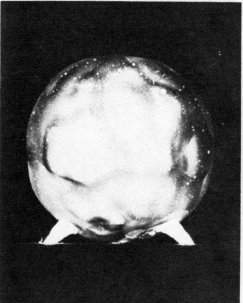

Nuclear fireball. High-speed photographs taken in the mid-1950s. Photographed for the U. S. Atomic Energy Commission by EG & G, Incorporated.

conventional psychological theory, caught as it is in the conceptual trap of Western European contemporary culture. Fortunately, there are some psychologists who have been dissatisfied with closed-score research and have broken out of the laboratory and ventured into the world. The first to break with the stimulus response school of psychology of vision were the transactional psychologists who produced a still controversial and much neglected body of knowledge and research. Started by Adelbert Ames and developed by men like Ittelson, Kilpatrick, and Cantril,

192

the transactionalists conducted hundreds of experiments in which they systematically altered the
spatial experience by manipulating key variables.

For the super-populated future, it is inevitable,
according to most environmentalists and planners, that we must seek ways of dealing with
massive urban densities. The new master plan for
New York City states: "Concentration is the
genius of the city, its reason for being, the source
of its vitality and its excitement. We believe the
center should be strengthened, not weakened and
we are not afraid of the bogey of high density."
However Jeffersonians and those who still long
for Wright's Broadacre City goals of every-man-
on-his-own-bit-of-nature might seek to naysay
this idea, the fact is that means must be found for
innovative and ecologically viable approaches to
man's living in urban situations with his fellow-
man. The options seem to be: stringently enforced
and universal population control; regional decentralization of urban areas; and new physical forms
for urban life. The first is a doubtful prospect, and

even under question from respected members of the scientific community. The second creates the vision of Constantinos Doxiadis's "Ecumenopolis," which might promise an endlessly proliferating web of two-dimensional urban networks and loss of still more open space.

The concept of creating new physical forms for urban life—and for utilizing these forms sympathetically as energizing transformers of our older urban areas—seems by far the most appropriate and contributory route to take in dealing with tomorrow's environment. The approach that appeals to many of the most creative environmental planners is the *megastructure,* which might be briefly defined as a three-dimensional matrix-system for the containment of man's activities—living, working, playing, worshipping, governing. The ideal of the megastructure is that of a neutral container, one which permits the additive inputs and mutual feedbacks of individuals and the community, acting strictly as a support (in the structural sense) and service armature (in terms of utilities, transit, and communications) for the city.

MIND

50. The Living Brain

W. GREY WALTER. W. W. Norton & Company, Inc., 55 Fifth Avenue, New York, N.Y. 10003; 1963; or *Real Time*. $2.25; 311 pp.

A key implication of scientific developments over the past twenty years is that one's own brain must now be included in any private philosophy. The thinking brain has just begun to discover, to look at, itself.

Grey Walter, a pioneer in electroencephalography, reviews the history of the brain's evolution, analyzes empirical data, and presents new models and concepts. JB

We shall be near the truth if we keep in mind that electrical changes in living tissue, the phenomena of animal electricity, are signs of chemical events, and that there is no way of distinguishing one from the other in the animal cell or in the mineral cell. The current of a nerve impulse is a sort of electro-chemical smoke-ring about two inches long travelling along the nerve at a speed of as much as 300 feet per second.

Regular or irregular, the alternation of day and night was probably the first pattern in time that impressed the human brain, accentuated by the pre-thermostasis imposition of sleep. There would be early recognition, too, of the patterned calls of animals, the warning sequence of a coming storm, memorable cries of defiance or distress; finally, most precious of all patterns in time, speech. Long before this, however, observation and memory of patterns in space would be highly developed, though limited in practice to two dimensions—the relative position of places, spoors, waterholes, caves. Early in our history we must have found safety and satisfaction in remembering and reproducing simple patterns.

What, then, is the function of these elaborate electrical structures in the economy of brain physiology? What process can require so laborious a transformation? To what end does the brain construct these transient fabrics of hard-earned energy?

To answer this question we may ask another, easier to answer but often neglected. What *specific* property has the brain that other systems have not? Is the "great ravelled knot" of the brain different in kind, or only in size, from its stalk, the spinal cord?

The answer is clear and opens a wide door to truth. The brain can learn—NO other structure can. So rare and so precious is this learning, so delicate and so elegant is the electric weaving we have seen, that to associate the two is more than tempting—it seems a marriage of necessity.

The scheme of learning elaborated here involves two main groups of operations, one selective and the other constructive. In the latter group, the change of state induced by a series of observed coincidences in no way resembles the coincidences themselves; it is a formal, symbolic change, a signal of signals. When several such mechanisms are operating together in parallel and in series a new aspect of the constructive process emerges—abstraction. The several learning circuits are really extracting from a selection of events the features that are common to them in time and space—they are, in effect, *recognising a pattern*. It was found in a previous chapter that pattern is hard to define except as something memorable; here, starting from a different standpoint, we have reached the same conclusion—the raw material of learned behaviour is symbolic abstracted pattern.

When tracing the processes of learning in a previous chapter, a point was reached where it could be said that the critical operation was the recognition of pattern, an abstraction. This was advanced without thought of any parallel in the evolution of the brain itself; but there is in fact a very striking one, an abstraction at a critical phase which may be regarded as a functional recapitulation of the organ's growth. Freed by homeostasis for intellectual pursuits, the supreme abstraction of the brain was indeed the mind. And *mens sana* until recently has been the only watchword. But changes are taking place in which the material success of psychosurgery is significant. From the confusion of metaphysics and psychoanalysis, abstractions of an abstraction, the thinking brain has turned eagerly to the first possible glimpses of itself. The millennial period of its unconscious evolution ends before the mirror; a new phase begins.

Any discussion of mind except as a function—the supreme function—of brain, lies beyond the scope of this work and must always remain outside the purview of physiology. The physiologist, viewing in his modest workshop the inexplicable electric tides that sweep through the living brain, knows that the bobbing of his float must mean some Leviathan is yet uncaught; some great idea nibbles his bait and slides darkly behind the laughing waves. But he would be happier not to dub it Mind; he would prefer to call the one that got away—Mentality, thinking of it only as a relation of dimensions, in the same class as Velocity. We speak often of the "craze for speed," but only a truly mad mechanic would peer into his engine for the component of its velocity. So, even in a fever of interest in mental problems, no sane physiologist would look for a mechanism identifiable as Mind; but he may quite reasonably say: "At one time behaviour was *so;* later it was *thus*—the transformation of one mode into the other I will call *Mentality*."

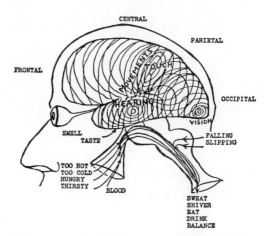

Figure 2. "...but the lake must be perfectly calm..." The upper brain is freed from the menial tasks of the body, the regulating functions being delegated to the lower brain.

Figure 7. "...the frequency of a rhythm is more significant than its amplitude...." Main Types of Brain Rhythms. Records showing the principal wave forms found in EEG's: (a) delta—0.5 to 3.5 cycles per second, (b) theta—4 to 7 cps, (c) alpha—8 to 13 cps, (d) higher frequency (beta)—14 to 30 cps.

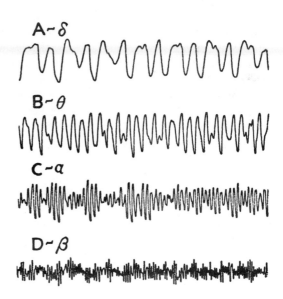

51. Programming and Metaprogramming in the Human Biocomputer

JOHN C. LILLY, M.D. Julian Press, 150 Fifth Avenue, New York, N.Y. 10011; 1972; or *Real Time*. (H) $8.00; (P) $4.95; 160 pp.

Lilly's giant step, stretching the empirical limits of the neuro-model of man until the whole construct begins to crack, explosively decreasing extant models of man and reality. Lilly's best work to date. JB

REVIEW BY GERD STERN. Although electric and cybernetic metaphors and analogues provide us with operating informations, many of us are still unable (because of educational and self-selective disfunctions) to sample, track, and hold these varieties of experience. John Lilly provides us with a focused, difficult, self-defining lexicon, which can be taken like medicine by accepting his working hypothesis, and evaluating the results after the transformation achieved by this self and new data dosage has been absorbed, or, less from the point of view of process, it can be taken as a travelogue.

A premise of the work is that we are all programmed computers and that we may well be the sum of our programs, nothing more, nothing less. The basic built-in programs are determined by survival needs. The learning to learn capabilities, model and language making consequences, are symbolized as metaprogramming, "An operation in which a central control system controls hundreds of thousands of programs operating in parallel simultaneously."

In his introduction Lilly lists thirty-seven basic assumptions. Number nineteen holds that "certain chemical substances have programmatic effects, i.e., they change the operations of the computer, some at the programmatic level and some at the metaprogrammatic level." As Lilly notes in his foreword, this work was completed just at the time laws were passed withdrawing funds and materials from researchers working with LSD-25 and other psychopharmacologically active drugs. A solid portion of the research base for The Human Biocomputer was accomplished using such substances.

Lilly's scientific responsibility as a researcher, coupled with a sensibility which will not phase out inexplicable phenomena, shifts the locus of his work from mechanistic construct to metaphysical design insight, open to the participating reader's input.

When one learns to learn, one is making models, using symbols, analogizing, making metaphors, in short, inventing and using language, mathematics, art, politics, business, etc. At the critical brain (cortex) size, languages and its consequences appear.

To avoid the necessity of repeating *learning to learn, symbols, metaphors, models* each time, I symbolize the underlying idea in these operations as *metaprogramming*. Metaprogramming appears at a critical cortical size — the cerebral computer must have a large enough number of interconnected circuits of sufficient quality for the operations of metaprogramming to exist in that biocomputer.

The use of the psychedelic agents (such as LSD-25) in the human subject shows certain properties of these substances in changing the computer's operations in certain ways. Some of these changes are mentioned above in passing; a summary of those found in the LSD state empirically are as follows:

1. **The self-metaprogram can make instructions to create special states of the computer;** many of these special states have been described in the literature on hypnosis.

2. These instructions are carried out with relatively short delays (minutes). The delays of course will vary with the complexity of the task which is being programmed into the computer. It also is a previous history of this same kind

of programming: the more often it has been done the easier it is to do again and the less time it takes.

3. **Only *taboo* or *forbidden* programs are not fully constructed:** there are peculiar gaps which give away the fact that there are forbidden areas. Within realizable limits most other programs can be produced.

4. When one first does enter into the storage systems the way the material is held in the dynamic storage is entirely strange to one's conscious self.

5. **Production of *displays* of data patterns, of instructions, or storage contents, or of current problems can be realized through such instructions.** [A "display" is any visual (or acoustic, or tactile, etc.) plotting of a set of discriminative variables in any number of dimensions of the currently available materials.] The motivational sign and intensity can be varied in any of these displays under special orders.

6. **More or less complete re-plays of past experiences important in current computations can be programmed from storage;** the calendar objective time of original occurrence seems a not too important aspect of the filing system; the level of maturation of the computer at the time of original occurrence is of greater import.

7. **Stored or filed occurrences, filed instructions, filed programs vary in the amount and specificity of positive and/or negative affect-feeling-emotion attached to each.** If too negative (evil, harmful, fearful) an emotional charge is attached, re-play can allow readjustment toward the positive end of the motivation-feeling-emotion spectrum. With the LSD-25 state the negative or the positive charge can be changed to neutral or to its opposite by special instructions. However, since most people wish to avoid the negative and encourage the positive once they obtain control over programming they tend to put a positive charge even on programs and metaprograms and the processes of creating them. (A chemical change may take place in signal storage (Fig. 1) as the sign of the motivational process shifts from negative to positive.)

VIEWS OF ORGANISM: MODELS

1. Physical-chemical: *series of millisecond to microsecond frozen* micro-pictures of patterns of neuronal activity, biochemical reserves, physical-chemical flows, energy-force-material exchange with outside sources-sinks; repeatability, reliability, signal/noise relations.

2. Physiological: partial integrated-over-time pictures of physical patterns: net results over seconds to days to years. Organism vs. environment generation of actions, signals.

3. Modern psychological: selection of certain aspects of physical physiological data and models which show properties of modifiability, CNS model making, model comparison, storage, *learning, memory, phychophysical*.

4. Classical psychological: mental, subjective, *inside view*, psychoanalytic, solipsistic, ego-centered, personal models.

5. *Evolutionary:* gradual formation of basic physical-chemical units into organic particles, cells, organisms; formation of genetic codes and cytoplasmic orders; increasing sizes of cellular aggregations; formation of species; changes to new species; evolution of CNS; evolution of man from anthropoids; origins of speech.

6. Social, anthropological

7. Basic particles → aggregates → cells → tissues organs →

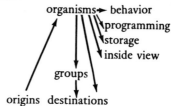

52. Physical Control of the Mind: Toward a Psychocivilized Society

JOSE M. R. DELGADO, M.D. (ed. by Ruth N. Anshen). Harper & Row, Publishers, 49 East 33rd Street, New York, N.Y. 10016; 1969; or *Real Time*. $7.95; 280 pp.

Delgado, a leading researcher in neurobehavior, writes about his discoveries and explores their relationship to possible societal problems foreseeable in the future. He's the man who implanted electrodes in the brain of a fighting bull and stopped his rage and charge with a flick of a switch. Most interesting is his work dealing with the rearrangement of patterns of hostility, fear, sex, etc. JB

Throughout the centuries, the most powerful intellects have attempted to comprehend the mysteries of their own functioning. Long ago Socrates, leading his desciples through the colonnades of Athens, propounded eternal questions which have been repeated throughout history in endless variety: What is life? What is soul? What is mind? The essence of man evolves from the existence of mental functions which permit him to think and remember, to love and hate, to believe in myths and in science, to create and destroy civilizations. It is remarkable that after hundreds of years of philosophical inquiry, and despite the impressive intellectual advances of our present era, the concept of the mind remains elusive, controversial, and impossible to confine within linguistic limits. It is also surprising that in spite of the importance of the mind for individual survival and for the preservation of civilization, our generation is mainly interested in atoms, cells, and stars, and directs so little effort toward the exploration of the inner space of the psyche.

Despite variations in wording and in meaning, most concepts of the mind share several qualities which may be summarized and interpreted as follows:

1. The definitions express what the mind *does*, but not what it *is*, or when or how it is formed.

2. Mental functions are described as active processes, not as passive objects.

3. The principal functions of the mind are *interpretation, storage, and retrieval of both inner and outer stimuli* through processes of thinking, remembering, feeling, willing, and other phenomena which are not well identified.

It had been generally assumed that mammals were born with most of their cerebral neurons present and that further development was limited to some synaptic elaboration of the already existing neuronal network. Recent studies performed with radio tracers have revealed, however, that at least in the hippocampus, olfactory bulb, and cerebellar cortex of mammals, *as many as 80 to 90 per cent of the neurons form only after the animal is born* (3). Experience provided by sensory inputs from the environment influences the number as well as the structual connections of these postnatal cells. Moreover, as Cajal suggested long ago, the microneurons of the cerebellum, which serve as association elements, develop after birth under the influence of the infant's behavioral activities. Therefore it can be said that the environment is absorbed as a structural part of the neurons in the developing brain.

SUMMARY

Autonomic and somatic functions, individual and social behavior, emotional and mental reactions may be evoked, maintained, modified, or inhibited, both in animals and in man, by electrical stimulation of specific cerebral structures.

Figure 13. Radio stimulation of Ludy in another red nucleus point 3 millimeters away produces only the simple response of yawning. If the monkey was sleeping, brain stimulation was less effective.

Physical control of many brain functions is a demonstrated fact, but the possibilities and limits of this control are still little known.

We may now be approaching a third equally momentous discovery about ourselves. The analysis of mental activities in the context of brain physiology indicates that our own self, our ego, is not so unique or even independent, as Freud pointed out many years ago. Study of the elements which constitute personal identity reveals the two classical factors of nature and nurture. These factors are given to, and not chosen by, the individual. The amino acids which form the genes are selected and assembled in the helix by natural chance, without intervention of the desires of the owner or the donors, and according to laws related to the history of protozoas, fishes, and apes, beyond the control or awareness of man. Genetically we are not the masters but the slaves of millennia of biological history.

The problem is that the universe has no center. Everything is relative and all that we can do is to compare the relations among given sets of values and express the result by mathematical formulas. If the size of all existing materials in the earth was suddenly reduced (or increased) 100 times (or any other amount), no human being would be able to detect the spectacular change because of the lack of units of reference. Two cars traveling at the same speed are motionless with respect to each other. While inside a jet airplane flying at 1,000 kilometers per hour, we may take a slow walk down the aisle at a speed of 1 meter per second. To say then that we are moving at 1,003.6 kilometers per hour would be meaningless unless we specified our points of reference. We do not have any absolute and immutable yardstick. The limitation of the world of physics is that it can be perceived only as the relativity of one value compared with another.

EXPERIMENTAL FACTS

Frog muscle contracted when stimulated by electricity. Volta, 1800; Galvani, 1791; DuBois Reymond, 1848.

Electrical stimulation of the brain in anesthetized dog evoked localized body and limb movements. Fritsch and Hitzig, 1870.

Stimulation of the diencephalon in unanesthetized cats evoked well-organized motor effects and emotional reactions. Hess, 1932.

In single animals, learning, conditioning, instrumental responses, pain, and pleasure have been evoked or inhibited by electrical stimulation of the brain in rats, cats, and monkeys. Delgado et al. 1954; Olds and Milner, 1954; see bibliography in Sheer, 1961.

In colonies of cats and monkeys, aggression, dominance, mounting, and other social interactions have been evoked, modified, or inhibited by radio stimulation of specific cerebral areas. Delgado, 1955, 1964.

In patients, brain stimulation during surgical interventions or with electrodes implanted for days or months has blocked the thinking process, inhibited speech and movement, or in other cases has evoked pleasure, laughter, friendliness, verbal output, hostility, fear, hallucinations, and memories. Delgado et al. 1952, 1968; Penfield and Jasper, 1954; see bibliography in Ramey and O'Doherty, 1960.

IMPLICATIONS

"Vital spirits" are not essential for biological activities. Electrical stimuli under man's control can initiate and verify vital processes.

The brain is excitable. Electrical stimulation of the cerebral cortex can produce movements.

Motor and emotional manifestations may be evoked by electrical stimulation of the brain in awake animals.

Psychological phenomena can be controlled by electrical stimulation of specific areas of the brain.

Social behavior may be controlled by radio stimulation of specific areas of the brain.

Human mental functions may be influenced by electrical stimulation of specific areas of the brain.

53. The Intelligent Eye

R.L. GREGORY. Weidenfeld & Nicolson Ltd., 11 St. John's Hill, London SW11 1XA; 1970; £2.10; 191 pp.

Seeing is believing, but don't look through your eyes for the truth, for the eyes see only what the brain transmits. Perception isn't a matter of input from sensory receptors, but a process, a "look-up system; in which sensory information is used to build gradually, and to select from, an internal repertoire of perceptual hypotheses—which are the nearest we ever get to reality."

Gregory is Professor of Bionics in the Department of Machine Intelligence and Perception, University of Edinburgh. His earlier book, *Eye and Brain*, covered experimental work in the psychology of seeing; this new work deals with the history and current state of the art of human perception. JB

A central problem of visual perception is how the brain interprets the patterns of the eye in terms of external objects. In this sense 'patterns' are very different from 'objects'. By a pattern we mean some set of inputs, in space or time, at the receptor. This is used to indicate and identify external objects giving rise to the sensory pattern. But what we perceive is far more than patterns—we perceive *objects* as existing in their space and time.

Some shapes are seen, at different times, in more ways than one. Just as the object-space reversible figures spontaneously change, so some shapes though continuously identified as object yet spontaneously change as to *what* object it is, or what position it is being viewed from. Here we must discuss the work of the psychologist who has devised the most striking demonstrations

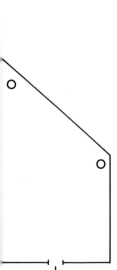

viewing point

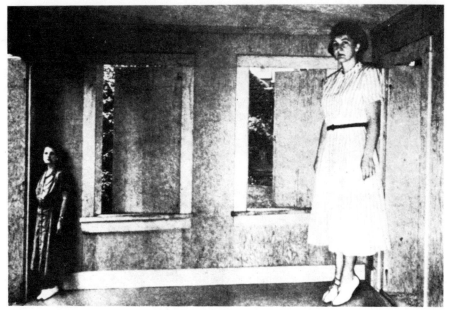

based on the essential ambiguity of objects—Adelbert Ames.

Ames started out as a painter, but ended by devising many of the best known 'visual demonstrations'. It has not, however, always been made clear what they demonstrate. Unfortunately Ames himself wrote very little: he was a visual man.

Ames made several models (sometimes full scale) designed to give the same retinal image as familiar objects, though the models were in fact of very different shapes. The models gave the same image as the familiar object only from one critical view point, and for a single eye. The best-known demonstration is the 'Ames room'. This gives the same image to an eye placed at the critical position as a normal rectangular room—but in fact it is very far from rectangular. The further wall recedes to one side, so that one of the far corners is much further from the eye than the other corner; but both corners subtend the same angle at the eye placed in the critical position; for as the further wall recedes it gets correspondingly larger. The Ames room is simply one of an infinite set of three-dimensional shapes giving the same image to the (critically placed) eye that it would receive from a normal rectangular room.

Pictures have a double reality. Drawings, paintings and photographs are objects in their own right—patterns on a flat sheet—and at the same time entirely different objects to the eye. We see both a pattern of marks on paper, with shading, brush-strokes or photographic 'grain', and at the same time we see that these compose a face, a house or a ship on a stormy sea. Pictures are unique among objects; for they are seen both as themselves and as some other thing, entirely different from the paper or canvas of the picture. Pictures are paradoxes.

No *object* can be in two places at the same time; no object can lie in both two- and three-dimensional space. Yet pictures are both visibly flat and three-dimensional. They are a certain size, yet also the size of a face or a house or a ship. Pictures are impossible.

The nervous system is so interconnected that an error in one part can affect some quite distant part, which may seem separate functionally and yet turn out to be associated in some subtle way. Even where there is a clear chain of processes along a single neural path (which is extremely rare) it is very difficult to locate a disturbance along the path. There are technical problems of recording activity within the nervous system, and there are also surprisingly difficult conceptual problems: especially when we do not know the function of each physical part of the system. The plumber has to know at least the rudiments of how thermostats, heating elements and taps work, to locate and correct even the simplest fault; but many of the basic functional processes of the nervous system remain mysterious and so it is very difficult to *locate functions*. Before they can be located they have to be defined and understood. A conceptual model of a system is vital for describing the functions of its parts.

Early descriptions of the Universe are egocentric and based on the physical size and capacities of man. Instruments allowed other references to be used, and so subtly displaced individual perception from the centre of the human view of the world. They showed that there are many things in the Universe not only too small or too distant to perceive, but also things immediately present whose presence could not be felt; such as the great sweep of the electromagnetic spectrum from X-rays to radio waves, with only one octave—light—sensed and so known to the brain without instruments.

Objects which are not classified for appropriate scaling constants cause great trouble. For example, it is not known whether the newly discovered stellar objects, quasars, are extraordinarily intense sources, and lying at correspondingly enormous distances, or whether they are in the normal range of brightness and so distance. The difficulty arises in their case because their spectra show a red shift of the lines, which would normally indicate a very high recession velocity, due to Doppler shift, itself believed to indicate great distance. So either there is some special reason for the red shift observed for quasars, or they are indeed very distant. But it is not yet agreed how the scaling constant should be set for quasars, and so it is not agreed whether quasars are incredibly bright and distant or whether they are nearer and of normal intensity, but have some peculiarity which upsets the generalised assumptions applied, apparently successfully, to other stellar objects for determining their distances.

54. Perception and Change: Projections for Survival

JOHN R. PLATT. The University of Michigan Press, 51 Weymouth Street, London W1N 3LE; 1970; £3.60; 178 pp.

The sciences must be viewed not merely as a basis for objective reality, but as the source of new perceptual modes and techniques. Platt, a biophysicist, presents approaches toward relating the conceptual advances of the twentieth century to the heuristic perceptions necessary for their basic understanding. JB

Not everybody would want a single universal suit, but it would be nice to have the option. It might not even be very hard to invent. But we still have prehistoric patterns of thought in what touches us most closely. Helicopters, *si;* clothes, *no.*

Perception is the first thing we experience and the last thing we understand. It is the beginning of knowledge and also, in some sense, the end of it. A more accurate understanding of perception might change our individual and social relations as dramatically as a more accurate understanding of motion a few hundred years ago changed our technological achievements.

Where in this approach is the "objective" physical world of Newton's laws and Dalton's atoms and Rutherford's nuclei? It is evidently in a simplified subsection of *our* subjective totality, subject to *our* decision as to whether we find it useful to believe in these atoms or not.

But are not the atoms, or the other fundamental particles of which the universe is supposed to be made, the realest things there are? Even within the framework of physical science there has always been some doubt. Ostwald and other great experimental chemists of the last century never thought that atoms were real. They said, as Laplace said of God, that "they had no need of that hypothesis." And our atoms today may dissolve at any moment into interferences of waves traveling at the speed of light or into some other bizarre reformulation, just as the Bohr orbits of 1912 dissolved into Schrödinger waves and then into Heisenberg matrices, more for reasons of elegance and unity than for any great improvement in prediction. I think this raises some serious questions for those who believe in physical science as the foundation of the world. What kind of primary reality is this, whose elements depend so much on time and taste, in successive new approximations to an ultimate description that they never reach?

Yet the most evident feature and the one least represented in our usual language is that all time is present together in this Now. We objectify the time of dates and memories and plans, but the remembering and planning is now. All time and space that is operationally real to us and actionable is present to us here and now, however diffuse this now may be. The storage in the network, or the feedback anticipation loops, are present storage and present loops. Anything that is not stored is not remembered; operationally in the present, it has not been. However much we may enjoy ordering and remembering the past and however much the scholars may try to make it more orderly and objective for us, "the only time there is, is now," as lovers say, and waterskiers, and preachers of conversion.

Our greatest achievements in science or in large-scale social organization are shaped by biological demands and emotions and the tissue structure within the human skull. They depend on our curiosity, speech, and reasoning, and on our ability or inability to teach, to learn, to plan, and to work together with other men. But at the same time, these new developments also react back and change man's biology, for they affect his foods and drugs, his houses and habitats, his health and diseases, his population pressures and wars, and his interrelations with the rest of mankind and with all the rest of the biological world of plants and animals that he multiplies or destroys.

TABLE 1

CLASSIFICATION OF PROBLEMS AND CRISES BY ESTIMATED TIME AND INTENSITY (U.S.)

Grade	Estimated Crisis Intensity (number affected times degree of effect)	Estimated Time to Crisis (if no major effort at anticipatory solution)		
		1–5 Years	5–20 Years	20–50 Years
1.	*Total Annihilation*	*Nuclear or RCBW Escalation*	*Nuclear or RCBW Escalation*	✝ *(Solved or dead)*
2.	10^8 *Great Destruction or Change (Physical, Biological, or Political)*	*(too soon)*	Participatory Democracy Eco-balance	Political Theory and Economic Structure Population Planning Patterns of Living Education Communications Integrative Philosophy
3.	10^7 *Widespread Almost Unbearable Tension*	Administrative Management Slums Participatory Democracy Race Conflict	Pollution Poverty Law and Justice	?
4.	10^6 *Large-Scale Distress*	Transportation Neighborhood Ugliness Crime	Communications-Gaps	?
5.	10^5 *Tension Producing Responsive Change*	Cancer and Heart Smoking and Drugs Artificial Organs Accidents Sonic Boom Water Supply Marine Resources Privacy on computers	Educational Inadequacy	?
6.	*Other Problems —Important, but Adequately Researched*	Military R&D New Educational Methods Mental Illness Fusion Power	Military R&D	
7.	*Exaggerated Dangers and Hopes*	Mind Control Heart Transplants Definition of Death	Sperm Banks Freezing Bodies Unemployment from Automation	Eugenics
8.	*Non-Crisis Problems Being "Overstudied"*	Man in Space Most Basic Science		

55. Mental Health Program Reports

Superintendent of Documents, U.S. Government Printing Office, Washington, D.C. 20402; 1971. $1.75; 388 pp.

The National Institute of Mental Health uses public money to fund research in the United States dealing with problems of mental health. These programs are aimed at developing manpower, stimulating further research, and providing delivery systems for mental health services.

Each year, the Institute publishes reports on research it is funding. The 1971 report, number 5 in their series, includes write-ups of the intellectual development of children, the long-term effects of LSD, evaluation of community mental health programs, and an entire section devoted to reports on biofeedback. Perhaps the most interesting report describes a program that trains Navaho medicine men, stressing the importance of psychic medicine to their community. ER

The restoration of a man's harmony with his family clan and universe is a goal that outreaches the more limited aim of medicine today. Yet for the Navaho, healing is total. Navaho medicine is central to Navaho community, family, and religious life and to the health of the tribe in an integrated manner that is quite unlike white medicine. NIMH aid in training medicine men in a region where the traditions have been on the verge of extinction is not only important for the psychic and physical health of the people in the area, but an important example of new paths that are possible in community mental health.

Within this NIMH program six medicine men (also known as singers) are each training two apprentices using the Rough Rock Demonstration School at Rough Rock, Arizona, as their group headquarters.

The Navaho medicine man is a combination of doctor, priest, consummate artist, and leader. In many of the ceremonies, conducted for a patient, tribal welfare is explicitly invoked. Perhaps because the Navahos were originally nomadic, they evolved no strong central leadership, and the medicine men became the main carriers of culture—the enlightened leaders of the group.

He will acquire hundreds of chants, learn intricate sand paintings, legends, and a pharmacopoeia consisting of 150-200 herbs. Each medicine man is a specialist, for not even the most learned man knows more than four or five of the elaborate ceremonials (depending upon the way they are cataloged, there are about 45-50).

The skills of the medicine men are varied, integrating both practical and symbolic remedies: They set fractured bones and administer a variety of herbs to counteract fever, insomnia, pain, but the most important impact is psychic. Depending upon the need of the patient, the singer draws from his complex of rituals, prayers, songs, and paintings, and dances.

Throughout our lives each of us is being trained in the way we use our nervous system, so that our sensory perceptions, our vision, the way we smell or hear or touch, as well as our mode of thinking, are finely tuned by the culture that surrounds us and by the people who directly influence our fate. We perceive selectively. We show habitual biases in our mode of thought. By adulthood our seemingly symmetrical brains are indeed very asymmetrical in the distribution of their functions. The giant cerebral hemispheres are quite specialized, and by adulthood our reliance upon the left or right hemisphere may be culturally biased. Dr. David Galin and Dr. Robert Ornstein have recently shown that normal adults tend to show relative activation in the left hemisphere when doing verbal problems and relative activation in the right hemisphere when presented with spatial tasks. The shift was observable in electroencephalographic recordings (EEGs) from the surface of the head.

————————

Most people in our technological society are rewarded for the kinds of mental activities that would be dominated by the left hemisphere, that is, analytic, verbal kinds of thinking. Artists, musicians, dancers, and children of the city ghettos, on the other hand, may be less skilled verbally but may be especially able to perceive relationships. Such people might be underrated on highly verbal tests of intelligence and may constitute a kind of "right hemisphere" culture. The work of Drs. Galin and Ornstein makes a preliminary step in asking whether individuals can be taught to selectively suppress or activate either hemisphere, and whether special educational techniques can be designed to help people who have a difficult time learning verbal skills or individuals for whom left-hemisphere dominance

is a hindrance, as it might be in learning music or sports.

————————

Life is a continuous, if random, education in which our nerves and flesh program responses to surprise, to anxiety, to delight, to all situations. The habitual manner in which the physiology reacts to stress may result in psychosomatic illnesses, for until now we have had no way to communicate with an individual about "unconscious" habits of capillary constriction, or gastric secretion, or muscle tension. However, an individual wearing electrodes, and hooked up to a receiver-amplifier known as a polygraph can be signaled each time he reduces his heart rate or tenses his forehead muscle, or when his brain emits an alpha rhythm (an even wave of about 60 microvolts in amplitude, and 9-13 cycles per second [cps]). Feedback can inform him each time he emits this rhythm, so that he can begin to identify the seamless, qualitative mental change that accompanies the signal. Instrumental conditioning is similar. An animal's brain waves may pass through a filter which activates a switch after it receives certain configurations and automatically opens a food hopper, rewarding the animal for that brain wave. Biofeedback and instrumental conditioning enable an individual to sense and control a formerly unknown internal state, to which we have had no access without instruments.

56. Shamanism: Archaic Techniques of Ecstasy

MIRCEA ELIADE. Routledge & Kegan Paul Ltd., 68–74 Carter Lane, London EC4V 5EL; 1964; £4.00; 610 pp.

Eliade is Chairman of the Department of History and Religions at the University of Chicago. This book is an authoritative work on ancient models of the transmission of consciousness centered on the activities of the Shaman, at once magician and medicine man, healer and miracle doer, psychopomp, priest, mystic, and poet. Just what the witch doctor ordered. JB

REVIEW BY JAY BAIL. Finally in paperback. This is the only book of its kind. An extensively researched, massively documented view of possession in various societies—from the American Indian, to African, Siberian, South American. "Shamanism is precisely one of the archaic techniques of ecstacy—at once mysticism, magic, and 'religion' in the broadest sense of the term . . . What we consider of greatest importance is presenting the shamanic phenomenon itself, analyzing its ideology, discussing its techniques, its symbolism, its mythologies." Easily a classic. What one is aware of throughout all the diverse practices and customs is the certainty, the utter certainty of the participants in the dances, the singing, the spirits, the healing. Within the immense differences and similarities that Eliade depicts with astonishing completeness is a sameness beneath, an attempt to structure world views, to change ordinary reality into functional points of ultra-reality. We need only watch the intense dedication, the focus of awareness in overcoming the nominal spread of the senses to realize exactly how deeply reality is the grid of our very arbitrary behavioral maps. Magical ceremonies, seances, mandalas, and the over-all symbolism so necessary to alter awareness. Over 600 pages of superb documentation.

It is as a further result of his ability to travel in the supernatural worlds and to *see* the superhuman beings (gods, demons, spirits of the dead, etc.) that the shaman has been able to contribute decisively to the *knowledge of death*. In all probability many features of "funerary geography," as well as some themes of the mythology of death, are the result of the ecstatic experiences of shamans. The lands that the shaman sees and the personages that he meets during his ecstatic journeys in the beyond are minutely described by the shaman himself, during or after his trance. The unknown and terrifying world of death assumes form, is organized in accordance with particular patterns; finally it displays a structure and, in course of time, becomes familiar and acceptable. In turn, the supernatural inhabitants of the world of death become *visible;* they show a form, display a personality, even a biography. Little by little the world of the dead becomes knowable, and death itself is evaluated primarily as a rite of passage to a spiritual mode of being. In the last analysis, the accounts of the shamans' ecstatic journeys contribute to "spiritualizing" the world of the dead, at the same time that they enrich it with wondrous forms and figures.

Quamaneq is a mystical faculty that the master sometimes obtains for the disciple from the Spirit of the Moon. It can also be obtained by the disciple directly, with the help of the spirits of the dead, of the Mother of the Caribou, or of bears. But there is always a personal experience; these mythical beings are only the sources from which the neophyte knows he is entitled to expect the revelation when he has prepared himself sufficiently.

Even before setting out to acquire one or more helping spirits, which are like new "mystical organs" for any shaman, the Eskimo neophyte must undergo a great initiatory ordeal. Success in obtaining this experience requires his making a long effort of physical privation and mental contemplation directed to gaining *the ability to see himself as a skeleton*. The shamans whom Rasmussen interrogated about this spiritual exercise gave rather vague answers, which the famous explorer summarizes as follows: "Though no shaman can explain to himself how and why, he can, by the power his brain derives from the supernatural, as it were by thought alone, divest his body of its flesh and blood, so that nothing remains but his bones. And he must then name all the parts of his body, mentioning every single bone by name; and in so doing, he must not use ordinary human speech, but only the special and sacred shaman's language which he has learned from his instructor. By thus seeing himself naked, altogether freed from the perishable and transient flesh and blood, he consecrates himself, in the sacred tongue of the shamans, to his great task, through that part of his body which will longest withstand the action of the sun, wind and weather, after he is dead."

In the archaic cultures communication between sky and earth is ordinarily used to send offerings to the celestial gods and not for a concrete and personal ascent; the latter remains the prerogative of shamans. Only they know how to make an ascent through the "central opening"; only they transform a cosmo-theological concept into a *concrete mystical experience*. This point is important. It explains the difference between, for example, the religious life of a North Asian people and the religious experience of its shamans; the latter is a *personal and ecstatic experience*. In other words, what for the rest of the community remains a cosmological ideogram, for the shamans (and the heroes, etc.) becomes a mystical itinerary. For the former, the "Center of the World" is a site that permits them to send their prayers and offerings to the celestial gods, whereas for the latter it is the place for beginning a flight in the strictest sense of the word. Only for the latter is *real communication* among the three cosmic zones a possibility.

Since the beginning of the century, ethnologists have fallen into the habit of using the terms "shaman," "medicine man," "sorcerer," and "magician" interchangeably to designate certain individuals possessing magico-religious powers and found in all "primitive" societies. By extension, the same terminology has been applied in studying the religious history of "civilized" peoples, and there have been discussions, for example, of an Indian, an Iranian, a Germanic, a Chinese, and even a Babylonian "shamanism" with reference to the "primitive" elements at-

tested in the corresponding religions. For many reasons this confusion can only militate against any understanding of the shamanic phenomenon. If the word "shaman" is taken to mean any magician, sorcerer, medicine man, or ecstatic found throughout the history of religions and religious ethnology, we arrive at a notion at once extremely complex and extremely vague; it seems, furthermore, to serve no purpose, for we already have the terms "magician" or "sorcerer" to express notions as unlike and as ill-defined as "primitive magic" or "primitive mysticism." We consider it advantageous to restrict the use of the words "shaman" and "shamanism," precisely to avoid misunderstandings and to cast a clearer light on the history of "magic" and "sorcery." For, of course, the shaman is also a magician and medicine man; he is believed to cure, like all doctors, and to perform miracles of the fakir type, like all magicians, whether primitive or modern. But beyond this, he is a psychopomp, and he may also be priest, mystic, and poet. In the dim, "confusionistic" mass of the religious life of archaic societies considered as a whole, shamanism—taken in its strict and exact sense—already shows a structure of its own and implies a "history" that there is every reason to clarify.

It is here that we see all the advantage of employing the term "shamanism" in its strict and proper sense. For, if we take the trouble to differentiate the shaman from other magicians and medicine men of primitive societies, the identification of shamanic complexes in one or another region immediately acquires definite significance. Magic and magicians are to be found more or less all over the world, whereas shamanism exhibits a particular magical specialty, on which we shall later dwell at length: "mastery over fire," "magical flight," and so on. By virtue of this fact, though the shaman is, among other things, a magician, not every magician can properly be termed a shaman. The same distinction must be applied in regard to shamanic healing; every medicine man is a healer, but the shaman employs a method that is his and his alone. As for the shamanic techniques of ecstasy, they do not exhaust all the varieties of ecstatic experience documented in the history of religions and religious ethnology. Hence any ecstatic cannot be considered a shaman; the shaman specializes in a trance during which his soul is believed to leave his body and ascend to the sky or descend to the underworld.

57. Zettel

LUDWIG WITTGENSTEIN (edited by G. E. M. Anscombe and G. H. von Wright, translated by G. E. M. Anscombe). Blackwell Scientific Publications Ltd., Osney Mead, Oxford OX2 0EL; 1967; £2.50; 124 pp.

At his death, in the early 1950s, Ludwig Wittgenstein had published only one book, his *Tractatus Logico-Philosophicus* in 1922. *Zettel* is not so much a book as a collection of fragments written and left by Wittgenstein in a file box.

While philosophers can and do spend much of their lives nit-picking over individual paragraphs in Wittgenstein's work, many bright young artists and writers are using his ideas to cut through all the waste and get to and through language and away from the outmoded concepts of philosophy. In this respect Wittgenstein is not so much a philosopher as "the last philosopher," or, even better, a poet. JB

60. Reality is not a property still missing in what is expected and which accedes to it when one's expectation comes about.—Nor is reality like the daylight that things need to acquire colour, when they are already there, as it were colourless, in the dark.

66. Psychological—trivial—discussions about expectation, association etc. always pass over what is really noteworthy and it is noticeable that they talk around, without touching, the *punctum saliens*.

410. A person can doubt only if he has learnt certain things; as he can miscalculate only if he has learnt to calculate. In that case it is indeed involuntary.

458. Philosophical investigations: conceptual investigations. The essential thing about metaphysics: it obliterates the distinction between factual and conceptual investigations.

605. One of the most dangerous of ideas for a philosopher is, oddly enough, that we think with our heads or in our heads.

606. The idea of thinking as a process in the head, in a completely enclosed space, gives him something occult.

706. Numbers are not fundamental to mathematics.

249. "Nothing easier than to imagine a four-dimensional cube! It looks like this:[1]

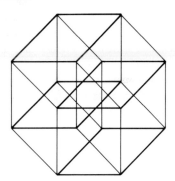

But I don't mean that, I mean something like

but with four dimensions!—"But *isn't* what I showed you like

[1] No drawing appears in the MS. at this place; the reader may imagine something appropriate. Of various possibilities, we have adopted a drawing by Dr. R. B. O. Richards. Eds.

58. A Wittgenstein Workbook

CHRISTOPER COOPE, Peter Geach, Timothy Potts and Roger White. Blackwell Scientific Publications Ltd., Osney Mead, Oxford OX2 0EL; 1970; £0.75; 51 pp.

Thinking and speaking take for granted basic assumptions about the nature of language and knowledge. Ludwig Wittgenstein set about to investigate those assumptions and catalogued his explorations so that others might be able to share in the work. At various stages in his career as a philosopher, Wittgenstein was "understood" by a number of different groups, each seizing upon an aspect of his work to support their own views.

The authors of A Wittgenstein Workbook, all members of the Department of Philosophy at the University of Leeds, England, have set out to provide a key of entry into Wittgenstein's often difficult considerations of language, consciousness and knowledge. This book treats all of Wittgenstein's writings as an entire body of work and traces his sources to show the continuity of his lifetime's investigations. ER

Overlooking his hard philosophical arguments, people come to regard the *Tractatus* as an arcane curiosity in the history of philosophy and the *Investigations* as a series of platitudes, and accordingly dismiss Wittgenstein's writings as something that a serious student of philosophy can with impunity ignore. For lack of this basic orientation, they have approached him expecting answers to the questions which were not his questions and have thereby overlooked the questions which he does raise and attempts to answer. Thus Carnap and others have seen in the *Tractatus* an attempt to supply prescriptions for an ideal language, whereas Wittgenstein from first to last was concerned to show how language as it is actually works.

There is a prevalent impression that Wittgenstein's later philosophy involved rejection of all or most of the doctrines of the *Tractatus*. To correct this, we have devised a programme of topics emphasizing those which are taken up in both the *Tractatus* and the *Investigations*, to the end that the changes in Wittgenstein's views may be set within a framework which shows the continuity of his thought (cp. his wish, expressed in his introduction to the *Investigations*, that the *Tractatus* and it might be published together in a single volume).

In addition to the point already made about the continuity of Wittgenstein's thought, we may specify: that the most important single influence on Wittgenstein was Frege, and that this is true of the late as well as of the early work, where the influence is so much closer to the surface; that the connexions between Wittgenstein's philosophy and other philosophies which go under the name of 'linguistic' or 'ordinary language' philosophy, such as the writings of Austin and his followers, rarely amount to more than surface similarities; and that Wittgenstein was constantly concerned to bring out logical differences (which, as he once said, are always *big* differences) rather than idiomatic niceties. We regard these beliefs as controversial only in that they have been controverted.

The basic texts used in the programme are the *Tractatus* and the *Investigations*; the earlier topics give prominence to the former, the later topics to the latter, but cross-references to relevant passages in the other work are given wherever possible. We have also drawn on the other published works of Wittgenstein (except *Philosophische Grammatik*, which appeared too recently) in an ancillary role, since they often provide substantial aid in understanding compressed or particularly difficult passages in the two main works. The *Notebooks* play this role in relation to the *Tractatus,* the *Blue and Brown Books* and *Zettel* in relation to the *Investigations,* while the *Philosophische Bemerkungen* provides an important link between the two main works. Occasional references have been made to *Remarks on the Foundations of Mathematics,* but for the most part we have avoided involvement in questions in the philosophy of mathematics. We have had to draw heavily on Wittgenstein's last work, *On Certainty,* for topic 9, because it contains Wittgenstein's most explicit discussion of scepticism. Obviously nobody can hope to profit by our references to Wittgenstein's texts unless he treats each book Wittgenstein wrote, not just as a source-book for discussion of a particular topic, but as a coherent book in its own right. We have had to exercise our judgment in drawing up a limited but useful list of references for each topic.

QUESTIONS:

1 Explain the difference between 'depict' (*abbilden*) and 'represent' (*darstellen*) in the *Tractatus,* also the difference between these and 'go proxy for' (*vertreten*).

2 'There must be something identical in a picture and what it depicts, to enable the one to be a picture of the other at all' (T:2.161). Elucidate.

3 'It is obvious that a proposition of the form "aRb" strikes us as a picture' (T:4.012). *How does it strike us as a picture?*

4 Must a picture consist of elements in relation representing things in an analogous relation?

5 Can a picture have a negation which is also a picture? (N:33, last paragraph; I:p.11, note).

6 What is the force of saying that a picture is a fact (T:2.141)?

7 On Wittgenstein's account of picturing, why isn't the world a picture of language?

8 'Every picture is also a logical picture' (T:2.182). Explain.

9 Is the picture below a picture of an impossible state of affairs?

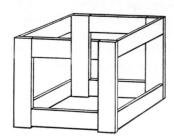

59. Insights and Illusions of Philosophy

JEAN PIAGET. Routledge & Kegan Paul Ltd., 68–74 Carter Lane, London EC4V 5EL; 1972; £2.50; 232 pp.

The past few years have seen a series of Piaget translations reach American bookstores. For all this, Piaget remains somewhat elusive. *Insights and Illusions of Philosophy* examines the philosophical position and intellectual development of this gifted thinker and is a good starting point for exploring his work. JB

REVIEW BY EDWIN SCHLOSSBERG. Each technique of exploration into understanding requires a theory of knowledge as well as a theory of operation—a standard of methodological verification. Often thinking about a subject is confused with the proof of the thinking. Often internal metaphysic is confused with external verification without note. Opinion becomes exchanged for refutable truth. These are problems which disturb Piaget and which cause difficulty in the pursuit of an effective psychology.

Piaget has worked for many years to develop a science of psychology based on the principles which he has developed under the heading of genetic epistemology. (Genetic epistemology is what one should refer to in discussing Piaget's work in psychology in order to clarify the science from the philosophy.) Piaget is adamant in his effort to create a science of psychology and not a philosophy, although he greatly respects philosophy in its proper place. Genetic epistemology is a science which seeks to study the development of cognitive stages in the mind through examination of the behavior of children. These stages are then associated with the structure of thought which is found in all aspects of intellectual activity.

Piaget is a deductivist—he seeks to know the science of a situation in order to develop a theory about it (good theory emerges from good science). Extending this to the thought that good philosophy emerges from good science, Piaget discusses the failures and successes based on this notion. It would be difficult to think of a case where the knowledge of a situation did not become the basis for the thoughts about it. Yet there are numerous cases where philosophy is thought of as the initiator or as the same structural activity as science and it is to this point that Piaget returns constantly.

As science moves from the experience of a sensation to the organization of experience through the development of complex systems, so the child develops his cognitive patterns from his initial sensory experience. This suggests a structural relationship between our developing ability as individuals and the development of knowledge in a society. Piaget seeks to make this relationship useful through empirical verification.

Intuition is indisputable as is instinct. Knowledge is testable and so falls under the scrutiny of verification. Introspection is essential to the development of thought—is important to the creation of beauty in a resonant voice—but is not essential for the development of a science of understanding behavior and cognitive patterns. This is an edge that Piaget focuses upon.

Piaget's text takes on some of the quality of a polemic about this edge and about the edge between science and philosophy—but that is its weakest point. The book provides an important insight into Piaget's teleological method and into the comprehensiveness with which he has approached the effort to understand how behavioristic relationship to thought in conceptual developmental stages can be associated with the over-all intellectual development of man. Piaget depicts his thinking in the tradition of philosophical and scientific psychology and makes this text an essential document if one is to understand the limits and uses of an intellectual construction based on observational study of cognitive activity.

The question whether below the microscopic level, physical reality exhibits an underlying determinism or a basic indeterminism would have been generally classified as "metaphysical" at the end of the last century. It is nonetheless a present-day problem in physics, one which L. de Broglie opposes to the position of the Copenhagen school. As for the problem of human freedom, it has by now been stripped of all scientific meaning, since any technique of verification only allows us to decide either for or against one of the proposed solutions and in such a field the evidence of the inner self is particularly suspect of partiality. Nevertheless, we discover that by an extension of Godel's theorem on the impossibility of demonstrating the non-contradiction of a system (sufficiently rich) by its own methods or by weaker methods, contemporary cybernetics raises the problem of determinism in limited but precise terms. A machine sufficiently complex to simulate an intellectual task, and rigorously determined as far as its mechanism and its interactions with the external world, cannot compute at a time t what its state will be at a time $t + 1$; it can only do this to the extent to which its determination, incomplete in itself, is subordinated to a machine of a higher order, but which is then no longer completely self-determined; and so on. We see once again that a problem without present meaning can suddenly acquire one as a result of advances in thought that were unforeseen.

As a subject metaphysics, together with psychology and scientific sociology, has the doubtful privilege that some people believe in it and others do not. A society of metaphysicians could come to agree on some extremely general principles, such as the existence of a boundary, between metaphysical problems and others, although they will fail to agree as to where the boundary is to be drawn and on its fixed or variable character. But the analogy ends here. When two psychologists disagree about a particular problem, which, of course, often happens, they can only, if personality factors do not enter to cause misunderstanding, be activated by an honest disagreement, since it will lead them to learn something about the facts and their interpretation. When two metaphysicians disagree, however honest and well-intentioned they may be, this disagreement depends, if there is no misunderstanding, on questions of conviction and not of verification or of logic. One can lessen the disagreement by clever argument, by an appeal to common values:

it cannot be reduced by a factual verification or a formal demonstration. If there existed for such metaphysical questions tests that were able to convince everyone, we would then speak of truth, pure and simple, and no longer of metaphysics. Descartes regarded the proposition *Je pense donc je suis* as incontrovertible, and my teacher Reymond saw in the *Cogito* the verification of a metaphysical hypothesis. But verification of what? If it is a question of clarifying the metaphysical meaning of "thinking" and "existing," the verifications become vague. If, on the other hand, it is a question of asserting that all knowledge is dependent on the existence of a subject: this is then the important discovery of the epistemological subject, but we are now concerned with epistemology and no longer with metaphysics.

The "philosopher" readily conceives of science in a positivist form and reduces it to a catalog of facts and laws. Scientific procedures are similarly only considered as techniques for the description of facts and the establishment of laws. This is why philosophy reserves for itself the right to discuss the value of science, and, hence, its *truth*.

It then criticizes science for not taking account of:

1. Man
2. Being, and also
3. The meaning of facts.

These three criticisms often amount only to one: ontology (or rather the ontic) brings us back to a metaphysics of meaning, and there is only one meaning for man. But:

(a) Either the clarification of meaning arises from a critique of knowledge; in this case philosophy is indistinguishable from epistemology;

(b) Either it goes beyond epistemological inquiry, the meaning then being constituted or exhibited in *praxis* and in *history* (cf. *Critique de la raison dialectique*).

But what is it which makes history or praxis intelligible? An immediate intuition? This is an epistemological concept, which there is every reason for discussing as such. The "necessity of things"? But then, why philosophers? (unless it is in order to philosophize about engagement, but then it is engagement and not philosophy which elaborates meaning).

In psychological circles ("psychology attracts psychopaths," Claparède said) one can certainly come across persons having the mentality of butterfly or postcard collectors, as sometimes happens in philosophical circles where one finds schizoids attaining "essences" much too easily. But to describe laboratory work in the way Sartre has done, definitely shows that he has not worked in one and that he has not the least idea what an experimental inquiry is.

A "fact" as conceived by scientists exhibits three characteristics of which we may ask whether the first and the third do not approximate to that which Sartre calls the "essence," the second serving as a control of the two others. Each scientific "fact" is: *(a)* an answer to a question: *(b)* a verification or a "reading off": *(c)* a sequence of interpretations, already implicit in the very manner of asking the question, as well (unfortunately or fortunately) as in the verification as such, or the "reading off" of experience, and explicit in the manner of understanding the answer given by reality to the question asked.

———————

Objectively, a fact can only be arrived at by systematically isolating the factors involved, and it required the genius of a Galileo to study successfully simple motions when the movements of everyday observation, like the fall of a leaf, are often of an inextricable complexity. As against this, logico-mathematical deduction starts immediately from simple operations like class-inclusion, the starting point of the syllogistic, or the addition of integers. In the case of psychology the isolation of factors is still much more complex, since they are organically related together into wholes difficult to vary systematically. I will always remember the surprise and admiration I felt in listening to Einstein at Princeton, who liked to be told the facts of child psychology (particularly the nonconservations), when he invariably concluded: "How difficult it is! How much more difficult psychology is than physics!" But one needs to be Einstein in order to grasp so quickly a difficulty that few people understand, and unfortunately not always the psychologists themselves. . . .

———————

One can finally ask if the opposition between scientists and philosophers does not often depend on the fact itself that science constantly progresses, despite its crises and temporary dead-ends, while the way of philosophy consists in constantly readjusting to a certain number of essential and almost permanent positions to the state of knowledge at a specific time, but always after it has been sifted and generally accepted. This would explain, on the one hand, the rarity of great philosophers compared with the number of innovators in all the particular fields of science. But it would above all explain the lack of understanding that the common sense of average philosophers shows (with respect to disciplines which are in a state of continual development, since their understanding of them, obtained solely from the reading of texts, is from this fact alone constantly being outdated. In this sense the disagreement could still continue for a long time, unless there was a radical reform of philosophical teaching that would allow students beginning their philosophical studies the opportunity of being introduced to the very practice of scientific inquiry.

60. Personal Knowledge:
Towards a Post-Critical Philosophy

MICHAEL POLANYI. Harper & Row, 49 East 33rd Street, New York, N.Y. 10016; 1964; or *Real Time*. (P) $2.95; 428 pp.
University of Chicago Press, 5801 Ellis Avenue, Chicago, Ill. 60637; 1958; or *Real Time*. (H) $10.75.

There's " know " where left to go. In other words, we're fast coming to the end of the epistemological road. Perhaps Polanyi's book is one of the last gasps. In any event, it's a big, impressive volume, covering a wide range of human knowledge in an attempt to show that scientific objectivity is both a delusion and a false ideal. In Polanyi's methodology, knowing is an involvement in the activities of appraisal and commitment, and this personal input is the bridge between the dogmatic concepts of the objective and the subjective. JB

In the Ptolemaic system, as in the cosmogony of the Bible, man was assigned a central position in the universe, from which position he was ousted by Copernicus. Ever since, writers eager to drive the lesson home have urged us, resolutely and repeatedly, to abandon all sentimental egoism, and to see ourselves objectively in the true perspective of time and space. What precisely does this mean? In a full 'main feature' film, recapitulating faithfully the complete history of the universe, the rise of human beings from the first beginnings of man to the achievements of the twentieth century would flash by in a single second. Alternatively, if we decided to examine the universe objectively in the sense of paying equal attention to portions of equal mass, this would result in a lifelong preoccupation with interstellar dust, relieved only at brief intervals by a survey of incandescent masses of hydrogen— not in a thousand million lifetimes would the turn come to give man even a second's notice. It goes without saying that no one—scientists included— looks at the universe this way, whatever lip-service is given to 'objectivity'. Nor should this surprise us. For, as human beings, we must inevitably see the universe from a centre lying within ourselves and speak about it in terms of a human language shaped by the exigencies of human intercourse. Any attempt rigorously to eliminate our human perspective from our picture of the world must lead to absurdity.

We shall find Personal Knowledge manifested in the appreciation of probability and of order in the exact sciences, and see it at work even more extensively in the way the descriptive sciences rely on skills and connoisseurship. At all these points the act of knowing includes an appraisal; and this personal coefficient, which shapes all factual knowledge, bridges in doing so the disjunction between subjectivity and objectivity. It implies the claim that man can transcend his own subjectivity by striving passionately to fulfil his personal obligations to universal standards.

The purpose of this book is to show that complete objectivity as usually attributed to the exact sciences is a delusion and is in fact a false ideal. But I shall not try to repudiate strict objectivity as an ideal without offering a substitute, which I believe to be more worthy of intelligent allegiance; this I have called 'personal knowledge'.

There is one more move to be made towards reopening this vision. I have shown in the last two chapters what I mean by the achievements of living things and have exhibited in these examples the logic of achievement. These were our results:

1. Living beings can be known only in terms of success or failure. They comprise ascending levels of successful existing and behaving.

2. We can know a successful system only by understanding it as a whole, while being subsidiarily aware of its particulars; and we cannot meaningfully study these particulars except with a bearing on the whole. Moreover, the higher the level of success we are contemplating, the more far-reaching must be our participation in our subject matter.

3. Therefore, to interpret systems that can succeed or fail in the more detached terms, by which we know systems to which no distinction of success or failure applies, is logically impossible. Systems that can succeed or fail are properly characterized by operational principles, or more generally, by certain rules of rightness; and our knowledge of any class of things that is characterized by a rule of rightness disappears when we attempt to define it in terms that are neutral to this rightness.

4. Accordingly, it is as meaningless to represent life in terms of physics and chemistry as it would be to interpret a grandfather clock or a Shakespeare sonnet in terms of physics and chemistry; and it is likewise meaningless to represent mind in terms of a machine or of a neural model. Lower levels do not lack a bearing on higher levels; *they define the conditions of their success and account for their failures, but they cannot account for their success, for they cannot even define it.*

A theory of evolution must explain, then, the rise of novel individuals performing new biotic operations. But the question how instances of new biotic operations come into existence, leads obviously back to the coming into being of life itself from inanimate origins. It is clear that for such an event to take place two things must be assured: (1) Living beings must be possible, i.e. there must exist rational principles, the operation of which can sustain their carriers indefinitely; and (2) favourable conditions must arise for initiating these operations and sustaining them. In this sense I shall acknowledge that the *ordering principle* which *originated* life is the *potentiality* of a stable open system; while the inanimate matter on which life feeds is merely a *condition* which *sustains* life, and the accidental configuration of matter from which life had started had merely *released* the operations of life. And evolution, like life itself, will then be said to have been *originated* by the *action* of an ordering principle, an action *released* by random fluctuations and *sustained* by fortunate *environmental conditions*.

61. Self and Others

R. D. LAING. Tavistock Publications Ltd., 11 New Fetter Lane, London EC4P 4EE; (H) 1969; £2.30; or Penguin Books Ltd., Harmondsworth, Middx; (P) 1971; £0.30; 169 pp.

Laing, an English psychoanalyst and psychiatrist, is interested in the extremes of human behavior, experience, and communication. He's looking for a unified theory of description, one that will reconcile artificial differences such as behavior-experience, perception-reality, me-you. JB

The psychoanalytic thesis can be stated thus: it is not *possible* to prove the existence of unconscious phantasy to the person who is immersed in it. Unconscious phantasy can be known to be phantasy only after the person's own emergence from it. This way of putting it is riddled with difficulties, and so is every other way. The situation is not assisted by the fact that the concept of unconscious phantasy has received very little scrutiny from an existential and phenomenological perspective. And yet no comprehensive account of human relations can ignore it.

One source of confusion is the particular dichotomous schema in which the whole theory is cast. This particular schema entails the distinction between 'the inner world of the mind', on the one hand, and 'the external world of the subject's bodily development and behaviour, and hence of other people's minds and bodies', on the other.

This contradistinction generates, in Isaacs's paper and in many psychoanalytic works, two opposed clusters of terms, namely:

inner	in contrast to	*outer*
mental	in contrast to	*physical*
mental activity	in contrast to	*external and bodily realities*
figment	in contrast to	*what can be touched, handled, seen*
psychical reality	in contrast to	*physical reality*
the inner world of the mind	in contrast to	*the external world of the subject's bodily development, and hence of other people's minds and bodies*
mind	in contrast to	*body*

Our perception of 'reality' is the perfectly achieved accomplishment of our civilization. To perceive *reality*! When did people stop feeling that what they *perceived* was *unreal*? Perhaps the feeling and the idea that what we perceive is real is very recent in human history.

Time is empty. It is as futile as it is inescapable. A false eternity, made out of all the time on one's hands which drags on eternally. It is an attempt to live outside time by living in a part of time, to live timelessly in the past, or in the future. The present is never realized.

The most significant theoretical and methodological development in the psychiatry of the last two decades is, in my view, the growing dissatisfaction with any theory or study of the individual which isolates him from his context. Efforts have been made from different angles to remedy this position. One may note, however, that there are formidable pitfalls. A schema may falsely fragment reality. There is a distinction between fragmentation that does violence to personal reality, and a legitimate analysis of one aspect of a situation at a time. One does not wish to sever 'mind' and 'body', 'psychic' and 'physical'. One must not treat 'persons' as 'animals' or 'things', but one would be foolish to try to disrupt man from his relation to other creatures and from the matter that is his matrix. It is immensely difficult not to subject unwittingly our human reality to such conceptual mutilation that the original is lost in the process.

62. On the Psychology of Meditation

CLAUDIO NARANJO and ROBERT E. ORNSTEIN. Allen & Unwin Ltd., 40 Museum Street, London WC1A 1LU; 1973; £3.75; 248 pp.

The rationality of Western man isn't the only alternative for humanity. Naranjo and Ornstein (in separate essays) explore (a) the non-religious spirituality of Eastern religions and philosophies and (b) the possibilities of integrating these techniques, with the technological ways of the West.

Naranjo is a Chilean psychiatrist known for his work and interest in psychedelics, and Ornstein is a research psychologist at the Langley-Porter Neuropsychiatric Institute. JB

The very diversity of practices given the name of meditation by the followers of this or that particular approach is an invitation to search for the answer of what meditation is *beyond its forms.* And if we are not content just to trace the boundaries of a particular group of related techniques, but instead search for a unity within the diversity, we may indeed recognize such a unity in an *attitude.* We may find that, *regardless of the medium* in which meditation is carried out— whether images, physical experiences, verbal utterances, etc.—the task of the meditator is essentially the same, as if the many forms of practice were nothing more than different occasions for the same basic exercise.

The negative way may seem opposite to the previously described approaches to meditation (upon externally given objects or upon internally arising mental contents), but this is only superficially so. Moreover, *the "negative" dimension of the meditation may be considered to be the invisible backbone sustaining both the concentrative and the expressive way of attunement.* It may be readily seen, in fact, that the concentrative effort involved in meditation upon a *single* object is of an eliminative nature. It is also clear that those forms of meditation involving the development of receptivity toward the unfolding of inner experience imply a passivity possible only through an active effort to eliminate the intrusion of thought on imagination. The practice in "letting go" that this meditation entails, in the sense of "surrendering to" or "allowing," cannot be completely divorced from a letting go in another sense, which is the essence of the negative way: letting go of habits, preconceptions, and expectations; letting go of control and of the filtering mechanisms of ego.

The way of Za-Zen may be regarded as the way of surrender of personal preferences: an emptying oneself of preconceptions (in the intellectual aspects), greed (in the emotional), and self-will, in order to discover that enlightenment bypasses or is not dependent on the satisfactions of those habits that we call our personality. As well as the movement of surrender or letting go of something, we can also see that there is place in meditation for an attitude of surrender *to.*

This might seem an attempt doomed to failure, if we consider that any surrender to our preferences is likely to leave us subject to those impulses in our personality that constitute the very prison or vicious circle that we want to transcend. If saying "No" to our little ego proves to be effective, could saying "Yes" to it be effective as well? In this, as in other things, paradoxes seem to be more compatible with empirical reality than with logical reasoning, and experience indicates that surrender *to* impulse may not be the blind alley that it seems to be.

Psychologically, continuous repetition of the same stimulus may be considered the equivalent of no stimulation at all. The two situations, which from the psychological and physiological points of view are quite similar, insofar as they restrict awareness to that of a single source of unchanging stimulation, also seem to produce the same effects. So we can say (within our frame of reference) that concentrative meditation is a practical technique which uses an experiential knowledge of the structure of our nervous system to "turn off" awareness of the external world and produce a state of blank-out or darkness, the "void," the cloud of unknowing. The techniques of concentrative meditation are not deliberately mysterious or exotic but are simply a matter of practical applied psychology.

We ordinarily speak of "seeing an image" on the retina of our eyes. More properly, we do not really "see" with our eyes but, rather, with the help of our eyes. The eyes and other sense organs should be considered information selection systems. We can trick the eye, for instance, in several ways. If we press on our eyelids with our eyes closed, we "see" a white light, and yet there is no physical light energy present. What we have done is to cause the cells in the retina to fire by pressure instead of by their usual source of stimulation, light energy. The cells in the retina fire and send signals up to the brain. Messages from the retina are interpreted as light by the brain, no matter how the message was brought about, and so we are tricked into "seeing." There are times when we do not even need our eyes to "see"— for instance, when we dream at night, or in the case of hallucinations, there is no light energy reaching our eyes.

To conclude briefly, "forgotten" esoteric disciplines are rich sources of information for contemporary psychology, and a new and extended view of the human capacity is emerging from the blend of contemporary and older psychologies.

Theoretically these older psychologies were the precursors of the modern analyses of the interactive nature of awareness. They also offer alternative conceptual models for human behavior (cf. Gurdjieff's division of man into several "centers"—motion, intellectual, emotional, and the "higher" ones). Their centuries-old non-dualistic approach to mind and body has only recently been accepted by science. They describe an extended set of variables that affect human behavior, which generally are not investigated as part of modern science. These psychologies also offer techniques for altering awareness and the "involuntary" aspects of nervous and glandular activity, which Western science has for a long time ignored. The study of accomplished practitioners of these disciplines may yield a glimpse of the scope of the mastery that may be achieved over these processes.

63. The Discontinuous Universe: Selected Writings in Contemporary Consciousness

Edited by SALLIE SEARS and GEORGIANNA W. LORD. Basic Books, Inc., 17–21 Sunbeam Road, London NW10; 1972; £4.65; 476 pp.

Whenever the scientists create a new world, the artists are usually right there with them, setting forth new forms which render this world visible to itself. This book is an anthology of short pieces taken from the work of forty original thinkers that the editors believe demonstrate the contemporary cultural drift beyond modernism to a consciousness of its own. Among those represented are Annette Michelson, Susan Sontag, N.O. Brown, Jorge Luis Borges, P.W. Bridgman, Wallace Stevens, Samuel Beckett, Claude Lévi-Strauss, Antonin Artaud, Eugene Minkowski, and Allan Kaprow.

Sallie Sears and Georgianna Lord are English teachers at State University of New York, Stonybrook, and City University of New York, respectively. JB

New music: new listening. Not an attempt to understand something that is being said, for, if something were being said, the sounds would be given the shapes of words. Just an attention to the activity of sounds.

Those involved with the composition of experimental music find ways and means to remove themselves from the activities of the sounds they make. Some employ chance operations, derived from sources as ancient as the Chinese *Book of Changes,* or as modern as the tables of random numbers used also by physicists in research. Or, analogous to the Rorschach tests of psychology, the interpretation of imperfections in the paper upon which one is writing may provide a music free from one's memory and imagination. Geometrical means employing spatial superimpositions at variance with the ultimate performance in time may be used. The total field of possibilities may be roughly divided and the actual sounds within these divisions may be indicated as to number but left to the performer or to the splicer to choose. In this latter case, the composer resembles the maker of a camera who allows someone else to take the picture.

John Cage

How literally does silence figure in art?

Silence exists as a *decision*—in the exemplary suicide of the artist (Kleist, Lautreamont), who thereby testifies that he has gone "too far"; and

in the already cited model renunciations by the artist of his vocation.

Silence also exists as a *punishment*—self-punishment, in the exemplary madness of artists (Hölderlin, Artaud) who demonstrate that sanity itself may be the price of trespassing the accepted frontiers of consciousness; and, of course, in penalties (ranging from censorship and physical destruction of artworks to fines, exile, prison for the artist) meted out by "society" for the artist's spiritual nonconformity or subversion of the group sensibility.

Silence doesn't exist in a literal sense, however, as the *experience* of an audience. It would mean that the spectator was aware of no stimulus or that he was unable to make a response. But this can't happen; nor can it even be induced programmatically. The non-awareness of any stimulus, the inability to make a response, can result only from a defective presence on the part of the spectator, or a misunderstanding of his own reactions (misled by restrictive ideas about what would be a "relevant" response). As long as audiences, by definition, consist of sentient beings in a "situation," it is impossible for them to have no response at all.

Susan Sontag

To see the gods dispelled in mid-air and dissolve like clouds is one of the great human experiences. It is not as if they had gone over the horizon to disappear for a time; nor as if they had been overcome by other gods of greater power and profounder knowledge. It is simply that they came to nothing. Since we have always shared all things with them and have always had a part of their strength and, certainly, all of their knowledge, we shared likewise this experience of annihilation. It was their annihilation, not ours, and yet it left us feeling that in a measure, we, too, had been annihilated.

Wallace Stevens

Newton's decisive realization was that the laws which govern the fall of a stone also determine the orbit of the moon around the earth and thus are applicable in cosmic dimensions also. In the years that followed, natural science began its victory march on a broad front into those remote regions of nature about which we may obtain information only by the detour of technology—that is, by using more or less complicated apparatus. Astronomy used the improved telescope to master ever more remote cosmic regions. Chemistry attempted to understand processes at the atomic level from the behavior of substances in chemical reactions. Experiments with the induction machine and the Voltaic pile gave the first insight into electrical phenomena that were still hidden from the daily life of that era. Thus the meaning of the word " nature " as an object of scientific research slowly changed; it became a collective concept for all those areas of experience into which man can penetrate through science and technology, whether or not they are given to him "naturally" in direct experience. The term *description* of nature also progressively lost its original significance as a representation intended to convey the most alive and imaginable picture possible of nature; instead, in increasing measure a mathematical description of nature was implied—that is, a collection of data concerning interrelations accor-ding to law in nature, precise and brief yet also as comprehensive as possible.

Werner Heisenberg

Our world is essentially the world of our perceptions, and the nature of this world is indelibly colored by the nature of the psychological present. But this psychological present is essentially different from the present of an idealized extension of our world of instruments. The psychological present is a smeared-out totality in which we grasp whole visual fields in a single glance as units, and *see* objects moving at a single instant of time, whereas instrumentally we find structure in this temporal amorphousness of a fineness of scale presumably limited only by the frequencies of the atoms of our nervous systems. These frequencies are of the order of 10^{13} per second, so that if we take the duration of the psychological present as of the order of 0.01 second, we have here the possiblity of instrumental detail nearly a million million times finer than that accessible to direct perception. There is room here for all the complexities of conscious experience, and for complexities not yet suspected.

P. W. Bridgman

And yet, and yet. . . . Denying temporal succession, denying the self, denying the astronomical universe, are apparent desperations and secret consolations. Our destiny (as contrasted with the hell of Swedenborg and the hell of Tibetan mythology) is not frightful by being unreal; it is frightful because it is irreversible and iron-clad. Time is the substance I am made of. Time is a river which sweeps me along, but I am the river; it is a tiger which destroys me, but I am the tiger; it is a fire which consumes me, but I am the fire. The world, unfortunately, is real; I, unfortunately, am Borges.

Jorge Luis Borges

64. Intuition

R. BUCKMINSTER FULLER. Doubleday & Company, Inc., 501 Franklin Avenue, Garden City, N.Y. 11530; 1972; or *Real Time.* $5.95; 190 pp.

There is only a limited amount of mind-bending information that any one person can shape in a lifetime. I don't even think it should be thought of in terms of information, but as effect. Fuller's effect has been profound; there isn't anyone around who has reached so many people. This new work, *Intuition,* is the basic book he's been writing for years.

I think the reason he keeps writing has to do with his notion that "idea" is a very hard, finite thing, that if you throw one out to the public, there is an inherent responsibility to keep it floating in the air, to constantly make it real, to state, restate, recapitulate at every possible opportunity. Thus every Fuller lecture, every Fuller book covers *all* the territory that he's covered, at least on the ideational level. This new work, written in a free form, is rewarding as a reading experience. My favorite Fuller books remain *Nine Chains to the Moon,* written by Fuller in 1937, plus the six-volume epic (co-authored with sociologist-futurist John McHale) *World Design Science Decade.* JB

In addition to inherent duality of Universe
There is also and always
An inherent *threefoldedness* and *fourfoldedness*
of initial consciousness
And of all experience.
For in addition to (1) action, (2) reaction, (3) resultant,
There is always (4) the a priori environment,
Within which the event occurs,
I.e., the *at-first-nothingness* around us
Of the child graduated from the womb,
Within which seeming nothingness (fourthness)
The inherently threefold
Local *event* took place.

———

Synergy is the *only* word that *means*
Behaviors of a whole system
Unpredicted by the separate behaviors
Of any of its parts.

———

Development is programable;
Discovery is not programable.
Since the behaviors to be sought
Are unknown,
Computers cannot be instructed

To watch out for them.
Computers can "keep track"
Of a complex of behaviors,
But only human mind can discern
The heretofore unknown
Unique interrelationships
Which exist *between* and not *of*
The separate bodies.

———

And the black void
Nothingness of night
Backdropping the fireworks
Is the omnipresent,
A priori mystery.
And the real beginning of education
Must be the experimental realization
Of absolute mystery.

———

I am now seventy-three years of age
And am eager to participate further
In humanity's designing functions—
That is, in metaphysically comprehending
And mastering in orderly ways
The physical energy Universe's
Inexorably expanding momentary disorders,
And am aware that humanity

R. BUCKMINSTER FULLER
INTUITION

The brain is a special case
Concept-communicating system
Very much like a television set.
It's not just a telegraph wire,
Not just a telephone,
It is sensorially conceptual as well.
It deals with our optical receipts
As well as with our hearing,
Our smelling
And our touching.
In effect we have a telesense station
Wherein we receive the live news
And make it into a video-taped documentary.
In our brain studio we have made a myriad of
such videoed recordings
Of the once live news,
All of which we hold in swiftly retrievable
storage.

———————————

Each one of these thinkable sets
Are what I call a *system*.
A system is a subdivision of Universe.
A system subdivides Universe
Into all of the Universe events
Which are irrelevant to the considered set
Because (a) they are outside the system,
Too macrocosmic and too infrequent
Either to fit into
Or to alter
The considered set.
Or irrelevant because (b) occurring
Too microcosmically remote
Within the system
And of too-high frequency
And of too-short duration
To be tunable with
Or to alter significantly
The considered think-set.

———————————

Is approaching a crisis
In which its residual ignorance, shortsightedness
And circumstance-biased viewpoints
May dominate,
Thus carrying humanity
Beyond the "point of no return"—
Enveloping his exclusively Sun-regenerated
Planetary home
In chain-reactive pollutionings
And utter disorder.

———————————

Entropy's behavior may be modernized to state
That every separately experienceable
And generalizably conceivable system in
Universe
Is continually exporting energies
While also always importing energies
At a concurrently accelerating and decelerating
Variety of local system rates,
Which also means
That all systems are continually transforming
Internally as well as externally,
And because the periodicity of importing and
exporting
Are both nonsimultaneous and unequal,
All the systems are tidally pulsative
At a variety of frequencies.

———————————

One physicist remarked recently,
"I am tiring of the nonsense legend
Which finds one end of Universe closed,
By a required beginning event
And the other end open to infinity."
The concept of primordial—
Meaning before the days of order—
Which imply an a priori,
Absolute disorder, chaos, a *beginning*
("The primordial ooze-gooze explosion")
Is now scientifically invalidated, passe.

Now I surmise
That the speculative thought
Of the human mind—
In contradistinction
To the physical experience recalls
Of the physical brain—
Is physically nondemonstrable,
Ergo, metaphysical,
But its teleological activity,
Which subjectively evolves generalizations
From multiplicities of special-case experiences
(And thereafter employs the generalizations
Objectively in other special-case physical
formulations)
Can be detected
Through man's intuitive recognition
Of the weightless pattern integrity per se,
Ever weightlessly, abstractly present in the
original
Discovering and inventing events.
Scientific generalizations
Have no inherent beginning or ending.
In discovering them
Mind is discovering a phase of Universe
That is eternal.
The physical human and its physical brain
Unmonitored by mind
Are not only less effectively syntropic
Than other biological species;
They are often consciously
Far more entropic
Than any other species
And are only subconsciously syntropic.

65. Mytholologies

ROLAND BARTHES (translated by Annette Lavers). Jonathan Cape Ltd., 30 Bedford Square, London WC1B 3EL; 1972; £2.50; 159 pp.

One problem in reading Barthes is in translating the original French into English—you can never be quite sure of what he's saying, or if the obscurities are in the translation, the French idiom, in the author, or ourselves. Still, he's saying *something* that must be read and dealt with. JB

REVIEW BY GERARD DOMBROWSKI. Roland Barthes's *Weltanschauung* centers around the concept that any whole or partial entity can be conceived of as a language in itself. An essay from this book considers Einstein's brain as myth, which for Barthes is language, and the perception is one of both magician and machine. Barthes has the propriety for doing this to many things: toys, cars, striptease, wrestling, detergents, cooking, film and our semi-divine reified hero, the Jet-Man. You almost have to read him with a half-cocked grin on your face; his phraseology is that unpredictable. I would almost draw parallels to Marshall McLuhan's disparate reverence for the bungholes in contemporary culture but the fear that this enormous presence could be dismissed as some pop patrician forces me to abandon comparative jingoism.

Barthes presently teaches the sociology of signs, symbols, and collective representations at the École Practique des Haute Études. He has also authored numerous books, among them a recently completed study of Japan. There are no boundaries in subject matter for this master sorcerer of the sidereal glance, or as Barthes himself says: "Products based on chlorine and ammonia are without doubt the representatives of a kind of absolute fire, a savior but a blind one."

Einstein's brain is a mythical object: paradoxically, the great intelligence of all provides an image of the most up-to-date machine, the man who is too powerful is removed from psychology, and introduced into a world of robots; as is well known, the supermen of science-fiction always have something reified about them. So has Einstein: he is commonly signified by his brain, which is like an object for anthologies, a true museum exhibit. Perhaps because of his mathematical specialization, superman is here divested of every magical character; no diffuse power in him, no mystery other than mechanical: he is a superior, a prodigious organ, but a real, even a physiological one. Mythologically, Einstein is matter, his power does not spontaneously draw one towards the spiritual, it needs the help of an independent morality, a reminder about the scientist's 'conscience' (*Science without conscience,* they said . . .).

There is a single secret to the world, and this secret is held in one word; the universe is a safe of which humanity seeks the combination: Einstein almost found it, this is the myth of Einstein. In it, we find all the Gnostic themes: the unity of nature, the ideal possibility of a fundamental reduction of the word, the unfastening power of the word, the age-old struggle between a secret and an utterance, the idea that total knowledge can only be discovered all at once, like a lock which suddenly opens after a thousand unsuccessful attempts. The historic equation $E = mc^2$, by its unexpected simplicity, almost embodies the pure idea of the key, bare, linear, made of one metal, opening with a wholly magical ease a door which had resisted the desperate efforts of centuries. Popular imagery faithfully expresses this: *photographs* of Einstein show him standing next to a blackboard covered with mathematical signs of obvious complexity; but *cartoons* of Einstein (the sign that he has become a legend) show him chalk still in hand, and having just written on an empty blackboard, as if without preparation, the magic formula of the world. In this way mythology shows an awareness of the nature of the various tasks: research proper brings into play clockwork-like mechanisms and has its seat in a wholly material organ which is monstrous only by its cybernetic complication; discovery, on the contrary, has a magical essence, it is simple like a basic element, a principal substance, like the philosophers' stone of hermetists, tar-water for Berkeley, or oxygen for Schelling.

———————

The *jet-man* is a jet-pilot. *Match* has specified that he belongs to a new race in aviation, nearer to the robot than to the hero. Yet there are in the *jet-man* several Parsifalian residues, as we shall see shortly. But what strikes one first in the mythology of the *jet-man* is the elimination of speed: nothing in the legend alludes to this experience. We must here accept a paradox, which is in fact admitted by everyone with the greatest of ease, and even consumed as a proof of modernity. This paradox is that an excess of speed turns into repose. The pilot-hero was made unique by a whole mythology of speed as an experience, of space devoured, of intoxicating motion; the *jet-man,* on the other hand, is defined by a coenaesthesis of motionlessness (*'at 2,000 km per hour, in level flight, no impression of speed at all'*), as if the extravagance of his vocation precisely consisted in *overtaking* motion, in going faster than speed. Mythology abandons here a whole imagery of exterior friction and enters pure coenaesthesis: motion is no longer the optical perception of points and surfaces; it has become a kind of vertical disorder, made of contractions, black-outs, terrors and faints; it is no longer a gliding but an inner devastation, an unnatural perturbation, a motionless crisis of bodily consciousness.

———————

The fashion for plastic highlights an evolution in the myth of 'imitation' materials. It is well known that their use is historically bourgeois in origin (the first vestimentary postiches date back to the rise of capitalism). But until now imitation materials have always indicated pretension, they belonged to the world of appearances, not to that of actual use; they aimed at reproducing cheaply the rarest substances, diamonds, silk, feathers, furs, silver, all the luxurious brilliance of the world. Plastic has climbed down, it is a household material. It is the first magical substance which consents to be prosaic. But it is precisely because this prosaic character is a triumphant reason for

its existence: for the first time, artifice aims at something common, not rare. And as an immediate consequence, the age-old function of nature is modified: it is no longer the Idea, the pure Substance to be regained or imitated: an artificial Matter, more bountiful than all the natural deposits, is about to replace her, and to determine the very invention of forms. A luxurious object is still of this earth, it still recalls, albeit in a precious mode, its mineral or animal origin, the natural theme of which it is but one actualization. Plastic is wholly swallowed up in the fact of being used: ultimately, objects will be invented for the sole pleasure of using them. The hierarchy of substances is abolished: a single one replaces them all: the whole world *can* be plasticized, and even life itself since, we are told, they are beginning to make plastic aortas.

———————

What is a myth, today? I shall give at the outset a first, very simple answer, which is perfectly consistent with etymology: *myth is a type of speech.*
Of course, it is not *any* type: language needs special conditions in order to become myth: we shall see them in a minute. But what must be firmly established at the start is that myth is a system of communication, that it is a message. This allows one to perceive that myth cannot possibly be an object, a concept, or an idea; it is a mode of signification, a form. Later, we shall have to assign to this form historical limits, conditions of use, and reintroduce society into it: we must nevertheless first describe it as a form.

———————

The starting point of these reflections was usually a feeling of impatience at the sight of the 'naturalness' with which newspapers, art and common sense constantly dress up a reality which, even though it is the one we live in, is undoubtedly determined by history. In short, in the account given of our contemporary circumstances, I resented seeing Nature and History confused at every turn, and I wanted to track down, in the decorative display of *what-goes-without-saying*, the ideological abuse which, in my view, is hidden there.

Right from the start, the notion of myth seemed to me to explain these examples of the falsely obvious. At that time, I still used the word 'myth' in its traditional sense. But I was already certain of a fact from which I later tried to draw all the consequences: myth is a language.

66. The Farther Reaches of Human Nature

ABRAHAM H. MASLOW. The Viking Press, Inc., 625 Madison Avenue, New York, N.Y. 10022; 1971; or *Real Time*. $12.50; 423 pp.

The late A.H. Maslow was greatly responsible for the start and perpetuation of the currently proliferating human potential movement. His work seems more subtle and intelligent than the ends to which it is used by a lot of his followers who are into easy answers and "one way" realities. JB

REVIEW BY ABBIE HOFFMAN. If one was pressed to name thinkers whose philosophy was best reflected in the past decade of social protest, two former Brandeis University professors would certainly rate high. Herbert Marcuse, by making Marxism relevant to a post-scarcity society, provided a theoretical base. Ideological commitment is not what produced the plethora of liberation movements and alternative communities but rather a unique birth of humanism in America. A humanism perhaps best reflected in the teachings of the late A.H. Maslow.

Rejecting much of the dark side of classical Freudian thought, Maslow turns to the study of healthy people to formulate a refreshingly optimistic view of humanity. In *The Farthest Reaches of Human Nature*, we are presented with a collection of the last refinements of Maslow's "Being Psychology"; the hierarchy of needs allowing us to better understand motivation; studies of self-actualization and creativity contributing to our search for a higher consciousness not separate from the reality of contemporary experience; his analysis of the "peak experience," that peculiar sort of religious ecstasy for the common folk.

Maslow was the ultimate Gestalt psychologist. This book is both a model and a demand for a science that accepts its basic responsibility as faith in the potential for human growth and understanding.

Psychology today is torn and riven, and may in fact be said to be three (or more) separate, noncommunicating sciences or groups of scientists. First is the behavioristic, objectivistic, mechanistic, positivistic group. Second is the whole cluster of psychologies that originated in Freud and in psychoanalysis. And third there are the humanistic psychologies, or the "Third Force" as this group has been called, a coalescence into a single philosophy of various splinter groups in psychology. It is for this third psychology that I want to speak. I interpret this third psychology to include the first and second psychologies, and have invented the words "epi-behavioristic" and "epi-Freudian" (epi = upon) to describe it. This also helps to avoid the sophomoric two-valued, dichotomized, orientation, for example, of being either pro-Freudian or anti-Freudian. I am Freudian and I am behavioristic and I am humanistic, and as a matter of fact I am developing what might be called a fourth psychology of transcendence as well.

_____

One main characteristic of the peak experience is just this total fascination with the matter-in-hand, this getting lost in the present, this detachment from time and place. And it seems to me now that much of what we have learned from the study of these peak experiences can be transferred quite directly to the enriched understanding of the here-now experience, of the creative attitude.

_____

Make the general assumption that no normative social thinking is possible until we have some idea of *the individual goal*, i.e., the kind of person to aim to be and by which to judge the adequacy of any society. I proceed on the assumption that the good society, and therefore the immediate goal of any society which is trying to improve itself, is the self-actualization of all individuals, or some norm or goal approximating this. (Transcendence of self—living at the level of Being—is assumed to be most possible for the person with a strong and free identity,i.e., for the self-actualizing person. This will necessarily involve consideration of social arrangements, education, etc., that make transcendence more possible.) The question here is: Do we have a trustworthy, reliable conception of the healthy or desirable or transcending or ideal person? Also this normative idea is itself moot and debatable. Is it possible to improve a society without having some idea of what one considers to be an improved human being?

CHARACTERISTICS OF BEING-COGNITION AND DEFICIENCY-COGNITION OF THE WORLD

B-COGNITION

1. Seen as whole, as complete, self-sufficient, as unitary. Either Cosmic Consciousness (Bucke), in which whole cosmos is perceived as single thing with oneself belonging in it; or else the person, object, or portion of the world seen is seen as if it were the whole world, i.e., rest of world is forgotten. Integrative perceiving of unities. Unity of the world or object perceived.

2. Exclusively, fully, narrowly attended to; absorption, fascination, focal attention; total attention. Tends to de-differentiate figure and ground. Richness of detail; seen from many sides. Seen with "care," totally, intensely, with complete investment. Totally cathected. Relative importance becomes unimportant; all aspects equally important.

3. No comparing (in Dorothy Lee's sense). Seen *per se* in itself, by itself. Not in competition with anything else. Sole member of the class (in Hartman's sense).

4. Human-irrelevant.

D-COGNITION

Seen as part, as incomplete, not self-sufficient, as dependent upon other things.

Attended to with simultaneous attention to all cause that is relevant. Sharp figure-ground differentiation. Seen imbedded in relationships to all else in world, as part of the world. Rubricized; seen from some aspects only; selective attention and selective inattention to some aspects; seen casually, seen only from some point of view.

Placing on a continuum or within a series; comparing, judging, evaluating. Seen as a member of a class, as an instance, a sample.

Relevant to human concerns; e.g., what good is it, what can it be used for, is it good for or dangerous to people, etc.

67. The Roots of Coincidence

ARTHUR KOESTLER. Hutchinson Publishing Ltd., 3 Fitzroy Square, London W1P 6JD; (H) 1972; £2.00; or Picador, Cavaye Place, London SW10 9PG; (P) 1974; £0.50; 159 pp.

A South American shaman was recently subjected to a variety of physiological tests while he mutilated his body with bicycle-wheel spokes. He bled very little during this self-mutilation, and his brain waves, blood pressure, pulse, heart rate, and other physiological indicators showed nearly no difference between when he was piercing his skin with the spokes and after he had finished. Was this man employing extrasensory perception?

Are the basics of psi phenomena rooted in our scheme for reality? Is physics occult? And if so, what about neurophysiology and molecular biology? Telepathy, clairvoyance, and precognition are beginning to become respectable just as space, time, and matter begin to disappear. What's going on here? ER

REVIEW BY BENNETT L. SHAPIRO. There are no accidents. Everything in the universe is somehow related to everything else. Only in the medium-sized world available to our everyday senses do things take on the hard, tangible qualities we are used to associating with " reality. " The irony is that the traditionally hard-nosed, positivistic science of physics has given the lie to our cherished nineteenth-century view of the nature of things, i.e. space, time, and matter. Heisenberg's Principle of Indeterminacy (Uncertainty) firmly maintains that " when we get down to the atomic level, the objective world of space and time no longer exists, " we can only refer " to possibilities not to facts. " Richard Feynman (Nobel Prize, 1965) proposed that " the positron is nothing but an electron which, for a while, is *moving backwards in time.* "

Yet an even more formidable obstacle to an appreciation of psi phenomena may be our own highly developed, rational, intellectual apparatus. " Sensitives " are by definition sensitive. Western culture and technology tends to cut people off from their more delicate feelings and perceptions of the natural universe. Here perhaps we can learn something from the cosmologists of ancient India. They had developed a view of the universe that in many ways fits quite neatly with the merging contemporary synthesis. There is no longer any question about the propriety of studying psi phenomena; it is now a question of how.

Thus we arrive at the paradoxical conclusion that physicalistic theories such as Adrian Dobbs', however ingenious, may explain the " extra " in extra-sensory perception, but leave the basic mystery of ordinary, sensory perception where it was before. But at least these theories, based on assumptions which sound weird but hardly more weird than those of modern physics, go a long way towards removing the aura of superstition from the " extra " in extra-sensory perception. The odour of the alchemist's kitchen is replaced by the smell of quark in the laboratory. The rapprochement between the conceptual world of parapsychology and that of modern physics is an important step towards the demolition of the greatest superstition of our age—the materialistic clockwork universe of early-nineteenth-century physics.

_____

The Greeks knew the electrical properties of amber—or *elektron*—but were not interested. For some two thousand years nobody was interested. When in the seventeenth century, experimenting with electricity became fashionable, previously undreamt-of phenomena were discovered, and scientists vied in proposing hypotheses to account for them—postulating effluvia, liquid fires, currents, fields, without turning a hair. Magnetism and gravity had a similar history: when Kepler suggested that the tides are due to attractive forces emanating from the moon, Galileo shrugged the idea off as an " occult fancy " because it involved action-at-a-distance and thus contradicted the "laws of nature"; but that did not deter Newton from postulating universal gravity. "*Hypothesis non fingo*" is perhaps the most shocking piece of hypocrisy ever uttered by a great scientist.

This does not mean that hypothesis-making is a free-for-all. To produce live rabbits out of a hat needs a skilled magician. Quantum physics may be mad, but it has method, and it works. I talked earlier on of a *negative* rapprochement between quantum physics and ESP, in so far as the surrealistic concepts of the former make it easier to suspend disbelief in the latter; if the former is permitted to violate the "laws of nature" as they were understood by classical physics a century ago, the latter may claim the same right. But to stress the point once more, this is merely a negative agreement, a shared disregard for ancient taboos, for a mechanistic world-view which has become an anachronism.

———————————

But the comparison is not quite fair because it is, as we have seen, much easier for a modern physicist than for a psychologist to get out of the grooves of causality, matter, space-time and other traditional categories of thought. The physicist has been trained to regard the world as experienced by our senses as an illusion—Eddington's shadow-desk, covered by the veil of Maya. But that does not worry him unduly, because he has created a world of his own, described in a language of great beauty and power, the language of mathematical equations, which tells him all he knows, and can ever hope to know, of the universe around him. Bertrand Russell did not mean to be ironical when he wrote: "Physics is mathematical not because we know so much about the physical world, but because we know so little: it is only its mathematical properties that we can discover."

Thus the physicist was able to discard, one by one, all commonsense ideas of what the world is like—without suffering any traumatic shock. One by one, matter, energy and causality were dethroned; but the physicist was richly compensated by being able to play around with such enticing Gretchens as the neutrino, and with such exhilirating notions as time flowing backward, ghost-particles of negative mass, and atoms of radium spontaneously emitting beta radiation without physical cause.

68. Medicine, Mind And Music: A Consideration of Their Links Through the Ages.

Edited and produced by GODDARD LIEBERSON. CBS Records, 51 West 52nd Street, New York, N.Y. 10019; 1971; or *Real Time*. $15; 2 records + 53 pp.

Goddard Lieberson is a CBS executive who gets to play creatively with the wealth of materials available to that corporation. Out of this creative activity has come a mixed media event: *Medicine, Mind and Music*, a set of records with an oversized book of texts and illustrations. This concept is a useful integration, in that the records are not the type that must be played with certain sections of the text, and vice versa.

The connections between medicine and music are traced historically and philosophically. Common ground is established between music and a variety of fascinating ills: cholera, odontology, suicide, sanity, narcosis, and others. Some of the recorded selections include plague songs, ancient hymns for health and songs of quacks and quick remedies. ER

To many people, this collection of writings, pictures and sounds joining the art of music to the art of medicine will seem curious, perhaps even eccentric. Yet, throughout history, in sometimes remarkable ways, music has often been utilized to demonstrate the sound medical principle of the placebo; particularly, if we accept the definition of a placebo as being a "non-something" (admittedly, usually in the form of a substance) which is presented to a patient as a potentially effective therapy. In primitive societies, and even in some not so primitive societies, music has been an essential part of many curative rituals and, like other placebos, has been dramatically successful with those disorders generally considered to be psychogenic. But even in cases where diseases have not been identified as psychological in origin, scientists have found the placebo factor to be an effective therapeutic agent.

Today, we may have become too sophisticated to react to such simple placebo devices as beautiful sound or exciting rhythmic patterns— though no one will deny the effect of these within other contexts—and placebos are now, for the most part, in the form of colored pills or acrid liquids. The latter are for those who believe a little suffering and discomfort are necessary for every cure, and on that basis we can provide a good deal of music which will meet the requirements.

In 1742, Johann Sebastian Bach published the longest and perhaps greatest variation work ever written for the keyboard—with the possible exception of Beethoven's variations on a waltz theme by Diabelli—the so-called "Goldberg Variations." They are one of the most immense, and at the same time most subtle, sets of variations in contrapuntal style. The theme, which is a sarabande, has no less than thirty-two measures divided into two sections of sixteen measures, each of which is repeated. Thirty variations follow the aria, which is repeated at the end. Since each variation has thirty-two measures, this makes a respectable total of nine hundred and sixty measures, not counting the repeats. Brahms' "Variations on a Theme by Haydn" contains only half as many. One would hardly expect to find such an enormous work to be connected historically with a case of insomnia. Yet, such indeed is its history. The variations are for the harpsichord and they were commissioned for performance by the harpsichordist Johann Gottlieb Goldberg, who was a pupil of Bach and a protégé of Count Hermann Karl von Keyserling. Goldberg himself was a prodigy, an outstanding harpsichordist and a composer. Johann Nikolaus Forkel, organist, historian of music at the University of Göttingen, and author of the first biography of Johann Sebastian Bach, engagingly recounts the origin of the work:

Drawing by Pieter Breughel (or pupil) showing bagpipe players and afflicted women. The inscription refers to the dance of the pilgrims on St. Jan's day and the healing of St. Jan's illness (epilepsy). *Albertina, Vienna.*

For this model . . . we are indebted to Count Keyserling, formerly Russian Ambassador at the Court of the Elector of Saxony, who frequently resided in Leipzig, and brought Goldberg with him . . . to have him instructed by Bach in music. The Count was often sickly, and had sleepless nights. At these times Goldberg, who lived in the house with him, had to pass the night in an adjoining room and play something to him. . . . The Count once said to Bach that he should like to have some clavier pieces for his Goldberg, which should be of such a soft and somewhat lively character that he might be a little cheered up by them in his sleepless nights. Bach thought he could best fulfill this wish by variations, which, because of the constant sameness of the fundamental harmony, he had hitherto considered an ungrateful task. But

as at this time all his works were models of art, these variations also became such under his hand. This is, indeed, the only model of the kind that he has left us. The Count thereafter called them nothing but *his* variations. He was never weary of hearing them; and for a long time, when the sleepless nights came, he used to say: " Dear Goldberg, do play me one of my variations. " Bach was, perhaps, never so well rewarded for any work: The Count made him a present of a golden goblet, filled with a hundred Louis d'ors. But their worth as a work of art would not be recompensed if the gift had been a thousand times as great.

If this report is based on fact, the world has never been more indebted to insomnia.

69. Steps to an Ecology of Mind

GREGORY BATESON. Intertext, International Textbook Co. Ltd., 450 Edgware Road, London, W2 1EG; 1972; £4.50; 517 pp.

Bateson, an anthropologist and systems theorist, reorders man's psyche in accordance with cybernetic modelling of the past quarter century. He always seems to be right on top of the most interesting work as it is conceived and as it unfolds. Currently, he is teaching at the University of California at Santa Cruz. JB

REVIEW BY ALAN SONDHEIM. On the surface, the essays in this book are concerned with a variety of apparently unrelated topics: primitive art and culture, a theory of schizophrenia, animal morphology, learning processes, etc. But Bateson applies a remarkably consistent methodology in most cases, and this methodology becomes the focal point of the work. Bateson's ecology is based on an analysis of order, logic, and structure. The emphasis, however, is on *processes:* growing, dividing, changing, perceiving. The result is a "cybernetic phenomenology," a re-presentation of various aspects of the subjective interplay of the individual and the world.

An enormous amount of work—essays spanning three decades of research—is presented. I particularly recommend "Style, Grace, and Information in Primitive Art." "Double Bind, 1969," "Conscious Purpose Versus Nature," and "Form, Substance, and Difference."

This book is recommended to anyone attempting a synthesis in the fields of anthropology, biology, or psychology. It should also be of considerable use to philosophers of science, and phenomenologists.

Returning now to the question of whether the fundamentals of science and/or philosophy were, at the primitive level, arrived at by inductive reasoning from empirical data, we find that the answer is not simple. It is difficult to see how the dichotomy between substance and form could be arrived at by inductive argument. No man, after all, has ever seen or experienced formless and unsorted matter; just as no man has ever seen or experienced a "random" event. If, therefore, the notion of a universe "without form and void" was arrived at by induction, it was by a monstrous—and perhaps erroneous—jump of extrapolation.

And even so, it is not clear that the starting point from which the primitive philosophers took off was observation. It is at least equally likely that dichotomy between form and substance was an unconscious *deduction* from the subject-predicate relation in the structure of primitive language. This, however, is a matter beyond the reach of useful speculation.

It is the very rules of transformation that are of interest to me—not the message, but the code.

My goal is not instrumental. I do not want to use the transformation rules when discovered to undo the transformation or to "decode" the message. To translate the art object into mythology and then examine the mythology would be only a neat way of dodging or negating the problem of "what is art?"

I ask, then, not about the meaning of the encoded message but rather about the meaning of the code chosen. But still that most slippery word "meaning" must be defined.

It will be convenient to define meaning in the most general possible way in the first instance.

"Meaning" may be regarded as an approximate synonym of pattern, redundancy, information, and "restraint" within a paradigm of the following sort:

Any aggregate of events or objects (*e.g.,* a sequence of phonemes, a painting, or a frog, or a culture) shall be said to contain "redundancy" or "pattern" if the aggregate can be divided in any way by a "slash mark," such that an observer perceiving only what is on one side of the slash mark can *guess,* with better than random success, what is on the other side of the slash mark. We may say that what is on one side of the slash contains *information* or has *meaning* about what is on the other side. Or, in engineer's language, the aggregate contains "redundancy." Or, again, from the point of view of a cybernetic observer, the information available on one side of the slash will restrain (*i.e.,* reduce the probability of) wrong guessing.

─────────────

The difference between the Newtonian world and the world of communication is simply this: that the Newtonian world ascribes reality to objects and achieves its simplicity by excluding the context of the context—excluding indeed all metarelationships—a fortiori excluding an infinite regress of such relations. In contrast, the theorist of communication insists upon examining the metarelationships while achieving its simplicity by excluding all objects.

This world, of communication, is a Berkeleyan world, but the good bishop was guilty of understatement. Relevance or reality must be denied not only to the sound of the tree which falls unheard in the forest but also to this chair which I can see and on which I am sitting. My perception of the chair is communicationally real, and that on which I sit is, for me, only an idea, a message in which I put my trust.

─────────────

Clearly there are in the mind no objects or events—no pigs, no coconut palms, and no mothers. The mind contains only transforms, percepts, images, etc., and rules for making these transforms, percepts, etc. In what form these rules exist we do not know, but presumably they are embodied in the very machinery which creates the transforms. The rules are certainly not commonly explicit as conscious "thoughts."

In any case, it is nonsense to say that a man was frightened by a lion, because a lion is not an idea. The man makes an *idea* of the lion.

─────────────

But in mental evolution, there is also an economy of flexibility. Ideas which survive repeated use are actually handled in a special way which is different from the way in which the mind handles new ideas. The phenomenon of *habit formation* sorts out the ideas which survive repeated use and puts them in a more or less separate category. These trusted ideas then become available for immediate use without thoughtful inspection, while the more flexible parts of the mind can be saved for use on newer matters.

In other words, the *frequency* or use of a given idea becomes a determinant of its survival in that ecology of ideas which we call Mind; and beyond that the survival of a frequently used idea is further promoted by the fact that habit formation tends to remove the idea from the field of critical inspection.

But the survival of an idea is also certainly determined by its relations with other ideas. Ideas may support or contradict each other; they may combine more or less readily. They may influence each other in complex unknown ways in polarized systems.

70. The Menninger Foundation

Box 829, Topeka, Kan. 66601.

The Menninger Foundation runs the Menninger Clinic, well known for psychiatric diagnosis and treatment. The Foundation also has been supporting research and investigation in a wide variety of areas. These include projects dealing with the cognition of twins; ways of viewing the life process; training for the voluntary control of the autonomic nervous system; stress and personality factors in thyroid dysfunction; investigation of familial structure; relationships among cognitive controls, vocational interests, and intellectual abilities; and evaluation of psychological testing scores against direct self-concept measures.

Other projects deal with migraines, hearing sensitivity in children, measuring patient in-hospital change, and relationships in unconscious processes. *Menninger Perspective* is published bimonthly for the members, employees, and alumni of the Foundation. ER

It is this question—"Is there a way to 'teach' or 'learn' creativity?"—which hopefully will be answered through work being done at The Menninger Foundation by Dr. Elmer Green, head of the psychophysiology laboratory.

Dr. Green and his colleagues, Alyce Green and Dale Walters, have proposed that increased creativity may be achieved by learning how to produce brain wave patterns thought to be associated with reverie and imagery, and a $72,379 grant from HEW's National Institute of Mental Health, Health Services and Mental Health Administration has been awarded them for investigation into that subject.

Well-known for his research of control over physiological processes using the autogenic-feedback-training techniques (self-motivated training), which utilizes visual or auditory displays to show what is happening in certain functions of the body as a person attempts to control them, Dr. Green has made numerous inroads into the study of voluntary control of internal states. Recently his work led to the experimental training of migraine headache sufferers, some who learned how to relieve their own symptoms through biofeedback techniques.

Now, Dr. Green hopes to develop a learning process to teach volunteers to control the production of theta brain waves, brain rhythms which are usually associated with "true" intuitive creativity. Theta waves often appear when a person is in a relaxed state of deep reverie or meditation—a state of consciousness little known in the Western world but common to Yoga practitioners and similar to some conscious dreamlike states in which hypnagogic images are perceived. However, while it takes months or years of practice by the Yogi to achieve this state, Dr. Green forsees his biofeedback-trained subjects needing only a matter of weeks to reach it.

Although The Menninger Foundation has long been synonymous with excellence in psychiatric care, few realize the extent and significance of research being conducted here—research designed to better understand complex mechanisms which link psychological and physiological functioning.

A small nucleus of men and more than $200,-000 worth of electronic equipment are being devoted to this study under the somewhat ponderous label, Psychophysiology Laboratory.

But even in this rather well-equipped lab, several projects are hampered for lack of necessary equipment, and funds for equipment continue to be a major problem.

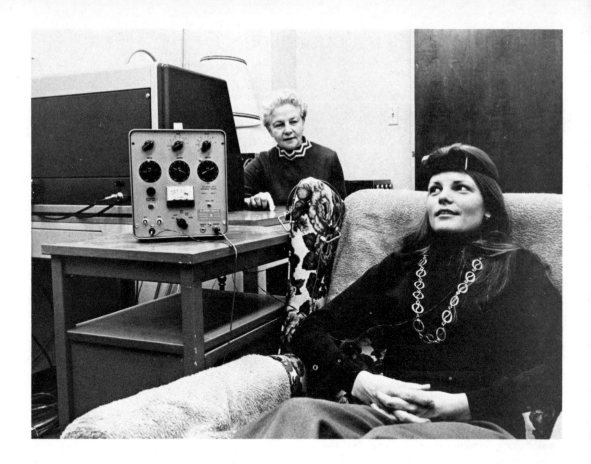

Mrs. Alyce Green of the Voluntary Control Project gives training instructions to the subject concerning the portable EEG feedback trainer used in developing voluntary control of beta, alpha, and theta brain waves.

To those who are unfamiliar with the complex terminology and imposing electronic equipment, the Psychophysiology Lab may seem a scientific ivory tower where researchers delve into realms of little practicality. On the contrary, data from these studies have tremendous practical application not only in areas of mental and physical health but in the study of education, the nature of creativity and many other fields as well. Inroads are being forged in fields previously shrouded in mystery.

"We all know there is such a thing as psychosomatic illness—why shouldn't there be psychosomatic health? If a person can make himself sick then he ought to be able to make himself well."

Dr. Green predicts that one day many heart, circulatory and psychosomatic diseases will be treated without pill or scalpel.

THE AUTOKINETIC PHENOMENON

A proposed project which may support Dr. Green's statement is being implemented by Dr. Harold Voth. Dr. Voth has long been interested in the autokinetic phenomenon—the apparent movement seen by almost anyone who looks steadily at a fixed pinpoint of light in otherwise total darkness.

The term "ego-close" was applied to those who perceive little or no movement and "ego-distant" to those who perceive movement.

The ego-close person is found to be more closely tied to external events and is more directly responsive to others around him—more influenced by his environment. He is less individualistic but is more in harmony with his surroundings and much more concerned with social ties.

The ego-distant person, on the other hand, is less subject to direct influence by social pressures and is freer to experience thought and fantasy. He is harder to know, more independent and more self-sufficient.

Dr. Voth stresses that autokinesis does not measure or indicate illness. He theorizes, however, that should illness develop, the amount and pattern of autokinesis may be a prediction of form and cause.

Based on this premise, Dr. Voth is planning further studies which may indicate that certain personality characteristics may predispose the individual to cancer. He suggests that certain unconscious conflicts may have something to do with cancer sites. For example, one form of conflict may be more related to cancer of the breast while another constellation of conflict may have more bearing on cancer of the cervix. Dr. Voth also suggests healthy emotional states may increase an individual's resistance to cancer.

"Why not?" he asks. "We know that individuals are more susceptible to other somatic illness when depressed. Why can't certain types of emotional conflicts make some parts of the body more vulnerable to cancer? and why can't healthy emotional states increase resistance?"

———————————

PERCEPTION AND BRAIN FUNCTIONING

The relationship between perception and certain types of brain wave activities is being investigated by Dr. Howard Shevrin and colleagues. Dr. Shevrin has been able to verify the relationship between certain forms of perception and a special brain wave called the average evoked response. The average evoked response makes it possible for the first time to study the brain's reaction to a specific stimulus.

71. A Separate Reality: Further Conversations with Don Juan

CARLOS CASTAÑEDA. The Bodley Head Ltd., 9 Bow Street, London WC2E 7AL; 1971; £2.25; 317 pp.

As Edmund Carpenter has noted, " for some anthropologists, the real world is not what is lived, but rather, it is the underlying structures (laws) that govern appearances. Thus they are bent on making anthropology a science of the same type as the physical sciences, for those too reject appearances and insist that reality is not in them but in the laws that govern them. "

Castañeda returns with Don Juan, the Yaqui sorcerer, master, and metaphysician to whom he apprenticed himself. The result is a special kind of anthropological trip, one that presents and illuminates the living reality, the human edge. JB

His premise was that a light and amenable disposition was needed in order to withstand the impact and the strangeness of the knowledge he was teaching me.

"The reason you got scared and quit is because you felt too damn important, " he said, explaining my previous withdrawal. "Feeling important makes one heavy, clumsy, and vain. To be a man of knowledge one needs to be light and fluid. "

"But if nothing matters, don Juan, why should it matter that I learn to see? "

"I told you once that our lot as men is to learn, for good or bad, " he said. "I have learned to see and I tell you that nothing really matters; now it is your turn; perhaps some day you will see and you will know then whether things matter or not. For me nothing matters, but perhaps for you everything will. You should know by now that a man of knowledge lives by acting, not by thinking about acting, nor by thinking about what he will think when he has finished acting. A man of knowledge chooses a path with heart and follows it; and then he looks and rejoices and laughs; and then he sees and knows. He knows that his life will be over altogether too soon; he knows that he, as well as everybody else, is not going anywhere; he knows, because he sees, that nothing is more important than anything else. In other words, a man of knowledge has no honor, no dignity, no family, no name, no country, but only life to be lived, and under these circumstances his only tie to his fellow men is his controlled folly.

"Death is a whorl, " he said. "Death is the face of the ally; death is a shiny cloud over the horizon; death is the whisper of Mescalito in your ears; death is the toothless mount of the guardian; death is Genaro sitting on his head; death is me talking; death is you and your writing pad; death is nothing. Nothing! It is here yet it isn't here at all. "

Don Juan looked at me and there was such sadness in his eyes that I began to weep. Tears fell freely. For the first time in my life I felt the encumbering weight of my reason. An indescribable anguish overtook me. I wailed involuntarily and embraced him. He gave me a quick blow with his knuckles on the top of my head. I felt it like a ripple down my spine. It had a sobering effect.

"You indulge too much, " he said softly.

72. Journey to Ixtlan: The Lessons of Don Juan

CARLOS CASTAÑEDA. Simon & Schuster, Inc., 630 Fifth Avenue, New York, N.Y. 10020; 1972; or *Real Time*. $6.95; 315 pp.

Volume three of Castañeda's encounters with Mexican-Indian *brujo* Don Juan, and perhaps the best. This is the most epistemological of the books, dropping the vision of a transcendent, drug-induced reality for the more finite reality of description. The parts of the book that deal with the descriptive process are surpassed only by the appendix of book one, in which Castañeda detailed a new descriptive anthropological structure for dealing with non-ordinary states of reality.

The interest aroused by these books makes one wonder just who this Don Juan really is. Here's the secret recipe: Take one part Buddha, add some Lao-tse, sprinkle with Ezra Pound, mix well with Clifford Irving, and serve with lots of dope. JB

He pointed out that everyone who comes into contact with a child is a teacher who incessantly describes the world to him, until the moment when the child is capable of perceiving the world as it is described. According to don Juan, we have no memory of that portentous moment, simply because none of us could possibly have had any point of reference to compare it to anything else. From that moment on, however, the child is a *member*. He knows the description of the world; and his *membership* becomes full-fledged, I suppose, when he is capable of making all the proper perceptual interpretations which, by conforming to that description, validate it.

For don Juan, then, the reality of our day-to-day life consists of an endless flow of perceptual interpretations which we, the individuals who share a specific *membership,* have learned to make in common.

The idea that the perceptual interpretations that make up the world have a flow is congruous with the fact that they run uninterruptedly and are rarely, if ever, open to question. In fact, the reality of the world we know is so taken for granted that the basic premise of sorcery, that our reality is merely one of many descriptions, could hardly be taken as a serious proposition.

"You see," he went on, "we only have two alternatives; we either take everything for sure and real, or we don't. If we follow the first, we end up bored to death with ourselves and with the world. If we follow the second and erase personal history, we create a fog around us, a very exciting and mysterious state in which nobody knows where the rabbit will pop out, not even ourselves."

"Look at me," he said. "I have no doubts or remorse. Everything I do is my decision and my responsibility. The simplest thing I do, to take you for a walk in the desert, for instance, may very well mean my death. Death is stalking me. Therefore, I have no room for doubts or remorse. If I have to die as a result of taking you for a walk, then I must die.

"You, on the other hand, feel that you are immortal, and the decisions of an immortal man can be canceled or regretted or doubted. In a world where death is the hunter, my friend, there is no time for regrets or doubts. There is only time for decisions."

"Well . . . are we equals?" he asked.

"Of course we're equals," I said.

I was, naturally, being condescending. I felt very warm towards him even though at times I did not know what to do with him; yet I still held in the back of my mind, although I would never voice it, the belief that I, being a university student, a man of the sophisticated Western world, was superior to an Indian.

"No," he said calmly, "we are not."

"Why, certainly we are," I protested.

"No," he said in a soft voice. "We are not equals. I am a hunter and a warrior, and you are a pimp."

My mouth fell open. I could not believe that don Juan had actually said that. I dropped my notebook and stared at him dumbfoundedly and then, of course, I became furious.

He looked at me with calm and collected eyes. I avoided his gaze. And then he began to talk. He enunciated his words clearly. They poured out smoothly and deadly. He said that I was pimping for someone else. That I was not fighting my own battles but the battles of some unknown people. That I did not want to learn about plants or about hunting or about anything. And that his world of precise acts and feelings and decisions was infinitely more effective than the blundering idiocy I called "my life."

I protested. My feeling was that my life was becoming increasingly more and more secretive. He said I had not understood his point, and that to be unavailable did not mean to hide or to be secretive but to be inaccessible.

"Let me put it another way," he proceeded patiently. "It makes no difference to hide if everyone knows that you are hiding.

"Your problems right now stem from that. When you are hiding, everyone knows that you are hiding, and when you are not, you are available for everyone to take a poke at you."

I was beginning to feel threatened and hurriedly tried to defend myself.

"Don't explain yourself," don Juan said dryly. "There is no need. We are fools, all of us, and you cannot be different. At one time in my life I, like you, made myself available over and over again until there was nothing of me left for anything except perhaps crying. And that I did, just like yourself."

"We're not talking about the same thing," he said. "For you the world is weird because if you're not bored with it you're at odds with it. For me the world is weird because it is stupendous, awesome, mysterious, unfathomable; my interest has been to convince you that you must assume responsibility for being here, in this marvelous world, in this marvelous desert, in this marvelous time. I wanted to convince you that you must learn to make every act count, since you are going to be here for only a short while, in fact, too short for witnessing all the marvels of it."

SCIENCE AND TECHNOLOGY

73. Passion to Know: The World's Scientists

MITCHELL WILSON. Weidenfeld & Nicolson Ltd., 11 St. John's Hill, London SW11 1XA; 1972; £4.75; 409 pp.

The late Mitchell Wilson entered a career in physics shortly after finishing his schooling. He went on to work with Enrico Fermi and I. I. Rabi, and to develop a passion for science. Later he became a novelist. Wilson has come back to science to call attention to the men and women he thinks are making the most powerful and important decisions of our time.

In *Passion to Know* Wilson creates still another mythic class of giants. His scientists are humble, proud, excellent, selfless and rarely take pride in their own discoveries, creations, or accomplishments. Wilson's portraits go beyond the personal elements deep into the work of scientists in the U.S., the U.S.S.R., France, England, Germany, Israel, Japan, Australia, and India. ER

Three crushing lessons lie in wait for almost every man if he lives long enough. He discovers that he is thoroughly resistible. He discovers that he is entirely replaceable. Most terrible of all, he discovers he is completely forgettable. One has to be an Einstein, a Shakespeare, a Rembrandt, a Mozart, or a Moliere to escape the fate of the millions of brilliant and talented men who, since the beginning of recorded history, were celebrated by their contemporaries, but already half forgotten on the way home from their funerals.

What interested me far more than celebrity was the differences in national styles in doing science; in the way young men and women selected themselves in different countries to be scientists; the different ways they educated themselves in science; how variously ideas could be translated into experiments, how differently experiments could be performed. Most important of all are the different ways in which various societies react to the results of these experiments.

To me, these differences are of prime importance—they reflect a society's past, and imply its future—because I am one of those who believe that the shape of any society in our time is determined far more profoundly by developments in its science and technology than by any political act or bill passed by that society's Parliament or Congress. Research work done in the 1930's in the United States in the development of synthetic plastics, electronics, aviation, the physics of the solid state and the atomic nucleus, has done more to shape the America of the 1970's than all the New Deal legislation under successive Roosevelt administrations.

This sense of being on the side of the future is probably what makes science seem always exciting and full of promise to the men who work in it. To the scientist, age comes as a surprise—a rather unfair surprise. He has been so busy all along with his eyes on the distant future that he is shocked to discover that his own biological life span has been ticking off on a far shorter time scale. The brilliant young men of twenty-five who worked out the elements of the quantum theory in the 1920's suddenly find themselves men of seventy when their once-strange ideas are at last being accepted as part of conventional thought. What a cruel joke it must seem to men who spent so much time being the radical young innovators! Hermann Minkowski, the mathematician who put Einstein's special relativity theory into the elegant form which gave rise to the idea of time as the "fourth dimension," sighed as he lay waiting for death: "What a pity to have to die just when relativity is about to be recognized!"

Why does a man become a scientist? Why does he devote his life to research in one particular discipline?

"I. I. Rabi at Columbia said flatly: 'Because physics is the only basic science there is. Everything else is to the right of it and depends on it. Nothing is to the left of it.'

"Max Perutz in Cambridge said just as flatly: 'Molecular biology is the basic science of life; it is now the only way one knows what one is talking about.'

"Allan Sandage at Mount Palomar says: 'Astronomy and cosmology—that's where the great questions still have to be answered.'

"Jacques Monod of the Pasteur Institute says: 'Why biology? Well, because I felt that was where the most work was to be done.' "

―――――――――――――――

A composer looked at me with surprise when I happened to mention that the scientist experienced creativity in exactly the same way as the artist. "But what does he create?" he asked. "I thought he dealt only with logical processes—deductions from experiment."

Creativity for the scientist does have certain characteristics that are unique. To begin with, the scientist picks his problem because he knows enough about it to know that no one knows very much about it—except that there are unanswered questions there. Out of insight or inspiration, he suggests a possible answer to one of the questions: for example, What *is* a possible structure for the atom? What *does* bind the atoms together to form molecules? By *what* means does the living cell store the chemical energy released within its walls? The creative moment occurs when the suggested answer is being formed. Naturally, the scientist would like to be proved right, and so the performance of the deciding experiment can never be the dispassionate exercise it is popularly thought to be. Experiment carries all the emotion of a contest. Objectivity lies in the scientist's willingness to accept, however reluctantly, evidence that his brilliant conception is wrong. Once nature gives its decision, there is no appeal. In fairly short order then, the scientist is ruthlessly informed whether his creation is valid or not. The artist, on the other hand, has no such objective standard. He can always find, or invent, an esthetic system to justify his creation.

74. Science and the Modern World

ALFRED NORTH WHITEHEAD. The Free Press, 866 Third Avenue, New York, N.Y. 10022; 1925; or *Real Time*. (P) $1.95; 212 pp.
The Macmillan Company, 866 Third Avenue, New York, N.Y. 10022; or *Real Time*. (H) $6.95.

Science, aesthetics, ethics, and religion are the basic human interests that suggest cosmologies and are, in turn, influenced by them. This work is a broad outline of the past three centuries in terms of how the cosmology derived from science has been asserting itself at the expense of older points of view with their origins elsewhere. Written in 1925, it is still up-to-date reading. JB

Primarily, the mental apprehension is aroused by the occurrences in certain parts of the correlated body, the occurrences in the brain, for instance. But the mind in apprehending also experiences sensations which, properly speaking, are qualities of the mind alone. These sensations are projected by the mind so as to clothe appropriate bodies in external nature. Thus the bodies are perceived as with qualities which in reality do not belong to them, qualities which in fact are purely the off-spring of the mind. Thus nature gets credit which should in truth be reserved for ourselves: the rose for its scent: the nightingale for his song: and the sun for his radiance. The poets are entirely mistaken. They should address their lyrics to themselves, and should turn them into odes of self-congratulation on the excellency of the human mind. Nature is a dull affair, soundless, scentless, colourless; merely the hurrying of material, endlessly, meaninglessly.

But we have to admit that the body is the organism whose states regulate our cognisance of the world. The unity of the perceptual field therefore must be a unity of bodily experience. In being aware of the bodily experience, we must thereby be aware of aspects of the whole spatio-temporal world as mirrored within the bodily life. . . . my theory involves the entire abandonment of the notion that simple location is the primary way in which things are involved in space-time. In a certain sense, everything is everywhere at all times. For every location involves an aspect of itself in every other location. Thus every spatio-temporal standpoint mirrors the world.

In the immediate past, and at present, a muddled state of mind is prevalent. The increased plasticity of the environment for mankind, resulting from the advances in scientific technology, is being construed in terms of habits of thought which find their justification in the theory of a fixed environment.

These instruments have put thought on to a new level. A fresh instrument serves the same purpose as foreign travel; it shows things in unusual combinations. The gain is more than a mere addition; it is a transformation. The advance in experimental ingenuity is, perhaps, also due to the largest proportion of national ability which now flows into scientific pursuits. Anyhow, whatever be the cause, subtle and ingenious experiments have abounded within the last generation. The result is, that a great deal of information has been accumulated in regions of nature very far removed from the ordinary experience of mankind. ------

A clash of doctrines is not a disaster—it is an opportunity. ------

Importance depends on endurance. Endurance is the retention through time of an achievement of value. What endures is identity of pattern, self-inherited. Endurance requires the favourable environment. The whole of science revolves round this question of enduring organisms.

75. Philosophy and Technology

Edited, with an introduction by CARL MITCHAM and ROBERT MACKEY. The Free Press, Distrib: Collier-Macmillan Publishers, 35 Red Lion Square, London WC1R 4SG; 1973; £5.85; 399 pp.

An interesting reader, chronologically re-creating the development of the philosophy of technology as a specific discipline. The essays are by twenty-four thinkers including Lewis Mumford, Jacques Ellul, Emmanuel Mesthene, and Lynn White, Jr. The book is divided into five major categories: conceptual, ethical, religious, existential, and metaphysical.

The editors of the volume are Carl Mitcham, an Instructor in Philosophy at Berea College, and Robert Mackey, a graduate student at Brandeis University. JB

The art of observation is not universal but specific for a given field or subject matter. Whenever observation plays a significant role in scientific investigation, it is selective observation directed toward perceiving some objects and their configurations and toward neglecting others. Observation, however, is not only a perceptual process but also involves some conceptual thinking. Certain types of observation are intrinsically connected with thinking in terms of certain categories.

In general, it seems to me that *specific branches of learning originate and condition specific modes of thinking, develop and adhere to categories through which they can best express their content and by means of which they can further progress.*

Henryk Skolimowski

So truth is not the same as effectiveness. And when we talk of knowledge we usually mean knowledge of truth. What I shall suggest is that knowledge of effectiveness is knowledge of truth too, even if it is on a different logical level. It is, so to speak, true knowledge of *what* is effective. It is not true knowledge of *why* it is effective; it does not *explain* anything. But it is part and parcel of the whole truth, nevertheless.

The ancients left us with an idea of knowledge as proved truths. Contemporary philosophy has smashed this idea to smithereens and decreed that only the tautologies of logic and mathematics can be proved, but tautologies like " all tables are tables " can hardly be knowledge, since they don't tell us anything. So a new conception of knowledge has arisen which discards proved truth and places the following mental reservation before all scientific assertions: " This is a hypothesis, the best we can suggest at the moment. It will be revised as soon as we have reason to doubt it. " Nowadays, then, knowledge with a capital K is generally taken to be putatively true statements; that is, statements tentatively advanced in the belief that they might be true and should be tested. Scientific knowledge is generally taken to be putatively true statements about the *structure of the world*. That water boils at 100°C. is not a truth about the structure of the world, but a contingent fact about our local environment. Technology, it seems to me, is closer to knowing a lot of things whose *logical* status is like that of water boiling at 100°C., rather than like Newton's laws or Einstein's mass-energy equations. That there is a difference of level between these will be clear. It is perhaps not so easy to specify. Put briefly in a way that should become clearer later on, I would say that science aims at true laws which cover the entire physical world and explain the facts of the case about it. Knowhow is knowing what works, how to do things in a small part of that world, with a precision as high as is demanded.

I.C. Jarvie

Due emphasis should be given to the fact that the greatest miracle wrought by the human mind, the science of physics, originated in technology. The young Galileo worked not at a university, but in the arsenals there that his mind was shaped.

In fact, the new technology proceeds in exactly the same way as the *nuova scienza*. The engineer no longer passes directly from the image of the desired end to the search for the means which may obtain it. He stands before the envisaged aim and begins to work on it. He analyzes it. That is to say, he breaks the total result down into the components which have formed it—that is, into its " causes. "

This is the method applied to physics by Galileo, who is known to have been an eminent inventor to boot. An Aristotelian scientist would not have thought of splitting a phenomenon up into its elements. Approaching it in its totality he also tried to find a total cause; for the drowsiness produced by poppy juice the *virtus dormitiva.* Galileo proceeded in the opposite way. When observing an object in motion he asked for the elementary and therefore general movements of which the concrete movement was made up. This is the new mode for thinking: analysis of nature.

José Ortega y Gasset

Early in the eighteenth century, Vico enunciated the principle that man can understand only what he has made himself. From this he reasoned that not nature, which as made by God stands over against man, but history, which is of man's own making, can be understood by man. Only a *factum*—what has been made—can be a *verum.* But in opposing this principle to Cartesian natural science, Vico overlooked that fact that, if only " has been made " is widened to " can be made, " the principle applies to nature even better than to history (where, in fact, its validity is doubtful). For according to the mechanistic scheme the knowledge of a natural event deals, as we have seen, not with the God-created part of the situation—the intrinsic nature of the substances involved—but with the variable conditions which, given those substances, determine the event. By reenacting those conditions, in thought or in actual manipulation, one can reproduce the event without producing the substratum. To understand the substratum itself is as much beyond man's powers as to produce it. But the latter is beyond the powers even of nature, which, once created in its substantial entities, goes on "creating" only by manipulating them—that is, by the shift of relations.

Hans Jonas

To hold that technology serves man's purposes is only to fall back into the difficulty that the structure of technology cannot be fixed. After all, man's purposes are not fixed for they focus sometimes on means, sometimes on products, and sometimes on other ends; and there is no longer the firm *a priori* distinction between means, products, and ends as there was in Aristotle's time. Today we have to acknowledge that technology *as such* cannot be isolated from the multiplicity of uses to which it is put. In the face of its complexity and dominance, it no longer makes sense to maintain that technology is simply a neutral instrument which, for better or for worse, serves man. If nothing more can be said than that technology is something neutral, we are abandoned to a haphazard scattering of goods and evils, of productive and destructive tendencies, and the structure of technology escapes us. Any meaningful discussion must proceed, therefore, from a position independent of the specific goods and evils of the technological complex. Technology is the encompassing unity of these opposites; it is the whole phenomenon which is in question, and not just certain of its aspects. To say, then, that technology is adequately grasped when it stands in the proper relation to man, when it is properly used by man, is really not to say anything at all. Consequently technology must be understood in such a way that we can overcome these defects and grasp it as a whole.

Webster F. Hood

76. Data: Mirrors of Science

R. HOUWINK. Elsevier Publishing Co., Chandos House, 2 Queen Anne Street, London W1M 9LE; 1970; £4.50; 213 pp.

R. Houwink, a retired chemical engineer, is an honorary director of Euratom, the European Atomic Energy Organization. His book, *Data: Mirrors of Science*, shows that the understanding of measurement and data comes most easily through comparison. An example is the data in the concept of a nanosecond. A nanosecond is a billionth of a second, or 10^9 second. The clarifying comparison is that as many nanoseconds are contained in one second as there are seconds contained in thirty years. ER

DATA AND IMAGES

Nothing can be more fatal to progress than a too confident reliance on mathematical symbols and data; for the student is only apt to take the easier course, and consider the data, and not the fact as the physical reality.
(Freely quoted after Lord Kelvin)

1.1 CONVERTING DATA INTO IMAGES

It is perhaps interesting to devise graphic or pictorial comparisons and interpretations that will make numerical data more understandable and meaningful than just numbers alone.

As an example, we read about the distances of stars in terms of light-years—even the nearest is about 4-1/2 light-years away from the solar system—and, perhaps on the same page, about the 100 kilometers (km) or 60 miles, separating two islands.

Now the light-year, 10 million million (10^{13}) kilometers (km), is 10^{11} times the distance between the islands, and while most of us can recognize the mathematical convenience of expressing the very large ratio in this way, we suffer meanwhile from a sort of " imagination vacuum " on making any attempt to visualize what 10^{11} is, taken purely as a number and neglecting its deeper implications. However, an image which perhaps helps in this case is comparison of the thickness of a human hair with the diameter of the Earth, for which the ratio is also 10^{11}

1.2 EASY TO KEEP IN MIND . . .

Keep in mind the number 3.5×10^9 (as an average between 3000 and 4000 million) and you have an idea of the order of magnitude of:
—the number of years which have elapsed since the earth solidified
—the number of people on the earth
—the number of cells in a man's brain
—the number of heart beats in a man's life.

Keep in mind the numbers ranging between 10^{11} and 10^{12} and you will have an idea of:
—the ratio between the diameter of the Earth and that of a human hair
—the ratio between the weight of the world's largest liner ever built, the Queen Elizabeth (83,000 brt) and that of a bee (1 gram)
—the number of gallons in a cubic mile (9×10^{11})

Keep in mind the numbers ranging between 10^{12} and 10^{13} and you will have an idea of:
—the number of cubic kilometers, contained in the Earth (10^{12})
—the annual electricity consumption in the world expressed in kilowatt-hours (4×10^{12})
—the number of kilometers in a light-year (10^{13})

8.26 LIVES SHORT AND LONG

We can take the present maximum lifetime which a man can expect as 120 years; calling this 1 minute, on a new time scale, the period of time since the solidification of the Earth (3.5×10^9 years ago) becomes 50 years.

The oldest material so far found which may be termed "living" is bacterial matter from Lower Cambrian salt beds which, on release from the mineral mass, resumes the normal life of this type of organism, even though it has been so long underground, and its total age can be represented by 10 years on our "compressed" time scale.

As to other long-lived organisms, Sequoia pines in California have lived for 1 "hour"—6000 real years—and in the animal world, turtles hold the crown. These slow-living reptiles may bridge a century or two, which ages up to 2.5 minutes on our scale, even more than the oldest human may expect.

8.27 ODD BITS

In one year there are as many generations of banana flies as the generations of man since the Crusades, 700 years ago.

A North African species of mice is capable of mating no less than 100 times in an hour.

A queen bee can lay her own weight in eggs in one single day. If a hen produced on this scale it would lay 45 eggs daily.

In the evolutionary history of the horse, the appearance of a recognizably different type of animal has, on the average, required 2.5 million years.

Camels, in their hump—or humps—have a most useful reserve source of water, for by the use in their bodies of the fat reserve from the humps, which may amount to 50 kg (110 lb), water is formed in the amount of around 50 liters (11 gallons).

White ants are so effective as excavators that, if they were scaled up to human size, they would have no difficulty in driving a tunnel of 100 meters diameter (about 330 feet).

Germinating grain gives out heat, in terms of calories per gram at about 70% of a man's heat output of 1 calories per gram (of body weight) per hour, thus at about the same rate as that for a snail.

In a European dairy herd, the cows yield about 6 to 7 times their own body weight in milk each year—4000 liters, about 900 gallons.

While a man is asleep, his heart, no larger than his fist, pumps about one teacupful (60 cm^3) of blood into his circulatory system per second. But if, after breakfast, he has to run to catch his morning train, the heart has to increase its output to a beer-bottleful (300 cm^3) per second.

In the past year your red corpuscles have traveled a distance equal to 2-1/2 times round the world.

In one year, you drink about 13 times your own weight of water, and breathe about 7 times your own weight of oxygen.

Ant hills, with a population up to about that of Amsterdam in Holland, or Vancouver, Canada, about 1 million, surely are among the world's largest houses.

Plankton in the Earth's seas and oceans takes up more of the element iron each year than the worldwide production of iron in blast furnaces.

77. Asimov's Biographical Encyclopedia of Science and Technology

ISAAC ASIMOV. Allen & Unwin Ltd., 40 Museum Street, London WC1A 1LU; 1967; £4.50; 805 pp.

Scientists are highly motivated people. Their sense of mental homeostasis is considerable. How else could Richard Feynman continue his Nobel Prize winning efforts at physics and still be ". . . renowned for his ability to handle the bongo drums at parties." Other aspects of theoretical physics, brought to light in this extraordinary volume, include the contributions of beer to the lives of James Joule and Niels Bohr. Joule was the son of a wealthy brewer and Bohr's pre-WWII institute for atomic studies was supported by Carlsberg.

Asimov provides 1195 biographical sketches running chronologically from the Third Egyptian Dynasty to twentieth-century astrophysics. Each entry contains Asimov's life portrait of the scientist, a brief explanation of the work accomplished, and, in many cases, apt anecdotal material. ER

[1] IMHOTEP (im-hoh' tep)
Egyptian scholar
Born: near Memphis
Flourished 2980-2950 B.C.

Imhotep is remarkable for being the first historic equivalent, known by name, of what we would today call a scientist. There was not to be another for over two thousand years.

The one definite feat that is attributed to him is that of being the architect of the "step pyramid" at the modern village of Sakkara (near the site of ancient Memphis) in Egypt. This was the earliest of the Egyptian pyramids, and if Imhotep was indeed the architect, he may be credited with a literally monumental first.

[138] BRUNO, Giordano
Italian philosopher
Born: Nola (near Naples), January 1548
Died: Rome, February 17, 1600

Bruno was born of very poor parents, was educated at the University of Naples, and entered a Dominican monastery. He held unpopular opinions with fearlessness and had the ability to attract huge audiences by his speaking and writing. (He had also developed a system of mnemonics—a memory course, so to speak—which proved most popular.)

Bruno preached the opinions of Nicholas of Cusa [106] concerning the infinity of space, the inhabitability of other worlds, the motions of the earth, and so on. His clearly expressed scorn of traditional opinions, even more in religion than in science, got him in trouble everywhere.

Changing his name to Filippo Giordano for safety, he fled first to Rome, then to Geneva. In Geneva, the Calvinists ejected him and he went to Paris where he was patronized by Henry III, but where the Aristotelians also ejected him. He wandered over Europe, lecturing at Oxford, England, in 1582 and in Germany for some years after 1586. In 1592 he was arrested in Venice by the Inquisition and charged with heresy.

[219] FAHRENHEIT, Gabriel Daniel (fah' ren-
hite)
German-Dutch physicist
Born: Danzig (now Gdansk, Poland), May 14, 1686
Died: The Hague, Netherlands, September 16, 1736

Early in life Fahrenheit emigrated to Amsterdam for a business education. By profession he was a manufacturer of meteorological instruments. Obviously one of the chief devices that can be used for studying climate is a thermometer. The thermometers of the seventeenth century, however, such as the gas thermometer of Galileo [146], were insufficiently exact for the purpose.

Fluid thermometers had come into use, but they used either alcohol or alcohol-water mixtures. Alcohol alone boiled at too low a temperature to allow high temperatures to be measured, and alcohol-water mixtures, which did a bit better in this respect, changed volume with changing temperature in too uneven a way.

[1069] GÖDEL, Kurt (ger'del)
Austrian-American mathematician
Born: Brünn, Austria-Hungary
(now Brno, Czechoslovakia),
April 28, 1906

Godel studied at the University of Vienna, obtaining his Ph.D. in 1930. He then joined its faculty.

In 1931 he published a paper which marked the culmination of the search for a new mathematical certainty, a search which had been going on for a full century, since Lobachevski [407] and Bolyai [442] had shattered the old certainty of Euclid [35].

With the establishment of non-Euclidean geometries, it had been realized that Euclid's revered axioms were insufficient. Men like Hilbert [752] had established new and far better axiom systems for geometry. Other mathematicians had used the symbolic logic of Boole [493] to try to establish axioms that would serve as a rigorous starting point for all of mathematics. Frege's [657] attempt had been frustrated by Russell [821], whose own attempt, with Whitehead [748], had been the most ambitious of all.

But two decades after the Russell-Whitehead structure had been published, Gödel advanced what has come to be called Gödel's proof. He translated the symbols of symbolic logic into numbers in a systematic way and showed that it was always possible to construct a number which could not be arrived at by the other numbers of his system.

What it amounted to was this: Gödel had shown that if you began with any set of axioms, there would always be statements, within the system governed by those axioms, that could be neither proved nor disproved on the basis of those axioms. If the axioms are modified in such a way that that statement could then be either proved or disproved, then another statement can be constructed which cannot be either proved or disproved, and so on forever.

In still other words, the totality of mathematics cannot be brought to complete order on the basis of any system of axioms. Every mathematical system, however complex, will always contain unresolvable paradoxes of the sort that Russell used to upset Frege's system.

Gödel had ended the search for certainty in mathematics by showing that it did not and could not exist, just as Heisenberg [1023] had done for the physical sciences with his Uncertainty Principle five years earlier.

Gödel formed a connection with the Institute for Advanced Studies at Princeton shortly after his paper was published. In 1940 he made the United States his permanent home and in 1948 he was naturalized an American citizen.

[1195] SAGAN, Carl (say'gan)
American astronomer
Born: New York, New York, November 9, 1934

Sagan obtained his Ph.D. at the University of Chicago in 1960.

He is primarily interested in planetary surfaces and atmospheres, a field which rose out of the doldrums with Kuiper's [1065] researches and the advent of rocketry. Thus, he worked out a greenhouse model for the atmosphere of Venus, accounting for the otherwise puzzling high temperature of the planet. He also found evidence for elevation differences on the surface of Mars and for organic molecules in the atmosphere of Jupiter.

Further in the periphery of his interests but possessing added glamour is the question of the probabilities of life on other planets and of the origin of life on ours. (It is not surprising that he is another of those scientists who are fond of reading science fiction.) He has been one of a group trying to form compounds from a system that mimics the conditions of the primordial earth, attempting to pass beyond the amino acids and into the building blocks of the nucleic acids. In 1963 he succeeded in detecting the formation of adenosine triphosphate (ATP), the prime energy-store of living tissue. Thus, it seems quite reasonable to visualize the formation of a chemical energy-store in the oceans, building up steadily at the expense of solar energy and serving as a ready source of energy for the production of complex nucleic acids and proteins; in short, for the production of life.

In 1968 he transferred his operations to Cornell University where he is an associate professor of astronomy and the director of its Laboratory for Planetary Studies. In 1969 he accepted a position of editor of the astronomical journal, *Icarus*.

78. Beyond the Observatory

HARLOW SHAPLEY. Charles Scribner's Sons, 597 Fifth Avenue, New York, N.Y. 10017; 1967; or *Real Time*. (H) $4.50; (P) $1.45; 223 pp.

Harlow Shapley was Director of the Harvard College Observatory for over thirty years. In this slim volume of essays, he surveys sociological aspects of various scientific disciplines that have captured his imagination. JB

I shall enumerate, without immediate explanation, the ten revelations or achievements of the twentieth century which seem to me to have most profoundly affected the lives and thoughts of mankind. Since this listing refers to the present century only, radioactivity, the origin of species (Darwinism), and spectrum analysis are not included.

1. Knowledge of the chemistry of life's origin
2. Cosmic evolution—neutrons to man and beyond
3. Relativity theories—special and general
4. The corpuscular sciences
5. Automation and computers (cybernetics)
6. Space exploration
7. Galaxies, quasars, and the expanding universe
8. Medical triumphs
9. Molecular biology—viruses and DNA
10. Exploration of the mind

I shall list here thirty facts that we can now deduce from appropriate studies of a single star image. The first eighteen of these facts can be discovered about any star.

1. The position in the sky with reference to other stars.
2. The apparent magnitude (brightness) with reference to stellar or artificial standards.
3. The color index (found by comparing the brightness in various spectrum intervals—that is, measuring the color tint: reddish, yellowish, greenish, or bluish).
4. The variability in light; it may be zero.
5. The spectral class in two dimensions.
6. The variability, if any, in spectrum class.
7. The chemical compositon of the stellar atmosphere and the consequent nature of the atomic transformations that maintain the radiation.
8. The approximate age.
9. Whether it is single or double (found in various ways).
10. The existence and strength of magnetic field.
11. The involvement with interstellar nebulosity.
12. The speed of rotation.
13. The tilt of the rotational axis.
14. The speed in the line of sight, and variations, regular or irregular, in that speed.
15. The cross motion—measurable only if the distance of the star is small or the speed is great.
16. The surface temperature.
17. The total luminosity (candle power).
18. The diameter.

The next eight facts can also be learned if the star is an eclipsing binary—a double star whose light varies because the two members of the system periodically eclipse each other.

19. The mean density of the two components.
20. The period of revolution.
21. The geometry of the eclipse—and whether it is total or partial.
22. The degree of darkening at the limb.
23. The ratio of the sizes of the two components.
24. The eccentricity of the relative orbit.
25. The inclination of the orbital plane.
26. The approximate distance.

---

79. Cosmic View: The Universe in 40 Jumps

KEES BOEKE. Faber & Faber Ltd., 3 Queen Square, London WC1N 3AU; 1957; £0.75; 48 pp.

Perception is a question of frame, of focus. Boeke who was a Dutch schoolteacher, presents us with a journey through the galaxy both without and within, in a series of drawings each seen from a point ten times farther out or ten times closer than the previous one. JB

We all, children and grownups alike, are inclined to live in our own little world, in our immediate surroundings, or at any rate with our attention concentrated on those things with which we are directly in touch. We tend to forget how vast are the ranges of existing reality which our eyes cannot directly see, and our attitudes may become narrow and provincial. We need to develop a wider outlook, to see ourselves in our relative position in the great and mysterious universe in which we have been born and live.

At school we are introduced to many different spheres of existence, but they are often not connected with each other, so that we are in danger of collecting a large number of images without realizing that they all join together in one great whole. It is therefore important in our education to find the means of developing a wider and more connected view of our world and a truly cosmic view of the universe and our place in it.

This book presents a series of forty pictures composed so that they may help to develop this wider view. They really give a series of views as seen during an imaginary and fantastic journey through space—a journey in one direction, straight upward from the place where it begins. Although these views are as true to reality as they can be made with our present knowledge, they portray a wonderland as full of marvels as that which Alice saw in her dreams.

1. The first picture, from which we start, is as we said already one of a child sitting in front of the school, with a cat on her lap. It is drawn on a scale of 1 to 10. This means that a centimeter on the drawing is in reality 10 centimeters. A centimeter (abbreviated "cm.") is the hundredth part of a meter, which corresponds to the yard as a unit of length. To be precise, a meter is 3.37 inches longer than 1 yard. One centimeter is therefore nearly 0.4 inch. In both length and height, the picture measures 15 centimeters, or nearly 6 inches. An arrow shows the direction of north.

1 cm. in picture = 10 cm. in actuality.   Scale of picture therefore = 1:10

6

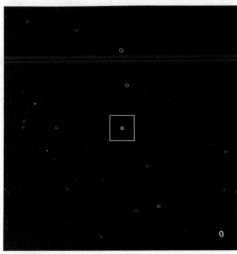

5. We have now jumped to a height of 50,000 meters or 50 kilometers, that is more than 30 miles, and we notice a second effect of our jumps: not only are all lengths we see reduced tenfold each time, but the area which comes into our field of vision increases a hundredfold. So the above illustration covers a square 15 kilometers on a side, and we see Bilthoven (1) as a suburb of Utrecht (2). A dotted wavy line symbolizes a radio wave of 298 meters wave length reaching Bilthoven from the transmitter southwest of Utrecht, called "Hilversum" after the town (3) where its studios are. The 1.5-centimeter square in the middle gives again, as it has done each time, a reduced representation of the preceding illustration. As this illustration contains a photograph of a detailed plan of Bilthoven, it just shows the houses, though very minutely.

1 cm. in picture = 10^5 cm. = 1,000 m. = 1 km.   Scale = 1:100,000 = 1:10^5

10

16. The tiny circle inside the smallest square now contains the whole field in which the vicissitudes of the solar system take place. If we continue the reckoning we used in drawings 4, 5, and 9, we should be now at a height of 5 million million kilometers above the horizon of that village in Holland from where we started. As we have imagined all along that we are making our trip without spending time, this means that it would have taken the light rays which we now see more than six months to cover the enormous distance from the earth, even though they travel at the rate of 299,800 kilometers per second! It also means that if we had a marvellously good telescope and could see details of events on earth, the events we watched would be those that happened more than six months ago!

1 cm. in picture = 10^{16} cm. = 100,000,000,000 km.   Scale = 1:10^{16}

21

26. In this last picture of the series at reduced scales, we naturally find that all galaxies and groups of galaxies, even the largest of them, are reduced to dots of various sizes. It goes without saying that the placing of them has been of necessity quite arbitrary. The object is merely to give a very faint idea of the inconceivably large number of galaxies in the midst of which our Milky Way is placed. The number of galaxies which are visible with our present telescopes is of the nature of a thousand million. The farthest of these would be at a distance from the earth of 2,000 million light years, that is, something like the length of a diagonal of the large square above. What is drawn here is therefore certainly less than what exists. For the galaxies would be much nearer to each other than the picture shows, and they would continue far beyond its confines. . . .

1 cm. in picture = 10^{26} cm. = about 100 million light-years.   Scale = 1:10^{26}

31

80. The View from Space: Photographic Exploration of the Planets

MERTON E. DAVIES and BRUCE C. MURRAY. Columbia University Press Ltd., 70 Great Russell Street, London WC1; 1972; £7.15; 163 pp.

The bigger the system at hand, the more available information and complexity. Going out to the solar-system model brings a new vantage to even the most casual interest. Since man wants to go to the planets, he sends surrogates first to make sure of what is going on out there.

The View from Space details the results that decades of research have revealed about the photographic and television data gathered from the earth, the moon and Mars, and goes on to speculate what might be found from investigations of Venus, Mercury, the sun, and the outer planets. Davies and Murray, from the Rand Corporation and Cal Tech, respectively, see space as a possible boon and a battleground, and evaluate many of the options inherent in both views. ER

Thus space is in some ways a mirror, reflecting the style, motivations, and even aspirations of the terrestrial societies which venture into it by the technologies, objectives, and priorities displayed there. The events in space of the last decade must be viewed in the context of the rivalry between the U.S. and the USSR—indeed this rivalry clearly has provided most of the priority for the development of space technology—but with very interesting national differences in approach,

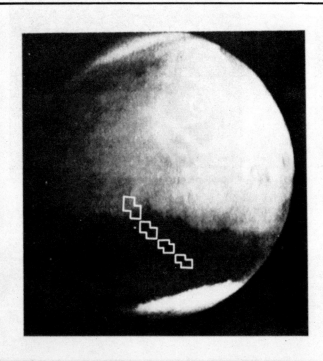

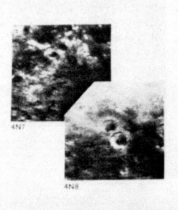

5.1 Mariner 4 frames located on Mariner 7 picture

scale, and emphasis. During the coming decades more countries will display their individual national signatures in the mirror of space.

Furthermore, space photography must itself be viewed in terms of the anatomy of space, of technological style, of relative use in exploration versus exploitation, and of its use in manned and in unmanned systems.

———————————

Mars is the only planet other than Earth that has so far been explored by means of close-up photography. After Mariner 4's first look, a pair of ambitious second generation photographic flybys were launched by the U.S. in the early spring of 1969 and returned two-hundred times the photographic data of Mariner 4, including not only a tenfold increase in resolution but also much-needed global photography. In addition, efforts are already underway for a pair of U.S. photographic

orbiters in 1971 as well as another pair in 1975 to support the first U.S. lander attempt. In each case, the choices of camera type, coverage/resolution combination, areas to be surveyed, and so on have been, or are being made, in the context of a variety of engineering, fiscal, and historical constraints as well as assessments of the probable scientific value of alternative schemes. Since the experience gained in the case of Mars may provide insight into photographic exploration of other planets and their satellites, and since the decision-making process in this part of the U.S. program can be reconstructed by us, it seems desirable to spend some time on this subject. First we shall review the background of the Mariner 4 photography experiment, and then proceed to the 1969, 1971, and 1975 missions which have evolved in succession from the original Mariner 4 success.

Eight of the 21 frames acquired by Mariner 4 on July 15, 1965, are shown in outline on frame 7F76 acquired by Mariner 7 on August 5, 1969. Processed and enhanced versions of the eight frames are reproduced to the right.

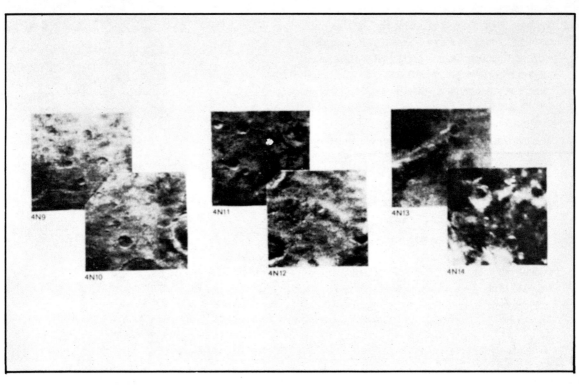

81. This Island Earth

Edited by ORAN W. HICKS. NASA. U.S. Superintendent of Documents, USGPO, Washington, D.C., 20402; 1970; $6.00; 182 pp.

Oran Hicks is an administrator at NASA's Office of Advanced Research and Technology. Several years ago he assembled *This Island Earth* as a result of the description of this planet by Apollo astronauts. With 150 color photographs, mostly of different parts of Earth from space, this book sets the planet as a whole, multicomplexed, self-organizing system. ". . .The changes that both natural and human forces bring about on the Earth's surface can best be grasped from the respectful distances inherent in Earth orbits. " ER

One way to see our neighborhood with a fresh eye is to approach it from afar. In fancy, let us assume that a spacecraft is approaching the solar system after a voyage across the inconceivable vastness of interstellar space. We may imagine— the details are not critical to the figure—that it carries extraterrestrial beings from a planet in orbit around Alpha Centauri B, 4.3 light-years away. They are creatures of a carbon-oxygen-hydrogen life form, entering the third millennium of scientific life on their home planet, and they have undertaken a hazardous and costly voyage for four powerful reasons. The first is that their scientists, studying a star later found to be called Sun and rivaling Sirius in brightness, have concluded that although 25 280 000 000 000 miles distant, it is nevertheless their nearest neighbor in the Galaxy. Very careful observation of the bright star's apparent movement might have led to a second reason for the voyage: such motion can be most reasonably explained by the presence around it of invisible planets of significant mass, and it is only on such bodies that the strange phenomenon of replicating organic cells called life can be imagined to exist. A third reason is that they have lately detected peculiar electromagnetic radiation from the vicinity of the bright star— radiation having a degree of organization that, their savants feel, is not easily explained by random mechanisms. The last and most powerful reason why they are aboard this space ark is that they have just lately achieved the technology that

makes exploration to the vicinity of the bright star possible.

―――――――――――

Quite the most remarkable aspect of this blue-white planet—making allowance for the fact that one does not know what Centaurians are accustomed to—is the compound that covers more than two-thirds of the planetary surface. By spectroscope it is a hydrogen-oxygen compound with the property of being a solid below about 32°F, a liquid up to 212°F (at 14.7 psi), and a vapor or gas above. In its liquid phase the compound is extremely reflective, sending a Sun glitter back to Centaurian eyes and sensors that is perhaps unique in the solar system. And although the remote sensors might not indicate it, this compound—known on Earth as water—is both a kind of near-universal solvent and an elixir of life.

The strange, dark, two-legged figure that clouds parted to reveal when an astronaut's camera looked west is the San Carlos Lake above the Coolidge Dam in eastern Arizona. No treasure like this water has been found on either the Moon or Mars. Some cultivation of the land can be noted along the Gila River. That river flows between the Piñaleno and the Gila mountains, two volcanic and complex ranges that enclose alluvium-filled basins.

A vertical line down the center of this color infrared photo is the boundary between New Mexico and Texas. The difference in the earth's appearance to the left and right of that line has been ascribed to different practices in those States in the use of well water for irrigation. Most of the vegetation was dormant when the picture was taken.

82. Violent Universe:
An Eyewitness Account of the New Astronomy

NIGEL CALDER. BBC Publications, 35 Marylebone High Street, London W1M 4AA; 1972; £1.90; 160 pp.

If you want to get into the Universe, but you don't have the thirty-five-dollar price of admission required for *The Atlas of the Universe*, try this book by Nigel Calder at about one-tenth the price. Of course, you could say that you're already *in* the Universe, or that you *are* the Universe. However, the Universe is, and has always been, tricky and elusive. Many strange new names continually pop up creating phenomena that can be described but not explained. It gets to the point that when we consider Universe as the all-inclusive concept, this very description is but one part of this whole describing the whole. But this means that it must be distinct from the whole. The whole thing is logically idiotic and so is the Universe, which is why it is so fascinating to think and write about.

This book by Calder is the best I've come across. Sections are devoted to exploding stars, exploding galaxies, exploding universe, and new laws for old. What comes through is the idea that Universe isn't a " thing " to be described and explained, but is a process that can be best dealt with through awareness of the frenetic and productive activities of " A Goggle of Astronomers " whose discoveries are coming so fast that a coherent world-view remains in the workings of our minds and is not yet dead material to be put on a piece of paper. This is indeed exciting. JB

This is astronomy today: a giddy intellectual game for great telescopes and great minds. What is at stake is nothing less than the imminent portrayal of a new and more vivid picture of the universe we inhabit, as astronomers routinely investigate cataclysms in the sky. It turns out that we live in a relatively peaceful suburb of a quiet galaxy of stars, while all around us, far away in space, events of unimaginable violence occur. There are objects so disorderly that they seem to violate even the laws of physics, as patiently elucidated and verified by ten generations of scientists on Earth.

Pulsars? Quasars? Galaxies? Do I presume that the reader already knows what these objects are? Certainly not, because the astronomers don't know! They are names given to phenomena observed in telescopes. They can be described but not yet explained. Pulsars, the discovery of which was announced by Cambridge radio astronomers in 1968, are 'pulsating radio sources', stars that broadcast great bursts of radio energy with the regularity of a ticking clock. They may be rapidly spinning stars, so crushed by their own gravity that a million tons of matter in them would fit in the volume of a pea. Quasars are ' quasi-stellar radio sources ' or ' quasi-stellar objects', discovered in the early 1960s. As their name suggests, they look like nearby stars, but they are far away and very bright—fantastic concentrations of energy that defy explanation.

The reader who recognises " galaxies " as a familiar term—for those vast collections of stars scattered like ships in the ocean of space—may be surprised to see them bracketed with the pulsars and the quasars, as unknown quantities. The reason is that ideas are being drastically revised, since an uproar of radio noise from the sky makes it plain that galaxies are something more than the sum of their component stars. Evidence now piles up, showing that galaxies can undergo violent changes, amounting in some cases to vast central explosions. The energy then radiated, and measured in the telescopes, is far greater than the normal stars themselves could produce. An obvious question is whether quasars are exploding galaxies.

With hindsight, we can say the present mystery of exploding galaxies began 18 years ago, in 1951.

189

That summer Graham Smith, then at Cambridge, measured the position of the second brightest radio source in the sky, Cygnus A, precisely enough for the distinguished American astronomer, Walter Baade, to train the new 200-inch Palomar telescope on the spot, and take photographs. Baade saw there was something unusual as soon as he developed the negatives. Right in the middle of the picture was what looked like a pair of galaxies pushed together, like a dumb-bell.

By misleading chance, the astronomer who first looked at this picture had for years speculated about the chances of galaxies colliding with one

Big Bang theory. The matter of the universe expands and disperses from a creative origin.

The telescope as a time machine

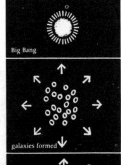

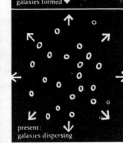

Oscillating Universe theory. The stuff of the universe, scattered by one Big Bang, eventually stops traveling outward and falls back together, causing another Big Bang from which a new universe can be made.

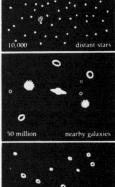

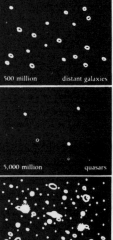

Steady State Theory. The matter of the universe, through expanding, is continuously replenished.

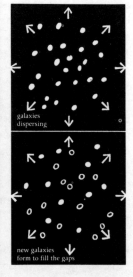

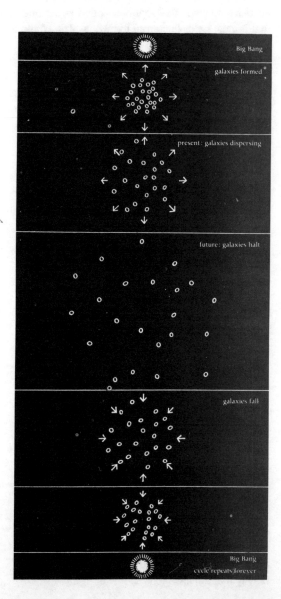

another while they moved about the universe at high speed. Baade quickly convinced himself, and then his colleagues, that Cygnus A was a pair of galaxies in collision—a traffic accident on a stupendous scale.

We cannot always believe our eyes, or trust to common sense. Just as an underwater swimmer has a very peculiar view of the world above the surface, so for men contemplating the universe the image is greatly distorted—despite the transparency of space. The effects can be weird and astronomers have to try to allow for them, in interpreting what they record in their telescopes.

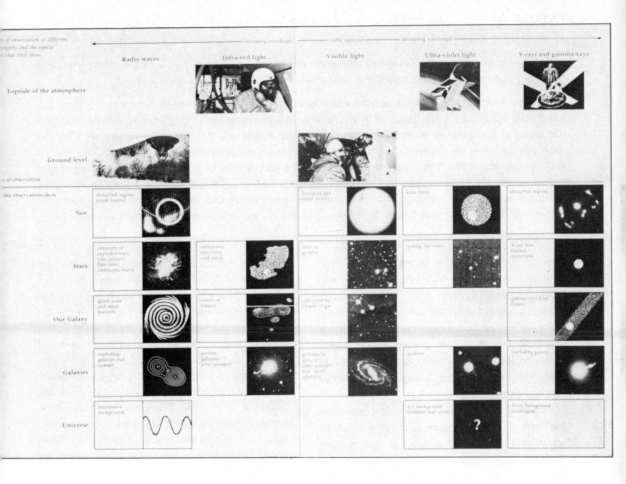

Means of observation at different wavelengths and the typical objects that they show.

83. The Atlas of the Universe

PATRICK MOORE. Mitchell Beazley Ltd., Artists House, 14 Manette Street, London W1V 5LB; 1970; £11.75; 272 pp.

A thirty-five-dollar look at the universe—and worth the price. Patrick Moore is a prolific author who has written so many books on outer space that the universe seems to be his private domain. JB

REVIEW BY JOHN LILLY. *The Universe,* and *the Atlas*: incredible! Man sits at a small desk on a small planet in a small solar system in a small galaxy in a small corner of a large universe. He sits and makes an atlas of a simulation of a universe, a fragmentary little picture from a vast set of possibilities. From a less cosmic view, this book is a trip, a turn-on, an authoritative guidebook to consensus reality, that part generated by *Astronomers* and *Artists.* The latest theories of origins, of earth's core, of galactic energies, of mappings of the space outside earth by light and radio waves, illustrated in color, galactic color. Pulsars and black holes are missing; their context is not. With this book you can trip into Olaf Stapledon's *The Starmaker* (Dover) and be sure that your God is large enough to include you and all else we newly know: here *It* is!

The last great astronomer of antiquity was Ptolemy of Alexandria (c. A.D. 120-180), who perfected the " world system " which bears his name. We know nothing about his life or his personality, but there can be no doubt of his genius, and our information about ancient science is due largely to the book which has come down to us by way of its Arab translation (the *Almagest*). The original version has been lost.

Ptolemy's theory sounds clumsy and artificial in the light of modern knowledge. Yet it must be remembered that it did at least fit the facts as Ptolemy knew them; it accounted for the movements of the planets and of the Sun and Moon, so that it did not appear in the least illogical. This should always be remembered. We have been able to build upon centuries of research and observation; the Greeks were, to all intents and purposes, starting from the beginning. Rather than criticize their mistakes, we should admire them for what they managed to accomplish.

Little progress was made for many centuries after Ptolemy's death. Then, with the Arabs, observation began again, and led on to the revolution in thought which was to overthrow the Ptolemaic theory.

All matter is made up of atoms, and there are only 92 different kinds of atoms known to occur naturally. These make up the elements, from No. 1 (hydrogen) up to 92 (uranium). The extra elements made artificially in recent years follow on from uranium in the sequence, and most of them are unstable.

This has an important bearing on the possibility of entirely alien life-forms. It seems likely that life, wherever it may be found, will be built of the same 92 elements that we know; and of these only one—carbon—is capable of forming the large, complicated atom-groups or molecules which are needed for life. The only other element with comparable ability is silicon, but the present evidence is against the idea of silicon-based life.

Much depends upon what is meant by " alien ". An intelligent being on another world need not have any physical resemblance to ourselves, and certainly need not be a biped; we must remember that even on Earth life takes diverse forms; there is not much outward resemblance between, say, a man and a jellyfish—and yet both are based upon carbon, and neither would be able to survive without water, an atmosphere, and an equable temperature range.

At present there is no evidence in favour of entirely alien forms. There have been suggestions that life on a giant planet such as Jupiter may be

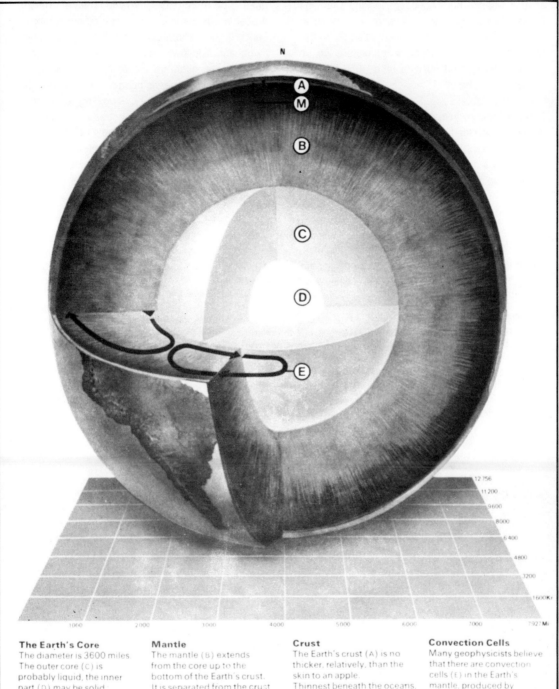

The Earth's Core
The diameter is 3600 miles.
The outer core (C) is
probably liquid, the inner
part (D) may be solid,
mainly nickel-iron. Specific
gravity: approximately 16.

Mantle
The mantle (B) extends
from the core up to the
bottom of the Earth's crust.
It is separated from the crust
by the Mohorovičić
Discontinuity (M).

Crust
The Earth's crust (A) is no
thicker, relatively, than the
skin to an apple.
Thinnest beneath the oceans,
it makes up less than 1 per
cent of the Earth by volume.

Convection Cells
Many geophysicists believe
that there are convection
cells (E) in the Earth's
mantle, produced by
temperature variations in
different regions.

ammonia-based, but evidence is lacking. Until and if fresh evidence is found, it is only sensible to assume that there are no entirely alien life-forms, however intriguing it might be to picture life on Venus which could survive in a pure carbon-dioxide atmosphere.

Radio astronomy investigations have cast serious doubt on the steady-state theory. The hypothesis assumes that the general distribution of the galaxies has always been the same as it is now, whereas on the evolutionary theory the galaxies used to be more closely crowded than at present. It seems that remote radio sources show significant differences in distribution from objects closer to us, and it follows that the universe is not in a steady state, although these observations themselves are by no means certain. There is also the oscillating or cyclic theory, according to which a period of expansion is succeeded by one of contraction; at intervals of perhaps 60,000 million years all the material in the universe comes together, after which the evolutionary cycle is repeated.

Map of the Milky Way

This map of the Milky Way was drawn by Martin and Tatiana Teskula at the Lund Observatory, Sweden. The co-ordinates refer to galactic latitude and longitude, measured from the galactic plane or mean plane of the Milky Way; the zero point for longitude is the intersection of the galactic plane and the celestial equator, at R.A. 18h.40., on the border of Aqüilla and Serpens.

The north galactic pole lies in Coma Berenices; the south galactic pole in Sculptor. In these areas the interstellar absorption is at its least, and it is possible to obtain a good view of external galaxies. Near the plane of the Milky Way, almost no galaxies are to be seen—not because they do not exist in these directions, but because their light is obscured by the material which is spread throughout our own galaxy. Astronomers often referred to this area of apparent emptiness as the "zone of avoidance."

The Milky Way itself is shown extending along the galactic equator; there are many bright stars, as well as gaseous nebulae. Various objects away from the Milky Way are identifiable on the maps, but appear to be somewhat distorted compared with their appearance on most charts, since they have been plotted on an unusual projection.

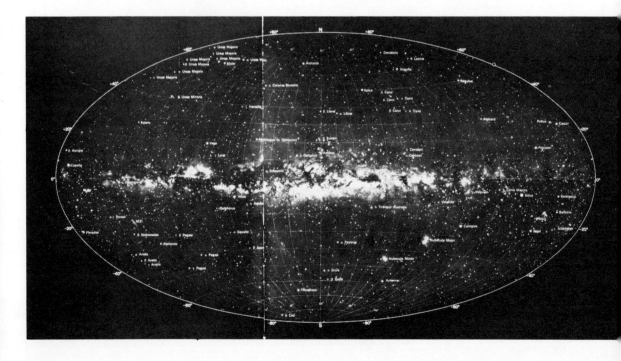

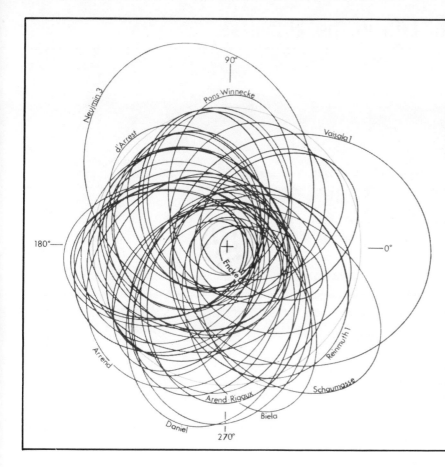

Families of Comets *left*

Orbits of the short-period comets classed as belonging to Jupiter's "comet family". It used to be thought that comets came from outer space, and were captured by the pulls of the planets, so that they were forced into elliptical orbits, but this theory is no longer accepted.

The first-discovered member of the family, Encke's Comet, has been seen at 50 separate returns, the last being that of 1970. Its distance from the Sun ranges between 31,500,000 miles and 381,300,000 miles. It is never visible to the naked eye, and there is evidence that its brightness is decreasing steadily, so that by the end of the century it may become a very faint object. Few of the comets in Jupiter's family ever develop tails.

Radio Map of Galaxy *right*

The radio map shows the distribution of the clouds of neutral hydrogen in the plane of the Galaxy. Each point has been assigned the maximum density which would be seen in projection against the plane; contours have then been drawn in accordance with the density scale to the lower left, giving the average number of atoms per cubic centimeter. Distances were inferred from the radial velocities of the clouds, measured from the Doppler shift in their radio frequency, with assumptions regarding galactic motions. In the region left blank, radial components of motion are so small the method fails.

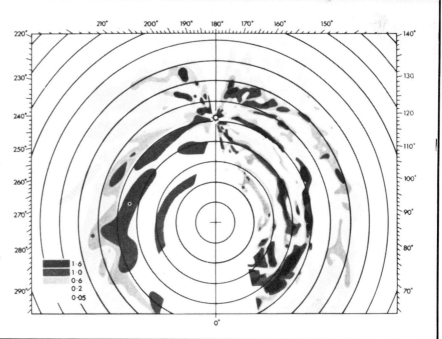

1·6
1·0
0·6
0·2
0·05

84. Intelligent Life in the Universe

I. S. SHKLOVSKII and CARL SAGAN. Dell Publishing Co., Inc., 750 Third Avenue, New York, N.Y. 10017; 1966; or *Real Time*. $2.95; 509 pp.

A panoramic view of natural evolution: the origin of the universe, the evolution of stars and planets, the beginnings of life on earth, and the development of intelligence and technical civilizations among galactic communities.

Shklovskii is a staff member of the Steinberg Astronomical Institute, University of Moscow. Sagan is Assistant Professor of Astronomy at Harvard University. Their collaboration resulted in a survey of present states of scientific knowledge and speculation (both philosophical and practical) about the near future. JB

The distinction between the Ptolemaic and the Copernican cosmologies is an interesting example of model-building, or hypothesis construction in science. Both the Ptolemaic and the Copernican views explained the motions of the planets. The heliocentric view of Copernicus was a simpler hypotheses. This in itself is not a demonstration of its validity. Nature may, after all, be complex. But if each view explains the planetary motions equally well, we certainly cannot be criticized if we think in terms of the simpler model. The Ptolemaic and Copernican pictures differed in another respect, however. According to Ptolemy, the Sun circled about the Earth, and inside the sphere of the Sun lay the sphere of Venus and Mercury. With such a geometry, it would be impossible for us ever to see the entire bright side of Venus. According to Copernicus, however, both Venus and the Earth circled the Sun. Since Venus was sometimes beyond the Earth and the Sun, it would be possible for us to see its bright side. Thus, when Galileo turned his telescope to Venus, and saw that its disk underwent phases from a "full Venus," corresponding to our full moon, to a "new Venus" (the dark side of Venus), corresponding to our new moon, it was clear that the Copernican hypothesis was vindicated. It does not follow that the Copernican view is completely valid in every respect; it is merely a model which conforms, with our desired degree of precision, to all the observations.

The possibility of life beyond the Earth evokes today strong and partisan emotions. There are some who want very much to believe that extraterrestrial life—particularly the intelligent variety—is common throughout the universe; and there are those who are committed to the view that extraterrestrial life is impossible, or so rare as to have neither practical nor philosophical interest. It seems to me appropriate that in this book more than passing attention be paid to such psychological predispositions.

The problem of his own beginnings has intrigued man since remotest antiquity. Of more recent origin—and of perhaps even greater fascination—is the question of life on other worlds beyond the Earth. It is our immense good fortune to be alive at the first moment in history when these tantalizing issues can be approached with rigor and in detail. To hold in our hands the keys to these ancient riddles is a triumph of the highest order; it heralds an age of exploration and discovery unsurpassed in the history of mankind.

When we look at Jupiter, we see a whirling, turbulent mass of clouds and gases. The atmosphere of Jupiter is composed primarily of hydrogen and helium, with smaller amounts of ammonia, methane, and probably water. The

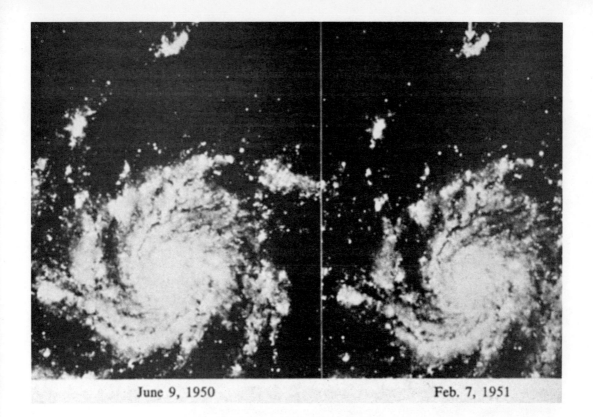

June 9, 1950   Feb. 7, 1951

Figure 7-2. Two photographs of the type Sc galaxy NGC 5457, in the constellation Ursa Major. The supernova is observed in one of the extensive spiral arms of this galaxy, which is also known as Messier 101. (Courtesy of Mount Wilson and Palomar Observatories)

Figure 23-1. Jupiter in blue light showing bands and belts parallel to the equator, and, in the upper left-hand corner, the Great Red Spot. (Courtesy of Mount Wilson and Palomar Observatories)

clouds of Jupiter are thought to be composed of frozen crystals of ammonia, but this is not certain. The temperature at the clouds is about -100°C. In this environment of unfamiliar substances and low temperatures, spots are observed suddenly to appear in the Jovian clouds. Due to the differential rotation of Jupiter (it rotates faster at the equator than near the poles), the spots are stretched out into the conspicuous, brightly colored bands which are one hallmark of the Jovian planets. The Great Red Spot of Jupiter . . . seen in the upper left central portion of Figure 23-1, is a generally brick-red feature observed probably for the last three centuries. It is of unknown composition and unknown origin.

As soon as the inhabitants of the contacted planet learn of the presence of intelligent beings near a particular star in their sky, they could begin their own intensive investigation. They might send modulated optical and radio transmission, and also their own automatic probe vehicles, in the direction of this star. It is conceivable that after several centuries, a lively two-way contact could be established between these civilizations, separated by a distance of, say, some tens of light years.

Note that for contact to be established, it is not necessary that the initial probe inform us of the success of its mission. If its mission is successful, the contacted civilization will make its own contact. The volume of information contained in such a probe could be so great that even a simple one-sided contact would be valuable.

It is also possible to conceive of a system of relay stations for the retransmission of signals obtained by the probe vehicle. The interstellar space vehicles used as relay stations would sequentially transmit the acquired information to the Earth.

At first, only civilizations relatively close to one another could be investigated by interstellar probes. However, we can assume that highly developed civilizations would investigate the universe in a systematic manner, without unnecessary duplication of contacts. As an end result, it is possible to postulate the existence of a vast network of intelligent civilizations in productive mutual contact.

85. Dividends From Space

F. I. ORDWAY, III, C. C. ADAMS, and M. R. SHARPE. Thomas Y. Crowell Company, 201 Park Avenue South, New York, N.Y. 10003; 1971; or *Real Time*. $10; 309 pp.

The United States has significantly reduced its space budget after great expenditures during the past decade. A good part of this reduction is the result of political pressure. The line of argument goes: how can we afford to send a couple of men to the moon for billions when we can't house, feed, and clothe all those here on Earth? A strong answer to this argument lies in the spinoffs from space exploration. When men were put into space, the resulting technology generated has had application far beyond the extant space program.

Ordway, Adams, and Sharpe, space scientists and historians, have produced an in-depth report on the secondary and tertiary consequences of the U.S. space program. They focus on products for home and industry; new applications in medicine; observation of the oceans, the land, and the atmosphere; and Earth-space-Earth communications. The appendix indicates information sources for space technology. ER

Space systems already have been utilized to help improve weather forecasting, to undertake national and international communications on an entirely new scale, and to assist in navigation. Itos satellites operated by the National Oceanic and Atmospheric Administration, for example, provide weather data to the National Environmental Satellite Service for worldwide analyses and forecasts, and the Nimbus program has shown the feasibility of obtaining global atmospheric temperature soundings from satellites. Continued advancement will permit, by about 1980, the development of comprehensive weather models with which we can make accurate 14-day weather forecasts and begin experiments in large-scale weather modification and climate control. Communications satellites, meanwhile, have evolved quickly from the Syncom of 1963 to the Intelsat IV models of today, each of which can provide almost 10 times as many channels or circuits as the most advanced transatlantic cable—and at a fraction of the cable cost. In the field of navigation, the Department of Defense has developed the Transit satellite, now being used by U.S. Navy ships and submarines, and the Department of Transportation has plans for an air traffic control satellite system. The latter concept, already demonstrated by NASA's application technology satellite, may be applicable to ships as well as to commercial aircraft.

With the development of satellites and remote sensors, we now have at our fingertips the tools necessary to survey and manage Earth's natural resources. This is a challenge of the first magnitude. Using multispectral sensor systems, it will be possible to take inventories of crops and timberlands and to monitor their health; to prospect for oil, natural gas, and minerals; and to mount programs for developing oceanic resources.

The potential of a global program for managing Earth resources to match the pattern of supply with the pattern of demand is so enormous that there is no question as to what must be done. Mother Earth can feed us all—even twice as many as we are now—if only we will stop exploiting her resources and start managing them. Can we afford to create a global resources management system? I think, and this book amply demonstrates, that we cannot affort *not* to develop one.

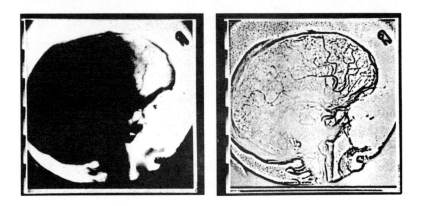

The technique of using computers to enhance the clarity of photographs returned to Earth from unmanned probes of the Moon and Mars also is being used to produce better x-ray pictures. Computer version (right) shows many details not visible in the original x ray at left. (Jet Propulsion Laboratory, California Institute of Technology)

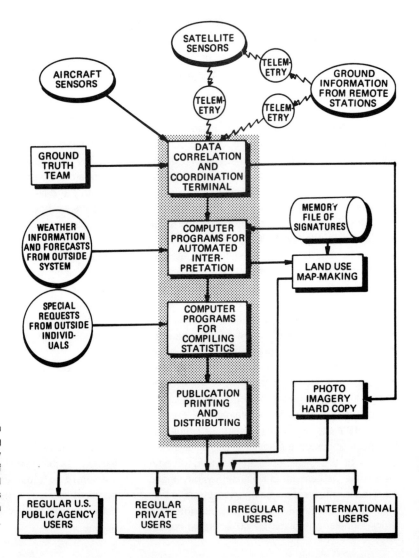

Earth resources information program for inventorying and evaluating productivity of the world's supply of food, fiber, and other natural resources, and to assess the interactions between man and his environment. (Richard P. McKenna)

TABLE I
TYPICAL APPLICATIONS OF REMOTE SENSORS

SENSING TECHNIQUE	AGRICULTURE AND FORESTRY	HYDROLOGY	GEOGRAPHY AND GEODESY	GEOLOGY	OCEANOGRAPHY
Photography, Visual	Crop and soil identification; Identification of plant vigor and disease	Identification of drainage patterns	Urban-rural land use, transportation routes and facilities	Identification of surface structures	Identification of sea state, beach erosion, off-shore depth, turbidity along coasts
Photography, Multispectral spectral	Crop and soil identification; Identification of plant vigor and disease	Moisture content of soils	Terrain and vegetation characteristics	Identification of surface features	Sea color as correlated with productivity
Infrared Imagery and Spectroscopy	Terrain composition; Plant vigor and disease conditions	Detection of areas cooled by evaporation	Surface energy budgets; Near-shore currents and land use	Mapping of thermal anomalies; Mineral identification	Mapping of ocean currents; Investigations of sea ice
Radar Imagery	Soil characteristics	Moisture content of soils; Identification of runoff slopes	Mapping of land ice; Cartography; Geodetic mapping	Surface roughness; Tectonic mapping	Sea state, ice flow, and ice penetration; Tsunami warning
Radio-frequency Reflectivity	Soil characteristics	Moisture content of soils	Land ice mapping and thickness of land ice; Penetration of vegetation cover	Measurement of subsurface layering; Mineral identification	Sea ice thickness and mapping; Sea state
Passive Microwave Radiometry and Imagery	Brightness temperature; Mapping of terrain	Snow and ice surveys	Snow and ice measurements	Dielectric constant; Measurement of subsurface layering	
Absorption Spectroscopy				Detection of mineral deposits; Trace metals and oil fields	Detection of concentrations of surface marine flora

Adapted from NASA Headquarters Manned Space Sciences and Applications, Washington, D.C.; and NASA Manned Spacecraft Center, Houston, Texas.

86. The Sources of Invention

JOHN JEWKES, DAVID SAWERS, RICHARD STILLERMAN. Macmillan International Ltd., Little Essex Street, London WC2R 3LF; 1969; £3.50; 372 pp.

Despite a pervasive permeation of all forms of news coverage, the political spectrum is vastly overrated if we are to look for some of the truly important events of the age. In fact, much of the really "good news" doesn't even qualify for the newspapers or the TV newscast. As for politics: nobody ever voted for the telephone, nobody ever voted for the automobile, nobody ever voted for railroads, xerography, television, and so on.

This work, originally published in 1958, deals with the phenomena of invention in the nineteenth and the twentieth centuries. The second edition considerably enlarges and updates the original group of sixty-one case histories. JB

What is an invention? Technical progress is an indivisible moving stream from which it seems impossible, except in an arbitrary fashion, to isolate one fragment for independent examination. Every item seems in the last analysis to be linked with every other item, so that nothing can be thought about or explained unless everything is taken into account. The windscreen wiper, the zip fastener, the jet engine, the cyclotron, nylon: all these have been described as inventions. Yet any definition that includes them all would seem to include also every technical or product variation that has ever occurred. Is the invention the idea; or the first conception of a way of using the idea; or the actual working utilisation of the idea; or the compounding together of two existing ideas; or the effective fusion of two ideas for a useful purpose? And if an invention cannot be defined, what becomes of the attempts to classify inventions? Thus the distinction between a 'cost reducing' invention and an invention which consists of a 'new product' seems theoretically valid. But in practice, every device for reducing cost is a new product. Every new product is a method of reducing cost in one form or another. A jet-engine aircraft for crossing the Atlantic in place of a sailing-boat is a new product but it is a new product only because it reduces the cost of the journey either in money or time or personal hazard or exertion. It is, indeed, not surprising that in the long history of patent litigation the efforts of the courts to define 'invention' have produced such contradictions and confusions.

Development is a term which is loosely used in general discussion to cover a wide range of activities and purposes, but all these activities seem to satisfy three conditions. One, development is the stage at which known technical methods are applied to a new problem which, in wider or narrower terms, has been defined by the original invention. Of course, it may happen that in the course of development a blockage occurs, existing technology may provide no answers, and then, what is strictly another invention is called for to set the ball rolling once more. Two, and consequentially, development is the stage at which the task to be performed is more precisely defined, the aim more exactly set, the search more specific, the chances of final success more susceptible to measurement than is true at the stage of invention. Invention is the stage at which the scent is first picked up, development the stage at which the hunt is in full cry. All the money in the world could not have produced nylon or the jet engine or crease-resisting fabrics or the cyclotron in 1900. At the time of writing it is possible to say that all the money in the world

TABLE IX

ESTIMATED COSTS OF SPECIFIC DEVELOPMENTS

	Period	Cost	Comments
Petroleum Cracking Processes[1]			
Burton	1909–13	$92,000	
Dubbs	1917–22	$6,000,000	'Development of New
Tube and Tank	1918–23	$600,000	Process' but not including
Houdry	1925–36	$11,000,000	'Major Improvements
Fluid	1938–41	$15,000,000	in the New Process'
T.C.C. and Houdriflow	1935–43	$1,150,000	
Fibres			
Du Pont Nylon[2]	1928–38	$1,178,000	Including Pilot Plant
Du Pont Orlon[2]	1941–7	$5,000,000	Including Pilot Plant and Market Development
Du Pont Dacron[2]	1947–50	$6–7,000,000	Including Pilot Plant
I.C.I. Terylene[3]	1941–9	£4,000,000	Including Pilot Plants
Television			
R.C.A.[4]	Up to 1939	$2,700,000	
E.M.I.[5]	Up to 1939	£550,000	
Moisture-proof Cellophane			
Du Pont[2]	1924–9	$250,000	Up to receipt of Basic Patents
Float Glass			
Pilkingtons[6]	1952–7	£500,000	Including Pilot Plant
	1952–67	£7,000,000	Including first Float Line
Surface Modified Float Process	1963–7	Nearly £1,000,000	
Video-Tape Recording			
Ampex[7]	1951–5	$1,000,000	Development costs of components 1956–60: $15 million
Diesel-Electric Locomotives			
G.M.[8]	1930–4	$4,000,000	
Missiles[10]			
Atlas		Over $3,000,000,000	
Atom Bomb[11]			
Electro-magnetic separation plant	Up to 1946	$304,000,000	
Gaseous diffusion plant	Up to 1946	$253,000,000	

Sources: 1. J. L. Enos, *Petroleum Progress and Profits* (M.I.T. Press, 1962), p. 238.
2. W. F. Mueller, *Rate and Direction of Inventive Activity* (National Bureau of Economic Research, 1962).
3. See pp. 310–12.
4. C. Freeman, 'Research and Development in Electronic Capital Goods', *National Institute Economic Review* (Nov. 1965).
5. Lord Brabazon, *The Brabazon Story* (Heinemann, 1956), pp. 151–2.
6. Private communication.
7. R. Houlton, 'The Process of Innovation', *Bulletin of Oxford University Institute of Economics and Statistics* (Feb. 1967).
8. Testimony of H. L. Hamilton. Hearings before the Sub-Committee on Anti-Trust and Monopoly of the Committee on the Judiciary, U.S. Senate, 84th Congress, 1st Session, Part 6.
9. R. Miller and D. Sawers, *The Technical Development of Modern Aviation* (Routledge and Kegan Paul, 1968), p. 267.
10. R. R. Nelson, M. J. Peck and E. D. Kalachek, *Technology, Economic Growth and Public Policy* (The Brookings Institution, 1967), p. 158.
11. L. R. Groves, *Now It Can Be Told* (Harper, New York, 1962), pp. 97 and 117.

may not produce a cure for most forms of cancer, or lead to the discovery of economical methods of storing electricity on a large scale. Three, development is the phase in which commercial considerations can be, and indeed must be, more systematically examined, the limits of feasibility imposed by the market are narrowed down. As one moves from invention to development the technical considerations give, way gradually to the market considerations.

The cases which are chosen for examination are listed below; from this list fifty-six of the most interesting histories, including the ten new ones, are printed in Part II and Part III.

Acrylic Fibres: Orlon, etc.
Air Conditioning
Air Cushion Vehicles
Automatic Transmissions
Bakelite
Ball-point Pen
Catalytic Cracking of Petroleum
'Cellophane'
'Cellophane' Tape
Chlordane, Aldrin and Dieldrin
Chromium Plating
Cinerama
Continuous Casting of Steel
Continuous Hot-Strip Rolling
Cotton Picker
Crease-resisting Fabrics
Cyclotron
DDT
Diesel-Electric Railway Traction
Domestic Gas Refrigeration
Duco Lacquers

Long-playing Record
Magnetic Recording
Methyl Methacrylate Polymers: Perspex, etc.
Modern Artificial Lighting
Moulton Bicycle
Neoprene
Nylon and Perlon
Oxygen Steel-making
Penicillin
Photo-typesetting
'Polaroid' Land Camera
Polyethylene
Power Steering
Quick Freezing
Radar
Radio
Rhesus Haemolytic Disease Treatment
Rockets
Safety Razor
Self-winding Wristwatch
Semi-synthetic Penicillins
Shell Moulding
Silicones
Stainless Steels
Streptomycin

Electric Precipitation
Electron Microscope
Electronic Digital Computers
Float Glass
Fluorescent Lighting
Freon Refrigerants
Gyro-Compass
Hardening of Liquid Fats
Helicopter
Insulin
Jet Engine
Kodachrome
Krilium

Sulzer Loom
Synthetic Detergents
Synthetic Light Polariser
Television
'Terylene' Polyester Fiber
Tetraethyl Lead
Titanium
Transistor
Tungsten Carbide
Wankel Engine
Xerography
Zip Fastener

The list of instances where a fresh and untutored mind has succeeded when the experts have failed, or have not thought it worth while trying, could be greatly extended. Some of them seem almost fantastic yet there is good authority for them; Gillette, the inventor of the safety razor, was a travelling salesman in crown corks. The joint inventors of Kodachrome were musicians. Eastman, when he revolutionised photography, was a bookkeeper. Carlson, the inventor of xerography, was a patent lawyer. The inventor of the ball-point pen was at various times sculptor, painter and journalist. The automatic telephone dialling system was invented by an undertaker. All the varieties of successful automatic guns have come from individual inventors who were civilians. Two Swedish technical students were responsible for the invention of domestic gas refrigeration; a twenty-year-old Harvard student for success in producing the first practical light-polarising material. The viscose rayon industry was largely the result of the work of a consulting chemist, a former glass blower and a former bank clerk. An American newspaperman is credited with being the father of the parking meter. J. B. Dunlop, one inventor of the pneumatic tyre, was a veterinary surgeon.

87. The Structure of Scientific Revolutions

THOMAS S. KUHN. University of Chicago Press Ltd., 126 Buckingham Palace Road, London SW1W 9SD; (H) 1970; £2.70; (P) 1970; £0.70; 210 pp.

Scientific changes as viewed through the ups and downs of paradigms: universally recognized scientific achievements that for a time provide model problems and solutions to a community of practitioners. JB

We have already seen, however, that one of the things a scientific community acquires with a paradigm is a criterion for choosing problems that, while the paradigm is taken for granted, can be assumed to have solutions. To a great extent these are the only problems that the community will admit as scientific or encourage its members to undertake. Other problems, including many that had previously been standard, are rejected as metaphysical, as the concern of another discipline, or sometimes as just too problematic to be worth the time. A paradigm can, for that matter, even insulate the community from those socially important problems that are not reducible to the puzzle form, because they cannot be stated in terms of the conceptual and instrumental tools the paradigm supplies. Such problems can be a distraction, a lesson brilliantly illustrated by several facets of seventeenth-century Baconianism and by some of the contemporary social sciences. One of the reasons why normal science seems to progress so rapidly is that its practitioners concentrate on problems that only their own lack of ingenuity should keep them from solving.

research. Anyone who has attempted to describe or analyze the evolution of a particular scientific tradition will necessarily have sought accepted principles and rules of this sort. Almost certainly, as the preceding section indicates, he will have met with at least partial success. But, if his experience has been at all like my own, he will have found the search for rules both more difficult and less satisfying than the search for paradigms. Some of the generalizations he employs to describe the community's shared beliefs will present no problems. Others, however, including some of those used as illustrations above, will seem a shade too strong. Phrased in just that way, or in any other way he can imagine, they would almost certainly have been rejected by some members of the group he studies. Nevertheless, if the coherence of the research tradition is to be understood in terms of rules, some specification of common ground in the corresponding area is needed. As a result, the search for a body of rules competent to constitute a given normal research tradition becomes a source of continual and deep frustration.

The determination of shared paradigms is not, however, the determination of shared rules. That demands a second step and one of a somewhat different kind. When undertaking it, the historian must compare the community's paradigms with each other and with its current research reports. In doing so, his object is to discover what isolable elements, explicit or implicit, the members of that community may have *abstracted* from their more global paradigms and deployed as rules in their

Discovery commences with the awareness of anomaly, i.e., with the recognition that nature has somehow violated the paradigm-induced expectations that govern normal science. It then continues with a more or less extended exploration of the area of anomaly. And it closes only when the paradigm theory has been adjusted so that the anomalous has become the expected. Assimilating a new sort of fact demands a more than additive adjustment of theory, and until that adjustment is completed—until the scientist has learned to see nature in a different way—the new fact is not quite a scientific fact at all.

Look first at a particularly famous case of paradigm change, the emergence of Copernican astronomy. When its predecessor, the Ptolemaic system, was first developed during the last two centuries before Christ and the first two after, it was admirably successful in predicting the changing positions of both stars and planets. No other ancient system had performed so well; for the stars, Ptolemaic astronomy is still widely used today as an engineering approximation; for the planets, Ptolemy's predictions were as good as Copernicus'. But to be admirably successful is never, for a scientific theory, to be completely successful. With respect both to planetary position and to precession of the equinoxes, predictions made with Ptolemy's system never quite conformed with the best available observations. Further reduction of those minor discrepancies constituted many of the principal problems of normal astronomical research for many of Ptolemy's successors, just as a similar attempt to bring celestial observation and Newtonian theory together provided normal research problems for Newton's eighteenth-century successors. For some time astronomers had every reason to suppose that these attempts would be as successful as those that had led to Ptolemy's system. Given a particular discrepancy, astronomers were invariably able to eliminate it by making some particular adjustment in Ptolemy's system of compounded circles. But as time went on, a man looking at the net result of the normal research effort of many astronomers could observe that astronomy's complexity was increasing far more rapidly than its accuracy and that a discrepancy corrected in one place was likely to show up in another.

This need to change the meaning of established and familiar concepts is central to the revolutionary impact of Einstein's theory. Though subtler than the changes from geocentrism to heliocentrism, from phlogiston to oxygen, or from corpuscles to waves, the resulting conceptual transformation is no less decisively destructive of a previously established paradigm. We may even come to see it as a prototype for revolutionary reorientations in the sciences. Just because it did not involve the introduction of additional objects or concepts, the transition from Newtonian to Einsteinian mechanics illustrates with particular clarity the scientific revolution as a displacement of the conceptual network through which scientists view the world.

But paradigm debates are not really about relative problem-solving ability, though for good reasons they are usually couched in those terms. Instead, the issue is which paradigm should in the future guide research on problems many of which neither competitor can yet claim to resolve completely. A decision between alternate ways of practicing science is called for, and in the circumstances that decision must be based less on past achievement than on future promise. The man who embraces a new paradigm at an early stage must often do so in defiance of the evidence provided by problem-solving. He must, that is, have faith that the new paradigm will succeed with the many large problems that confront it, knowing only that the older paradigm has failed with a few. A decision of that kind can only be made on faith.

88. From Watt to Clausius: The Rise of Thermodynamics in the Early Industrial Age

D. S. L. CARDWELL. Heinemann Educational Books Ltd., 48 Charles Street, London W1X 8AH; 1971; £5.00; 336 pp.

This book forces the reader to recognize what Cardwell calls "the true nature of scientific progress, which consists not in a series of deductions from an axiomatic system, given once-and-for-all, but in a resorting of knowledge in response to the changing experience of succeeding generations."

This work, a documentation of the rise of thermodynamics in the early part of the industrial revolution, reflects on the interplay between practical and theoretical developments, between science and technics. It is centered on two of the most important developments in modern thought: the Second Law of Thermodynamics, and the concept of entropy. Whereas Georgescu-Roegen in *The Entropy Law and the Economic Process* takes an established concept and applies it heuristically to a new area, Cardwell traces the development of the new thermodynamic science as well as its cosmological implications. During the first quarter of the nineteenth century a new cosmology, that of heat, displaced the mechanical clockwork cosmology of the seventeenth century. A new science was created with its own theoretical structures and experimental verification. It was based on the axiom of the conservation of energy. Cardwell makes the point that this was the very first time in history that such a thing had happened. An excellent book for an understanding of the practical and theoretical development of the concept of entropy.

Cardwell is Head of Department and Reader in the History of Science at the University of Manchester Institute of Science and Technology. JB

It is in one way unfortunate that the expression 'the scientific revolution", which is now often used to sum up the extraordinary progress made in the sixteenth century between the times of Galileo and Newton, should have been given so much *general* currency. It seems to imply that science was established in the seventeenth century, and that everything that has followed has amounted to an almost automatic, almost inevitable progress, thanks to the application of scientific method within the framework laid down by Newton and his contemporaries (regarded, of course, as mathematicians, chemists, 'physicists' etc.).

It is precisely this attitude that I wish to challenge. The progress of science has, I believe, at all times involved intense creative effort on the part of a small number of extremely able men, supported, or at least not hindered in their efforts, by the societies of western Europe. It is hardly an exaggeration to say that in almost every generation science has had to be recast and reinterpreted, sometimes very fundamentally indeed.

Thus even the least historically minded know something of the changes wrought in physics by relativity and the quantum theory, which were initiated at the beginning of this century. It has been said that these were the first radical breaks in Newtonian science since its establishment in the seventeenth century. But this was not the case. Relativity and quantum theory were major transpositions in a nineteenth-century physics that had long outgrown Newtonianism. The major topics of nineteenth-century physics were energy, thermodynamics and field theory. To the extent that these can be traced back to the sixteenth century, Huygens and Leibnitz, and not Newton, were among the ancestors of the first; Descartes, Huygens, and perhaps Hooke, of the last. I shall argue that the second of these three, thermodynamics, originated substantially (but not of course wholly) in the power technologies of the eighteenth and early nineteenth centuries—and these had virtually nothing to do with Newtonianism.

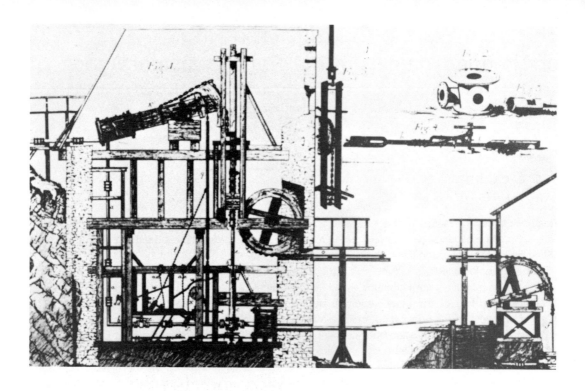

Column-of-water engine at Schemnitz in about 1770. The water is led in by the pipe *a* to the vertical cylinder *c*, fitted with the piston *d*. *A* is a large counterbalance of the sort that was common in early Newcomen engine practice. The oscillations of the piston are transmitted by the connecting rods *o* to the pump rod *f*. This engine should be compared with the much more advanced one illustrated by A. M. Heron de Villefosse (Plate XVI)

Generally speaking, then, seventeenth-century theories of heat combined the idea of a subtle fluid with that of the motion of its constituent corpuscles or atoms. In this respect there was no essential difference between the views of Galileo, Descartes, Boyle and their numerous disciples. Nevertheless, from their rather diffuse notions two distinct and indeed rival theories could be deduced, which were later to become increasingly important. According to the first theory there was no 'subtle fluid', and the phenomena of heat were to be accounted for by some function of the motions of the atoms that constitute all material bodies. But the atoms remained scientifically inscrutable until Daltonian chemistry was accepted, and the unknown function of their motions was not understood until the concept of *energy* was established in the nineteenth century. The second theory ignored atoms and their motions and concentrated on the more tangible notion of a 'subtle fluid' whose presence accounted for the phenomena of heat. As we have remarked, this hypothesis developed in the course of the eighteenth century into the caloric theory. Mathematicians and physicists tended to favour the first theory while chemists came increasingly to accept the second. But we must remember that few men, if any, held wholly consistent theories throughout their scientific careers—or even for any considerable portion of them. Men's views and ideas change; they modify their hypotheses in the light of their own experiences, reflections and discussions. And men do not always write as clearly as the historian would wish; sometimes because they lack literary facility, sometimes—perhaps usually—because of confusion in their own thoughts and sometimes because they do not want to commit themselves too strongly to a theory about which they may have secret doubts.

One possible explanation for this apparent separation of science and technology was political. England, with the most advanced industrial technology, and France, the leading scientific nation,

were at war during the first decade-and-a-half of the nineteenth century. Although 'the sciences were never at war' in the sense that books and periodicals were exchanged and very distinguished scientists became temporary honorary neutrals for the purpose of visiting enemy countries, the inevitable hindrances to the free communication of other ideas and to intercourse at lower social levels must have retarded the progress of science in relation to technology. Not that there was lack of interest or effort; on the contrary, with the possible exception of Fourier virtually every distinguished French physicist, theoretical or experimental, concerned himself to some extent with the problems of the steam-engine. But apart from peace between the nations, further advances were necessary in the technology of heat-engines, and then a wide diffusion of knowledge of these advances. Above all, science awaited the genius of one remarkable man who was to weld all these disparate elements into one great system of thought.

The development of European technics has resulted in a dramatic widening of man's horizons and an increased understanding of the world he inhabits. Just as the great geographical discoveries of the fifteenth century radically changed man's knowledge of his world, informing him of new continents and oceans undreamed of by the old writers, shifting his vision from the confines of his own back-yard to a rich and diverse world (and incidentally making things like the Copernican revolution acceptable and fruitful) so too the development of machines like the steam-engine in the eighteenth century almost forced man to recognise the enormous power, the *puissance,* of heat, the grand moving-agent of the universe. The sight of a primitive steam-engine tirelessly pumping ton after ton of water out of a mine, or of a crude early locomotive hauling a train of trucks along a rough, uneven railway-track, did more for science than all the speculations of the philosophers about the nature of heat since the world began.

The last of the line. This steam engine, built by Galloway's, was one of the last to be installed in a cotton mill (Messrs. Melland's, Elm Street, Burnley). It had previously been displayed, as an example of engineering skill, at the Empire Exhibition, Wembley, in 1924.

Steam is admitted to the high-pressure cylinder, on the left, at about 165 p.s.i. The low-pressure cylinder, on the right, works on the uniflow principle. Power for the textile machines is taken by means of rope-drive from the large flywheel in the background.

89. The Extension of Man: The History of Physics Before the Modern Age

J. D. BERNAL. Weidenfeld & Nicolson Ltd., 11 St. John's Hill, London SW11 1XA; 1972; £2.95; 317 pp.

A presentation of physics as the extension of the human sensory-motor arrangement. Bernal starts with this proposition and proceeds slowly to build the world . . . from ancient times through the end of the nineteenth century. He approaches this subject through analysis of the state of the art of mathematics, astronomy, mechanics, dynamics, pneumatics, magnetism, electricity, and optics as they were viewed in various periods of recorded history. Although this is a historical book, the approach taken by Bernal makes it an intriguing introduction to the fundamental concepts of physics. One realization comes through very strongly: that physics doesn't belong to some all-pervasive reality surrounding us, but is a centuries-old process of one scientist-alchemist-astrologer communicating the results of his work to an associate, whether he be sitting at the next bench, or in some distant land hundreds of years later.

The late J.D. Bernal is the author of the epic four-volume series *Science in History* (M.I.T. Press). This newest book stems from a recording of lectures given to physics students in England. JB

The reason why we can block out this particular part of knowledge and experience and call it *physics* is because it deals primarily with what might be called *the extension of the human sensory-motor arrangement.* A man may be deprived of everything, deprived of tools or clothes—in the definition of the Yahgans of Tierra del Fuego for a poor man, he is " body only "—yet he possesses a most complete set of *physical apparatus* in the shape of sense organs to register the external world and muscular effectors to change it. It is true that he also possesses an even more elaborate *chemical apparatus* for digestion and the maintenance of metabolism. But while the latter became intelligible very recently, and then only partially, by sophisticated biochemistry, the physical sensory-muscular apparatus is comparatively understandable, or at least it was there that man's rational understanding of his world which we call *physics* began.

Heraclitus and Empedocles and others thought the world was full of little seeds that could be turned into anything. But Democritus took a very rigid view and said that there were just hard, unbreakable, *uncuttable* things—*a-tomos*—and that by arranging them in various geometrical figures, you could produce all the various appearances that were seen. The appearances were real because they were made of real things, they were made of atoms. But what about all the rest of the world? Democritus argued that there was simply no rest of the world. The rest of the world was just nothing, emptiness. The world consisted of the atoms and the void. The atoms, of course, did not stand still, they moved around forming new combinations. These are very general ideas; if you try to follow them too far you get into difficulties—and the Greeks certainly did.

The fundamental advances were discoveries that destroyed the Greek world view, first, through the development of anatomy, the working of the human body, and second, through the discovery by experiment and observation of how the solar system works. Previously, things above, celestial things, were for observation only and the people on earth could not be expected to understand how such divine objects moved. This was expressed by saying that they were moved by angels or they were moved by celestial mechanisms, at any rate they were moved by some kind of mechanism which we did not have on earth.

With the developments of this period, particularly the work of Kepler, we get the picture, which was completed by Newton, of the dynamics

TABLE I

Period 4000 BC	Mathematics	Astronomy	Mechanics	Dynamics	Pneumatics and Heat	Magnetism and Electricity	Optics
Ancient and Classical 500 AD	Arithmetic Geometry	Movement of heavens Shape and size of earth	Spring bow Lever Wheel Pulley Wedge Screw	Resisted motion Sound as vibration (Pythagoras)	Bellows Pipes Pumps Archimedes Principle	Magnet and amber	Shadows Mirrors Plane and curved
Mediaeval and Arabic 1450 AD	Arabic numbers Algebra	Navigational astronomy	Horse harness *Gearing* Water and windmills Clocks Pumps	Motion of projectiles	*Gunpowder*	*Compass*	Lenses Eye spectacles
Renaissance 1600 AD	Equations	*The solar system* (Copernicus)	Parallelogram of forces (Stevinus)		Pumps for mines	*Laws of magnetism* (Gilbert)	Perspective
1700 AD	Analytical geometry (Descartes) *Calculus* (Newton)	Elliptical orbits (Kepler) Satellites (Galileo)	Elasticity (Hooke)	Pendulum Law of fall (Galileo) *Laws of motion* Gravitation (Newton)	*Vacuum* (Torricelli) Barometer Gas laws (Boyle) Thermometer	Frictional electricity	*Telescopes* Microscopes Velocity of light Colour *Double refraction* Interferences
1800 AD	Differential equations	Solution of longitude problem	Strength of materials (Smeaton) (Coulomb)	Generalisation of mechanics (Laplace) (Hamilton)	*Steam engine* Specific and latent heat (Black) Condenser (Watt) Heat from friction (Rumford)	Conduction (Grey) Electricity (Franklin) Condenser Laws of force (Coulomb) *Batteries and Currents* (Volta)	Achromatism
1890 AD	Harmonics (Fourier)	The stellar system Nebulae (Herschel)	Structural calculations Fluid motion Turbines		*Mechanical equivalent* (Joule) Second law of thermodynamics (Carnot)	Electromagnetism (Ampère) (Faraday) Telegraph Dynamo *Maxwell's equations*	Polarisation *Wave Theory* Photography Electromagnetic theory

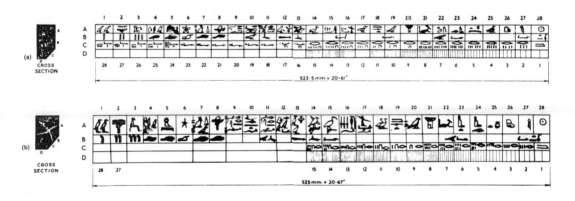

Egyptian measures of length. The ancient Egyptian primary unit of length was the cubit—the length of the forearm. Thus the hieroglyphic sign for the cubit was the forearm and all the subdivisions of digits or fingers, palms, great and little spans, and the foot can be seen in these royal cubits of Amenhotep 1 (a) and of his vizier (b) c. 1500 B.C.

of the earth being transferred to the heavens. Incidentally, this work completes the circle to the extent that the discovery of how the heavens work was considered as the main object of science, physics. This was because the motions of the heavens were considered to be intrinsically at the beginning of the problem, the most important things there were in the universe. The whole fate of life and everything else was tied up with the movement of the heavens: the heavens ruled the earth. Therefore, whoever understood how the heavens worked, would understand everything on earth.

Thus, we have the solar system established, but now comes the question of the other aspect of the theory, to which I referred earlier—the foundation of dynamics. I will go back a little. The real foundation of modern dynamics was to be found in the cannon ball. Aristotle had some very good ideas about dynamics: everything fell to its natural place; the natural place of everything was according to the element; if it was an earthly thing, a solid thing, it fell to the ground or right through the sea to the bottom; if it was fire it went upwards. But what about what is called 'violent motion'? What about throwing a stone or shooting an arrow? Well, it was very difficult to explain that on Aristotelian grounds, so the theory was that natural motion was all right—the stone fell, and the heavier the stone the faster it fell—but violent motion was much more difficult to explain. Aristotle argued this way: you threw a spear, the spear penetrated the air, the air which was displaced from the front end of the spear came round to the back end of the spear and pushed it along. It did not do this for very long because it tired of it and, ultimately, the spear always fell to the ground. This satisfied most people for about 2,000 years, though some did have doubts about it.

———————————

It was, however, from the study of X-rays that the real clue to the new physics was to come. The fact that electrical discharges gave rise to fluorescent phenomena, discovered by Röntgen, led almost accidentally to that of similar fluorescent appearances produced spontaneously from certain minerals, in particular, those containing uranium. This observation, first made by Becquerel, was to lead to the discovery of radioactivity and the impermanence of atoms. It is somewhat ironical that the atom was first accepted just at the time when it was demonstrated as impermanent. The explanation was to come in the first place from the experiments of Rutherford and was then established by Bohr. This gave rise to the whole of nuclear physics of today, including atomic disintegration and the principle of indeterminacy: the picture of the atom as a miniature solar system containing a highly charged and heavy nucleus surrounded by a planetary system of electrons. This concept, which had first appeared in an entirely hypothetical and analogical form in Newton's work, a new paradigm, was to prove the beginning of a new era in physics, and its application in the form of nuclear energy and the atom bomb was to transform the whole of the prospects—good and evil—for humanity.

90. Physics in the Twentieth Century

VICTOR F. WEISSKOPF. M.I.T. Press, 126 Buckingham Palace Road, London SW1W 9SD; 1972; £3.60; 368 pp.

My own rule of thumb for paying attention to a book (or for including it in *Real Time*) is that it provide but a single significant idea. In other words, that it tell me something I didn't already know. This has little to do with the traditional way of dealing with the extant categories established for "book" or "literature." In many respects this book is quite technical, but it's worth the effort. JB

REVIEW BY ALAN SONDHEIM. Weisskopf's subject is quantum mechanics—its structure, philosophy, and social significance. The book is divided into four sections: "Fundamental Questions," "Survey Essays," "Special Approaches," and "General Essays."

The first section may well be the most interesting. Here, the concept of the "quantum ladder" is developed. The "world" is considered as a series of levels, characterized by the amount of energy needed to disrupt them. These levels are discrete, not continuous; because of this, reality is divisible into qualitatively different forms. (For example, all gold atoms possess the same "intrinsic" properties, and, further, no atoms can be half gold and half another element.) This interpretation of quantum mechanics stresses a systems conceptualization of the world (as opposed to an interpretation based on the familiar uncertainty principle).

The second section presents a technical exposition of recent developments in various areas of quantum and particle physics; the third presents, with remarkable clarity, a number of essays for the general reader. "How Light Interacts with Matter" and "Fall of Parity" are of particular interest; the concluding section features a series of articles on the role of science and the scientist.

Physics in the Twentieth Century is recommended to anyone interested in quantum mechanics or systems theory—or to anyone interested in unusually lucid scientific prose. Victor Weisskopf, a leader in atomic and particle physics, was, for five years, head of the Center for European Nuclear Research (CENR).

One main feature of classical physics is the divisibility of each process. Every physical process can be thought of as consisting of a succession of partial processes. Theoretically at least, each process can be followed step by step in time and space. The orbit of an electron round the nucleus may be thought of as a succession of small displacements. The electron of a given charge may be thought of as consisting of parts of a smaller charge. This is the point to be discarded if one wants to understand what we see in nature: quality, specificity, and individuality.

The individuality and the stability of the quantum states have definite limitations. The atom has a unique and specific shape only as long as it is not disturbed by outside effects strong enough for an excitation of higher quantum states. Under very energetic interference from outside, the individuality of the quantum effects disappears completely and the system acquires the classical continuous character (often referred to as the correspondence principle). Hence the quantum character of mechanical systems is limited; it is exhibited only as long as the disturbing factors are weaker than the excitation energy to higher quantum states. This excitation threshold depends on the character of the system. It is always higher, the smaller the spatial dimension of the system. For example, it needs very little energy to change the quantum state of a large molecule; it needs much more to change the quantum state of an atom; and it needs many thousand times more energy to produce a change within the atomic nucleus. We arrive at a characteristic sequence of conditions which we may call the "quantum ladder."

Quantum physics is very different from classical physics. How do you see the difference?

I like to say it in the following way: Before we got to quantum theory our understanding of nature did not correspond at all to one of the most obvious characters of nature, namely the definite and specific properties of things. Steam is always steam, wherever you find it. Rock is always rock. Air is always air. This property of matter whereby it has characteristic properties seems to me one of the most obvious facts of nature. Yet classical physics has no way of accounting for it. In classical physics, the properties are all continuous.

What do you mean by "continuous"?

There are no two classical systems that are really identical. Take the planetary systems of stars, of which we all know that there are billions. According to our present knowledge, you can be sure that no two of them are exactly identical. In some, the sun will be a little larger, in some the planets would be a little larger, the orbits would be a little different . . . . Why? . . .Classical physics allows us an immense range of possibilities. The behavior of things depends on the initial conditions, which can have a continuum of values.

Now quantum theory changes this fundamentally, because things are quantized. No longer is "any" orbit possible, only certain ones, and all the orbits of a particular kind are the same. Thus in quantum theory it makes sense to say that two iron atoms are "exactly" alike because of the quantized orbits. So, an iron atom here and an iron atom in Soviet Russia are exactly alike. Quantum theory brought into physics this idea of identity.

Bohr introduced the term *complementarity* for this complex state of affairs. He was so fascinated with this new mode of arguing that he tried to apply it to some other aspects of human thought. For example, the problem of free will can be looked at in a similar way. The awareness of personal freedom in decision is an experience as clear and as factual as any other. When it is analyzed, however, by following up each step of decision making in its causal connection, the phenomenon of free decision is no longer apparent. A related complementarity is found in the well-known paradox of thinking about the thinking process and also in the juxtaposition of reasoning and acting. We can never analyze the actual process of the thinking that does the analysis; we can never act if we constantly think about the possible consequences of our acts; we have no time to reason during the process of acting. The legal and the humanitarian approach to a human conflict often shows similar features of contradiction that should be resolved by a complementary approach.

Indeed, today one is able to give a reasonably definite answer to the question what matter is made of. One begins to understand the essence of life and the origin of the universe. Only a renunciation of immediate contact with the "one and absolute truth," only endless detours through the diversity of experience could allow the methods of science to become more penetrating and their insights to become more fundamental. It resulted in the recognition of universal principles such as gravitation, the wave nature of light, the conservation of energy, heat as a form of motion, the electric and magnetic fields, the existence of fundamental units of matter (atoms and molecules), the living cell, the Darwinian evolution. It reached its culmination in the twentieth century with the discovery of the connections between space and time by Einstein, the recognition of the electric nature of matter and of the principles of quantum mechanics, providing the answers of how nature manages to produce specific materials, qualities, shapes, colors, and structures, and finally the new insights into the nature of life provided by molecular biology. A framework has been created for a unified description and understanding of the natural world on a cosmic and microcosmic level, and its evolution from a disordered hydrogen cloud to the existence of life on our planet. This framework allows us to see fundamental connections between the properties of nuclei, atoms, molecules, living cells, and stars; it tells us in terms of a few constants of nature why matter in its different forms exhibits the qualities we observe. Scientific insight is not complete, it is still being developed, but its universal character and its success in disclosing the essential features of our natural world make it one of the great cultural creations of our era.

91. The Nature of Physical Reality

HENRY MARGENAU. McGraw-Hill Book Company (UK) Ltd., McGraw-Hill House, Shoppenhangers Road, Maidenhead SL6 2QL; 1959; £1.90; 479 pp.

What has happened in this century is that our methods of experimentation and exploration have far outreached our means for representation and description. Margenau, a physicist, attempts to take stock, to consolidate, to build a frame from which new discussions can commence. This is a book to read for a grounding in both the empirical and the epistemological aspects of theoretical, experimental, and mathematical physics. JB

Our knowledge of what is real also changes in time. In fact this knowledge populates the world with entities whose lifetime may be long or short; the Greek elements, phlogiston, the ether, and now the electron and other so-called "elementary" particles—are they to be rejected as constituents of reality because of the transitory role they play in physical theories?

Two lines of evidence serve to corroborate this assertion, one empirical and scientific, the other epistemological. The first notes that external things are divisible, perhaps indefinitely divisible. This, though superficially contradicting the naive version of the atomic hypothesis, is the seeming verdict of modern physics, which indicates that even reputedly elementary particles can be divided or forced to change their identities under sufficiently energetic treatment. Whether this expectation is borne out by experimentation or not, the fact is that particles of atomic magnitude according to present conception—protons, neutrons, electrons, mesons—are not perceptible in the same sense as the objects they compose, and if present theories are correct, they will never be thus perceptible. In the face of this circumstance we are forced to recognize that the parts of the real are not real themselves or at any rate are real in some other sense. But this concession tends to dissolve the allegedly irreducible quality of whatever it is that assails us from without.

We should be foolish to leave science aside merely because it fails to speak directly about reality, for what it says is so strong with significance as to make it worth while for us to examine what it implies metaphysically. Most interesting is the *way* in which it ascertains its truths. In a sense to be made clear by the detailed subsequent discussion, reality cannot be abstracted from finite existence; as it is the number-generating *process* that points to and defines infinity, so it is the *methodology* of science that defines physical reality. A considerable part of this book, therefore, must be devoted to methodology, viewed as a part of metaphysics.

The lesson to be learned is simple: In basic matters we must discipline our intuition and rely more heavily on abstract thought. In essence, the new analysis ceases to specify x as a function of t; but it does state the probability w that the electron be at x. Thus it describes the *smear*; if, for example, w is constant, the electron is equally likely to be encountered anywhere on the circle; if w is large in a certain region, the electron is more likely to be encountered there in measurements. The new description implies nothing about the place of an electron at every instant, for it talks about happenings when observations are made.

Modern physics is an indictment of the universal adequacy of common sense. It cautions against too glib an acceptance of the so-called "deliverances" of our senses. And for that reason the foregoing considerations have an enormous bearing on the problem of the present chapter: the character of what is immediately given in experience.

Location is not one of the properties of bare experience, though elements within experience may or may not have location. It is therefore never necessary to say *where* experience is. Nor is there anything *external* to experience, for such a spatial attribute can at best be only a metaphor. However, in saying this we do not surrender what is commonly meant by an "external object" if that term is correctly understood. The adjective *external* as used is in fact gratuitous, added perhaps for the sake of emphasis, but not with metaphysical deliberation, and implies a quality peculiar to certain things *of* our experience. We shall call this quality *objectivity,* and we shall indeed find room for it, the rules certifying what is objective in things being a major part of the epistemology here presented. The problem of externality thus becomes the problem of objectivity.

Ability to invest objectivity with meaning is what saves the present approach from landing us in Berkeleian idealism. Berkeley's error was to regard experience as not significant in itself, as requiring transcendental stabilization, which it attained by being the thought of God. For Kant, on the other hand, significance is an essential element of experience, an element with which experience is born and which is attached a priori in different measure to different parts of it. The point we shall endeavor to make is that experience does not come with predetermined significance nor without any significance whatever: significance has to be determined within it, has to be discovered by procedures of which we all are vaguely cognizant and which reach highest precision in the methods of the theoretical sciences.

92. Physics and Beyond: Encounters and Conversations

WERNER HEISENBERG (ed. by Ruth N. Anshen, tr. by Arnold Pomerans). Allen & Unwin Ltd., 40 Museum Street, London WC1A 1LU; 1971; £3.00; 247 pp.

Encounters with reality involve locating the separation between objective and subjective features. This is a situation faced by Heisenberg throughout his long career as an atomic physicist. He's at it again with his autobiography, seeing his life and scientific career not as a simple continuous narrative of place and time, but as illuminating encounters and discussions with his friends and fellow scientists. JB

Science is made by men, a self-evident fact that is far too often forgotten. If it is recalled here, it is in the hope of reducing the gap between the two cultures, between art and science. The present book deals with the developments of atomic physics during the past fifty years, as the author has experienced them. Science rests on experiments; its results are attained through talks among those who work in it and who consult one another about their interpretation of these experiments. Such talks form the main content of this book. Through them the author hopes to demonstrate that science is rooted in conversations.

———————

"In relativity theory," I told Walter, "the experiments you have mentioned, together with other experiments, caused Einstein to discard the prevailing concept of simultaneity. That in itself was exciting enough. Every one of us thinks that he knows precisely what the word 'simultaneous' means, even if it refers to events that take place at great distances. But we are mistaken. For if we ask how one determines whether two such events are, in fact, simultaneous and then evaluates the various means of verification by their results, nature herself informs us that the answers are not at all clear-cut but depend on the observer's state of motion. Space and time are therefore not independent of each other, as we previously believed. Einstein was able to express the 'new' structure of space and time by means of a simple and coherent mathematical formula. While I was ill, I tried to probe into this mathematical world,

which, as I have since learned from Sommerfield, has already been opened up fairly extensively and has therefore ceased to be unexplored territory.

———————

From Bohr's remarks it was quite obvious that he was familiar with all the doubts we ourselves had been expressing. But to make doubly sure that I had understood him, I asked: "If that is all we can do, what is the point of all those atomic models you produced and justified during the past few lectures? What exactly did you try to prove with them?"

"These models," Bohr replied, "have been deduced, or if you prefer guessed, from experiments, not from theoretical calculations. I hope that they describe the structure of the atoms as well, but *only* as well, as is possible in the descriptive language of classical physics. We must be clear that, when it comes to atoms, language can be used only as in poetry. The poet, too, is not nearly so concerned with describing facts as with creating images and establishing mental connections."

———————

"We cannot observe electron orbits inside the atom," I must have replied, "but the radiation which an atom emits during discharges enables us to deduce the frequencies and corresponding amplitudes of its electrons. After all, even in the older physics wave numbers and amplitudes could be considered substitutes for electron orbits. Now, since a good theory must be based on directly observable magnitudes, I thought it

217

more fitting to restrict myself to these, treating them, as it were, as representatives of the electron orbits. "

" But you don't seriously believe, " Einstein protested, " that none but observable magnitudes must go into a physical theory? "

" Isn't that precisely what you have done with relativity? " I asked in .some surprise. " After all, you did stress the fact that it is impermissible to speak of absolute time, simply because absolute time cannot be observed; that only clock readings, be it in the moving reference system or the system at rest, are relevant to the determination of time. "

" Possibly I did use this kind of reasoning, " Einstein admitted, " but it is nonsense all the same. Perhaps I could put it more diplomatically by saying that it may be heuristically useful to keep in mind what one has actually observed. But on principle, it is quite wrong to try founding a theory on observable magnitudes alone. In reality the very opposite happens. It is the theory which decides what we can observe. You must appreciate that observation is a very complicated process. The phenomenon under observation produces certain events in our measuring apparatus. As a result, further processes take place in the apparatus, which eventually and by complicated paths produce sense impressions and help us to fix the effects in our consciousness.

" But I myself find the division of the world into an objective and a subjective side much too arbitrary. The fact that religions through the ages have spoken in images, parables and paradoxes means simply that there are no other ways of grasping the reality to which they refer. But that does not mean that it is not a genuine reality. And splitting this reality into an objective and a subjective side won't get us very far.

" That is why I consider those developments in physics during the last decades which have shown how problematical such concepts as 'objective' and 'subjective' are, a great liberation of thought. The whole thing started with the theory of relativity. In the past, the statement that two events are simultaneous was considered an objective assertion, one that could be communicated quite simply and that was open to verification by any observer. Today we know that 'simultaneity' contains a subjective element, inasmuch as two events that appear simultaneous to an observer at rest are not necessarily simultaneous to an observer in motion. However, the relativistic description is also objective inasmuch as every observer can deduce by calculation what the other observer will perceive or has perceived. For all that, we have come a long way from the classical ideal of objective descriptions.

" In quantum mechanics the departure from this ideal has been even more radical. We can still use the objectifying language of classical physics to make statements about observable facts. For instance, we can say that a photographic plate has been blackened, or that cloud droplets have formed. But we can say nothing about the atoms themselves. And what predictions we base on such findings depend on the way we pose our experimental question, and here the observer has freedom of choice. Naturally, it still makes no difference whether the observer is a man, an animal or a piece of apparatus, but it is no longer possible to make predictions without reference to the observer or the means of observation. To that extent, every physical process may be said to have objective and subjective features. The objective world of nineteenth-century science was, as we know today, an ideal, limiting case, but not the whole reality. "

93. The Born-Einstein Letters: The Correspondence Between Albert Einstein and Max and Hedwig Born 1920-1955

Macmillan International Ltd., Little Essex Street, London WC2R 3LF; 1971; £3.85; 240 pp.

Einstein's $E = MC^2$ reduced (or perhaps enlarged) the "objective world" to a fictive state. The irony of this collection of letters is that while relativity theory changed extant notions of objective reality, the two men were themselves true believers and defenders of such a reality, and—particularly in Einstein's case—spent the better part of their lives attempting to prove it.

This collection is noteworthy not just for the personal insight into the lives of Einstein and Born, but also for the running commentary by Born on over thirty years of developments in modern physics. JB

I too committed a monumental blunder some time ago (my experiment on the emission of light with positive rays), but one must not take it too seriously. Death alone can save one from making blunders. I greatly admire the sure instinct which guides all of Bohr's work. It is good that you should be working on helium. The most interesting thing at the moment is Gerlach's and Stern's experiment. The orientation of atoms without collisions cannot be explained by means of radiation, according to current reasoning; an orientation should, by rights, last more than a hundred years. I made a little calculation about it with Ehrenfest. Rubens considers the experimental result to be absolutely reliable.

Make sure you use the money for the purchase of the X-ray apparatus quite soon. Why is it taking so long?

> Kindest regards to you all
> Yours
> *Einstein*

Here Einstein admits that the considerations which led him to the positive-ray experiments were wrong: 'a monumental blunder'. I should add that now (1965), when I read through the old letters again, I could not understand Einstein's observation at all and found it untenable before I had finished reading. This is, of course, quite simply because we have learned a good many things about the propagation of light during the intervening forty-odd years. The same is true of the idea that the laws of the propagation of light in transparent media have nothing to do with quanta but are correctly described by the wave theory (Maxwell's equations and their relativistic generalisations for moving bodies). It is quite possible that Laue had already realised this at that time, and used it in argument against Einstein's ideas.

Dear Borns

Your letter, dear Mrs Born, was really excellent. Indeed, what causes the sense of well-being inspired by Japanese society and art is that the individual is so harmoniously integrated into his wider environment that he derives his experiences, not from the self, but mainly from the community. Each of us longed for this when we were young, but we had to resign ourselves to its impossibility. For of all the communities available to us there is not one I would want to devote myself to, except for the society of the true searchers, which has very few living members at any time.

The letter from my wife to which Einstein replied is missing. The basic reason for the dispute between us on the validity of statistical laws was as follows. Einstein was firmly convinced that physics can supply us with knowledge of the objectively existing world. Together with many other physicists I have been gradually converted, as a result of experiences in the field of atomic quantum phenomena, to the point of view that this is not so. At any given moment, our knowledge of the objective world is only a crude approximation from which, by applying certain rules such as the probability laws of quantum mechanics, we can predict unknown (e.g. future) conditions.

————————

In an obituary that Einstein wrote for Ernst Mach, he says: 'concepts which have proved useful for ordering things easily assume so great an authority over us, that we forget their terrestial origin and accept them as unalterable facts. They then become labelled as " conceptual necessities ", " *a*

priori situations ", etc. The road of scientific progress is frequently blocked for long periods by such errors. It is therefore not just an idle game to exercise our ability to analyse familiar concepts, and to demonstrate the conditions on which their justification and usefulness depend, and the way in which these developed, little by little, from the data of experience. In this way they are deprived of their excessive authority. Concepts which cannot be shown to be valid are removed. Those which had not been coordinated with the accepted order of things with sufficient care are corrected, or they are replaced by new concepts when a new system is produced which, for some reason or other, seems preferable. "

International Solvay Conference, Brussels, 23-29 October, 1927

(Back, left to right): A. Piccard, E. Henriot, P. Ehrenfest, Ed. Herzen, Th. de Donder, E. Schroedinger, E. Verschaffelt, W. Pauli, W. Heisenberg, R.H. Fowler, L. Brillouin; (middle): P. Debye, M. Knudsen, W.L. Bragg, H.A. Kramers, P.A.M. Dirac, A.H. Compton, L.V. de Broglie, M. Born, N. Bohr; (front): I. Langmeir, M. Planck, Madame Curie, H.A. Lorentz, A. Einstein, P. Langevin, Ch. E. Guye, C.T.R. Wilson, O.W. Richardson

94. Why Fusion?

WILLIAM C. GOUGH. Division of Technical Information, U.S. Atomic Energy Commission, Washington, D.C. 20545; 1970; 76 pp.

William C. Gough is in the Division of Research at the U.S. Atomic Energy Commission, Washington, D.C. His booklet takes a non-technical look at the sources of energy and resources available on a global scale, and proposes that controlled thermonulcear fusion would be a near-infinite way to meet our power and energy needs. Gough, along with Ben Eastlund, also developed the concept of the fusion torch, which uses the fusion process to close the materials cycle between wastes and raw materials. Fusion energy breaks down waste products, bringing them back to the raw-materials stage, thus providing new "natural resources."

Controlled thermonuclear fusion is a man-made imitation of the way in which the sun produces energy. It's also the same energy system as that found in the detonation of hydrogen bombs. ER

POLLUTION

Lets look at the question of pollution. We really don't use anything up; actually all we do is alter its form. Figure 14 is a plot of the refuse production per person in the U.S. versus time. These data were obtained before the Solid Wastes Program of HEW made a careful study. That study showed we are already generating 7 pounds of household, commercial, and municipal wastes per person per day. And that if you add on the wastes being produced by the industries that provide our high standard of living you must add another 3 pounds, so each person in this country is now responsible for about 10 pounds of waste per day. Some interesting numbers for total waste production in the United States were given for 1967: household, commercial and industrial total 360 million tons per year. To that add agriculture waste which is 550 million tons, animal waste (for all the fine steaks we eat)—1-1/2 billion tons, and mining wastes—over 1.1 billion tons. So the grand total is something like 2-1/2 billion tons per year.

Now what do we do with all this? There are really three sinks we can put it in. We can put it in the ocean, and that's what we do with a lot of it. We essentially use the rivers as a means of transporting the wastes to the ocean. This creates what is commonly known as water pollution. Another way is to burn it and this, of course, releases particulate matter and CO and other gases to the air. We looked at how much CO would be released in the year 2000 if all of the municipal refuse was burned and it was 444 million tons per year, just from the U.S. alone. Another alternative is to bury it. From Figure 15 we see that between 1965 and 2000, 10 billion tons would be accumulated just from the municipal refuse. If all this were compacted and disposed of by sanitary landfill, it would require burial to a depth greater than 10 feet in a land area the size of the State of Delaware. If a burial depth of 20 feet were used, the land area could be reduced to the size of the State of Rhode Island. The average composition of municipal refuse is shown in Figure 16. The refuse is mostly paper, but it does contain much valuable material such as metal. Practically everything that we use reappears in our wastes. From Figure 17, you see that the municipal refuse is not too bad an ore with almost 7% iron plus a number of other valuable elements, if they only could be recovered at low cost.

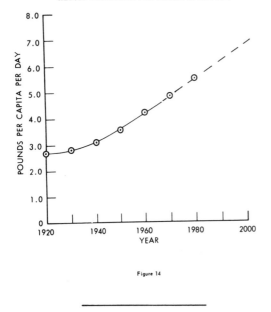

Figure 14

LIMITED ENERGY SOURCES

FOSSIL FUELS:
    CONCERN: A LIMITED AND IRREPLACABLE NATURAL RESOURCE
    QUESTION: ATMOSPHERE CO_2 BUILDUP - EFFECT ON WEATHER, PH OF OCEAN,
              PHOTOSYNTHESIS
FISSION WATER REACTORS:
    CONCERN: USE OF IRREPLACABLE U-235 "SEED - CORN" - ONLY 1-2% EFFICIENCY
              FOR RECOVERING FUEL'S HEAT CONTENT
    QUESTION: FUEL AVAILABILITY AT LOW COST

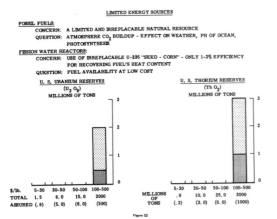

$/lb.	5-30	30-50	50-100	100-500
TOTAL	1.5	8.0	15.0	2000
ASSURED	(.8)	(5.0)	(6.0)	(500)

MILLIONS OF TONS	5-30	30-50	50-100	100-500
	.6	10.0	25.0	3000
	(.2)	(3.0)	(8.0)	(1000)

Figure 22

"INFINITE" ENERGY SOURCES

MAJOR:

    FISSION BREEDER REACTORS:
        QUESTION: FISSION PRODUCTS, SAFETY, AND RADIOECOLOGICAL CONCEN-
              TRATION PROCESSES, PROLIFERATION OF NUCLEAR MATERIAL

    SOLAR ENERGY:
        QUESTION: TECHNOLOGICAL ABILITY TO ECONOMICALLY AND EFFICIENTLY
              CONCENTRATE THE LOW RADIATION ENERGY DENSITY

    FUSION REACTOR:
        QUESTION: ADEQUATE SCIENTIFIC UNDERSTANDING OF PLASMA PHYSICS
              (CONFINEMENT AND SCALING LAWS)

MINOR:

    OTHER ENERGY SOURCES:
        INSUFFICIENT TO MEET FUTURE DEMANDS

	WORLD POWER CAPACITY THOUSANDS OF MW
WATER	2,900
TIDAL	1,100
GEOTHERMAL	10
WIND	NEGLIGIBLE

BUT: WORLD ENERGY REQUIREMENTS = 30,000
     BY YEAR 2000

Figure 23

In Figure 23, we have what I will call the "infinite energy sources." First, there will be the fission breeder reactors whose development is further advanced than for any of the other major "infinite energy sources." The questions raised for long-term use are on handling of fission products since every ton of uranium produces a ton of fission products. There is safety, which is being worked on hard to eliminate any potential hazards. The radiological concentration processes—an area where scientific data is still not fully known. Also, the proliferation of nuclear material requires careful study.

In solar energy, the main question that remains is our ability to economically and efficiently concentrate the low radiation energy density that is coming in from the sun. There are proposals for the use of satellites to avoid problems created by weather on earth. Maybe there could be research and development programs on how to obtain more efficient solar energy. Almost no effort is being devoted to harnessing solar energy.

For controlled fusion we need a better understanding of the plasma to control confinement and establish scaling laws. Right now we're getting confinement times which are better than needed, but we have to put all three properties—confinement, temperature and density—into one device and then check the scaling laws. This is the current world objective. Each of these three "infinite" energy sources requires extensive engineering and materials' development—and fusion is at an early stage.

Looking at other energy sources you find ones that are infinite but insufficient to meet future annual demands. Water—if you took all the water power that could be developed in the world you could produce only about 1/10 of the world's energy requirements for the year 2000. Geothermal, or wind power, will not meet or come close to meeting the needs that we are going to be facing in this world. We have a very limited choice. We don't have many options. And none of these options are guaranteed at this moment. Environmental limitations could further restrict us. If we don't get an unlimited energy source that is relatively inexpensive or at least somewhere close, we will be in trouble. We will be unable to support the large world population at a standard of living anywhere near what we have now in this country or even what less fortunate countries now hope to obtain.

95. National Accelerator Laboratory

P.O. Box 500, Batavia, Ill. 60510.

The frontiers of theoretical physics lie in the domain of high-energy particle interactions. Such events are produced by, and studied at, accelerator facilities. Such a facility at Stanford is of the linear type in that the particles move at high energy in a straight line. The National Accelerator Laboratory is currently the largest facility of its kind, and will for the next few years be the highest energy machine in the world. It accelerates protons to energy levels of 300 billion electron volts (300 GeV), and hopes to be able to reach energies of 500 GeV in the near future. It reaches these energies by propelling the particles in a circular motion and then arranging collisions with other particles.

This type of reaction is part of the sub-microscopic world that high-energy physics has been seeking to fathom since the introduction of quantum mechanical theory earlier this century. It is in this nether world that time seems to disappear, that the number of particles produced in collisions increases as a function of the energies involved, and that the possibility remains to produce and identify such mysterious postulations as tachyons, particles that travel faster than the speed of light.

What is to be seen during these enormously powerful pulsating interactions is, hopefully, a surprise. If the physicists involved knew exactly what they were looking for they wouldn't have had to build accelerators. ER

The accelerator now in the final stages of construction and tune-up at the National Accelerator Laboratory will become, when fully operating, the highest energy machine in the world, producing protons of 500-GeV energy. It is located on a 6800 acre site near Batavia, Illinois, about 35 miles west of Chicago. The sponsoring organization is the Universities Research Association, a group of 52 universities engaged in high-energy physics research widely spread across the United States, and one in Canada. All supporting funds come from the U. S. Atomic Energy Commission. The project was authorized by the U. S. Congress in 1968 and approximately $200 million have been allocated up to this time. The accelerator is scheduled for full operation in 1972.

The machine is an alternating gradient proton synchrotron of very large orbital radius. It incorporates many new and simplifying features which differ markedly from those of earlier AG synchrotrons. Acceleration is achieved in three steps: a 200-MeV proton linac about 150-meters long; a fast-cycling 8-GeV "booster" synchrotron of 75-m orbital radius; and a "main ring" synchrotron of 1000-m orbital radius which accelerates the protons to their final energy. The high energy particles will be ejected at one point in the ring as an emergent beam extending for 3 km, along which will be switching magnets to direct the beam against a sequence of target stations at which research experiments will be performed.

Bending magnets in Interior of Main Accelerator at National Accelerator Laboratory. The Main Accelerator is four miles in circumference; 1.24 miles in diameter. NAL Photo.

One of the first photographs taken with the thirty-inch bubble chamber at NAL June 15, 1972. A two-hundred GeV proton enters the chamber and interacts with the liquid hydrogen. The resulting collision produces a spectacular event with ten visible nuclear fragments emerging. The tracks are nearly thirty inches long.

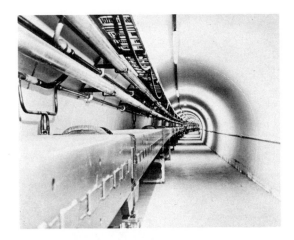

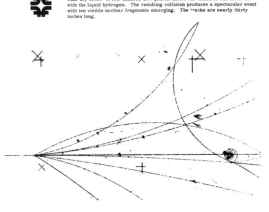

One of the first photographs taken with the thirty-inch bubble chamber at NAL June 15, 1972. A two-hundred GeV proton enters the chamber and interacts with the liquid hydrogen. The resulting collision produces a spectacular event with ten visible nuclear fragments emerging. The tracks are nearly thirty inches long.

Aerial view of main accelerator at National Accelerator Laboratory, near Batavia, Illinois. The main accelerator is four miles in circumference; 1.24 miles in diameter. In foreground (right) is the Central Laboratory Area including the pre-accelerator, the Linac, Beam Transfer, and Central Laboratory building (under construction). NAL Photo. Tony Frelo.

96. Oak Ridge National Laboratory

Oak Ridge, Tenn. 37830.

The Oak Ridge National Laboratory is a research and development facility operated by Union Carbide Corporation for the U.S. Atomic Energy Commission. The Lab's director is Alvin Weinberg, a scientist and philosopher of science.

The major concerns at Oak Ridge involve energy and the environment. There is ongoing R&D dealing with breeder reactors, both salt and liquid-metal types; controlled thermonuclear fusion; and the environmental considerations inherent in the nuclear production of power. Other areas of work include cancer research, thermal-effects research, and participation in the International Biological Program.

Review is a quarterly periodical published for the employees of Oak Ridge National Laboratory and those associated with the Lab. ER

OTHER COOPERATIVE EDUCATIONAL AND RESEARCH ACTIVITIES

UNISOR (University Isotopes Separator Oak Ridge) involves a group of 11 universities which have banded together and raised money to procure an on-line isotope separator (90° Danfysik design) to be used in conjunction with the ORNL cyclotron (ORIC). The Laboratory has

FUSION BY LASER A new concept evolved during this past year by investigators at the Oak Ridge National Laboratory envisioned controlled thermonuclear reactions taking place through the interactions of laser light with deuterium-tritium ice pellets of small sizes. They found that it is possible theoretically to extract useful energy from these pellets when the laser light is converted into particle energy. The containment of the reaction products as plasma created by such an illumination expands rapidly, and the shock wave that occurs as this plasma grows would be contained within a spherical reactor vessel that makes use of present heavy steel technology and of the molten metal technology developed in the AEC reactor program. Reactors of fairly small sizes (up to 100 MW) and of low costs for the boilers of such reactors seem very reasonable. This schematic shows the boiler region of such a reactor complex. The lithium that has been heated through the interaction of these particles with the contained lithium goes into a heat exchanger where it is converted into steam to create electrical energy. The evolution of this concept will depend upon the development of suitably shaped and intense laser pulses of high efficiency.

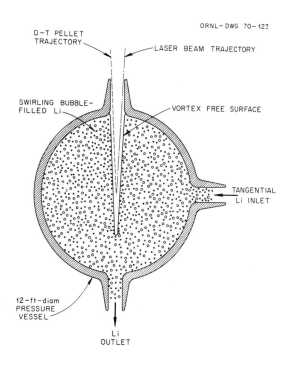

ORNL–DWG 70–123

D–T PELLET TRAJECTORY

LASER BEAM TRAJECTORY

SWIRLING BUBBLE-FILLED Li

VORTEX FREE SURFACE

TANGENTIAL Li INLET

12–ft–diam PRESSURE VESSEL

Li OUTLET

assisted the project in important ways, including the building and equipping of experimental areas needed to house the separator. AEC is contributing both operating and capital money. We expect that the UNISOR experimental program, using its unique facility, will start during the first part of 1972, delving especially into the properties of many nuclear species lying far from stability. These unknown nuclei can be produced by use of the prolific heavy-ion beams now available on ORIC; and their properties can be studied effectively through the on-line mass separator techniques (Fig. 10).

The Southern Regional Demographic Group is an organization of demographers in the South, which is affiliated with ORAU and with ORNL. The group, whose president is Everett S. Lee of the University of Georgia and ORNL, encourages cooperative studies in demography of the South. Our Laboratory helps the group by making available to it our computing facilities and our bank of census tapes; the group helps the Laboratory establish contact with distinguished demographers who advise us on demographic problems in civil defense, urban development, and reactor siting.

WHERE DO WE GO FROM HERE?

In some degree, what may at times appear to be a scattering of our efforts is illusion: energy and the environment are intimately connected, as is the environment with cancer; energy with water; environment with the city, and so on. I therefore would look upon these new salients as enriching and deepening our capacity to respond to national needs—in reintegrating at the working level the fragments into which socio-technological problems are split by bureaucracy. Moreover, the alignment in Washington *is* changing.

I remind you again that *atomic* has been struck from an important section of the Atomic Energy Act, and that we have been encouraged by AEC to work with other agencies.

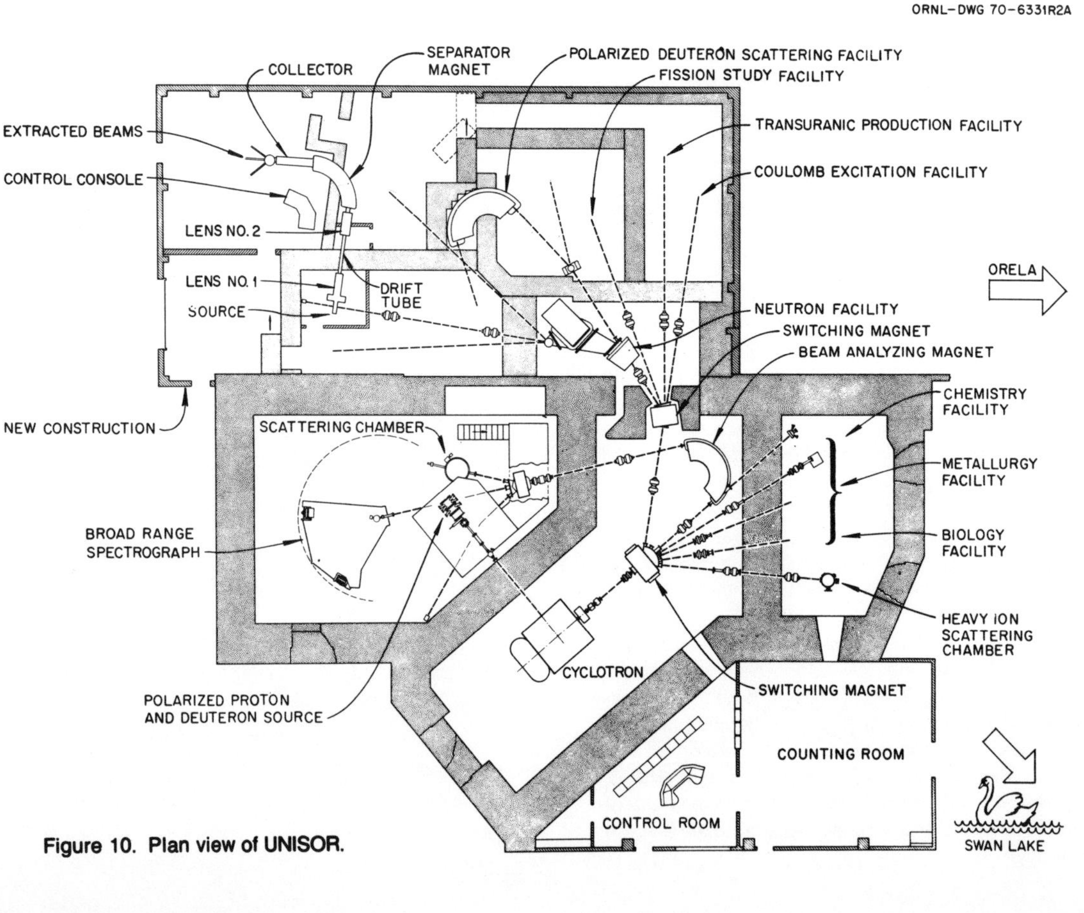

ORNL–DWG 70–6331R2A

Figure 10. Plan view of UNISOR.

97. The Computer from Pascal to Von Neumann

HERMAN H. GOLDSTINE. Princeton University Press, Distrib: Oxford University Press, Ely House, 37 Dover Street, London W1X 4AH; 1973; £6.25; 378 pp.

The history of the computer from the nineteenth-century analytical engine of Charles Babbage through the developments during World War II. The effect of the "computer revolution" has been an irreversible alteration of our own image. For example, the model for the computer was partly inspired by the operation of the brain, now the operation of the brain is accounted for as a mimic-model of the modern-day computer. New technology = new perceptions.

Goldstine provides a firsthand account of the latter stages of the development of the computer. His personal contribution was as a member of the wartime group that produced the ENIAC (Electronic Numerical Integrator & Calculator). This device was operational by December 1945, but even before it was completed, ideas for its improvement were proliferating. The principal source for those ideas was John von Neumann, who became Goldstine's chief collaborator, and whose genius provided answers for numerous problems that many regarded as insurmountable. The collaboration resulted in EDVAC (Electronic Discrete Variable Computer) which was another step toward the prototype of the present-day computer.

Most of the really fantastic things that have happened in computer technology have occurred since World War II, but this history provides the ground from which this activity was generated. Herman Goldstine has been an IBM Fellow since 1969. JB

Prior to Galileo (1564-1642) there were of course intellectual giants, but his great contribution was to mathematicize the physical sciences. Many great scientists before him had investigated nature and made measurements, but the world needed Galileo to give these data "the magic touch of mathematical formulation."

It is worth recalling that prior to this time the state of mathematics in Europe was not substantially more advanced than that in the Arab world, based as it was on European and Chinese ideas and concepts. Then suddenly, as a result of a bringing together of mathematics and physics, something happened in Europe that started science on the path that led from Galileo to Newton. This melding of practical and empirical knowledge with mathematics was the magic touchstone. In about 1580 François Vieta (1540-1603) in an earth-shaking discovery introduced the use of letters for unknowns or general parameters into mathematics. The subjects we now call algebra and arithmetic were called by him *logistica speciosa* and *logistica numerosa*, respectively. He was followed, from our point of view, by John Napier, Laird of Merchiston (1550-1617), who in 1614 invented logarithms and who also was perhaps the first man to understand, in his *Rabdologia* in 1617, the use of the decimal point in arithmetical operations; and by Edmund Gunter (1581-1626), who in 1620 invented a forerunner of the slide rule, which was actually invented by William Oughtred (1575-1660) in 1632 and independently by Richard Delamain, who also published the first account of the industrument in 1630. The discovery of Rene Descartes (1596-1650) of analytical geometry in 1637 is perhaps the next great milestone on the road to the joint discovery of the calculus by Newton and Leibniz. The last stepping stone in that great chain lying between Descartes and Newton and Leibniz is, for our parochial purposes, Pascal's adding machine in 1642.

In 1833 during a hiatus in his development of the Difference Engine, Babbage conceived his *chef d'oeuvre*, his Analytical Engine. This was to be in concept a general purpose computer, very nearly in the modern sense. It was very close in spirit to

Reconstruction of machine designed and built in 1623 by Wilhelm Shickard of Tübingen. Writing to the astronomer Johann Kepler, Schickard proudly proclaimed that it "immediately computes the given numbers automatically, adds, subtracts, multiplies, and divides. Surely you will beam when you see how (it) accumulates left carries of tens and hundreds by itself or while subtracting takes something away from them." (Phot: IBM)

As we mentioned above when the discussions leading up to von Neumann's *First Draft* had taken place it had been against a background of complete mutual openness and desire to produce the best possible ideas. Later it turned out that Eckert and Mauchly viewed themselves as the inventors or discoverers of all the ideas and concepts underlying the EDVAC. This view was strenuously opposed by von Neumann and me. A meeting on this subject took place in Washington in March 1946, attended by us, Col. Gillon, and two representatives of the Patent Branch. As a result of this meeting von Neumann submitted material stating that he had contributed three ideas to the EDVAC. As formulated by the lawyers it stated his claims as:

1. A new code for enabling the operation of the EDVAC.
2. The serial performance or progression through the system of the various arithmetical operations required for the solution of a whole problem.
3. The use of the "iconoscope" [by which was understood the electron beam oscilloscope substantially as used in video systems] as a memory device.

---

the Harvard-IBM machine, Mark I, about which we shall speak at a later point. This machine was to be the goal of his life, and he worked at it until his death in 1871; and after that his son H. P. Babbage carried on the work, building pieces of the device himself and presenting them to the Science Museum in London.

The basic idea of this machine was totally different from that of his earlier Difference Engine. In this new one he saw rather clearly some of the ideas that characterized the modern computer. He got his idea from observing the Jacquard attachment to the loom which revolutionized the textile industry in 1805.

Von Neumann's keen participation and leadership of the logical design work on the EDVAC became a source of substantial conflict between him and me on one side and Eckert and Mauchly on the other. While these matters did not come to a head until later, perhaps it is as well to finish off the subject at this time.

Finally, we may well ask why the computer only came into its own with the advent of electronics. The answer of course is because of speed. But why is speed so important? Clearly, it was not merely to do quicker those problems already being done by more primitive means. That is to say, the whole point of great increases in speed is to handle totally novel situations not possible before. Once one can predict the weather 24 hours in advance in a quarter of an hour, it is not worth a great deal to be able to cut this to one second; but it would be worth enormous amounts if one could predict the weather for 30 days in advance in a quarter of an hour.

We may summarize the pre-electronic days of digital computing by recognizing that in that era electromechanical digital computers eased man's burden in a significant but modest number of ways without however creating a new way of life for him. It was not until the electronic era that totally new burdens could be undertaken by machines to better mankind's way of life.

98. Doubt and Certainty in Science: A Biologist's Reflections on the Brain

J. Z. YOUNG. Oxford University Press (Galaxy Books), Ely House, 37 Dover Street, London W1X 4AH; 1960; £0.75; 168 pp.

A heady attempt at the creation-realization of a non-animistic model of human capacity and potential. Young, Professor of Anatomy, University College, London, thinks we can get along just fine without our minds. He proceeds to postulate an information model for talking not about "mind," but what the brain is doing. Originally delivered as the Reith Lectures on the B.B.C. in 1950, the work has had a great influence on the ideas of contemporary thinkers by creating a conceptual framework in an area that virtually begged for new models and language. JB

The biologists' question about man is, therefore, how does he get his living on the earth? What are the means by which the continuity of human life is ensured? In answering it some biologists might say: 'Man is an omnivorous, terrestrial, bipedal mammal', or some such talk. I believe that such phrases show where we biologists have all been wrong. We have been concentrating on those features of man that are obviously like those of animals; his digestion, his locomotion, and so on. We have been very much more loath to realize that we can apply the same methods also to his higher functions. Eating and walking are not the really important features of man. We all recognize that it is far more significant that he is, shall we say, a thinking creature, or a worshipping one. What we have not sufficiently considered is that it is just these traits of what we commonly call man's mind that are also his most peculiar and important *biological* characteristics. These are the features by which he gets his living: they are the very ones that should most attract our attention as biologists.

Consider first that without leaving the topic of the brain we can at least begin to discuss many, perhaps all, human activities. The method that I am going to suggest as a working basis is to organize *all* our talk about human powers and capacities around knowledge of what the brain does. When the philosopher studies the way in which people think, let him consider what activity this represents in the brain: for certainly there is some. When the theologian studies the fact that human beings tend to organize their activities

Figure 4. Diagram of the nervous system of an octopus

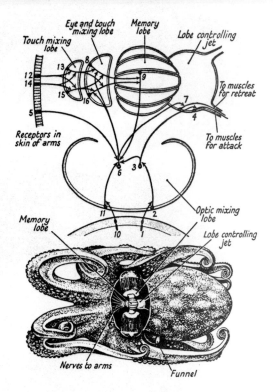

Figure 9. Diagram to show some of the pathways involved in a response such as shouting a warning to a child seen about to cross a road.

The inverted image thrown onto the retina of the eye causes a discharge of impulses in the optic nerves, which end in the thalamus. From here, further impulses are sent to the cortex, at the back of the head. The cells of this optic receiving area send impulses to the optic mixing areas, and from here they go to many other parts of the cortex. The complicated activity thus set up fits with the existing brain rules to produce impulses in the output fibers of the cortex, such as those shown leading to the motor cells that activate the muscles of the tongue and larynx. The arrangements for providing feedback at various stages are shown, including the receptors in the muscles.

Many other parts of the cortex would be involved besides those here drawn, and of course instead of the few cells shown millions would be active.

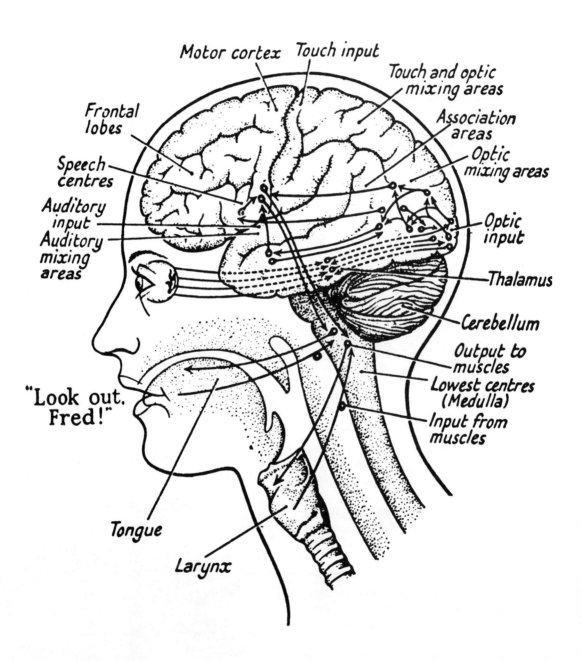

around statements about gods, let him consider the activity that this involves in the brain. When the educationist and psychologist follow the ways in which the child grows to his mature powers and later perhaps goes astray, let them consider the process of the development and decay of the activities of the brain.

I shall try to show how it comes about that we speak of ourselves as distinct entities, set in our bodies, able to communicate with others like ourselves. I shall try to show how our brains make us able to communicate by comparing one thing with another. In early stages of human communication man described the action of all bodies as caused by spirits or powers resident within them. Recently we have learned that it is better not to use this animistic way of speaking about physical things. Perhaps therefore we do not even need to do it when talking about ourselves, or each other. We may be able ultimately to dispense with the concept of mind altogether.

Human society has long been a self-regulating system and we can say that it preserves itself by conveying information to its members and receiving information from them. Human tools are also self-regulating, in so far as they convey to us sufficient power or information to ensure that we return to them the power and information needed for their continuance. This is the relationship, for example, between a man and his watch. Many people have feared that as our tools become more complicated they will control us instead of the other way round. There is indeed a sense in which as they become more fully self-regulating they become more independent and more able to tell us things that are useful. It is perhaps natural for each generation to fear its products, but surely it is more satisfactory to welcome their independence and the new information that they provide as an aid to the continuation of the whole system.

In order to have some picture of how the brain works it is useful to think of it as a gigantic government office—an enormous ministry, whose one aim and object is to preserve intact the country for which it is responsible. Ten million telegraph wires bring information to the office, coded in dots. These correspond to the sensory or input fibres reaching the brain. In the office one must try to imagine nearly 15,000,000,000 clerks, that is to say more than six times more people that there are at present in the whole world. They correspond to the cells of the brain, and we can imagine them sitting in closely packed rows, as the brain cells are arranged. Every clerk has a telephone and receives coded messages either from outside the office or from some other part of it. So each nerve-cell of the brain receives nerve-impulses, either from the sense organs or from other brain cells near to it or far away. Each clerk spends most of his time sending code messages on his telephone to some other group, which may be near or far. So every nerve-cell has an outgoing fibre, which may be long or short. But the clerks can also influence their neighbours by whispering 'silence'; obviously if a group of them starts doing this then a wave of quiet will pass over that area and it will send out no messages for a while.

This is where the biologist steps in, for his business is the description of living organisms, such as these observers—the physicists. He insists that he finds that they are not all alike. They differ, for example, in their brains and the rules that are in them. It is not adequate, therefore, to define truth as that which can be observed and verified by anyone. The biologist goes on to suggest that we are mistaken in this emphasis on individual observers. They are not the basic units of life. Each individual is part of a much larger system, which continues over millions of years, changing slowly by the process of evolution. This maintenance of continuity is the most fundamental feature that the biologist can see, and he suggests that all human action should be spoken about relative to it.

99. Of Molecules and Men

FRANCIS CRICK. University of Washington Press, Seattle, Wash. 98105; 1966; or *Real Time*. (H) $3.95; (P) $1.95; 99 pp.

Francis Crick was joint winner of the Nobel Prize in Medicine in 1962 for the discovery of the structure of DNA. His coworker James Watson (author of *The Double Helix*) presents Crick as a witty and provocative character, whose personality has a lot to do with the successful effort. In this concise book, a summary of contemporary thought, Crick manages to show the value of putting hypotheses in general language, while pointing out that the problems raised by the new biology will rival those presented by the rise of modern physics. JB

It is notoriously difficult to define the word "living." In many cases we all know whether something is alive or dead. You are alive; cats and dogs are alive; whereas a rock or a pane of glass is dead. But the word "dead" is a bad one, because it half implies that the object was once alive and is now dead. It is interesting that there is no *simple* word for something that is not alive and never has been. In the old game, the question was "Animal, Vegetable, or Mineral?" and here the word "mineral" does service for the sense we want. Notice, too, the useful distinction between "animal" and "vegetable." I remember once declaring a passion for oysters, and being told by a young woman, "I could never eat anything that's alive." She was munching salad at the time, which is certainly vegetable and, as I shall argue, can well be considered to be alive.

The ultimate aim of the modern movement in biology is in fact to explain *all* biology in terms of physics and chemistry. There is a very good reason for this. Since the revolution in physics in the mid-twenties, we have had a sound theoretical basis for chemistry and the relevant parts of physics. This is not to be so presumptuous as to say that our knowledge is absolutely complete. Nevertheless quantum mechanics, together with our empirical knowledge of chemistry, appears to provide us with a "foundation of certainty" on which to build biology. In just the same way Newtonian mechanics, even though we know that it is only a first approximation, provides a foundation for, say, mechanical engineering.

The other great field of knowledge that will undoubtedly expand and that is associated with molecular biology concerns the origin of life. However we define the point of origin, it was a step that took place an exceedingly long time ago, probably about three or four thousand million years ago. We have a general picture of what the world was like at that time. In particular we believe that the atmosphere did not contain oxygen and was reducing in nature, and that under the action of electrical discharges and of ultraviolet light the gases of the atmosphere were converted into simple organic compounds. These then dissolved in the sea so that the primitive oceans of that period can be thought of as a rather dilute soup, consisting of many different rather simple organic molecules.

One might wonder why the soup did not go bad, but the answer is quite obvious. There was no living thing to make it go bad! It is true that most of these chemical molecules are, on a long-time scale, somewhat unstable and would break down by themselves. Presumably some sort of steady state was reached between the synthesis of molecules by electric discharges and similar processes, and their spontaneous breakdown to other compounds.

But leaving aside all these fancier applications we have to realize, as has already been stressed by a number of people, that machines are going to take on many of the functions of human beings, and that it is going to be quite disturbing for us to associate with them. There are people, Fred Hoyle for example, who believe that machines will eventually take control of our civilization; but even if that does not happen it could be argued that what will arise is a symbiosis between machines and men, in which the main function of the men will be to reproduce and to tend the machines. I doubt myself whether we shall reach quite such a stage, but nevertheless I am convinced that it is going to be quite upsetting having to associate with very complicated and sophisticated machines, and that this development is likely to happen during our own lifetime.

The most striking thing about the work of the last thirty years on ESP has been its complete failure to produce any technique whatsoever which is scientifically acceptable. There is no known way, by a special screening procedure, by the use of drugs, or by any other method, to discover people who can communicate in this way, and be proved to skeptical observers to do so. Not one truly reproducible experiment has been devised although the record is thick with fakes and sloppy experimentation. We must conclude either that the phenomenon does not exist, or that it is too difficult to study by present methods, or that the people who work on these problems are hopelessly third-rate. ESP has all the appearance of a completely "void" science, like astrology, in which no genuine experiments exist, and the only "results" are due to bad experimentation or to faking either by subject or experimenter, conscious or unconscious. This background level, incidentally, occurs in all genuine subjects—there is about one fake in biochemistry every year or so—but in respectable sciences the "noise" is well below the level of the "sense." In ESP the sense seems to be absent, and only the noise remains.

100. The Double Helix: Being a Personal Account of The Discovery of The Structure of DNA

JAMES D. WATSON. Weidenfeld & Nicolson Ltd., 11 St. John's Hill, London SW11 1XA; (H) 1968; £1.75; or Penguin Books Ltd., Harmondsworth, Middx; (P) 1970; £0.25; 226 pp.

Watson won a Nobel prize for his part in the discovery of the structure of DNA, the molecule of heredity. This book is a personal account of the interactions of the people involved in the quest. The main point is that science is not some abstract monolith, but a situation in which particular people think certain thoughts and communicate them to others. JB

Before my arrival in Cambridge, Francis only occasionally thought about deoxyribonucleic acid (DNA) and its role in heredity. This was not because he thought it uninteresting. Quite the contrary. A major factor in his leaving physics and developing an interest in biology had been the reading in 1946 of *What Is Life?* by the noted theoretical physicist Erwin Schrödinger. This book very elegantly propounded the belief that genes were the key components of living cells and that, to understand what life is, we must know how genes act. When Schrödinger wrote his book (1944), there was general acceptance that genes were special types of protein molecules. But almost at this same time the bacteriologist O. T. Avery was carrying out experiments at the Rockefeller Institute in New York which showed that hereditary traits could be transmitted from one bacterial cell to another by purified DNA molecules.

Given the fact that DNA was known to occur in the chromosomes of all cells, Avery's experiments strongly suggested that future experiments would show that all genes were composed of DNA. If true, this meant to Francis that proteins would not be the Rosetta Stone for unraveling the true secret of life. Instead, DNA would have to provide the key to enable us to find out how the genes determined, among other characteristics, the color of our hair, our eyes, most likely our comparative intelligence, and maybe even our potential to amuse others.

I retained a slight hope that I might profit from the meeting on the structures of biological macromolecules. Though I knew nothing about the X-ray diffraction techniques that dominated structural analysis, I was optimistic that the spoken arguments would be more comprehensible than the journal articles, which passed over my head. I was specially interested to hear the talk on nucleic acids to be given by Randall. At that time almost nothing was published about the possible three-dimensional configurations of a nucleic-acid molecule. Conceivably this fact affected my casual pursuit of chemistry. For why should I get excited learning boring chemical facts as long as the chemists never provided anything incisive about the nucleic acids?

From my first day in the lab I knew I would not leave Cambridge for a long time. Departing would be idiocy, for I had immediately discovered the fun of talking to Francis Crick. Finding someone in Max's lab who knew that DNA was more important than proteins was real luck. Moreover, it was a great relief for me not to spend full time learning X-ray analysis of proteins. Our lunch conversations quickly centered on how genes were put together. Within a few days after my arrival, we knew what to do: imitate Linus Pauling and beat him at his own game.

James D. Watson
and Francis Crick

Conceivably a few additional X-ray pictures would tell how the protein subunits were arranged. This was particularly true if they were helically stacked. Excitedly I pilfered Bernal's and Fankuchen's paper from the Philosophical Library and brought it up to the lab so that Francis could inspect the TMV X-ray picture. When he saw the blank regions that characterize helical patterns, he jumped into action, quickly spilling out several possible helical TMV structures. From this moment on, I knew I could no longer avoid actually understanding the helical theory. Waiting until Francis had free time to help me would save me from having to master the mathematics, but only at the penalty of my standing still if Francis was out of the room. Luckily, merely a superficial grasp was needed to see why the TMV X-ray picture suggested a helix with a turn every 23 $\overline{A}$ along the helical axis. The rules were, in fact, so simple that Francis considered writing them up under the title, "Fourier Transforms for the Birdwatcher".

Elizabeth and I flew off the following afternoon to Paris, where Peter would join us the next day. Ten days hence she was sailing to the States on her way to Japan to marry an American she had known in college. These were to be our last days together, at least in the carefree spirit that had marked our escape from the Middle West and the American culture it was so easy to be ambivalent about. Monday morning we went over to the Faubourg St. Honore for our last look at its elegance. There, peering in at a shop full of sleek umbrellas, I realized one should be her wedding present and we quickly had it. Afterwards she searched out a friend for tea while I walked back across the Seine to our hotel near the Palais du Luxembourg. Later that night with Peter we would celebrate my birthday. But now I was alone, looking at the long-haired girls near St. Germain des Prés and knowing they were not for me. I was twenty-five and too old to be unusual.

101. Beyond Reductionism:
New Perspectives In The Life Sciences

Edited by ARTHUR KOESTLER and J. R. SMYTHIES. The Macmillan Company, 866 Third Avenue, New York, N. Y. 10022; 1970; or *Real Time.* (H) $8.95, 438 pp.

Beacon Press, Inc., 25 Beacon Street, Boston, Mass. 02108; 1970; or *Real Time.* (P) $3.95, 438 pp.

This book presents the controversial papers and discussions of fifteen scientists who gathered together at a 1968 symposium to attempt a refutation of the mechanistic world view of reductionism. The empirical limits of the mechanistic sciences can be stretched just so far: we've come to the end of the epistemological trail. Koestler believes that the life sciences are still locked into the mechanistic concepts of nineteenth-century physics, resulting in what he terms a "crudely reductionistic philosophy." He goes on, "But up to now, no coherent alternative world-view is in sight. There is a groping for a new synthesis, but also a strong feeling that it should not be a premature, abortive synthesis. . . . If a new synthesis is to emerge, it will emerge from the laboratories."

The reductionist sciences of the nineteenth and twentieth centuries have built up a picture of man as nothing more than passive automata controlled by environment, or as a mere sum of many kinds of quantified measurement. Science isn't humanism. These pictures of man, although offensive to the corporate human ego, nevertheless have served well on the empirical level. When they stop being useful they should be discarded, and new methodologies adopted from which, no doubt, new pictures of who we are will emerge. This book is one step along that process, a series of negations of the old methodology. But it is not even necessary to paint the new picture of man. This will reveal itself to us without our even knowing it. JB

Neo-Darwinism or the "Synthetic Theory" of evolution has incorporated genetics, cytology, molecular biology, physiological and population genetics, into its framework. For the present purpose it will suffice to outline briefly the main differences between the Neo-Darwinist and Darwin's original theory.

First, Darwin's rather vague concept of hereditary variation has been replaced by the concept of mutation in modern genetics and molecular biology. Mutation (in its principal form) is defined as a change in a chromosomal gene, ultimately of a DNA molecule. Secondly, the Darwinian conception of selection as a bloody "struggle for survival" was replaced by that of differential reproduction, that is, those mutants gradually prevail that produce the largest number of offspring. Thirdly, instead of the survival of the fittest or best adapted individual, what really matters according to the modern theory is rather a continuous change in the gene pool, the genetic constitution of populations.

L. von Bertalanffy

At this point, I would like to stress that no data support the view that brain cells contain "memory molecules" that store information in a linear way, i.e. record and reproduce it tape-recorder fashion. This is biological nonsense. In current literature, such views are seen, but they do little more than add to the confusion. As will be seen, RNA and proteins in brain cells do respond to the establishment of new behaviour, but the mechanism and its regulation still remain to be elucidated.

Proteins are probable candidates as executive molecules in a mechanism for acquisition and retrieval of memory. They have a high specificity and could respond rapidly in millions of brain cells to a trigger mechanism.

Holger Hyden

The concept of the holon is meant to supply the missing link between atomism and holism, and to supplant the dualistic way of thinking in terms of "parts" and "wholes", which is so deeply engrained in our mental habits, by a multi-level, stratified approach. A hierarchically-organized whole cannot be "reduced" to its elementary parts; but it can be "dissected" into its constituent branches of holons, represented by the nodes of the tree-diagram, while the lines connecting the holons stand for channels of communication, control or transportation, as the case may be.

Arthur Koestler

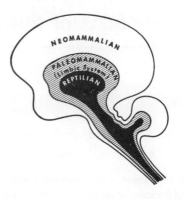

Schema of "holonarchic" organization of the three basic brain types which, in the evaluation of the mammalian brain, become part of man's inheritance. Man's counterpart of the old mammalian brain comprises the so-called limbic system which has been found to play an important role in emotional behavior. (From MacLean, 1966.)

The trouble about trying to discuss such situations in terms of the Theory of Games is that although that branch of mathematics has got such an interesting title, which seems to promise such a lot, in practice as far as I can make out it contains almost no theorems. There is one, a Theorem of Minimax Strategy, which essentially teaches you how to play safe. But beyond that the content of the Theory of Games seems to be almost non-existent, except for discussions of elaborate ways of formulating problems, which you then find you can't solve.

C. H. Waddington

In the popular language of today, the reptilian and the old and new mammalian brains might be regarded as biological computers, each with its own subjective, gnostic, time-measuring, memory, motor and other functions (MacLean, 1966b). On the basis of behavioural observations of ethologists, it may be inferred that the reptilian brain programmes stereotyped behaviours according to instructions based on ancestral learning and ancestral memories. In other words, it seems to play a primary role in instinctually determined functions such as establishing territory, finding shelter, hunting, homing, mating, breeding, imprinting, forming social hierarchies, selecting leaders and the like. In the experimental situation the presentation of a dummy or a fragment of a dummy may release the sequential acting out of an instinctual form of behaviour. Indeed, a mere phantom is sometimes sufficient to trigger the entire copulatory act.

Paul O. MacLean

Strongly believing, as I do, that the unique functions of the brain rest crucially upon the particular connections of its parts in addition to its chemical composition, I see drugs as capable of inhibiting or facilitating the processes involved in those connections but hardly capable of generating them *de novo* and without the genetic or experiential processes which make them adaptive. My belief that specific memories lie in specific patterns of connection in the brain and not in specific molecules, would make me incredulous of the possibility that experiential information can be transmitted from one individual to another by the transfer of a chemical substance however macromolecular. On the other hand, I would quite readily accept the possibility that certain drugs could slow or accelerate the process of making these connections and thus speed or retard the rate of learning. In fact, the hypothesis I have presented, is based upon the possibility that endogenous biogenic amines in the brain are engaged in just that activity. Again, regarding affective state in man as inextricably bound to the apperceptive mass of the individual, I would find it difficult to believe that a drug could establish or correct an affective state out of context with the experience and the intellectual processing which are necessary to generate it.

Seymour S. Kety

237

102. Genetics of the Evolutionary Process

THEODOSIUS DOBZHANSKY. Columbia University Press Ltd., 70 Great Russell Street, London WC1; 1972; £2.15; 505 pp.

A lot of information about important questions in the most lively field of scientific inquiry today: the biological sciences in general and the biological theory of evolution in particular. Dobzhansky's book deals with biology's several hierarchically superimposed levels of integration of structures and functions: molecular, cellular, individual, populational, and ecosystemic.

Although theories of evolution in biology have been around for a long time, it's only in the past quarter century that the physical basis of heredity, and hence evolution, was uncovered by the work of Watson and Crick in decoding the double-helix structure of DNA. Novel insights, and new problems as well, have resulted from this work, and it is in these directions that Dobzhansky applies his thinking. Some areas of discussion: results of discoveries of the molecular geneticists, lingering misconceptions about the biological theory of evolution and its genetic aspects, the profound truths of the linear conception of time which evolutionary theory confirms, the crucial importance of DNA and RNA in explaining the unity and diversity of life, and an inquiry into the peculiar myths that have arisen around the question of the races of mankind.

Dobzhansky, a Nobel Laureate, is a Professor at the Rockefeller University in New York. JB

A man consists of some seven octillion (7×10^{27}) atoms, grouped in about ten trillion (10^{13}) cells. This agglomeration of cells and atoms has some astounding properties; it is alive, feels joy and suffering, discriminates between beauty and ugliness, and distinguishes good from evil. There are many other living agglomerations of atoms, belonging to at least two million, possibly twice that many, biological species. What is most remarkable is that the individuals of every one of these species are so designed that they are able to live and reproduce in some existing environments. In other words, each species is adapted to a certain way of life. How has this come about? How can agglomerations of atoms accomplish any of these things?

Two kinds of answers have been proposed. Vitalists assume that living bodies are formed through the intervention of occult forces, variously called entelechy (Aristotle, Driesch), *vis essentialis* (C. F. Wolff), psyche, or inherent directiveness (Sinnott). Mechanists, on the other hand, claim that all biological structures and processes are only highly elaborate patterns of physical and chemical phenomena. Life can be understood without recourse to the assumption of any transcendental powers.

The evolutionary world view assumes a linear, instead of a cyclic, concept of time. Things, especially living things, were different in the past and will be different in the future. History is not an illusion, not a tedious return of past states. It is evolution, which has brought about the present state and will usher in the future states of the world. Because of an egregious miscomprehension, some Christians have fought Darwin's evolutionary interpretation of the living world, and eventually of the universe as a whole, though a linear concept of time is basic to Christian religious thought. At any rate, in biology nothing makes sense except in the light of evolution. It is possible to describe living beings without asking questions about their origins. The descriptions acquire meaning and coherence, however, only when viewed in the perspective of evolutionary development.

This book presents an outline of the biological theory of evolution, with special emphasis on its genetic aspects. The general principles of the biological theory are widely, but not universally, accepted among present-day biologists. A stridently dissenting voice is, for example, that of Koestler (1967). Though not himself a biologist, this author lists, as the first of the "monumental superstitions" on which "the citadel of orthodoxy" in modern science is built, the view "that biological evolution is the result of random mutations preserved by natural selection." I shall endeavor to show that Koestler's view and similar ones result from a monumental miscomprehension of what the biological theory of evolution really is.

———————

The term mutation subsumes a variety of phenomena. In the inclusive sense, any change in the genotype not due to gene recombination is a mutation. Chromosomes, as well as self-producing cytoplasmic organelles, undergo mutational changes. Gene mutations are caused by alterations within genetic materials; chromosomal aberrations involve loss, multiplication, or rearrangement of genes in the chromosomes. A synopsis of the kinds of mutations may be as follows:

I. *Gene mutations,* or point mutations in older genetic literature—changes caused by substitution, addition, or deletion of nucleotides within a section of the DNA or the RNA of a gene.

II. *Structural Chromosomal Changes,* affecting the arrangement of genes in the chromosomes.

  A. Changes due to loss or reduplication of some of the genes.

    a. *Deficiency* (deletion). A section containing one gene or a block of genes is lost from one of the chromosomes. If a normal chromosome carries genes *ABCDEFG,* the deficient chromosome may contain only *ABEFG.*

    b. *Duplication.* A section of a chromosome may be present at its normal location in addition to being present elsewhere. If a normal chromosome has genes *ABCDEFG,* the duplication may be *ABCDCDEFG* or the equivalent. Studies of chromosomes in the salivary gland cells of certain flies have shown that in the "normal" chromosomes certain sections are represented two or more times in the haploid set. Such "repeats" are duplications that have become established in the phylogeny of these flies.

  B. Changes due to an alteration in the arrangement of the genes.

    a. *Translocation.* Two chromosomes, with genes *ABCDEFG* and *HIJK,* may exchange parts, giving rise to "new" chromosomes having *ABCDJK* and *HIEFG.*

    b. *Inversion.* The location of a block of genes within a chromosome may be changed by rotation through $180°$. The resulting chromosome carries the same genes as the original one, but their arrangement is modified, for instance, from *ABCDEFG* to *AEDCBFG.*

    c. *Transposition.* A block of genes is moved to a new position within a chromosome, for instance, *ABCDEFG* to *ADEFBCG.*

III. *Numerical Changes,* affecting the number of chromosomes.

  A. *Aneuploidy.* One or more chromosomes of the normal set may be lacking (monosomics, nullosomics) or present in excess (trisomics, tetrasomics, etc.).

  B. *Haploidy.* Higher organisms are mostly diploid during a major part of the life cycle, that is, they possess two chromosomes of each kind in the nuclei of most cells. Gametes, as well as gametophytes in plants, are haploid and carry one chromosome of each kind. Under experimental conditions some diploid organisms have produced haploid aberrants, which have a single set of chromosomes in the tissues that are normally diploid.

  C. *Polyploidy.* Normally diploid organisms may give rise to forms with more than two sets of homologous chromosomes. Such forms are known as polyploids.

———————

Evolution is a creative process, in precisely the same sense in which composing a poem or a symphony, carving a statue, or painting a picture are creative acts. An art work is novel, unique, and unrepeatable; a copy of a painting, however exact, is only a reproduction of somebody's creation. Some creativity is possible, however, in playing music, the performer adding his own to that of the composer. The evolution of every phyletic line yields a novelty that never existed before and is a unique, unrepeatable, and irreversible proceeding. As we have seen above, only a most elementary component of the evolutionary process, a mutation followed by selection of a single gene allele, may be recurrent. An evolutionary history is a unique chain of events.

103. Biology and the Future of Man

Edited by PHILIP HANDLER. Oxford University Press, Ely House, 37 Dover Street, London W1X 4AH; 1970, £5.75; 1971, £2.25; 967 pp.

Several years ago, The Committee on Science and Public Policy of the National Academy of Sciences organized twenty panels of authorities to examine the present state of knowledge in the life sciences. The result is this encyclopedic volume under the editorship of Philip Handler. This book may be considered as the ultimate single volume on biology. A list of the chapter headings indicates the range of work: Molecular Biology; Materials of Life; Cells—The Units of Life; The Origins of Life; The Biology of Development; Function of Tissues and Organs; Biological Structures—From Molecules to Man; The Nervous System; The Biology of Behavior; What Is Ecology; Heredity and Evolution; The Diversity of Life; Digital Computers and the Life Sciences; On Feeding Mankind; Science and Medical Practices; Renewable Resources; Biology and Industrial Technology; Environmental Health; and Biology and the Future of Man. Each chapter, the result of the activities of the individual panels, serves as a mini-book in itself. The book is uniformly well written and in most cases accessible to the lay reader. JB

In Man's View of Himself. Perhaps the most important result of the growth of evolutionary biology and an understanding of the mechanisms of heredity and evolution is a change in man's view of himself, of his place in the living world, and of his responsibility for its continuance.

Man used to regard himself as somehow apart from the animals and plants, following a set of rules that were different from those followed by the rest of nature. Then the study of comparative anatomy made him realize that he is similar in many structural ways to the other animals. The study of physiology showed similar mechanisms of blood circulation, of muscle contraction, of digestion, and of other body functions. Comparative biochemistry demonstrated the basic similarity of chemical mechanisms, reaction sequences, and metabolic patterns in all living organisms. The study of evolution revealed that all these similarities were the consequence of a common origin.

The interrelatedness of all life is now regarded as a part of the beauty and excitement of nature. We thereby understand ourselves better. The view has practical consequences in that we can learn a great deal about ourselves by studying other organisms. Man, knowing that he is a part of nature, realizes his dependence on the natural environment. We realize that we cannot change

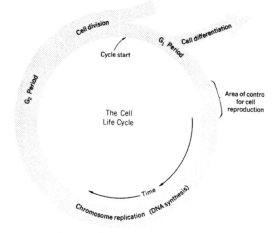

The diagram describes the process of the cell through its life cycle. Cell reproduction is regulated by interruption of cycle process at a still unidentified control point in the G_1 phase. The total time for one traverse through the cycle varies enormously from one cell type to another but is typically ten to fifteen hours in a mammalian cell undergoing unrestricted reproduction. See text for discussion of the cell life cycle. (Courtesy David M. Prescott)

this radically from the environment in which man evolved without generating serious problems.

———————————

Fortunately experience has shown that for many of the problems of human life, it is possible to find in animal life models that represent close analogies to the human situation. This is true not only for physical and physiological characteristics, but also for pathological states, behavioral patterns, and social organization. By taking advantage of this fact, it should be possible to create a new scientific discipline that will provide an ecological basis for environmental biomedicine. Ecological biomedical science might investigate such problems as:

1. Lasting effects of early influences, i.e., the effects exerted by the total environment on the organism during the formative stages of its development
2. Effects of relative degrees of isolation or crowding on hormonal activities and behavioral patterns
3. Effects of housing conditions and environmental stimuli on the development of sense organs and of various physiological processes
4. Delayed and indirect effects of biologically active substances, such as drugs and environmental pollutants
5. Long-term consequences of toleration of injurious agents
6. Adaptive potentialities

Until the laws of physics and chemistry had been elucidated, it was not possible even to formulate the important, penetrating questions concerning the nature of life. For centuries students of biology, in considering the diversity of life, its seemingly utter distinction from inanimate phenomena, and its general unlikelihood, found it necessary, in their imagination, to invest living objects with a mysterious life force, "vitalism," with which all living organisms were endowed. But in the late eighteenth century, Lavoisier and Laplace were able to show that, within the not inconsiderable

Automatic system for chromosome mapping. (From Argonne National Laboratory and J. W. Butler, *Developments in Industrial Microbiology* 8:370)

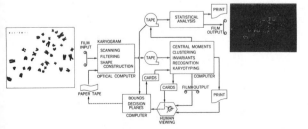

limits of error of the methods available to them, the recently formulated laws of conservation of energy and mass were valid also in a living guinea pig. The endeavors of thousands of life scientists over the next two centuries have gone far to document the thesis thus begun. Living phenomena are indeed intelligible in physical terms. And although much remains to be learned and understood, and the details of many processes remain elusive, those engaged in such studies hold no doubt that answers will be forthcoming in the reasonably near future. Indeed, only two truly major questions remain enshrouded in a cloak of not quite fathomable mystery: (1) the origin of life, i.e., the events that first gave rise to the remarkable cooperative functioning of nucleic acids and proteins which constitutes the genetic apparatus, and (2) the mind-body problem, i.e., the physical basis for self-awareness and personality. Great strides have been made in the approaches to both of these problems, as summarized in Chapters 6 and 9. But the ultimate explanations are perceived very dimly indeed.

What is Life? The most concise, unambiguous, and general definition of life that can be given at the present time is based on the *genetic* properties of living things. According to this view, the unique attribute of living matter, from which all of its other remarkable features derive, is its capacity for self-duplication with mutation. That is to say, living systems are systems that reproduce, that mutate, and that reproduce their mutations. Reproduction by itself is not a sufficient criterion for life. Many nonliving systems are self-propagating to a greater or lesser degree: crystals, for example, or even better, flames, which not only reproduce (by means of sparks) but also show metabolism and growth. Systems such as these increase by the same exponential law that describes the growth of living populations. But nonliving systems, being immutable, are incapable of evolution. Living things, on the other hand, are endowed with a seemingly infinite capacity to adapt themselves to the exigencies of existence. The endless variety and complexity of living organisms, the apparent purposefulness of their structure and behavior, are consequences of their mutability. *Any* system that has the capacity to mutate blindly in many directions and to reproduce its mutations must evolve.

2 East 63rd Street, New York, N.Y. 10021. *The Sciences;* **$6, monthly.**

The basic function of the New York Academy of Sciences is to organize scientific meetings on specialized subjects in the sciences. The Academy has over twenty-six thousand members, world wide. Each year some fifteen conferences are held on topics ranging from genetic manipulation to brain dysfunction to environmental safeguards.

The Academy publishes a magazine—*The Sciences*—for the general public. This periodical presents brief articles on contemporary scientific developments and often asks leading scientists to speculate on future changes and transformations. ER

MAN REVISED

"What a piece of work is a man!" says Hamlet, "how infinite in faculty! in form and moving, how express and admirable!" But in a rapidly evolving technological society, the paragon of animals is hard-pressed to master his environment—or himself. Physiologically and psychologically, he has proven something less than a perfect specimen for ending war and racial strife, controlling population, or maintaining the ecology. Ancient problems of disease haunt him and new problems of space exploration are spectres in his future.

Techniques for improving on nature may be developed to solve these problems in the future. Anticipating a brave new world, THE SCIENCES has asked several distinguished scientists in various disciplines what single alteration they would make in the human body, with a particular emphasis on changes useful at this time in history. We suggested that previous evolutionary functions of an organ or organ system be disregarded and that innovation be the guide. Here are their responses, some controversial, comments on a controversial body. MI

ON LINE AT SLEEP

If one believes H. G. Wells' admonition that "History is a race between education and catastrophe," then the single most important need of mankind is immediate and massive education.

One human alteration that might allow us to facilitate this would be the ability to make a direct connection between the human brain and a computer programmed with a vast amount of information relevant to the solutions of man's current problems.

If it were possible to create such a human alteration—a connection between the human neural system and an electronic device—so that people could learn perhaps during their sleep and carry on productive work during their waking hours, we could produce a mankind that would be able to solve all the physical and social problems that the human race faces today.

Of course, I do not overlook the danger of the wrong information being programmed into human beings. But then we do that today without the help of computers.

GLENN T. SEABORG

Dr. Seaborg, nobelist for chemistry, is Chairman of the U.S. Atomic Energy Commission

CEREBRAL CONTRACEPTION

Changes in the human body must take place by the adoption of advantageous or neutral point mutations into the genome of the species. The alternatives are plastic surgery or an act of God, and He does not seem to be prone to intervene at the DNA level. The rate of adoption of point mutations is about one per 1 to 2 years in human

DNA, which contains about three billion base pairs. A major change for voluntary temporary sterility (for population control) could be achieved by cortical control of the ejaculatory mechanism of the seminal vesicles replacing the present autonomic innervation. (No picture by your artist of the matter under discussion is needed for your readers, assuming that they are New York theater-goers.) The change is in the correct evolutionary direction because voluntary musculature is "newer" than smooth muscle. The innervation could come from the anterior rami of the first four sacral nerves. With the changes in musculature, and the establishment of a new center in the cerebral cortex, about 10,000 point mutations would be needed. These could be accepted at a maximum rate of one per year, so stick around until the year 119,969.

THOMAS H. JUKES

Dr. Jukes, a biochemist, is Associate Director of the Space Sciences Laboratory, University of California, Berkeley

REMEMBRANCE OF THINGS PAST

The biological imperfection of man, at the present state of his evolution, has been discussed at great length. Our critics unfairly neglect the other side of the equation: the complexity of the problems we face. Man is the only intelligent creature on this planet; as soon as his rational functions evolved to the point that culture was possible, he was bound to explore and inhabit the biosphere to the very margins of possibility, and these margins are neither always comfortable nor assuredly durable. Man is likely to press against similar margins whatever improvements he evolves or designs.

I can, however, think of one function we lack by contrast to electronic computers, namely INNOCENCE. No complex program ever works as an immediate outcome of its prior design. However, computer programs can be perfected ("debugged") by repetitive trial and error—the disasters being subject to erasure so that the system memory is restored to a standard condition. This stabilizes the problem so that it can often be solved. The human condition suffers from the fact that our sins and our guilt are cumulative; we may assuage, we may forgive, but have no way to forget.

JOSHUA LEDERBERG

Dr. Lederberg, nobelist for medicine, is Executive Head of the Department of Genetics at the Stanford University Medical Center School of Medicine

CUT DOWN TO SIZE

I see little long-term advantage in very special adaptations or appendages for man, since his greatness is in the generality of his faculties and their adaptability. Man should be smaller in size, and have a much longer life cycle than in the past, including in particular a longer time before senility and a much slower reproductive cycle.

In the past, man's size needed to be reasonably large so that he could exert the physical force necessary to do work and fight enemies; the application of intelligence and the development of tools has completely changed this. Suppose that man's scale-size, with exception of the brain, were reduced by a factor of two. The area on the surface of the earth needed for living structures would then be reduced by a factor of four, and the volume occupied by man a factor of eight. Food requirements would decrease about fourfold and the drain on other resources, for example on fuel, would be very much decreased.

Since training, education, and wisdom are such important parts of man's present and future, it would be highly desirable to extend man's effective working life and the length of his memory so that the required period of training is a less dominating fraction of his entire career. A longer life would also give him a better perspective in a rapidly changing world, allowing a lengthened time span for consideration of any given situation. Continued effectiveness of an individual over many years, with any incapacitation, old age, and death setting in suddenly rather than gradually, would be ideal. Small size and long life would, of course, very much facilitate long space journeys, to mention one of man's most recent challenges.

Less dangers from outside forces and more dangers from man himself mean that birth rates should be very much reduced. One useful way of achieving this would be to have the period of fertility much shorter and occurring somewhat later in life, after the age required for preliminary education and training.

CHARLES H. TOWNES

Dr. Townes, nobelist for physics, is Professor at Large at the University of California, Berkeley

The main result of my research, stretching over more than five decades, is a deep admiration for the harmony and perfection of nature. When I received your letter asking me whether I could improve on nature, I gave serious thought to the question. The result was a negative one: I could not. In a way, this result is a positive one, under-lining the perfection of nature. Living systems have a built-in mechanism for improving them-selves which we understand but partly. It had all the time, millions or billions of years, to do its work. It seems difficult to add to it.

One might easily be tempted to think up attrac-tive changes. Undoubtedly, it would be nice to be able to fly. However, if one pursues the con-sequences of these changes, one soon is willing to dispense with them.

My inability to improve on nature only made my silent admiration deeper.

ALBERT SZENT-GYÖRGYI

Dr. Szent-Györgyi, nobelist for medicine, is Direc-tor of the Institute for Muscle Research at The Marine Biological Laboratory, Woods Hole, Massachusetts

Any attempt to alter the human body is a *biolog-ical, intellectual and ethical monstrosity.*

RENÉ DUBOS

Dr. Dubos, a bacteriologist, is Professor at The Rockefeller University

105. The Case of the Midwife Toad

ARTHUR KOESTLER. Hutchinson Publishing Ltd., 3 Fitzroy Square, London W1P 6JD; (H) 1971; £2.00; or Pan Books Ltd., Cavaye Place, London SW10 9PG; (P) 1974; £0.50; 187 pp.

This is the best book of its kind since *The Double Helix*, Watson's story of the discovery of the structure of DNA.

In 1926, Viennese biologist William Kammerer shot and killed himself, thus climaxing a controversy over the evolutionary significance of his experiments dealing with inherited characteristics of the midwife toad. Kammerer was a Lamarckian, believing that the efforts of the parents are not entirely wasted, that some of the benefits derived from them are transmitted to their offspring, and that this is the principle active cause of evolution from amoeba to man. This thesis runs contrary to Darwinism, which is based on random mutations and haphazard variations produced by blind chance. Kammerer's experimental evidence, used as proof of the Lamarckian thesis, was questioned by William Bateson (father of Gregory Bateson), the English scientist who eventually narrowed the battlefied down to a trap and managed to center the entire debate over the origin of the species on the case of the veracity of Kammerer's work with the nuptial pads of the midwife toad. Kammerer's evidence had been deliberately falsified by either himself, a lab assistant, a museum official, or someone out to do him in. The result was his suicide, but, as Koestler points out, many questions of evolutionary significance were raised by his work, and have as yet to be answered.

This book offers a picture of the fascinating interaction of current social ideas and the interpretation of scientific fact. The Darwinists had a modern mechanistic answer to evolution, backed by several different kinds of "quantified verification"—Mendel's laws, the new statistical approach to genetics, and the breaking of the genetic code. These approaches all fit well into Darwinistic dogma and tended to be regarded as an easy proof. Lamarckism was considered disreputable as it postulated a principle in nature without being able to offer a mechanism which could account for it.

The story, thanks to Koestler, did not end with Kammerer's death. JB

Kammerer's undoing was a grotesque amphibian creature: the midwife toad *Alytes obstetricans,* or, more precisely, its so-called nuptial pads—small callosities with horny spines on the male's forelimbs which give it a better grip on the female while mating. These pads Kammerer claimed to be proof of the inheritance of acquired characters, while his opponents denied their existence.

According to the Lamarckians, evolution progresses stepwise, in the commonsense manner in which a bricklayer builds: each generation profits from the accumulated experience of its forbears. The neo-Darwinian theory, on the other hand, postulates that the parents can transmit through the channels of heredity only what they have inherited themselves and nothing else—none of the new acquisitions in skills or bodily

features that they have made in their lifetime. One might compare this doctrine to a law which decrees that a man can leave to his heirs only what he himself had been left by his parents, neither more nor less—not the added wealth he had acquired, not the house he had built, not the patents of the inventions he made; nor the debts he had incurred.

Moreover, to all appearances, Darwinism offered a 'modern', mechanistic explanation of evolution, which Lamarckism was unable to do. The discovery of Mendel's Laws, the statistical approach to genetics, and finally the breaking of the 'genetic code' imprinted on the chromosomes, seemed to be as many confirmations of Darwin's prophetic foresight. The mechanism of evolution which he had proposed may have been crude, in need of modifications and refinements; but the Lamarckians could offer no mechanism at all which would be in keeping with modern biochemistry. Random mutations in the chromosomes, triggered by radioactivity, cosmic rays, excessive heat or noxious chemicals, were scientifically acceptable as a basis on which natural selection could operate. But no acceptable hypothesis was forthcoming to explain how an acquired bodily or mental feature could cause an alteration in the genetic blueprint, contained in the micro-structure of the chromosomes in the germ-cells. That evolution should operate through a process which permits the offspring to benefit from useful changes in its forbears was an idea that might appeal to commonsense, but to the scientist at his microscope it was technically unimaginable and had to be rejected. It smacked of the ancient notion of a miniature homunculus, encased in the sperm or ovum as an exact replica of the person who carried it—including his or her 'acquired characteristics'; so that the individual who grew out of the homunculus would bear the mark of everything that had happened to its parents.

Then, in the 1950s, came another dawn: the discovery by Crick and Watson of the chemical structure of DNA, the nucleic acid in the chromosomes, carrier of the 'hereditary blueprint'. The Weismann doctrine, that nothing that happens to an organism in its lifetime can alter that blueprint, was now elevated into Crick's so-called 'Central Dogma', which states that 'information can flow from nucleic acids to proteins [i.e. from blueprint to building block] but cannot flow from protein to nucleic acid'. But dogmas are brittle structures. On June 25, 1970, the *New Scientist* announced: 'Biology's Central Dogma Turned Topsyturvy.' *The Times* Science Report followed suit: 'Big Reverse for Dogma of Biology.' The report concluded:

> It is too early to say what consequences may follow from the demonstration that DNA can be copied from RNA, but at least the central dogma now seems to be an oversimplification.

Only a fool or a fanatic could deny the revolutionary impact of Darwinism on our outlook. If I have concentrated on its shortcomings, it is partly because of that philosophical bias to which von Bertalanffy alluded; and partly for reasons explained in the opening pages of this essay. The totalitarian claim of the neo-Darwinists that evolution is 'nothing but' chance mutation plus selection has, I think, been finally defeated, and a decade or two from now biologists—and philosophers—may well wonder what sort of benightedness it was that held their elders in its thrall. Darwinian selection operating on chance mutations is doubtless a part of the evolutionary picture, but it cannot be the whole picture, and probably not even a very important part of it. There must be other principles and forces at work on the vast canvas of evolutionary phenomena.

106. On The Track of Unknown Animals

BERNARD HEUVELMANS. Paladin Books, Park Street, St. Albans, Herts; 1970; £0.60; 306 pp.

An abridged edition of the 1955 book recently published in paperback for the general reader. It's a masterpiece in mammology. JB

REVIEW BY MICHAEL PERKINS. "Even without Antarctica, the regions that are little known amount to no less than *one tenth* of the land surface of the globe." In those regions—interior Africa, Australia, and the Amazon basin, etc.—it is still possible that large animals roam that have not yet been pinned into the zoological hierarchy. Almost two dozen important animals have been discovered only within the last one hundred years, including the giant panda, captured for American zoos in the nineteen thirties.

Heuvelmans' thesis is a refutation of a statement made in 1812 by Baron Georges Cuvier, the "Father of Paleontology," who pronounced: "there is little hope of discovering new species of large quadrupeds." He follows it with challenges to successive generations of orthodox zoologists who have held the same stiff line against recognition of the Nittaewo, the lost people of Ceylon, described as perfect human beings but smaller than pygmies, being reddish, hairy, and the possessors of long claws; the orang pendek, the ape men of Sumatra, the Abominable Snowman, the Australian bunyips, and the giant anaconda.

"Authorities" are the enemy in this book, and the heroes are natives, explorers, and legend. Immediate response is opposed to intellectualized distancing, and the result is mystery. Despite the fantastic elements of his story, Heuvelmans makes a good case for his findings that there are many unknown animals left, and that zoology is a stodgy, hardly exact science. Science hasn't pinned us all down yet—or at least not those of us with tails.

"Living fossils" can best be defined as *stationary* species. There are quite a number of types of animal whose evolution seems to have stopped long ago, for their structure has not altered appreciably since distant ages. Admittedly it is not always easy to say for certain that an organism has not changed for millions of years, for our knowledge of past creatures is often slender and based on no more than a shell, a skeleton, or a mere impression in the mud. We cannot be sure that the flesh which has perished has not undergone any change in its physiology or cellular structure. We may also grant the name to creatures which have preserved a set of important and archaic characteristics, though they would be "living fossils" only in respect to these particular features.

The hoatzin *(Opisthocomus hoatzin)* of the Amazon is a good example of this. When fully grown it looks ordinary enough, like a sort of crested pheasant, yellowish in color with an olive back and dull red belly. But the young bird still has well-developed claws on the first two fingers of its wings, thus betraying its distant origin. When hoatzin chicks use their clawed wings to climb branches, crawl on the ground, or swim after tadpoles, they look just like little reptiles, and remind one irresistibly of the archaeopteryx, the reptile-bird of the Jurassic, when birds had teeth.

The young hoatzin still has claws on its wings.

The hoatzin has also preserved other significant archaic features. It does not cry like a bird, but croaks like a frog and gives off a strong smell of musk like a crocodile and some of the turtles. To deny that it is a " living fossil " would be absurd.

———————

The *orang pendek,* according to reports, is a very shy biped which speaks an unintelligible language. It is between 2 feet 6 inches and 5 feet high. Its skin is pinkish brown and, according to most versions, covered all over with short dark brown to black hair. It has a head of jet-black hair forming a bushy mane down its back. It has no visible tail. Its arms are not as long as an anthropoid ape's. It hardly ever climbs in trees, but walks on the ground. It is supposed to walk with its feet reversed, the heels facing forward.

———————

It may seem odd that the first unknown animals to be investigated should be described as " people. " But from India to the Malay Archipelago we shall constantly run up against the same question about the mysterious creatures reported to live there: are they men or beasts?

Asia may still hide unknown apes whose mental development is higher than that of the anthropoid apes and thus comes close to our own. Or it may be inhabited by men more primitive than the Australian aborigines, the Veddahs, or the African Bushmen, and still at the Neanderthal stage. Or yet again, a few survivors of those strange ape men, the Java Man and the Peking Man, may linger on today not far from the places where their bones were found.

The first place in which " beast men " are reported to have survived into historical times is India. Pliny the Elder wrote at the very beginning of the Christian era:

> *Duris* maketh report, That certaine Indians engender with beasts, of which generation are bred

The indris, the largest known living lemur.

certaine monstrous mungrels, halfe beasts and halfe men.

———————

We can now even give a detailed description of the giant biped anthropoid of the Himalayas, a survivor of the giant primates which once ruled a large part of the earth. Only four are so far known to paleontology: the Chinese Gigantopithecus, of which we have only a few molars and a jawbone, the Java Meganthropus, represented by a fragment of jawbone with its teeth, the Tanganyika Meganthropus, consisting only of jaw and facial bones, and the South African Paranthropus, of which several skulls and a biped's pelvis have been excavated. If I seek to relate the snowman to the Gigantopithecus it is obviously for geographical reasons and because most reports of its size agree with Dr. Broom's estimate of that of the Chinese giant.

107. Factors in the Transfer of Technology

Edited by WILLIAM H. GRUBER and DONALD G. MARQUIS. The M.I.T. Press, 126 Buckingham Palace Road, London SW1W 9SD; 1969; £5.85; 289 pp.

Last year's spaceship is this year's new-model washing machine. In fact, it takes about a generation for the major technological systems developed for military use to filter through for general use. For instance, the technical work done on anti-aircraft devices to enable the effective tracking of enemy planes during World War II became the feedback technology for individual electric thermostats.

This book is the first serious study to examine the transfer of technology—the multilateral flow of information and techniques across the boundaries of science, technology, and the practical world. JB

Some models were developed during the last day of the conference, and these models are referred to in a number of the papers. The models are briefly summarized here so that the reader may have an understanding of a model when it is mentioned in one of the papers. The presentation of the models at this point also permits the specification of definitions and concepts that are frequently used in the papers that follow. The development of the models at the conference was an attempt to provide a framework for further analysis on the problem of the transfer of technology.

MODEL I

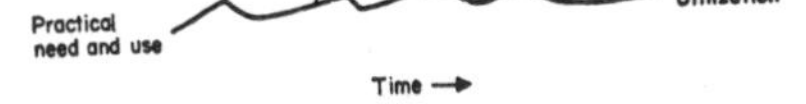

Figure 1. Science, technology, and the utilization of their products, showing communication paths among the three streams: (a) science to science; (b) science to technology (slow); (c) science to technology (fast gap filling); (d) technology to science (e.g., instruments); (e) technology to technology; (f) use to use (diffusion); (g) technology to use; (h) science to use (e.g., cod liver oil treatment of rickets). For an extended analysis of the "Communications Patterns In Applied Technology," as related to this model, see the Marquis and Allen (1966) paper by that title in *The American Psychologist*, 21 (November 1966).

Given any bit of technical information, is it possible to evaluate the probability that this bit will be transferred into another use? Are there critical factors that should be investigated during the development of a transfer model? Assume that there is technical information available that is relevant to a given project. Model II provides a sequential series of probabilities that might be considered in order to determine whether the given technical information would be transferred into a new use that would itself result in eventual diffusion.

MODEL II

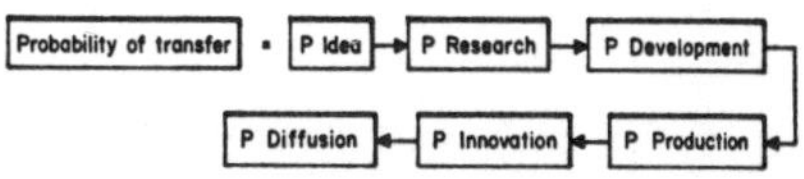

Model II examines the sequence of events within the organization structure of a given potential recipient or user of existing technology. There is an entry point, the probability of someone in the organization having the idea to examine a new

piece of technical information. The remaining set of probabilities focuses on the sequence from the point of entry of the idea into consideration through to the point of success in diffusion. Model II, therefore, has two critical links with the outside world, one at the point of entry and one at the point of marketing the output of the inventive effort.

For reasons which will become apparent as we go along, these three aspects of the process of innovation may be conveniently referred to by using names borrowed from zoology: (1) the phase of *mutation,* (2) that of *selection,* and (3) that of *diffusion* and eventual *dominance.* During the phase of mutation, a pool of novel variants (or mutants) is created, on which the intelligence and experience of the practical man can proceed to exercise itself; in the phase of selection, those variants which do not meet the immediate demands of the situation in question are weeded out, and a few meritorious ones are selected for incorporation into practical use—that is, for perpetuation within the current tradition of concepts and techniques; and finally, in the phase of ecological diffusion and dominance, those variants which have been successful within a limited environment (or niche) either spread or fail to spread throughout the larger human environment.

This study has measured the relative performance of six channels in transferring technical information. The research technique employs the vehicle of parallel R and D projects to provide a control over the substance of the problem and a relative evaluation of solutions. Data are gathered by means of Solution Development Records and lengthy interviews with the engineers. The ideas considered for solution to each problem are thus associated with the channels whence they came, and measures of performance are generated for the channels.

The principal conclusions of the study are

1. There is a serious misalignment between the quality of the ideas generated through the channels studied, and the frequency with which these channels are used by engineers.

2. Literature is not greatly used, and is mediocre at best in its performance.

3. Better performing groups rely more than the poorer performers upon sources within the laboratory (the technical staff, and other company research programs) as contrasted with sources outside the laboratory.

4. A mismatch in information coding schemes appears to be responsible for the ineffectiveness of communication across the organizational boundary. The possible existence of key individuals (technological gatekeepers) shows promise of providing a means of surmounting this organizational boundary impedance.

Technology may be defined as the means or capacity to perform a particular activity. The transfer of technology must then mean the utilization of an existing technique in an instance where it has not previously been used. This transfer may be merely the acceptance by a user of a practice common elsewhere, or it may be a different application of a given technique designed originally for another use.

The acceptance by a user of a common practice is called " adoption, " and the spread of such adoptions the " diffusion of technology. " The application of technology in a new way is properly labeled an " innovation. " A transfer of technology occurs in both adoption and innovation in the sense that a decision is made to use a form of technology where it has not previously been utilized.

This focus on the science-technology relationship may be summarized as follows:

1. The immediate contribution of science to technology is in the training of personnel to be employed in applied projects.

2. The longer run contribution occurs after a necessary lag between discovery and utilization has occurred.

3. In cases where technology discovered a science gap and needed science is specified, then there may be relatively rapid transfer from science into technology under the spur of mission-oriented organization.

This application of the research findings on the transfer of science to technology indicates the usefulness of such research. In a field heretofore dominated by opinion, the basis for an operational understanding of the process of transfer has been reached.

108. Bell Telephone Laboratories

Mountain Avenue, Murray Hill, N.J. 07974.

American Telephone and Telegraph is one of the world's largest companies. The Bell Telephone Laboratories constitute the research and development division of this corporation. With a budget in excess of $350 million annually (from both AT&T and Western Electric), and over seventeen thousand employees, Bell Labs pursues specific objectives in research, systems engineering, and design and development.

The men and women working at Bell Labs have changed all our lives. Their research and works have led to the development of the transistor, the solar battery, sound motion pictures, stereo sound, and the first active communications satellite—Telstar.

The breadth and range of this research ranges from the development of magnetic bubbles that may eventually shrink the computer to palm size, to the work of an acoustical engineer in the development of equipment that creates auditory illusions. And, of course, great assortments of improved telecommunications technology for the extension of our ears and our eyes. ER

BELL LABORATORIES ROLE IN THE BELL SYSTEM

BELL LABS' MISSION: To undertake the basic research, development, and design, and systems engineering, necessary to provide the Bell System—and, in turn, society—with new and improved equipment and services for communication.

OWNERSHIP OF BELL LABS: Jointly shared by AT&T, parent company of the Bell System, and Western Electric, manufacturing and supply unit of the System.

AT&T SUPPORTS: All research and fundamental development in fields such as physics, chemistry, metallurgy, electronics. Also, systems engineering. Total budget for these activities in 1971: $136,-300,000.

WESTERN ELECTRIC SUPPORTS: Specific development and design of components, equipment and systems. Certain other engineering and manufacturing services. Total budget for these activities in 1971: $218,200,000.

OBJECTIVES: *Research*—new knowledge in basic sciences as a foundation for new communications systems and facilities. *Systems engineering*—

technical planning with respect to development projects to be undertaken. Considers new knowledge and opportunities for its use in service of Bell System customers. *Specific development and design*—leads directly to new systems and facilities. Constitutes the bulk of BTL's development activities. *Business information systems programs*—develops systems for the Operating Companies to enable them to better handle increasing business information needs.

HIGHLIGHTS OF OUR TECHNICAL HISTORY

1925: "Orthophonic" phonograph demonstration is results of Bell Labs development in technique and equipment for high-fidelity sound reproduction.

1926: First full-length motion picture with synchronized sound presented by Warner Brothers using recording and reproducing equipment developed by Bell Laboratories.

1927: Two-way radio telephone service initiated between New York and London · First demonstration of transmission long distance television over wires · C. J. Davisson experiments in electron diffraction demonstrate the wave nature of matter.

1929: First public demonstration of transmission of color television.

1930: Negative feedback amplifier invented by Harold Black; eventually makes possible transcontinental multichannel telephone systems.

1931: Teletypewriter exchange service begins using Bell Laboratories-designed switching networks.

1933: Radio astronomy is born with Karl Jansky's study of stellar noise · First stereo reproduction of symphonic music—then called " auditory perspective "—transmitted via underground cable from Philadelphia to Washington.

1936: First demonstration of a coaxial cable system—New York to Philadelphia.

1937: Clinton J. Davisson is co-recipient—with G. P. Thomson of Great Britain—of Nobel Prize for work done at Bell Laboratories in 1927.

1938: First electrical relay-type digital computer developed by George Stibitz · First " terrain clearance indicator " or altimeter for aircraft demonstrated.

1968: Call-a-matic ® telephone, first repertory dialer, developed · Dial Tone First service has successful field trial.

1969: Discovery of magnetic bubbles—tiny cylinder-shaped areas of magnetism, which can be manipulated in magnetic materials and used for memory and other data applications · Traffic Service Position System—a new electronic system automating many details of long distance calling and freeing the operator for more personal service to customers— put in service in Morristown, N. J. · Waterproof cable, filled with petroleum jelly and polyethylene mixture developed.

1970: First commercial Picturephone service begins operation in Pittsburgh, Pa. · No. 2 ESS, small electronic central office, put in service in Oswego, Illinois · First semiconductor laser to operate continuously at room temperature demonstrated.

CONTRIBUTIONS TO NEW INDUSTRIES AND NEW PRODUCTS

VACUUM TUBES: First commercial cathode ray tube; magnetrons; closed-spaced triode; traveling-wave tube; klystron. A $40 million annual industry.

LASERS: First continuously operating gas laser; carbon dioxide laser; several hundred other gas and solid-state type lasers.

SEMICONDUCTORS: Transistors; single crystal germanium and silicon; epitaxial materials; zone refining; oxide masking; integrated circuits; silicon target tube for Picturephone ® camera; electroluminescent diodes.

SUPERCONDUCTIVITY: Over 100 superconducting materials discovered since 1950.

THERMISTORS: Basic discovery of nickel-manganese-cobalt-oxide system.

QUARTZ CRYSTALS: Synthetic material processes; theory; circuit applications; commercial hydrothermal growth process.

ACOUSTICS: Audiometer; high-fidelity recording and reproduction; sound motion pictures; sound spectrograph; artificial larynx; vocoders.

DATA COMMUNICATIONS: Telephotography and facsimile; TWX; data sets; data terminals; teletypesetter; audio response units.

DIGITAL COMPUTERS: First relay computer; information theory; memory technology; programming languages; error-detecting and error-correcting codes; on-line graphics terminals; computer animation, speech and music.

Magnified magnetic bubbles (the light circles) are shown moving through a circuit pattern formed on a thin epitaxial film of uniaxial garnet. The Y and Bar circuit elements are part of an experimental shift register made at Bell Labs. One bubble, somewhat elongated, can be seen in transition from one pole to the next. The bubbles are three ten-thousandths of an inch in diameter. Photo 8.7-36, November 1970, Bell Laboratories.

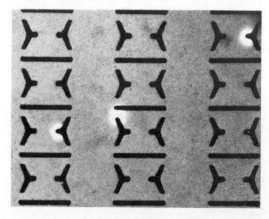

109. The Salk Institute for Biological Studies

P.O. Box 1809, San Diego, Calif. 92112; 1970 (Gaffron).

The Salk Institute is a residential center where the new advances in the life sciences are studied and weighed with special attention given to moral, social, and ethical implications. The institute publishes a series of Occasional Papers to "assure the dissemination of contemporary thinking upon the broader implications" of contemporary life-science research. The first two papers in this series are Jacques Monod's "From Biology to Ethics" and Hans Gaffron's "Resistance to Knowledge," the latter of which is excerpted here. ER

Experimenting with social institutions.—Many of the troubles assailing us today may well be called eternal, for they are not too different from those that plagued our ancestors 3000 years ago. What is new are the solutions to such problems that have become available in our time through biology and psychology. Just as it took some effort to persuade people to abandon traditional quackery in favor of modern medicine, just as virtually every man now believes that the earth rotates once in a day, in clear contradiction to what he sees, so we must persuade the people that it is time to supplant some old prejudices by new ones. It is time that they learn to believe what they already know superficially about such matters as evolution, inheritance, psychology, or even physics.

The technical world has outpaced all norms of earlier ages. Now even religions have to adjust themselves to changes in human conditions everywhere in the world, and ours also are in for revision. When objective science has become so influential, free discussion about the most suitable among religious ideologies and value systems is one of the conditions for civilized progress.

Because a few of the behavioral experiments performed in the laboratory with persons who volunteer as guinea pigs are harrowing and often somewhat painful, the thought persists that much greater and unforeseeable damage to society may result if we experiment deliberately with social institutions and populations in the open. People forget that customs, fashions and morals change all the time (unless protected by law), not because of farsighted intention, but rather in the manner of contagious diseases. It stands to reason that the clumsiness of our judicial procedures, particularly in reversing decisions that do not work out right, are the source of much avoidable unhappiness.

Truth to tell, the evolution of the species is not the central problem of biology, not any longer. The frontiers of this discipline, the limits of its *terra incognita* lie nowadays at the two poles of evolution: at the prime sources of emergence and at the most highly refined manifestations of teleonomy. In other words, two problems: that, on the one hand, of the appearance of the very first structures endowed with the capacity for self-reproduction; on the other, that of the functioning of the most highly evolved among teleonomic structures, namely, the central nervous system.

It remains, nevertheless, that although our theoretical generalizations are bringing a wide range of possible applications to light, thus far the essential role of the allosteric interactions has been experimentally demonstrated only at the cell level. Multicellular organisms succeeded in emerging thanks only to the development of new networks of coordination. In order of complexity, we should differentiate between:

1. Coordinations which result from direct, contactual interactions between cells.

2. Endocrine correlations.

3. The nervous system.

All these systems function through the intermediary of chemical signals which, in the last analysis, act at the cellular level. How these signals act within the molecule—whether they are mediators of the nerve impulse, like acetylcholine, or hormones such as the steroids—is still almost completely unknown. It is tempting to suppose that these bodies might play the part of allosteric ligands, which would imply that, without significance in and of themselves, their interpretation as signals would depend exclusively on the cellular program. Thus might one be able to expain how a single body can produce different primary effects, depending on the tissue or the recipient organ.

These for the time being are no more than speculations. It is certain, however, that embryology, endocrine physiology, neurophysiology and molecular biology must now join forces in this domain to seek the solution to these basic teleonomic problems.

Let us say that I would be surprised—and my faith in the unity of the living world deceived—if man's central nervous system, this prodigious organism of teleonomic coordination, did not in fact use the allosteric interactions already discovered through bacteria as a means of molecular communication.

————————————————

In the ethic of knowledge the single goal, the supreme value, the "sovereign good" is not, let us admit it, the happiness of mankind, still less mankind's temporal power or comfort, nor even the $\gamma\nu\omega\theta\iota$ $\sigma\epsilon\alpha\upsilon\tau o\nu$, The Socratic "know thyself," it is objective knowledge itself. I feel that this has to be said; that this ethic has to be systematized, its social, moral and political consequences distinguished; that we have to broadcast it and teach it; for, creator of the modern world, it alone is compatible with that world. There must be no hiding that this is a severe and constraining ethic which, though respecting man as the sustainer of knowledge, defines a value superior to man. It is a conquering ethic and in some ways Nietzschean, since its core is a will to power: but power only in the noosphere. An ethic which will therefore teach scorn for violence and temporal domination. An ethic of personal and political liberty; for to contest, to criticize, to question constantly are not only rights therein, but a duty. A social ethic, for objective knowledge cannot be established as such elsewhere than within a community which recognizes its norms.

To the men of today what ideal is there to propose, what ideal above and beyond themselves, if not the reconquest, through knowledge, of the nullity of which they themselves have been the first discoverers?

110. Scientific American

Scientific American, Inc., 415 Madison Avenue, New York, N.Y. 10017; $10, monthly. Scientific American Offprints; W. H. Freeman and Co. Publishers, 660 Market Street, San Francisco, Calif. 94104; $0.25 offprint.

Scientific American is a monthly magazine carrying feature articles on contemporary trends in science and technology. Authors of the articles are the men involved in the ongoing research being described. The illustrations and design, both conservative in nature, amplify and augment the over-all presentation.

Once a year, in the September issue, *Scientific American* devotes an entire issue to a single theme. Such issues have been concerned with the cities, the oceans, the biosphere, energy, and power. Over eight hundred reprints from the magazine are available in an individual format. ER

THE FASTEST COMPUTER

BY D.L. SLOTNICK

ILLIAC IV is made up of 64 independent processing units that by operating simultaneously will be capable of solving complex problems in a fraction of the time needed by any other machine

The computer ILLIAC IV, which is now nearing completion, is the fourth generation in a line of advanced machines that have been conceived and developed at the University of Illinois. ILLIAC I, a vacuum-tube machine completed in 1952, could perform 11,000 arithmetical operations per second. ILLIAC II, a transistor-and-diode computer completed in 1963, could perform 500,000 operations per second. ILLIAC III, which became operational in 1966, is a special-purpose computer designed for automatic scanning of large quantities of visual data. Since it processes nonarithmetical data it cannot be compared with the earlier ILLIAC'S in terms of operational speed. ILLIAC IV, employing the latest semiconductor technololgy, is actually a battery of 64 "slave" computers, capable of executing between 100 million and 200 million instructions per second. Even that basic rate, although it is faster than that of any other computer yet built, does not express the true capacity of ILLIAC IV.

Unlike its three predecessors and all computers now on the market, which solve problems by a series of sequential steps, ILLIAC IV is designed to perform as many as 64 computations simultaneously. For such a computing structure to be utilized efficiently the problem must be amenable to parallel, rather than sequential, processing. In actuality problems of this kind constitute a considerable part of the total computational spectrum, ranging from payroll calculations to linear programming to models of the general circulation of the atmosphere for use in weather prediction. For example, a typical linear-programming problem that might occupy a large present-generation computer for six to eight hours should be solvable by ILLIAC IV in less than two minutes—a time reduction of at least 200 to one.

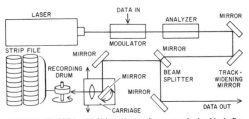

ARCHIVAL MEMORY is a new high-capacity secondary memory, developed by the Precision Instrument Company. The beam from an argon laser records binary data by burning microscopic holes in a thin film of metal coated on a strip of polyester sheet, which is carried by a rotating drum. Each data strip can store some 2.9 billion bits, the equivalent of 625 reels of standard magnetic tape in less than 1 percent of the volume. The "strip file" provides storage for 400 data strips containing more than a trillion bits. The time to locate data stored on any one of the 400 strips is about five seconds. Within the same strip data can be located in 200 milliseconds. The read-and-record rate is four million bits a second.

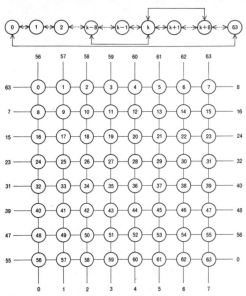

ARRAY OF 64 PROCESSING ELEMENTS in ILLIAC IV is connected in a pattern that can be regarded in either of two ways, which are topologically equivalent. The elements can be viewed as a linear string (*top*) with each processing element connected to its immediate neighbors and to neighbors spaced eight elements away. Equivalently, one can regard the processing elements as a square array (*bottom*) with each element connected to its four nearest neighbors. One can imagine the array rolled into a cylinder so that the processing elements in the top row connect directly to those in the bottom row. The last processing element in each row is connected to the first in the next row to produce a linear sequence.

83

EXPERIMENTS IN TIME REVERSAL

With the presumed symmetry of charge and parity disproved, rigorous tests have been made of nature's indifference to which way time flows. No proof to the contrary has yet appeared but the hunt for it goes on

BY OLIVER E. OVERSETH

The arrow of time, to use that marvelous phrase of Sir Arthur Eddington's, points in an obvious direction. It is aimed toward the future, over which we can hope to exert some control, and away from the irretrievable past. All of us vividly recognize which way time flows; we take considerable comfort, for example, in our confidence that the carefully arranged marriage of gin and vermouth is not going to be suddenly annulled in our glass, leaving us with two layers of warm liquid and a lump of ice. It is a curious fact, however, that the laws that provide the basis for our understanding of fundamental physical processes (and presumably biological processes as well) do not favor one direction of time's arrow over another. They would represent the world just as well if time were flowing backward instead of forward and martinis were coming apart rather than being created.

This symmetry of the basic laws of nature with respect to the direction of the flow of time has long been a principle of physics. Eddington himself touched on time at considerable length (in his Gifford Lectures of 1927). After discussing the physical and philosophical foundations of the then new theories of relativity, gravitation and quantum mechanics, he concluded: "The laws of nature are indifferent as to a direction of time. There is no more distinction between past and future than between right and left."

Today we have come to realize that the laws of nature are *not* indifferent to right and left, and we now suspect that they also make a distinction between past and future. As a result of recent findings in elementary-particle physics the principle of the symmetry of the flow of time has been seriously challenged. An intense search is now under way to see if violations of the principle can be detected experimentally. Workers in the fields of atomic, nuclear and high-energy physics have undertaken a multipronged attack on the problem. No violation has yet been confirmed, but there is good reason to believe an asymmetry exists. It may be very small and difficult to detect, or perhaps we have not yet looked in the right places.

In this article I should like to show how physicists conduct the search for violations of what is known as time-reversal invariance and to summarize the results of some of the most significant tests.

EFFECTS ON PUBLISHING

The effects of electronic typesetting *cum* computer on publishing are likely to be substantial. The public hunger for printed information is seemingly insatiable; historically the supply has generally run behind the demand. Within the past decade book publishing has doubled in the U.S., and the sales of newspapers and periodicals have increased by 50 percent or more. Printing, the eighth-largest industry in the nation, is growing faster than other manufacturing industries. Its total sales now amount to more than $15 billion a year, of which $5.5 billion is spent for newspapers, $5.3 billion for general printing, $2.5 billion for periodicals and $2 billion for books.

Electronic typesetting will undoubtedly foster a considerable increase in the demand for and volume of printed material, since it reduces the cost of printing and speeds up the output.

60 Garden Street, Cambridge, Mass. 02138.

Short-lived phenomena include comets, earthquakes, tidal waves, volcanic eruptions, the creation of islands in the sea, the disappearance of lakes, oil spills, pollution, and plagues. The Center maintains a communications network linking some 2,500 volunteers from almost 150 countries. ER

| EVENT | 61-70 | WALAGA METEORITE FALL | 23 JULY 1970 | 975. |

EVENT NOTIFICATION REPORT

The following cable was received from professor Pierre Gouin on 22 July 1970:

" ON 19 APRIL A STONEY METEORITE FELL IN WALAGA PROVINCE· IN SOUTHWEST ETHIOPIA AT APPROX 1700 LT. GOUIN HAS OBTAINED A 2.3 KILO FRAGMENT. A 300 GRAM SAMPLE AIRMAILED TO SAO ON 22 JUL. GOUIN TO INVESTIGATE AREA OF FALL TO OBTAIN DATA ON OTHER FRAGMENTS."

TYPE OF EVENT	ASTROPHYSICAL
DATE OF OCCURRENCE	19 APRIL 1970
LOCATION OF EVENT	WALAGA PROVINCE, SOUTHWEST ETHIOPIA
REPORTING SOURCE	GEOPHYSICAL OBSERVATORY. HAILE SELLASSIE I UNIVERSITY
SOURCE CONTACT	PROFESSOR PIERRE GOUIN. DIRECTOR, GEOPHYSICAL OBSERVATORY HAILE SELLASSIE I UNIVERSITY, P.O. BOX 1176 ADDIS ABABA, ETHIOPIA

SMITHSONIAN INSTITUTION
CENTER FOR SHORT-LIVED PHENOMENA
60 Garden Street
CAMBRIDGE MASSACHUSETTS 02138
UNITED STATES OF AMERICA
CABLE SATELLITES NEW YORK
TELEPHONE (617) 864-7911

soo-slp-5

| EVENT | 5-70 | FLORIDA BEACHED WHALE MORTALITY | 12 JANUARY 1970 | 845. |

EVENT NOTIFICATION REPORT

About 150 Black Pilot whales have beached along a two mile stretch on Fort Pierce North Beach. The majority of them range from 15 to 20 feet in length, 3 to 4 feet high, and are estimated to weight 1500 pounds each. It is believed that due to the cold water from the unusually cold weather (26° F.) that the bull leader of the herd of Black Pilot whales was looking for warmer water or was sick. When they are sick whales tend to beach themselves. If he was looking for warmer water it would have been an accidental beaching; whereas if he was sick it would have been on purpose. And naturally, the rest of the whales followed him.

Yesterday the Department of Natural Resources marine patrol had boats out trying to pull them back out into the water. They did manage to tie ropes to the tails of about 35 young bulls and pull them out into deep water, but as soon as the whales were free they immediately turned around and swam back onto the shore faster than the boats could head them off, and beached themselves again. Only three didn't rebeach immediately, and they were found on Palm Beach later. They died because of dehydration. The ones that were still alive were sounding and making a special kind of sonar type noises.

TYPE OF EVENT	BIOLOGICAL
DATE OF OCCURRENCE	11 JANUARY 1970
LOCATION OF EVENT	FORT PIERCE, FLORIDA, USA
REPORTING SOURCE	MISS PAT QUINA FORT PIERCE NEWS-TRIBUNE
SOURCE CONTACT	MR.JERRY ROGERS STATE DEPT. OF NATURAL RESOURCES MARINE DIVISION TALLAHASSEE, FLORIDA

SMITHSONIAN INSTITUTION
CENTER FOR SHORT-LIVED PHENOMENA
60 Garden Street
CAMBRIDGE MASSACHUSETTS 02138
UNITED STATES OF AMERICA
CABLE SATELLITES NEW YORK
TELEPHONE (617) 864-7911

soo-slp-5

SMITHSONIAN INSTITUTION
CENTER FOR SHORT-LIVED PHENOMENA

EVENT NOTIFICATION AND INFORMATION CARD SERVICE
ORDER FORM

Please enter my subscription to the Center's short-lived event notification and information card service in the following categories for a period of one year. Mark an X in category/issue frequency desired.

Average Issues/Yr.	Event Categories	Annual Subscription Rate Issue Frequency		
		Daily	Weekly	Monthly
100	Earth Science Event Cards	$40 ☐	$20 ☐	$10 ☐
100	Biological Science Event Cards	$40 ☐	$20 ☐	$10 ☐
40	Astrophysical Science Event Cards	$20 ☐	$10 ☐	$ 5 ☐
10	Urgent Archaeological/Anthro-pological Event Cards	$10 ☐	$ 5 ☐	$ 5 ☐
250	All Event Cards Issued by the Center	$100 ☐	$50 ☐	$25 ☐

EVENT CARD ISSUE FREQUENCY		AUDIENCE
Daily	Event cards in selected categories issued daily as events occur; airmailed within 24 hours of receipt of information by the Center.	Research scientists, government agencies, laboratories and environmental research centers with fast response capabilities; news media.
Weekly	Event cards in selected categories issued during past week; mailed on Friday afternoon each week.	Teachers, schools, and college departments and students participating in science programs
Monthly	Event cards in selected categories issued during past month; mailed on the last day of the month.	Libraries, archives, statisticians, and documentation centers.

Payment Enclosed ☐   Please Bill Me. ☐

Name_____

Address_____

City, State, & Zip Code_____

If payment is enclosed, send check, money order, or purchase order with this card to: SMITHSONIAN INSTITUTION, CENTER FOR SHORT-LIVED PHENOMENA, 60 GARDEN STREET, CAMBRIDGE, MASSACHUSETTS, 02138. Please make checks payable to the Smithsonian Institution.

112. New Scientist

New Science Publications, 128 Long Acre, London WC2E 9OH; weekly, £9.75 per year.

New Scientist is a weekly British scientific periodical offering original articles on new research by scientists from all over the world. Recently *New Scientist* was merged with the previously monthly *Science Journal* to form one weekly magazine. Each issue contains a very thorough review of scientific information and data reported in other international journals. *New Scientist* is a complete science news service. ER

THE FUTURE OF THE BRAIN SCIENCES

A new science is in the process of being born. The offspring of many parent disciplines, its target is the brain. Where does this fledgling science stand today?

Understanding that unpromising lump of grey matter wherein our consciousness resides must surely rank as the greatest intellectual challenge remaining to Man, now that the golden days of molecular biology are fading slowly into the establishment. The ground has been prepared; the tools are at hand; the first sketchy hypotheses are being formed; and the workers—from every conceivable scientific discipline—are assembling. We have invited some of these researchers to take a look at the brain, and in particular its key attributes of learning and memory, from their several points of view. The result is a tentative though as yet incomplete manifesto for a scientific revolution

TOWARDS THE TERABIT MEMORIES

JOSEPH HANLON staff writer for Computerworld

Two technologies new to the computer world—lasers and videotape—have made it possible to store, on-line, more than 10^{12} bits of data. The cost per bit of such memories is so low that the major expense will be inputting the data, rather than storing or retrieving it

One of the great promises—and threats—of the computer has been its supposed ability to disgorge instantly vast amounts of information at the press of a button. But the reality of the situation has been less exciting. Until now, few computers could have immediately accessible (on-line) more than the 38 million words in the Encyclopaedia Brittanica. To store more information, one had to go off-line and keep tapes or disc packs on a shelf just like library books.

But two new technologies—lasers and videotape—have finally fulfilled the original promise. Memory units now available can store, on-line, some 3×10^{12} bits of data. A "bit" is equivalent to an on-off switch, and it takes eight bits for each letter, so a typical five letter word would require 40 bits. Thus the new memories will store between 10^{10} and 10^{11} English words—more than in 1000 encyclopaedias.

Typical on-line mass memories

memory type	millions of bits on-line	approximate access time in seconds
Core	64	0.00001
Disc	6400	0.04
IBM data cell	26 000	0.4
RCA magnetic card	34 000	0.5
Laser	1 000 000	9.0
Videotape	3 000 000	15.0

THE WATERFRONT OF NOW

NORMAN GRIDGEMAN Biometrician with the Canadian National Research Council, Ottawa

Energy for the world's technology

3 The future of world energy — Sir Harold Hartley, CH, FRS

The world will need to draw on all the available sources of energy to meet its growing appetite. With the possible exception of natural gas, reserves should be adequate for at least 30 years

5 Rise of the total energy concept — William Short

The use of one fuel to supply all kinds of energy improves overall fuel efficiency, but is hindered in Britain by restrictions on the sale of electricity

11 Progress for coal — Leslie Grainger

Coal will remain valuable chiefly as a fuel, its competitiveness maintained by improved mine productivity and by combustion in fluid-bed burners. Current research, on such themes as obtaining chemicals and structural materials from coal digests, is opening up new lines for the future

16 Fuel cells in perspective — Colin Clow, Dr Hans Espig, and Dr Derek Gregory

What problems remain to be solved before the fuel cell becomes a practical, economic power source?

18 Looking ahead with nuclear power — Philip Searby

Even after 20 years of intensive development, nuclear power is still in its infancy. Last year it supplied barely two per cent of the world's electricity. It is now growing rapidly and costs will fall as fast reactors take over from thermal reactors

---

Simultaneity implies the coincidence in time of events in separate places. But just how much significance can we attach to this concept in a real world?

I believe that time is something that we can see

Anonymous symposiast

I do not believe in time

Vladimir Nabokov

Ever since the establishment of a finite speed for light and the subsequent unfolding of evidence that many celestial objects are light years away, we have been entertaining the whimsy of "seeing" the past when such objects come into our vision. A typical illustration is that of a star in a remote corner of the universe, and of imagining that in fact it ceased to exist (by explosion, say) aeons ago, so that we are now looking at a heavenly ghost. The interesting thing about this notion is its endurance. It is still popular today—two generations after being scuppered by Einstein's Special Theory of Relativity. That is why, with grave deliberation, I use the word "whimsy", and why I believe a new attempt at explication to be worth while.

BETWEEN MAN AND MACHINE

. . . or how to get on with a computer

LEARNING TO LIVE WITH THE COMPUTER

The Earl of Halsbury

TEMPERING THE REVOLUTION

J. Malcolm Rigby

THINKING WITH THE MACHINE

Robert Parslow

PHYSICISTS AS INFORMATION ENGINEERS

Dr Keith Roberts

START OF A LIFELONG PARTNERSHIP

John Barker

THE MACHINE'S INTELLIGENT ROLE

Dr Rodney Burstall

WHAT SHOULD SCIENTISTS COMMUNICATE?

DR MARTIN SHERWOODS Senior assistant editor at the Royal Institute of Chemistry

Scientific papers should contain only "pure, storable data", without intellectual introspection

If, in their research papers, scientists were to discuss in hypothetico-deductive terms what they did, would anyone benefit? Personally, I believe that most of them would get it wrong. It would all be done by hindsight, and trying to go backwards down an "uncharted by-way of thought" to see where it began is not the scientist's job. It is the historian's. The scientist should not be discouraged from doing it if he is prepared to devote sufficient time and effort to it. If he sits down to write something specifically on the subject, as Watson attempted to do in The Double Helix, he may enrich society in his attempt. But it would benefit nobody if every scientist felt it obligatory to dash off a few hasty philosophical thoughts in every paper he wrote, in order to conform to a trend.

Instead of trying to replace what is bad in scientific papers at present with something different but just as bad, scientists should concentrate on refining the scientific paper so that it comes closer to being pure, storable data. Whether they like it or not, scientists are probably being pushed this way already by the demands of computerized information systems. Instead of letting themselves be pushed, they should start to move voluntarily in this direction. This would make the writing of scientific papers easier and could facilitate their publication. And it might even give those scientists with a bent for it more time to think seriously about the nature of science and scientific problems. They could then present their views to a general audience which probably is interested, rather than to other scientists who, as literature searchers, are not.

STRANGENESS, QUARKS AND THE EIGHTFOLD WAY

DR GERALD L. WICKS Nuclear physicist currently working as assistant science editor of New Scientist

The theoretical work of Murray Gell-Mann, the 1969 Nobel prize winner for physics, has unified much of elementary particle physics and provided the incentive for many famous experiments

Gell-Mann, a 40-year-old professor of physics at the California Institute of Technology, was awarded his Nobel prize for "contributions and discoveries concerning the classification of elementary particles and their interactions". The citation is necessarily vague due to the quantity and diversity of ideas that originated with Gell-Mann.

Another famous contribution of Gell-Mann's was the invention of "quarks" as the bases of elementary particles. Again, this idea was independently derived, this time by George Zweig at CERN. Quarks were named by Gell-Mann from a passage in James Joyce's Finnegan's Wake. They have the unusual property of fractional electrical charge (see "A new model of fundamental particles", New Scientist vol. 43, p.526). Recent evidence indicated that the first quarks may have been detected. (See New Scientist, vol. 43, p.510.) Also noteworthy are Gell-Mann's elucidation in collaboration with A. Pais of the dynamics of neutral K mesons and the role of isotope spin in weak decays.

As can be seen, theorists do not generally work in a vacuum. It is difficult to point at a physical theory and say "this is uniquely Gell-Mann". However, it can be said that Gell-Mann has had a finger in every important theoretical pie over the last 15 years. His creativity must have been directed in some way by the aphorism of Buddha that led to the name eightfold way. "Now this, O monks, is noble truth that leads to the cessation of pain; this is the noble Eightfold Way: namely right views, right intention, right speech, right action, right living, right mindfulness, right concentration."

113. Changes

Orba Information, Ltd., 418 Saint Sulpice Street, Montreal 125, Canada; $150, 104 issues.

Changes is an information service from Montreal published twice a week. The editors read through a variety of important international newspapers, trade and popular periodicals, and scientific and technical journals, searching for articles relating to scientific and technological change. These articles are then abstracted into brief precis of about fifty words each. Sixty such abstracts are selected for each issue and sent out to subscribers. ER

C8988 LASER SYSTEM MAKES FILM FROM TV SIGNALS

A "Laser Color Recorder," recently developed and now being tested by CBS, is the first system to make high-quality films from TV signals. The system uses standard color film and is expected to be extremely economical.

VIDEA 1000 (first Laser System. . .)
DEC 71, p.1; 1/2"

C8982 SCANDAL PREDICTED IN ORGANIC FOODS

There will soon be a scandal in the US concerning increasingly popular organic foods, following which the industry will emerge in mass-marketing form under new government regulations, predicts marketing authority E.B. Weiss. Weiss says that much chemically grown food is claimed to be organic, since organic food sells for higher prices. This fact will soon become an issue for consumer groups, says Weiss.

ADVERTISING AGE (Look Out for. . .)
6 DEC 71, p.44, col.1; 36" + pic.

C8741 ELECTRICITY SPEEDS UP BONE HEALING

Low-ampere electric currents have been successfully used to speed up the healing of bone fractures, three University of Pennsylvania surgeons have found. A 10-microampere current constantly passed through the fractured bone may eventually reduce healing time by one-half and may be used to replace bone grafting.
JOURNAL OF THE AMERICAN MEDICAL ASSOCIATION (Electric Current Hastens. . .)
22-28 NOV 71, p.1128, col.1; 1 1/2p. + diag.

C8657 DUTCH CLINIC TREATS CRIMINALS AS PATIENTS

Henri van der Hueven Klinick, Utrecht, Holland, is perhaps the world's most enlightened penal institution. Seventy murderers, sexual offenders and other psychopaths, both men and women, are treated as patients rather than criminals. The rooms and wards are left unlocked at night, and there are more staff at the institution than there are prisoners. *(The Guardian,* Manchester)

ATLAS (Unlocking The Penal. . .)
NOV 71, p.28, col.1; 34" + pic.

E0982 NEW SPENT SULFITE PROCESS FOR PULP & PAPER INDUSTRY

Spring Chemicals Ltd., Toronto, is offering to the pulp industry a new spent sulfite liquor process that is applicable to all but sodium-based pulping processes. The company claims efficient recovery of chemicals and maximum assurance of meeting pollution control regulations.

ENVIRONMENTAL SCIENCE & TECHNOLOGY
(Spring. . .)
NOV 71, p.1142, col.3; 3"

E0985   ANIMAL WASTES CONVERTED TO
         CRUDE OIL IN US

Scientists at the US Bureau of Mines' Energy
Research Center have developed a process to
convert animal wastes into oil. Manure is put
under a pressure of 200 lbs. per square inch,
with carbon monoxide added at a temperature
of 750° F. Two tons of dry manure can produce
one tone of crude oil and one ton of water.

JAPAN TIMES (Turning. . . .)

14 NOV 71, p. 5, col. 7; 10"

E0988   CARBON MONOXIDE LEVELS GO
         DOWN AS TRAFFIC SPEED
         INCREASES

The density of carbon monoxide on congested
roads seems to lessen considerably when traffic
travels fast, according to a recent survey by the
Tokyo Bureau of Environmental Protection.
Noting this phenomenon, Chicago plans to
increase the speed of traffic flow by 10% in
order to reduce the carbon monoxide.

JAPAN TIMES (Pollution. . . .)
14 NOV 71, p. 2, col. 3; 6"

114. Nature

Macmillan Journals Limited, 4 Little Essex Street, London WC2R 3LF; Subscriptions: Brunel Road, Basingstoke, Hants. Weekly, £22 per year.

Current environmental feelings tend to produce complaints about living in a plastic environment. This insight capitalizes on the fact that trees, meadows, mountains and rivers are natural and buildings, highways, factories, and billboards are not natural. Things produced by chemical, biological, and electrical forces other than man himself are, in this case, judged to be natural, whereas the things and objects that man creates are unnatural, hence "plastic."

  What this argument misses is that everything shares natural roots and origins. Artificial distinctions traced back lead to artificial distinctions. Nature, perhaps the most prestigious scientific journal in the English language, surveys the entire scene of nature, especially man-made objects and effects. ER

SUGAR AND DISEASE

JOHN YUDKIN

Queen Elizabeth College, University of London

Professor Yudkin discusses whether the intake of dietary sugar is linked with some diseases.

The view that sugar (sucrose) may cause disease is not generally accepted; first, because few realize the size of the contribution of sucrose to the diet in Western countries, and second, because of the widespread belief that sucrose has the same effects in the body as has any other metabolizable carbohydrate.

  The average intake of sucrose in Western countries, which in the early 1700s was about 2 kg a year, is now about 50 kg a year (Fig. 1). This is usually between 15% and 20% of the energy value of the diet. In Britain, it is a higher percentage than that provided by bread and flour, or by meat, poultry and fish, or by milk, cheese and eggs. In some people, especially teenage boys, the average intake can supply up to 50% of calories.

  Sucrose has a wide range of unique chemical, biological and metabolic properties[1] and an increase of sucrose in the diet, largely at the expense of starch, is not simply the replacement of one carbohydrate by another. Sucrose taken in addition to other foods already adequate in cal-

ories is likely (but not certain) to give rise to obesity: taken instead of other foods, it reduces the nutrient content of the diet, since sucrose holds the unique position of a food component that supplies calories without nutrients, that is, "empty calories". Although there is no significant prevalence of nutritional deficiency in Britain,

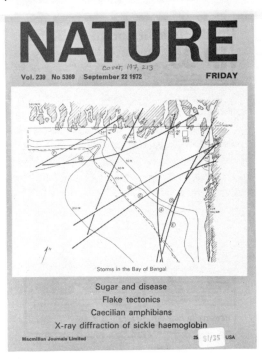

NATURE

Vol. 239   No 5369   September 22 1972   FRIDAY

Cover; 197, 213

Storms in the Bay of Bengal

Sugar and disease
Flake tectonics
Caecilian amphibians
X-ray diffraction of sickle haemoglobin

Macmillan Journals Limited   25   51/35   USA

desirable foods are displaced by sugar-rich foods, which leads to a decrease in consumption of meat and fruit. Although only limited statistics are available they reveal that these falls are associated with a rise in the consumption of foods and drinks containing sugar consistent with an increase in the standard of living and sophistication of food technology.

If we are concerned about the nutritional adequacy of our diets we should be more concerned about the displacement of nutritious foods by sugar than about the possible reduction in the nutrient content of foods by production or processing methods.

Deadly Surges in the Bay of Bengal: Dynamics and Storm-tide Tables

During the 1960s alone about 400,000 people died in the exceptionally high tides which swept in along the low lying northern coast of the Bay of Bengal under the force of tropical cyclones. Over half of these lives were lost in the single surge caused by the storm of November 1970. Such loss of life can be prevented only by depopulation of the area, construction of permanent defences, or by prediction of and protection against individual storms. The latter involves the identification and survey of a severe cyclone, forecast of the development and course of the storm, prediction of the sea level response, warning of danger, and protection of the survivors. We have considered the problem of sea level dynamics and prediction, and using simple mathematical models have studied the characteristics of the surge and found the sea level response to a number of model cyclones moving across the Bay along a variety of paths. Our results are summarized in a form which is handy for immediate incorporation into a warning programme.

Elementary Particles and Cosmology

On page 86 of this issue of *Nature*, Hoyle and Narlikar put forward the idea which they have been studying for a decade or so now that local phenomena cannot be understood in isolation from the rest of the universe. Most, though not all, of their previous work in connexion with this hypothesis has been devoted to showing how it predicts and illuminates generally accepted theory. Their work on electrodynamics, for example, has shown how the influence of the rest of the universe, through an interaction whose structure is much simpler and more elegant than conventional local theory, leads nonetheless to the right answer—namely, the same predictions as Maxwell's theory. The distinctive and controversial character of their work lies chiefly, though not entirely, in the conditions on the structure of the universe over large distances and times (in the future as well as in the past) which make such a deduction possible. The importance of the present article lies in the fact that it purports to explain a phenomenon which local theory has always regarded as given and inexplicable. If explanations of this type are successful they will establish not merely that one can use theories which treat the universe as a whole, but that one must do so.

It is a paradoxical feature of modern theoretical physics that the possibility of large scale concerted cosmological interaction should still be controversial. It would be possible to construe the progress of physics from Copernicus to Dirac as the lingering demise of this possibility. Copernician heliocentricity ended mundane cosmological purpose. Newtonian action at a distance which kept the planets in their new courses soon gave way to Laplacian field theory in which the intervening space was filled by fields described by differential equations so that each part acts only on neighboring points—a change only in mathematical method certainly, and not in hypothesis, but one without which Einsteinian gravitational theory would not have been psychologically possible or plausible. That theory (or mathematical method) was so successful that it was applied to electrodynamic interactions as soon as they were discovered. Maxwell went so far as to assert that electromagnetic fields are the sole reality and that material charges are mere vortices which happen to exist in them. In modern times matter has lost its solidity and given way to space-filling fields. Physics, then, has been increasingly concerned with continuity and local interaction and less with interaction between discrete particles at a distance.

115. Science News

Science Service, Inc., 1719 N Street, N.W., Washington, D.C. 20036; Subscription Department, 231 West Center Street, Marion, Ohio 43302. Weekly, $10 per year.

Science News is one of the most compact of the weekly scientific publications. Usually running sixteen pages, *SN* manages to provide an overview of the most important scientific research reported in the previous week, as well as several in-depth articles, a review of the physical, social and/or behavior sciences, and listing of new books and films of interest to scientists. ER

LEAD LEVELS IN HAIR
LOWER NOW THAN IN 1871

Concentrations of lead in the atmosphere have risen steadily since 1940, says the National Academy of Sciences. Even so, human absorption of environmental lead may have decreased significantly in the past 50 years, according to a report in the Oct. 6 SCIENCE. The research is based on comparisons of the lead content of antique and contemporary samples of human hair. The presence of lead in the hair reflects the prior presence of lead in the blood because during growth the emerging hair accumulates and retains heavy metals such as lead.

Advertisements for samples of old hair produced 130 specimens (from museums and private individuals) dated between 1871 and 1923 (the year tetraethyl lead was introduced into gasoline). Contemporary hair samples were collected from rural and urban barber shops. Donald Weiss of Newton, Pa., and Bert Whitten and David Leddy of Michigan Technological University in Houghton, Mich., used atomic absorption spectrophotometry to analyze the lead content of the hair. They found the amount of lead in antique hair to be as much as 10 times the amount in 1971 samples—both rural and urban. Whitten admits that the technique may not be sensitive enough to detect small differences (significant differences were not found between urban and rural samples), but the difference between pre- and post-1923 samples was obvious.

ATTENDING AN OPEN MEETING OF A FORMERLY CLOSED SCIENCE COMMITTEE: A REPORTER'S VIEW

BY EVERLY DRISCOLL

Executive Order 11671, signed by President Nixon in June, opened to the press meetings of advisory committees to Federal agencies. Two weeks ago, Everly Driscoll, SCIENCE NEWS' space sciences editor, traveled to Houston to attend the first meeting of the NASA Physical Sciences Committee held since the executive order was issued. Following is her personal report on the meeting. (Reports on the scientific matters discussed will appear in future issues.)

"We'll feel our way along this morass somehow," sighed William A. Fowler, chairman of the physical sciences committee, an advisory group to NASA, at the start of its first open meeting. Seven of the 12 committee members were present, plus the usual NASA personnel, a scientist who wished to present the details of an experiment he wants to fly on Apollo 17, and one member of the press. The meeting had been announced only three days before in the Federal Register. NASA plans in the future to give a one-week to two-week notice, says one official.

On this rather humid Texas day, the committee was meeting for the first time at the Lunar Science Institute in Houston. The institute used to be the mansion of James Marion West ("Silver Dollar Jim"). It overlooks Clear Lake, adjacent to the Manned Spacecraft Center (MSC), and is the site for many of the lunar and planetary "think" sessions, where scientists meet to discuss, most often in private, their latest experimental results and theories. The Italian Renaissance-styled mansion is almost clubby in decor.

Fowler began by rearranging the approved agenda to accommodate an executive session he now felt he needed because a member of the press was present. (Executive sessions are not open to the public.) It was already obvious that even without the unscheduled executive session, the committee would have a hard time completing all items on the agenda in two days. If a closed session were worked in, something would have to go. "We won't get around to the 'thrust for space research in the 1980's' [item 7 on the agenda]. We have too many problems left in the 1970's," the chairman noted. "We have to have an executive session," Fowler said to the senior NASA official present. "Does Homer Newell [associate administrator for NASA who has to approve advisory committee agendas] have to approve an executive session?" The answer was yes.

While the NASA official looked through the text of the Presidential order for the rules governing closed meetings, the chairman listed four items he wanted to discuss: the atomic clock experiment proposal, problems of the physics and astronomy program, the composition and function of the committee, and the current NASA budget problems.

"I don't understand why some of these items should be discussed in executive session," one committeeman said. Answer: "I rule these sound to me like executive session and that's that. They can fire me." (Laughter because he had already announced his plan to retire from the committee.) According to interpretation of the Presidential order by the NASA official present, the consideration of the proposed clock experiment for Apollo 17 and the role and membership of the committee could be discussed in a closed session. He left the meeting to make one of several calls to Newell in Washington.

"It appears to me we must become guardhouse lawyers very quickly," quipped one scientist.

"It sounds to me that if there is no public interest in the items, we will discuss them in public; if the public is interested, we will do it in private," observed another. "Things *are* confusing."

Evidently the scientists had decided business as usual. They had not staged the meetings, softened their criticisms or camouflaged their doubts. That they would go underground had been my principal fear.

116. American Scientist

155 Whitney Avenue, New Haven, Conn. 06510. Published bimonthly, $12 per year.

American Scientist is one of a number of scientific magazines published by scientist-journalists reporting on currently completed scientific research for the benefit of other scientists. Though *AS* is available to the general public it is not well known. This lack of public familiarity is due more to deficiencies in publicity than to any editorial policies.

Six times a year the Society of the Sigma Xi produces issues of *AS* each containing eight to ten full length articles on current research findings as well as a variety of news and review features. ER

PLATE TECTONICS AND SEA-FLOOR SPREADING

DAN P. MCKENZIE

Simple geometric ideas have led to a profound understanding of continental motions and the creation and destruction of sea floor

Until about 1960 the possibility that the continents might have drifted huge distances in the course of geological time excited all earth scientists, but produced more imaginative speculation and bitter controversy than sound scientific argument. In the last ten years, however, two instrumental developments have completely changed this situation, and it is now possible to describe the motions of the continents and the evolution of the ocean basins between them in the most remarkable detail. The two new developments were the installation of standardized seismic stations on a global scale to record earthquake waves and the systematic measurement of the earth's magnetic field at the sea surface using proton magnetometers. Both were closely connected with, and to a considerable extent paid for by, the armed forces of the United States, and without this data the advances of the last ten years could not have taken place. Like all major scientific advances, the history of the discoveries is unrelated to the logical development of the theory, and there now seems little purpose in following the various attempts that were made to produce a consistent framework for understanding the tectonics of the earth before plate tectonics was formulated.

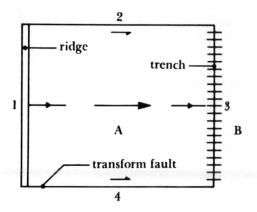

Plate *A* is moving to the right relative to plate *B*. It is being formed along the ridge (1), sliding on transform faults (2 and 4), and being destroyed along the trench (3).

ONE BRAIN—TWO MINDS?

MICHAEL S. GAZZANIGA

The behavioral consequences of sectioning the cerebral commissures raise fascinating questions about the physical basis of conscious behavior

The idea of consciousness stands out alone as man's most important, most puzzling, and most abused problem. Most other human ideas pale in complexity next to this one and to the long series of associated questions surrounding the nature of brain and mind. Indeed, upon studying the problem and reading the literature, one cannot help but conclude that the only subjects of greater

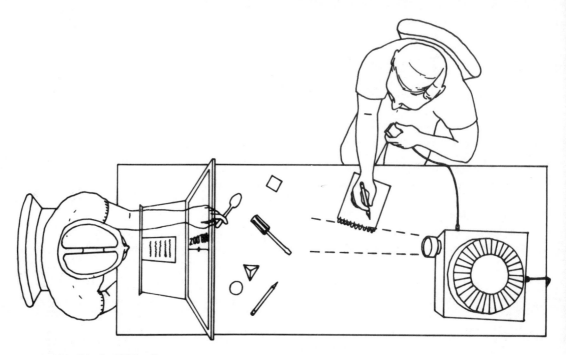

Using an apparatus especially designed for testing split-brain patients, visual stimuli can be presented to one or the other hemisphere exclusively. Tactual testing is also possible by allowing exploration of objects presented out of view to either hand. In testing right-hemisphere function, pictures or words are quick-flashed to the left visual field. The subjects invariably say they saw nothing or will make a guess. Yet the left hand, which sends its touch information to the right hemisphere, will be able to retrieve the object described. After the task is correctly completed, the subject will still deny knowledge of the specific aspects of the event, because the activity was carried out by the disconnected right hemisphere, which is now disconnected from the left speech hemisphere, which is the half brain talking to the experimenter.

mystery are the articles written about or around the problem of consciousness.

It is difficult if not impossible with our present knowledge to define explicitly what is meant by conscious experience. What I mean by the term can be illustrated by considering what you the reader presently feels. It is the dimension which makes you more like a dog than a computer. Since this is hardly a sophisticated or formal notion, we talk about the *functions* of conscious-

ness in order to make the subject of consciousness scientifically manageable. Thus eating, drinking, reading, loving are all analyzed in their separate parts. By studying these aspects of conscious activity we hope to gain some understanding of the whole idea of consciousness. In real terms, of course, how such processes relate to brain mechanisms remains unknown. Yet it is these kinds of questions that arise when considering the problems of the bisected brain in both animal and man.

117. The Closing Circle

BARRY COMMONER. Jonathan Cape Ltd., 30 Bedford Square, London WC1B 3EL; 1972; £2.50; 326 pp.

The Great Society of technology and affluence is a fraud. The " wealth " produced can be seen as a short-term rape of our finite resources. But the solutions to these problems lie not so much in direct action as in reformulation of our systems, starting with the economy.

Barry Commoner, Director of the Center for the Biology of Natural Systems, at Washington University, St. Louis, is a biologist, ecologist, and educator. His influence lies both in his conceptual strength and his abilities and talents to articulate and publicize his ideas. JB

After the excitement of Earth Week, I tried to find some meaning in the welter of contradictory advice that it produced. It seemed to me that the confusion of Earth Week was a sign that the situation was so complex and ambiguous that people could read into it whatever conclusion their own beliefs—about human nature, economics and politics—suggested. Like a Rorschach ink blot, Earth Week mirrored personal convictions more than objective knowledge.

Living things, as a whole, emerged from the nonliving skin of the earth. Life is a very powerful form of chemistry, which, once on the earth, rapidly changed its surface. Every living thing is intimately dependent on its physical and chemical surroundings, so that as these changed, new forms of life suited to new surroundings could emerge. Life begets life, so that once new forms appeared in a favorable environment, they could proliferate and spread until they occupied every suitable environmental niche within physical reach. Every living thing is dependent on many others, either indirectly through the physical and chemical features of the environment or directly for food or a sheltering place. Within every living thing on the earth, indeed within each of its individual cells, is contained another network—on its own scale, as complex as the environmental system—made up of numerous, intricate molecules, elaborately interconnected by chemical reactions, on which the life-properties of the whole organism depend.

This is where matters stand at this time. After persistent, intensive efforts to control photochemical smog, Los Angeles has exchanged a small improvement in the level of one noxious agent, PAN, and a larger decrease in carbon monoxide levels, for a serious increase in the level of another toxic agent, nitrogen dioxide. The battleground is now located in Detroit, where the automobile industry is yet to be convinced that air pollution control requires a drastic revision of the engines that drive its vehicles.

The most blatant example of the environmental crisis in the United States is Lake Erie, a huge inland sea large enough to symbolize the permanence of nature. Lake Erie has been a major natural resource for a rich region comprising a half dozen large cities with a population of thirteen million, a huge and varied industry, lush farm lands, and profitable fisheries. But in the process of creating this wealth, the lake has been changed, so polluted that the original biological systems that maintained the social value of the lake have largely been killed off. The fate of Lake Erie is a measure of the damage we inflict on our natural resources in order to create the nation's wealth.

In the last decade, the people living near Lake Erie have had ample evidence of its deterioration. Nearly all the beaches they once enjoyed have been closed by pollution; each summer huge mounds of decaying fish and algae pile up on the shore; the once sparkling water is dense with muck; oil discharged into one of its tributary rivers has burst into flame. Lake Eries's living balance has been upset and if the lake is not yet "dead," it certainly appears to be in the grip of a fatal disease.

––––––––––––

We return now to the one remaining, profoundly basic, sector of the man-nature system—the ecosphere and the earth's mineral resources. Here matters are very different. First, this is the only part of the over-all system that is not created by human effort. It pre-existed human beings on the earth; its fundamental properties were established long before the appearance of man. And, in contrast to the human sectors of the system, this natural segment is intrinsically *incapable of continued growth or expansion.*

––––––––––––

The environmental crisis is somber evidence of an insidious fraud hidden in the vaunted productivity and wealth of modern, technology-based society. This wealth has been gained by rapid short-term exploitation of the environmental system, but it has blindly accumulated a debt to nature (in the form of environmental destruction in developed countries and of population pressure in developing ones)—a debt so large and so pervasive that in the next generation it may, if unpaid, wipe out most of the wealth it has gained us. In effect, the account books of modern society are drastically out of balance, so that, largely unconsciously, a huge fraud has been perpetrated on the people of the world. The rapidly worsening course of environmental pollution is a warning that the bubble is about to burst, that the demand to pay the global debt may find the world bankrupt.

TRENDS

118. Things to Come:
Thinking About the 70's and 80's

HERMAN KAHN and B. BRUCE-BRIGGS. Macmillan International Ltd., Little Essex Street, London WC2R 3LF; 1972; £2.50; 262 pp.

Most thinking about the future is couched in safe predictions about the year 2000, that never-never land of the millennium that recedes quickly into a mystical thereafter. Not so for Herman Kahn and B. Bruce-Briggs, respectively director of, and historian at, the Hudson Institute think tank. *Things to Come* looks at the dangerous period, the next two decades. Most of us will be alive to see how these possible futures match with the coming realities. ER

REVIEW BY BENNETT L. SHAPIRO. "Thinking about the future can tell us a lot about the present." Equally, thinking about the present can tell us a lot about the past. This is one of the largest obstacles we face in trying to plan for the future. The much discussed increase in the rate of change, particularly technological, and the increased rate and volume of communications in our time, make it imperative for us to escape from the trap created by viewing the world through the famous "rear-view mirror." One of the most effective ways to do this is demonstrated throughout this lively book. We must focus clearly on our current situation, define the elements present and then create alternative futures with various combinations (extrapolations, etc.). The resulting scenarios do not predict *the* future but possible futures. With these possibilities made explicit we can plan more effectively. Simple, neat, even elegant; but the catch is that many of the people using future studies as a policy formulating tool are crippled by what Kahn and Bruce-Briggs (with a tip of the hat to Veblen) call educated incapacity. This is a formidable stumbling block on our road to paradise. Educated incapacity is "an acquired or learned inability to understand or see a problem, much less a solution." Sic semper expertise. The result of our modern educational system, educated incapacity (similar to Whitehead's paradox) prevents the exercise of the necessary imagination and creativity we need. History is not discontinuous.

WHY EDUCATED INCAPACITY?

1. Classic tendency to exercise favorite or accustomed muscles (skills or formulations)
2. Normal parochial professionalism and emphasis
3. Misleading or constraining bureaucratic or organizational ground rules or commitments
4. Misplaced glamor or incentives
5. Ideological (political or apolitical) biases
6. Insufficient imagination, courage, expertise, etc., for useful innovation or creativity
7. An increasing use of irrelevant experience and intuition: a growth of simplistic, theoretic, illusioned, and/or wishful thinking and utopian objectives; and a general lack of reality testing and hard-headed or "tough-minded" analysis (perhaps most important of all)

In 1985 the people of the world will be more culturally similar than they have been at any time in the history of mankind. Even the recently Stone Age natives of New Guinea will participate in the world economy, the world culture, and world society. To a remarkable degree, this "global metropolis" will be Americanized in that it will be a mass culture, mechanized, pragmatic, and cheerfully anarchistic; fundamentally philistine by highbrow cultural canons; and irreverent by traditional social standards.

MACRO-HISTORICAL PERSPECTIVES ON CHANGE

1. Static, traditional, and/or repetitive
2. Progressive: the multifold trend, progress, rev-

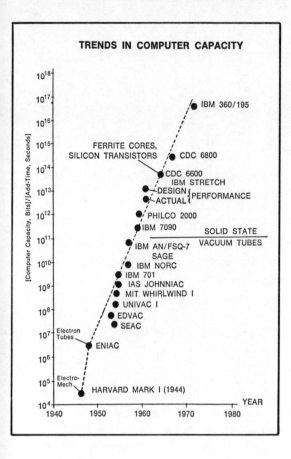

TRENDS IN COMPUTER CAPACITY

olution of rising expectations, utopian, chiliastic, culminating point

3. Decay: not competitive, "hubris," lost golden age, nostalgia, conservatism

4. Cyclic: rise and fall, growth and decay, fluctuation, "regular" ebb and flow

5. Patternless, unpredictable, and incomprehensible

6. Typical (empirical) patterns: the multifold trend, irregular ebb and flow, empirical and analytic trend analysis, typical or phenomenological scenarios

7. Eclectic and syncretic: the multifold trend, other trend analyses, other typical patterns, metaphors and analogies, some current speculations on decline and/or rebirth

119. Between Two Ages

ZBIGNIEW BRZEZINSKI. The Viking Press, Inc., 625 Madison Avenue, New York, N.Y. 10022; 1970; or *Real Time*. (H) $7.95; (P) $2.45; 334 pp.

Brzezinski is the director of the Research Institute on Communist Affairs at Columbia University. His book points out how political entities will no longer be calling the shots toward the end of the twentieth century. This is the "technetronic" era (new technology and electronics), and "the social, political, and economic changes will follow rather than lead the technological changes." JB

The transformation that is now taking place, especially in America, is already creating a society increasingly unlike its industrial predecessor. The post-industrial society is becoming a "technetronic" society: a society that is shaped culturally, psychologically, socially, and economically by the impact of technology and electronics—particularly in the area of computers and communications. The industrial process is no longer the principal determinant of social change, altering the mores, the social structure, and the values of society. In the industrial society technical knowledge was applied primarily to one specific end: the acceleration and improvement of production techniques. Social consequences were a later by-product of this paramount concern. In the technetronic society scienctific and technical knowledge, in addition to enhancing production capabilities, quickly spills over to affect almost all aspects of life directly. Accordingly, both the growing capacity for the instant calculation of the most complex interactions and the increasing availability of biochemical means of human control augment the potential scope of consciously chosen direction, and thereby also the pressures to direct, to choose, and to change.

Between Two Ages
America's Role in the Technetronic Era
Zbigniew Brzezinski

For Norbert Wiener, "the locus of an earlier industrial revolution before the main industrial revolution" is to be found in the fifteenth-century research pertaining to navigation (the nautical compass), as well as in the development of gunpowder and printing. Today the functional equivalent of navigation is the thrust into space, which requires a rapid computing capacity beyond the means of the human brain; the equivalent of gunpowder is modern nuclear physics, and that of printing is television and long-range instant communications. The consequence of this new technetronic revolution is the progressive emergence of a society that increasingly differs from the industrial one in a variety of economic, political, and social aspects.

Eventually, these changes and many others, including some that more directly affect the personality and quality of the human being himself, will make the technetronic society as different from the industrial as the industrial was from the agrarian.* And just as the shift from an agrarian economy and feudal politics toward an industrial society and political systems based on the individual's emotional identification with the nation-state gave rise to contemporary international politics, so the appearance of the technetronic society reflects the onset of a new relationship between man and his expanded global reality.

The crucial breakthrough in the development of human self-awareness on a mass scale came with the great religions—the first universal syntheses that simultaneously expanded man's vision both vertically and horizontally: vertically, to define in extended and complex terms man's

*We are talking here about *our* history—of our historical civilization Claude Lévi-Strauss is otherwise quite right in pointing out that " . . . it is forgotten that each of the tens or hundreds of thousands of societies which have existed side by side in the world or succeeded one another since man's first appearance, has claimed that it contains the essence of all the meanings and dignity of which human society is capable and, reduced though it might have been to a small nomad band or a hamlet lost in the depths of the forest, its claim has in its own eyes rested on a moral certainty comparable to that which we can invoke in our own case. But whether in their case or our own, a good deal of egocentricity and naivety is necessary to believe that man has taken refuge in a single one of the historical or geographical modes of his existence, when the truth about man resides in the system of the differences and common properties " *(The Savage Mind,* Chicago, 1968, p. 249).

relationship to a God that was not a small group's alone *but everyone's;* horizontally, to articulate a series of imperatives that governed man's obligations to man on the grounds that all shared the divine spark. Universalism thus emerged as a state of mind even at a time when man was still provincial and isolated in mutually exclusive social-cultural compartments.

It is increasingly difficult for institutions to assert dogmatically the pristine purity of the doctrines that they claim to embody. This is as true of the Christian churches as of communist parties. In some of the more advanced countries this difficulty also involves—especially on the part of the young—a crisis in allegiance to the procedures of liberal democracy.

Today the relationship of ideas to institutions is turbulent: institutions resist ideas lest they lead to changes that undermine the institutions, and the exponents of ideas rebel against institutions because of the intellectual constraints said to be inherent in their existence.

Contemporary America is in transition from the industrial to the technetronic age. As the world's first post-industrial society, the United States is no longer shaped by the same forces that have stimulated social change in the advanced countries ever since England first confronted the machine. This broad transformation is causing a crisis of established American values and institutions, particularly the tradition of liberal democracy, and as the nation's two-hundredth birthday approaches, it therefore calls for a redefinition of the American system.

120. The Age of Discontinuity: Guidelines to our Changing Society

PETER F. DRUCKER. William Heinemann Ltd., 15–16 Queen Street, London W1X 8BE; (H) 1969; £3.15; or Pan Books Ltd., Cavaye Place, London SW10 9PG; (P) 1971; £0.60; 402 pp.

During the industrial era, the wheel, as symbol of continuity, was a predominant image. The electronic age, symbolized by simultaneity, by totality, has given us new models to play with, and "continuity" isn't among them.

Drucker, Professor of Management at NYU Business School, sees discontinuities in four major areas: (1) genuinely new technologies; (2) a change from an international to a "world" economy; (3) an increasingly pluralistic society, and (4) the emergence of knowledge as the central capital, the cost center, and the crucial resource of the economy. JB

The world of the New Left and of the hippies, of Op Art and of Mao Tse-tung's Cultural Revolution, of H-bombs and moon rockets, seems further removed from the certainties and perceptions of the Victorians and Edwardians than they were from the Age of the Migration at the end of antiquity. But in the economy, in industrial geography, industrial structure, and industrial technology, we are still very much the heirs of the Victorians.

Measured by the yardsticks of the economist, the last half-century has been an Age of Continuity—the period of least change in three hundred years or so, that is, since world commerce and systematic agriculture first became dominant economic factors in the closing decades of the seventeenth century.

The world economy is not yet a community—not even an economic community. Yet the existence of the "global shopping center" is a fact that cannot be undone. The vision of an economy for all will not be forgotten again. On the contrary, the worldwide communication of goods, services, standards of living, and ways of life will become ever more pervasive.

To develop into a genuine community, the world economy needs to mature the institutions that it has today only in embryonic form. It needs

a money and credit system to provide circulation of purchasing power and investment. The very rich can, perhaps, prosper without it. For it is to them that money and credit flow in the absence of an adequate system. But the poor are deprived even of the little they have unless there is a functioning and well-managed monetary system.

Today it is the workingman in the developed countries—and even the poor on relief in these countries—who are the "rich" in the world. The world has become divided into nations that know how to manage technology to create wealth, and nations who do not know how to do this. Within the rich nations technology has succeeded to an amazing extent in overcoming the cleavage between the rich and the poor, not by making the rich poorer, but by making the poor richer. It has thereby overcome to a very large extent that haunting specter of the nineteenth century: class war within industrial society. But this has been replaced by a gap in income and opportunities between nations and cultures which never existed before.

We need a theory of economic dynamics in addition to the theory of equilibrium, which is all we have now. We need a theoretical understanding of technological innovation as an economic event and its integration into economic theory and economic policy. We need a model of the world economy and an understanding of the complex relationships between the world economy and the domestic economy. Finally we need a theory of microeconomic behavior, that is, of the behavior of the actors—the "organisms"—of the economy. For it is the microeconomy, in the end, that produces economic results, goods and services, jobs and incomes.

What has emerged in this half-century is *a new pluralism*. There is little left of the structure that our seventeenth-century political theory still preaches, a structure in which government is the only organized power center. It is totally inadequate, however, to see just one of these new institutions—business, for instance, or the labor union, or the university—and proclaim it *the* new institution.* Social theory, to be meaningful at all, must start out with the reality of a pluralism of institutions—a galaxy of suns rather than one big center surrounded by moons that shine only by reflected light.

*I must plead guilty to having done this myself—twenty-odd years ago. In *Concept of the Corporation* (New York: John Day, 1946) I called big business the "determining" institution of our time. However, the other institutions were then barely visible; the crystalline structure of our society had not yet become apparent. There is little excuse today, however, for such oversimplification as that in John Kenneth Galbraith's latest book, *The New Industrial State* (Boston: Houghton Mifflin, 1967), which fails to notice any institution except business.

In fact, most of us today realize that to turn an area over to government creates conflict, creates vested and selfish interests, and complicates decisions. We realize that to turn something over to government makes it political instead of abolishing politics. When the garbage collectors went on strike against the City of New York in the winter of 1968, many good liberals seriously proposed turning garbage collection over to "free enterprise" to "ease the tension." We realize, in other words,.that government is no alternative to decision. It does not replace conflict of interests by rational decision making.

But the greatest disappointment, the great letdown, is the fiasco of the welfare state. Not many people would want to do without the social services and welfare benefits of an affluent modern industrial society. But the welfare state promised a great deal more than to provide social services. It promised to create a new and happy society. It promised to release creative energies. It promised to do away with ugliness and envy and strife. No matter how well it is doing its jobs—and in some areas in some countries some jobs are being done very well—the welfare state turns out at best to be just another big insurance company, as exciting, as creative, and as inspiring as insurance companies tend to be. No one has ever laid down his life for an insurance policy.

121. The Coming of the Golden Age:
A View of the End of Progress

GUNTHER S. STENT. Natural History Press, 277 Park Avenue, New York, N.Y. 10017; 1969; or *Real Time*. (H) $4.95; (P) $2.50; 146 pp.

Stent is a Professor of Molecular Biology at the University of California, Berkeley. He presents us with two books in one: (I) "The Rise and Fall of Molecular Genetics," a comprehensive review of progress in the field over the past one hundred years, and (II) "The Rise and Fall of Faustian Man," which deals with the self-limited aspect of the will to power and the inevitable end of "progress" as it has been constituted over the past few centuries. JB

Thus we now realize that this problem actually amounts to the attempt to discover a primitive system which is capable of carrying out *both* the autocatalytic and the heterocatalytic reactions nowadays accomplished by the DNA→RNA→ protein triad. That is, any evolutionary development by natural selection already demands a self-reproducing, mutable genetic system which encodes *information* for and can give expression to the characters that are being selected. There is no guarantee, of course, that the first system of this sort formed on the primitive Earth were nucleic acids and proteins. However, it seems that for the present the most promising attack on the problem of the origin of life is to probe into the origin of the genetic code and into how it could have arisen without, like Athena, having sprung full-blown from Zeus's head. Now that this problem has been clearly posed in molecular terms, it can hardly be very long until its solution is at hand. Perhaps a paradox might still be hidden here, but unless extra-terrestrial life becomes available for study, it is not easy to imagine how a paradox connected with the origin of life could ever come into focus sufficiently clearly to reveal "other" physical laws.

The Coming of the Golden Age $2.50
a view of the end of progress

Gunther S.Stent

Bohr, an enthusiastic skier, sometimes used the following simile, which can be understood perhaps only by fellow skiers. When you try to analyze a Christiania turn in all its detailed movements, it will evanesce and become an ordinary stem turn, just as the quantum state turns into classical motion when analyzed by sharp observation." This attitude would mean nothing less than that searching for a "molecular" explanation of consciousness is a waste of time, since the physiological processes responsible for this wholly private experience will be seen to degenerate into seemingly quite ordinary, workaday reactions, no more and no less fascinating than those that occur in, say, the liver, long before the molecular level has been reached. Thus, as far as consciousness is concerned, it is possible that the quest for its physical nature is bringing us to the limits of human understanding, in that the brain may not be capable, in the last analysis, of providing an explanation of itself. Indeed, Bohr ended his 1932 lecture with the thought that "without entering into metaphysical speculations, I may perhaps add that any analysis of the very concept of an explanation would, naturally, begin and end with a renunciation as to explaining our own conscious activity." Perhaps *this* then is the paradox: There exist processes which, though they clearly obey the laws of physics, can *never* be explained.

It seems that the most meaningful definition of progress can be made from the purview of its very mainspring, namely the will to power. That is, the "better" world is one in which man has a greater power over external events, one in which he has gained a greater dominion over nature, one in which he is economically more secure.

This definition makes progress an undeniable historical fact. Furthermore, it makes possible the claim that progress will end, since the assertion that there is to be no further increase in power over external events is meaningful, even if it were untrue. This definition does not, therefore, encompass such wholly internal aspects of the human condition as happiness. Hence, it is a totally amoral view of progress, under which nuclear ballistic missiles definitely represent progress over gunpowder cannonballs, which in turn represent progress over bows and arrows.

As far as culture is concerned, the Golden Age will be a period of general stasis, not unlike that envisaged by Meyer for the arts. Progress will have greatly decelerated, even though activities formally analogous to the arts and sciences will continue. It is obvious that Faustian Man of the Iron Age would view with some considerable distaste this prospect of his affluent successors, devoting their abundance of leisure time to sensual pleasures, or what is even more repugnant to him, deriving private synthetic happiness from hallucinatory drugs. But Faustian Man had better face up to the fact that it is precisely *this* Golden Age which is the natural fruit of all his frantic efforts, and that it does no good now to wish it otherwise. Millennia of doing arts and sciences will finally transform the tragicomedy of life into a happening.

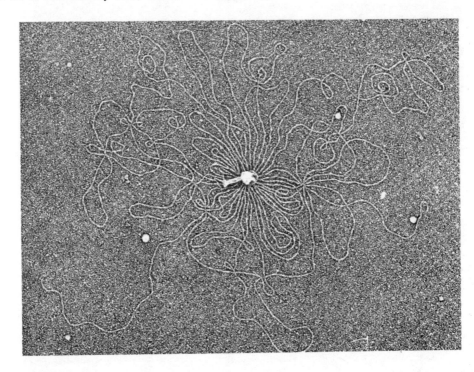

122. The Mature Society

DENNIS GABOR. Secker & Warburg Ltd., 14 Carlisle Street, London W1V 6NN; 1972; £2.75; 208 pp.

Gabor's interpretation of the effect of technology on our daily life. This is a book of cultural philosophy that makes best sense when read in tandem with *Innovations,* Gabor's earlier work. JB

REVIEW BY ARIE KOPELMAN. Gabor's focus is " the problem of men and women living a peaceful and contented life at a high level of material comfort and security without the daily struggle of life. "

Nimbly digesting economics, econometrics, labor relations, productivity, public finance, and technology, Gabor plots the surprisingly modest socio-economic adjustments required to produce material abundance in a relatively free society. Basic elements include: (1) technological and productivity growth patterns within existing potentials, (2) retraining of redundant production employees and papercrats, as successfully practiced in Sweden, and (3) prevention of ecosystem disaster through serious application of emerging computer-planning techniques to resource utilization, capital investment, and population growth, etc. (as in the Forrester projections for the Club of Rome).

Gabor foresees these adjustments as leading to a twenty-four-hour work week with a concomitant extension of "leisure time." He fears the resultant malaise as future men lose the vitality generated by their feeling of material contribution to the commonweal. Recognizing, indeed emphasizing, the moral questions thus raised, he would combat malaise with (1) freedom, since the " continual conflict and strife in a free society provides the *excitement* which is a necessity for Irrational Man, " (2) hope, e.g. for escape from boredom via opportunities for changing occupations at some reasonable intervals, and (3) happiness as a function of creativity stimulated through educational reforms, personal contacts, and plays.

The obvious inability here to deal seriously with the underlying moral issues raised is merely evidence that futuristic constructs provide no more of an answer to ennui than present socio-economic structures, with good reason. Internal processes may be colored, but are rarely consumed, by externalities. Whether the individual human system transmits or merely absorbs is as much a function of today's free choice as tomorrow's morality. Gabor says essentially nothing about the sense reactivities of people's minds. Ultimately, however, that is where the humane survival issue must be joined.

Till now man has been up against Nature; from now on he will be up against his own nature.' The age-old enemy, poverty, is defeated in one-quarter of the world, almost all the ailments which used to kill one-half of the people in childhood are eliminated; there is no enemy left but man. We have every right to be proud when we look back, none at all for pride when looking forward. The tragic situation has arisen that the very talents which have made the naked ape the master of the Earth are now turning against him; his fighting temper, his restless quest for novelty, his craving for excitement and adventure, even his virtues— such as the love and care for his progeny, and his social instincts which make him willing to sacrifice himself for his tribe or for his nation.

In 1971 the SST was defeated by a narrow vote in the US Congress. This was historically the first instance of a parliament calling a stop to 'technological progress', and it can be argued that the correct decision was made for not quite the right reasons. It was a majority of conservationists and environmentalists which brought the SST to a halt, not the determination to stop a line of development which was driving *ad absurdum.* Because what will come after the 350-500 seat jumbo and the supersonic plane? The 1000-seat jumbo, and the hypersonic plane? And after that?

However much the technologists would hate to admit it, some time the aircraft industry must settle down on a stationary basis, building planes only for replacement, with small improvements, like the motor car industry. It will not have the advantage of the motor industry, which can keep up an exaggerated production by creating fashions, because the customers of the aircraft industry are commercial airlines which must make a profit, and are not as gullible as the general public.

So far, what is called in the English-speaking countries the 'Protestant ethic' has been sufficient as a moral mainstay; it will not be sufficient in the future. It needed only a minimum of human decency to recognize that the 'toiling masses', who by producing goods maintained the whole of the society, deserved social justice. But when, by the progress of technology, the toiling masses are no longer needed, justice will have to find other foundations than in the times of economic scarcity. We have come a long way since Herbert Spencer loudly protested against 'pampering the poor' from the rates paid by the affluent. Assistance not only to the unemployed, but also to the unemployable, is now paid in all civilized countries, but only to an extent which keeps them well below the poverty level. When, as can be expected, their number increases and their standard of living is raised to a decent level, we can expect not only protestations but strong resistance from people who by old-fashioned standards consider themselves thoroughly ethical.

For a generation, or perhaps two, in the age of transition towards a mature society, we must make use of high-energy individuals, and play the economic game more or less according to the traditional rules, but there can be no doubt that during this time interest in the economic drive will gradually fade out. Once the new education has inculcated *responsibility* into everyone, without the straitjacket of the age of scarcity, the economy can be allowed to become as smoothly efficient and imperceptible as the water supply of big towns used to be before the increasing danger of modern pollution. What will the high-energy individuals do then? We need not worry; the management of restless, Irrational Man will never be easy!

The mature society must offer a great diversity of ladders, in administration, the sciences, the arts, sports, entertainment, and other lines of values yet to be invented. Needless to say, it must be a *multidimensional* world of values; the one-dimensional scale of pay, already less important than it was 50 years ago, is bound to become unimportant in an age of material abundance. But let us be clear about it—however many avenues we offer towards success there is no success unless others fail. It is a distinction to be a member of a national academy only because there are so many who have not made it. The more just the method of election or promotion, the worse the fate of the unsuccessful, who cannot console themselves that they are victims of intrigues. If we wish for a world in which ambition can be rewarded by distinction, we cannot wish for a world without frustration, because distinction is a thing which cannot be democratically distributed. We cannot have excellence *and* equality.

Higher education must be split into two branches. There should be universities of the traditional type for the gifted minority, to prepare them for intellectually exacting professions. For the less gifted majority the mass university should be the entrance into the permissive society. Its assignment will be less vocational training than giving them a taste for culture and life-long self improvement. It may teach them foreign languages, preparing them for years spent abroad, making them citizens of the world. The mass university must be an agreeable place, to which the students will be glad to return later in their sabbatical years.

Those capable of it must be given a chance to change their occupation in middle life. Nobody ought to be tied for life to a monotonous production job. Service occupations must be made rewarding by the opportunity for personal contacts, and by social esteem for those who are good at it. Almost everybody ought to take a turn at them.

Life must be made richer by not only tolerating nonconformists, but by actively encouraging those who can creatively add to its diversity.

Finally two short slogans, which could go a long way if they were obeyed:

Excellence instead of quantitative growth.
Possession instead of consumption.

The first is an advice to the industrial elite, the second to everybody. Possessions which do not wear out, not only material possessions such as beautiful habitations, but also arts, knowledge and the memory of a life rich in fulfilments.

123. The Future of the Future

JOHN McHALE. George Braziller, Inc., 1 Park Avenue, New York, N.Y. 10016; 1969; or *Real Time*. (H) $7.95; 322 pp.

Ballantine Books, Inc., 101 Fifth Avenue, New York, N.Y. 10003; (P) $1.50 or *Real Time*.

Technology is already globalized in terms of usage. In this sense nations are already obsolete: airport operations, computers, telegraph systems, will work alike whether it be New York or Tokyo. John McHale, Director of the Center for Integrative Studies, State University of New York, Binghamton, deals with the sociocultural impact of new, emerging technologies and technological change. His book is an exploration of the utilization of man's resources on a global scale. McHale points out that it's not just a matter of projecting present-day facts and figures into the future. It's also a question of knowledge, and "knowledge is not just accumulation of new facts, but reduction of unrelated and irrelevant facts into new conceptual wholes. New, simple, and inclusive concepts (i.e., $E = MC^2$, RNA/DNA) make an enormous number of 'facts' obsolete. The information explosion = conceptual implosion." JB

Culturally, however, the idea of the future, in the sense that we now employ it, is relatively new in human experience. Most previous societies operated with quite different models—of the past, present, and future of man, of society, and of the universe.

For some, the future was largely a continuation of the past beyond a relatively unchanging and unchangeable present. Their purview of any future state was limited by their consciousness of time, by constraint within the narrow margins of survival in the present, and by the lack of adequate symbols and images to communicate radically different future states.

In all these dimensions, past, present, and future have no actual fixed time locus. The future is compounded of past and present. The past is constantly re-created in the future. Past, present, and future commingle in any one conscious instant.

For various social purposes (scientific, historical, or religious), we assume various modes in which events are connected in time. In our present Western mode, time is unilinear in that the past comes before the present and the future follows upon the present. So pervasive is this mode that it is difficult for us to imagine a practical way of relating events other than in such a sequence.

The Romantic attitude of the nineteenth century has evolved into many peculiarly contemporary forms. Thus the Romantic of today has often fallen in love with "the mechanical bride" and her key-punched IBM progeny. The latent fear of individually fallible reason, per se, is displaced by an absolute trust in the security and value neutrality of instrumented process or in a systems mystique whose scientific laws are taken as both moral force and infallible truth. The kingdom of Boheme, largely evacuated by the artist, has been invaded and developed into a sanctuary by the young, whose romantic unreason often proceeds from more reasonable and humane premises than that of their reasonable elders.

In general, much of our present computer usage simply regards the machine as a superfast and efficient clerical assistant. However, the real trend is (1) toward a closer individual/computer rapport so that the computer will become a generalized intelligence amplifier, and (2) toward specific types of computer systems that assume the routine operations and maintenance of all the basic physical metabolism of human society.

This aspect of automation is easier to grasp, and as it becomes discernible, it proceeds slowly to assume its proper niche. The rate of integration of automated procedures into productive use is presently masked by inadequate economic criteria and indicators, but is reflected in the following figures. :

	No. of Computers, 1966	Growth Rate	No. of Computers, 1970
United States	27,000	10–13%	45,000
Western Europe	6,000	20–22	18,000
Japan	1,900	20	4,575
Canada	900	23–25	3,000
Australia	280	35	1,000
Latin America	200	7	440

In the United States alone the Federal Government uses 2,600 computers and spends over $2 billion annually to acquire and operate this equipment.

The extent to which automated systems have now assumed the operation of the *invisible metabolies* of advanced societies is more far reaching. Apart from completely automated factories and continentally linked automatic inventory, dispatch, and other control operations, the whole energy conversion, transmission, and distribution system of vast areas are increasingly under automated control. Over 80 percent of electrical capacity in the United States is, for example, controlled presently by such systems. The inter-continental telephone linking service is an increasingly automated system in terms of its myriad switching and individualized calling stations. . . . Much of the sociology of work and leisure is still primarily the study of those social roles that arise from the classification of men by gainful occupation, or in which all other activity is interpreted in relation to work, as traditionally defined. They are based on the model of economic man.

Figure 51. E. S. Mills, R. L. Butterton, Douglas Missile & Space Systems Development, Interplanetary Mission Life Support System 1965; NASA; ASD Report TR 61-363.

Figure 10a. Sensory Extension. The most abrupt and fundamentally important of the transitions that lead up to our present world developed in the sciences in the late-nineteenth century and became first evident in the technology of World War 1. Experimental science began to extend its measureable range into the invisible subsensorial world of atomic, molecular, and "radiation" phenomena.

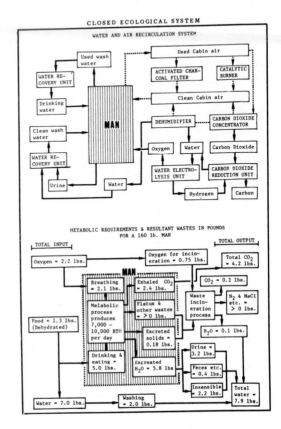

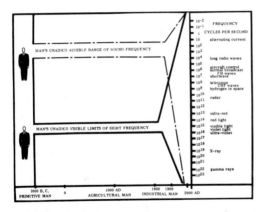

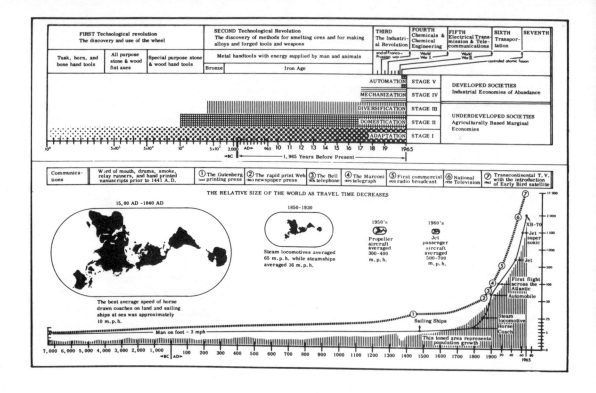

74. Global Development. "Science, Engineering and the Future of Man," by W. Taylor Thom, Jr.; *Science and the Future of Mankind,* World Academy of Art and Science, 1963; *International Industrial Development Center Study,* Stanford Research Institute, 1962.

This radical change, which is also occurring in other countries, from product- and market-oriented economies to service- and welfare-oriented systems whose mainspring is no longer economically motivated, profoundly alters the importance and status relation of occupational roles. The more valuable work, even economically, is in human service, whether directly in teaching, welfare, or other public service or indirectly in the expansion of knowledge and the exploration of othe physical, intellectual, or social frontiers.

Work, as previously defined, is no longer the central life interest. It has lost its relation to the compulsive work ethic, to the principle of nationality and efficiency, and the notion of time as money, that is, as a scarce commodity and socially significant unit.

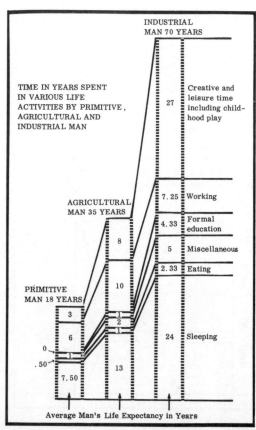

Figure 80.

284

124. World Facts and Trends:
Where Man Is Headed—A Multidimensional View

JOHN McHALE. Macmillan International Ltd., Little Essex Street, London WC2R 3LF; 1973; (H) £2.95, (P) £0.90; 95 pp.

Wallace Stevens pointed out that when the facts stop, imagination stops. McHale lays claim to the world of facts, pursuing research and evaluation of data and the subsequent trends that reveal themselves. McHale is a British futurist-sociologist, and Director of the Center for Integrative Studies at State University of New York, Binghampton. His work deals with hard, finite, exact measures of the real world, and he is consistantly the most rewarding thinker-writer in his field. JB

REVIEW BY ARIE KOPELMAN. In the era of the manic enumerator on the one hand and the exoteric perceptual psycho-conceptualizer on the other, McHale's volume reawakens the value, and possibly the poetry, of basic data examination.

Essentially, this is an illuminating synthesis pertaining to ecological resources. However, it describes not so much "the facts " but, as McHale puts it, " their consideration within the overall global context. " "The facts' are nonetheless set forth in brief and fascinating detail, covering atmospheric, terrestrial, marine, biophysical, and technological resources with superb use of illustrative materials.

McHale's distinguishing characteristic is his professionally detached world view, which is welcome in a field where public dialogue is frequently graced more by rhetoric than by reality. His methodology depends on relating one ecological subsystem to another and thereafter to existing and projected levels of technology. Not surprisingly then, this volume yields, directly or by inference, some interesting challenges to commonly held preconceptions including (just as examples) the following:

(1) Some of the long-term solutions to world-wide pollution problems as a function of increasing population may lie in *increased* industrialization in the less developed countries.

(2) The apparently rapid depletion of petroleum and natural gas reserves may be less of a threat to our energy resources than to our conservation of certain irreplaceable metal ores.

(3) The population situation may be misstated as a problem of growth outpacing either the available living space or food supply since (a) land-supply problems may be exaggerated, and (b) food supplies historically have tended to respond well to demand crises while major potential food sources (i.e. the oceans) remain untapped.

The emphasis in McHale's work is on physical trends. His indication that this emphasis will be adjusted in future editions merely underlines the crucial need for a parallel synthesis of socio-psychological and cultural-economic trends since, obviously, the question of ecosystem preservation and utilization is ultimately governed by the operation of individual and collective human decision-making matrices.

The last third of the twentieth century has become increasingly characterized as the age of critical transition, revolution, and discontinuity. In this situation, two major aspects of change are now crucial. One is the explosive growth in man's actual and potential capacities to interfere on a large scale with the natural environmental processes. The other is the lag in conceptual orientation toward these capacities and in the cognitive understanding of the social processes through which we may manage change more effectively. In both cases, the conceptual grasp of the rate and magnitude of ongoing changes and their potential consequences is one of our survival imperatives.

There are three great evolutionary transitions in the human occupancy of the earth which are critical to our understanding of change:

1. THE AGRICULTURAL REVOLUTION. Man achieved a greater degree of long-range predictive control over his food supply through entering into a more directly symbiotic relation to intensive local land use. This gave rise to the early city civilizations, and so forth.

2. THE INDUSTRIAL REVOLUTION. This freed man from direct dependence on his own and animal muscle energies and, to a degree, freed him from local dependence on the land itself.

3. THE ECOLOGICAL REVOLUTION. In the past hundred years various successive and overlapping strands of the industrial-social-electrochemical and electronic revolutions have been developed, placing man and his systems at magnitudes capable of large-scale interference with the overall ecological balance of the earth.

The prime vehicle for all our environmental interpretation and the basis for human action is some form of language. Both verbal and non-verbal symbolic languages " order " our perception of the environ and control the interpretation and communication of what we perceive. Language constructs our reality.

It is suggested that man stopped " physically " evolving about 150,000 years ago and now tends to offload his evolution socially through various extensions. Much of his apparently irrational behavior is explicable as " instinctual " responses which were biologically meaningful, but which are no longer appropriate to his changed condition. Fears and insecurities expressed in certain " dominance, territoriality, crowd, and flight responses, " which had great survival value in past states, may often act to negative advantage in the present unless positively channeled and/or symbolically transformed when they may become sources of social energy.

Man's ecological expansion has been partic-

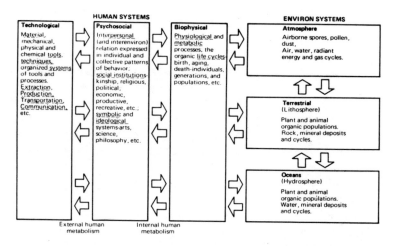

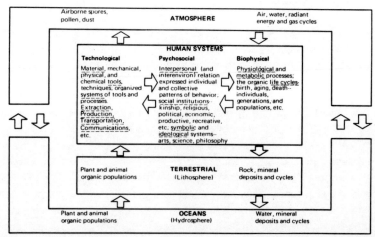

ularly characterized by the way in which accumulated knowledge about the environ is preserved and passed on through succeeding generations. This forms part of the major evolutionary step in the adaptability of the organism. This function of transmitting social and cultural experience and of regulating social interaction through symbolic extensions has led to the complex growth of human institutions, of human society. His evolution is more directly that of a psychosocial and increasingly conscious development.

Income energies are the naturally recurring energies available to man by tapping into the regenerative cycles in the ecosystem and include:

1. photosynthesis: we have hitherto considered this energy conversion process only in its food energy cycling role. There are many other ways in which energy may be directly extracted from vegetation product cycles; e.g., through fuels from wood and other sources; by microbial action in "biological fuel cells," etc.

2. other direct solar energy uses: through concentrating lenses and reflectors into cooling devices; through photoelectrical and photochemical fuel cells, etc.

3. hydrological: as derived from the earth's gravitational system through rivers, dams, etc., and the direct use of tidal and wave power; also various modes of tapping into the hydrological cycle of evaporation precipitation.

4. wind: though this is intermittent and variable, improvements in storage capacities may enable this source to be more widely used.

5. temperature: temperature differentials between atmospheric and earth/water surfaces yield energy potentials of considerable magnitude.

6. geothermal: tapping directly into the heat of the earth either through naturally occurring volcanic sources of hot gases and water or by drilling artificial vents for similar purposes.

7. other "unconventional" sources: magnetophydrodynamics, thermionics, etc.

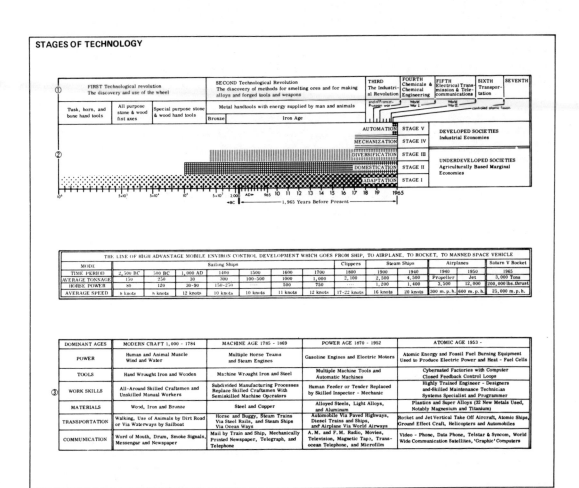

STAGES OF TECHNOLOGY

MODE	Sailing Ships							Clippers	Steam Ships		Airplanes		Saturn V Rocket
TIME PERIOD	2,500 BC	500 BC	1,000 AD	1400	1500	1600	1700	1800	1900	1940	1940	1950	1965
AVERAGE TONNAGE	150	250	30	300	100-500	1000	1,000	2,100	2,500	4,500	Propeller	Jet	3,000 Tons
HORSE POWER	80	120	30-90	150-250	....	500	750	....	1,200	1,400	3,500	12,000	200,000 lbs.thrust
AVERAGE SPEED	6 knots	6 knots	12 knots	10 knots	10 knots	11 knots	12 knots	17-22 knots	16 knots	20 knots	300 m.p.h.	600 m.p.h.	25,000 m.p.h.

THE LINE OF HIGH ADVANTAGE MOBILE ENVIRON CONTROL DEVELOPMENT WHICH GOES FROM SHIP, TO AIRPLANE, TO ROCKET, TO MANNED SPACE VEHICLE

DOMINANT AGES	MODERN CRAFT 1,000 - 1784	MACHINE AGE 1785 - 1869	POWER AGE 1870 - 1952	ATOMIC AGE 1953 -
POWER	Human and Animal Muscle Wind and Water	Multiple Horse Teams and Steam Engines	Gasoline Engines and Electric Motors	Atomic Energy and Fossil Fuel Burning Equipment Used to Produce Electric Power and Heat - Fuel Cells
TOOLS	Hand Wrought Iron and Wooden	Machine Wrought Iron and Steel	Multiple Machine Tools and Automatic Machines	Cybernated Factories with Computer Closed Feedback Control Loops
WORK SKILLS	All-Around Skilled Craftsmen and Unskilled Manual Workers	Subdivided Manufacturing Processes Replace Skilled Craftsmen With Semiskilled Machine Operators	Human Feeder or Tender Replaced by Skilled Inspector - Mechanic	Highly Trained Engineer - Designers and-Skilled Maintenance Technician Systems Specialist and Programmer
MATERIALS	Wood, Iron and Bronze	Steel and Copper	Alloyed Steels, Light Alloys, and Aluminum	Plastics and Super Alloys (32 New Metals Used, Notably Magnesium and Titanium)
TRANSPORTATION	Walking, Use of Animals by Dirt Road or Via Waterways by Sailboat	Horse and Buggy, Steam Trains Via Steel Rails, and Steam Ships Via Ocean Ways	Automobile Via Paved Highways, Diesel Trains and Ships, and Airplane Via World Airways	Rocket and Jet Vertical Take Off Aircraft, Atomic Ships, Ground Effect Craft, Helicopters and Automobiles
COMMUNICATION	Word of Mouth, Drum, Smoke Signals, Messenger and Newspaper	Mail by Train and Ship, Mechanically Printed Newspaper, Telegraph, and Telephone	A.M. and F.M. Radio, Movies, Television, Magnetic Tape, Transocean Telephone, and Microfilm	Video - Phone, Data Phone, Telstar & Syncom, World Wide Communication Satellites, 'Graphic' Computers

125. World Dynamics

JAY W. FORRESTER. Wright-Allen Press, Inc., Distrib: John Wiley & Sons Ltd., Baffins Lane, Chichester, Sussex; 1972; £4.25; 142 pp.

J.Z. Young tells us that the brain works through a complex system of model making. Bateson, Lilly, and others have indicated that the cybernetic model is best for dealing with human organisms and the systems that human/human interface creates. Forrester takes the cybernetic model back to the cybernetic, man-made hardware and returns with a series of models all indicating that certain growth patterns are no longer indicative of health but now reflect potential decay. New approaches are needed. ER

REVIEW BY BENNETT L. SHAPIRO. Most literate people in America have by now heard of (and forgotten) the Club of Rome study *The Limits of Growth*. It received an inordinate amount of publicity, virtually all of which emphasized the rather gloomy, not to say macabre, future in store for mankind if certain trends continue, e.g. population growth, pollution, food and resource shortages. This study was, in turn, based on Jay Forrester's earlier work *World Dynamics* (chapter four of which is called "The Limits of Growth").

World Dynamics is the most recent and sophisticated example of the trend toward rationalization of social dynamics that has been developing in the post-war period. The chief difference between Forrester's work and that of most of his predecessors is that he has made more of an impression on the public consciousness. This is, in itself, extremely significant. Consider that the fundamental thesis he is promoting contains a truly revolutionary view of future planetary development. He is saying that the exponential growth that we have come to associate with the only religion of modern times (the idea of progress) cannot continue. Our messianic efforts to extend the blessings of the faith to all humanity lead nowhere but to hell. The simplistic and somewhat hysterical reduction of the issues to a growth versus no growth dichotomy is typical of the thinking of the vested interests of corporate capitalism. (It appears somewhat ironic that Forrester is Professor of Management at M.I.T.'s Sloan Graduate School.) The obvious answers will not suffice. We must begin in earnest a fundamental analysis of our society in terms of the institutions and policies that shape our current practice of spastic reaction to the daily emergency. The case is here presented for superseding this pattern with a more profound understanding of social dynamics using computer simulations and modeling as a prime tool.

Over the last several decades interest in economic development, population growth, and the world environment has expanded rapidly. As world-wide stresses have increased, many individuals and organizations have begun to study and to influence the changing aspects of the world situation. But it seems fair to observe that most of the activity has been addressed to separate facets of the world system. Little has yet been done to show how the many actions and forces are affecting one another to produce the total consequences that we observe. Now however, many persons are coming to believe that the interactions within the whole are more important than the sum of the separate parts. This book was undertaken as one step toward showing how the behavior of the world system results from mutual interplay between its demographic, industrial, and agricultural subsystems.

It is certain that resource shortage, pollution, crowding, food failure, or some other equally powerful force will limit population and industrialization if persuasion and psychological factors do not. Exponential growth cannot continue forever. Our greatest immediate challenge is how we guide the transition from growth to equilibrium. There are many possible mechanisms of growth suppression. That some one or combination will occur is inevitable. Unless we come to understand and to choose, the social system by its internal processes will choose for us. The internal mechanisms for terminating exponential growth appear highly undesirable. Unless we understand and act soon, we may be overwhelmed by a social and economic system we have created but cannot control.

Initially the characteristics of social systems began to emerge from the modeling of corporate policy structures. Often we have gone into a corporation which is having severe and well-known difficulties. The difficulties can be major and obvious like falling market share, or low profitability, or instability of employment. Such difficulties are known throughout the company and by anyone outside who reads the management press. The first step in understanding such a company is to discuss with people in key decision points the actions they are taking to solve the problem. Generally speaking we find that people perceive correctly their immediate environment. They know what they are trying to accomplish. They know the crises which will force certain actions. They are sensitive to the power structure of the organization, to traditions, and to

their own personal goals and welfare. In general, when circumstances are conducive to frank disclosure, people can state what they are doing and can give rational reasons for their action. In a troubled company, people are usually trying in good conscience and to the best of their abilities to solve the major difficulties. From such an organization one can take the policies that are well-known and are being followed at the various points in the organization. The policies are being followed on the presumption that they will alleviate the difficulties. These policies are then combined into a computer model to show the consequences of how the policies interact with one another. In many instances it then emerges that the known policies describe a system which actually causes the troubles. In other words, the known and intended practices of the organization are often fully sufficient to create the difficulty, regardless of what happens outside the company or in the marketplace. In fact, a downward spiral develops in which the presumed solution makes the difficulty worse and thereby causes redoubling of the presumed solution so that matters become still worse.

Complete diagram of the world model interrelating the five level variables—population, natural resources, capital investment, capital-investment-in-agriculture fraction, and pollution.

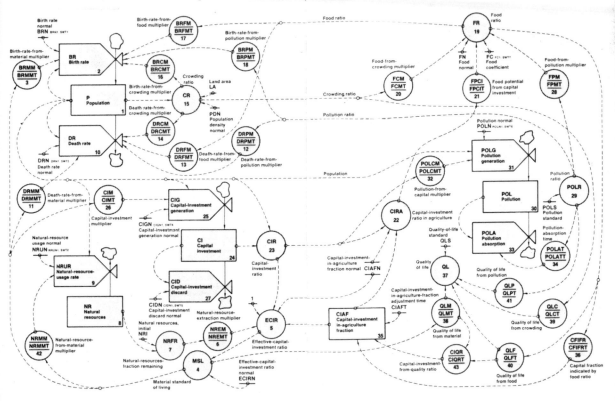

126. Innovations: Scientific, Technological and Social

DENNIS GABOR. Oxford University Press, Ely House, 37 Dover Street, London W1X 4AH; 1970; £0.75; 113 pp.

This little book lists and describes 137 recent innovations (scientific, technological, and social): such developments as fission power, petroleum technology, supersonic air transport, automation in the home, transplants, teleshopping, student violence, lifelong education. The point of it all is that it is a discontinuous world, one in which new facts of science and technology constantly demand the evolution of frameworks within which they may be properly considered.

One lesson in this book is the impossibility of prediction. In the discontinuity of perception affected by rapid technological change, any dogmatic prediction will in a very short time place the " futurist " in the position of the librarian who classifies experience with one-hundred-year-old subject categories.

Gabor won a Nobel Prize for his development of holography photography. JB

When *Homo sapiens* appeared on the Earth, more or less in his present shape, innovation began. Early Man was equipped with the same sort of brain that later could write the *Principia Philosophiae Naturalis* and the *Principia Mathematica,* but the brain was almost empty. First had to come the greatest of all inventions: language; then tools, weapons, and a primitive social organization suitable for agriculture and the domestication of animals. Then, much later, came writing, and what we now call history.

Traffic jams and deaths on the road or in the air, to which we could add the problems of pollution of the air, the rivers, the lakes, and the sea, take us to what is probably the most important difference between the inventions of the past and of the present day. *The most important and urgent problems of the technology of today are no longer the satisfactions of primary needs or of archetypal wishes, but the reparation of the evils and damages wrought by the technology of yesterday.*

---

55. *Programmed mechanical hands*

The most advanced of these robots is the UNIMATE (Consolidated Controls Corporation, Bethel, Connecticut, U.S.A.) The inventor is George Devol. It has motions humanoid in form, simulating the waist, shoulder, elbow, wrist and fingers, with a great variety of 'hands'. The 'hand' is taken once, slowly, through the operations which it must perform; afterward, the speed can be set, and the robot will go through a series of up to 200 separate steps at any speed, and for any time. The steps are stored in a magnetic memory, the actuation is hydraulic. For instance, the UNIMATE can pick up an ingot from a rack or chute, put it in a die casting machine, pull out the still red-hot casting and place it in another rack, in an empty place, taking account of the castings which it has previously put in, until the rack is full. In this and many other applications, it achieves a consistency beyond that of the best human operator, 24 hours per day. Workers and even labour unions in the United States have, surprisingly, taken kindly to this robot. They consider it as a willing slave, not as a blackleg.

---

67. *Wide-angle stereoscopic projection*

Leonardo da Vinci, and many imaginative writers after him, dreamt of a picture which surrounds the viewer from all sides, so that he is in the midst of the happenings. It has been mentioned before that such a system, with the viewer freely moving, comes up against a formidable information-bottleneck. But if the viewer keeps still, or if he moves only a little, one has to present him with only twice the information which he is capable of taking in with one eye, and this can be accommodated in two 35-mm films. A device which can accomplish this consists of a projector with two wide-angle ('fisheye') lenses, the same as the objectives through which the films were taken, so that the distortion is compensated; every ray goes back in the projection where it came from in the taking. The screen is almost hemispherical, and sends back every ray from the left-eye projector into a strip sufficiently wide to cover the left eye of the viewer who sits below the projector, and similarly for the right eye. This system is under active development. It ought to be a teaching device of unmatched power.

---

100. *Creation of some sort of artificial life*

When Wohler synthesized the first organic compound, urea, in 1828, there were some people who believed that the next step would be the *homunculus*. After 150 years of progress we have become more modest in our aims; we would be satisfied with some sort of virus, or even a self-reproducing molecule. Such a discovery would have a rather exceptional standing in biology; it would be a scientific achievement of the highest order, but for the start at least without great social consequences. (In old times, when religions were interpreted dogmatically, the impact would have been tremendous.) The opinions show a remarkable consensus.

It is a commonplace in our days that social development has not kept up with the explosive progress of science and technology. It was probably J. M. Keynes who put the chief reason for this into clear, quantitative terms. Very few people change their view and values after their school days. Something like twenty-five years elapse between the university and the graduate obtaining a position of consequence. If during this time the technological basis of society has significantly changed, the conditions are given for a serious mismatch. The great originator of the quantum theory, Max Planck, has expressed a similar thought: 'Theories win recognition not so much by acceptance, as by the dying off of their opponents'. This is rather too pessimistic, and in fact if the time lag in science and technology were as great as in the institutions, we would have far less of a problem.

291

127. The Economics of Abundance: A Non-Inflationary Future

ROBERT THEOBALD. Pitman Publishing Corp., 6 East 43rd Street, New York, N.Y. 10017; 1970; or *Real Time*. $5.95; 151 pp.

Our economic thinking is scarcity oriented to such a degree that even the contemplation of an era of abundance demands a new conceptual framework and terminology. Theobald calls it "socioeconomics," and proceeds to trace the relationship between our economic vulnerability and the rise of cybernetics. His conclusion: we can no longer think of "economics" as being a subject unconnected to the fabric of our social structures and societal systems. JB

The world's abundance-economic systems therefore require immediate change. We face a system break—a change from one system, in which a particular set of understandings and rules worked effectively, to a fundamentally new system, which requires new understandings and policies. Mankind has already undergone two such system breaks in the past—one from hunting and gathering to agriculture, and the other from agriculture to industry. The present, third system break is from industry to cybernation: the combination of men with machine systems. Controlling and benefiting from cybernation will be possible only if we learn to communicate more honestly and efficiently than we do today.

The main socioeconomic reinforcement for scarcity economics is the measuring systems that we have created to evaluate "success" and "failure." We measure success by the rate of growth in Gross National Product, failure by high unemployment rates. In abundance regions it is still essentially assumed, despite all the evidence to the contrary, that if a high rate of growth is being attained, improvement in educational, social, and ethical patterns will occur. While support for this view has admittedly diminished following the social developments which have accompanied the economic boom of the sixties, we have not yet abandoned this belief.

John Cage, the artist, has stated that "Mea-surements measure measuring means." In other words, what and how we measure explains more about our culture than statistical changes in the measurements. We measure economic growth because we have been convinced that it is the important reality. It is only recently that we have begun to search for new measurements which will enable us to discover the implications of changes in our social relations, in our educational skills, and in our ethics. We are now learning that improvements in these patterns do not necessarily occur if there is economic growth. Indeed, we have increasingly clear evidence that economic growth may be negatively correlated with societal, educational and ethical changes.

It is now argued, with increasing frequency, that economics has become an obsolete science, that policies for the emerging era cannot be formulated with the industrial-era tool of economics, that economics is adapted only to scarcity conditions. Instead of challenging economists to extend their theory to cover the new realities, this kind of criticism states flatly that economics has become inapplicable, and implicitly assumes that economic thinking will simply "go away" because it has been dismissed as irrelevant.

This view ignores the existing reality of economic dominance of our present thought patterns. A time will come when we are so accustomed to a state of abundance that we are unaware of its existence; but in order to reach that time we must become highly aware of abundance now. This can only be done if we develop out of economics into · socioeconomics. Scarcity-economic thinking has not automatically diminished in the face of negating reality and will not do so; it must be shown that a serious consideration of what we already know in economics will force us to move on to socioeconomics.

The science of cybernetics is based on a simple core statement. Any social, or other, system must be able to adapt to changing circumstances if it is to survive. There are two critical steps in this continuing process; one can start examining the process from either point:

1. There must be the possibility for effective decision making. This requires that some parts of the system take the responsibility for decisions about the situation as it confronts them. The more flexible the system, the more the decision about responsibility for action will necessarily be based on self-perception and self-motivation.

We can contrast the system involved in the " decision " of a tree to grow its leaves in the spring with the decision of the society to do something about pollution. In the case of the tree, an automatic mechanism is triggered by the warmer weather or some other change in the seasonal pattern. (If the weather is prematurely hot early in the year, the tree may " decide " wrongly.) In the case of pollution, some individuals must decide that it is *their* responsibility to alert the society to the dangers of pollution. Until they begin to do so, they cannot be certain that the task is essential or that the channels exist to make possible effective communication.

2. Decisions always entail consequences. *Even* if the decision made is ideal and provides a maximum favorable response (a situation seldom realized in complex human systems), the decision will necessarily change the initial situation, and further action will inevitably be required.

In the more probable case, the decision will have been less than ideal, and there will be a necessity for correction of the original decision. In either case, *accurate* feedback will be required to permit evaluation of the new situation brought into existence by the decision.

The channels for feedback may be fixed, as in the case of a tree, or they may be open and uncertain, as when people are trying to draw the attention of the society to the issue of pollution. Those engaging in drawing the attention of the society to new issues will have to evaluate highly contradictory feedback patterns if they are to determine the effectiveness of their previous action. It must be particularly noted that in today's conditions the problems of decision makers in evaluating feedback are made even more complicated because of its deliberate distortion.

128. Rapid Population Growth: Consequences and Policy Implications (Volume I: Summary and Recommendations)

Prepared by the National Academy of Sciences. The Johns Hopkins Press, Baltimore, Md. 21218; 1971; or *Real Time*. $2.45; 105 pp.

It is now common knowledge that the twentieth century has seen, and will continue to witness, a meteoric rise in human population. In 1970 there were approximately three and one-half billion people on earth. That figure is expected to double by the end of the twentieth century.

What are the economic implications of seven billion people? What happens to society and the quality of life when population increases at such rapid rates? The Agency for International Development commissioned the National Academy of Sciences to explore some potential answers and scenarios. ER

Many people believe, as Malthus did at first, though he later changed his mind, that the numbers of human beings will always increase up to a level set by the available food supply, or by enemies and disease. " Gigantic, inevitable famine stalks in the rear of misery and vice to limit the numbers of mankind." Even though death rates today are lower than they have ever been, and the proportion of the world's human population that is seriously malnourished is probably less than at any time since the Old Stone Age, the belief is widespread that uncontrolled population growth in the earth's poor countries is leading to catastrophe. It is possible, however, to take a different view, based on what we know about the history of human populations and on the behavior of many people at the present time—a view that social inventions will lead to a deliberate limitation of fertility by individual couples. At the same time the technical potentialities exist, not only to feed all human beings, but greatly to improve the quality of human diets, at least until the end of this century. During the next 20 years no change in human fertility patterns can have much effect on the dimensions of the world food problem. And the natural resources available to present technology are sufficient to allow a vast improvement in the standard of living of all the people who will inhabit the earth 20 to 30 years from now. This is not to say that such an improvement in diets or standard of living will inevitably occur. It will depend on the improvement of social and economic institutions, and on the growth of cooperation and interdependence among the peoples of the world.

MEASURING CHANGES IN QUALITY OF LIFE

Measuring changes in the quality of life should take account of both improvements and deteriorations. It should be a *weighted* average taking account of differences in preferences and reactions at specified levels of cost, and perhaps of intensities of such preferences (which surely

TABLE 2

Population Densities in Certain Developed and Less Developed Countries

	Population 1965	Total Area	Cultivated Area	Density on Total Area	Density on Cultivated Land
	Millions	Millions of Hectares		Persons/Hectare	
LESS DEVELOPED COUNTRIES					
People's Republic of China	730	956	145	0.7	5
India	483	304	162	1.6	3
Pakistan	115	95	29	1.2	4
Indonesia	105	149	18	0.7	5.8
Philippines	32	30	11	1.1	2.9
Thailand	31	51	10	0.6	3.1
Republic of China (Taiwan)	12	3.6	1	3.3	12
Ceylon	11	6.6	2	1.7	5.5
Ghana	8	24	5	0.3	1.6
Madagascar	6	59	3	0.1	2
Tanzania	11	94	9	0.1	1.2
United Arab Republic	30	100	3	0.3	10
Mexico	41	197	11	0.2	3.7
Brazil	81	851	19	0.1	4.3
Colombia	16	114	5	0.1	3.2
DEVELOPED COUNTRIES					
Soviet Union	234	2240	230	0.1	1
United States	195	936	185	0.2	1
Japan	98	37	6	2.7	16.3
France	49	55	21	0.9	2.2
West Germany	57	25	8	2.3	7.1
United Kingdom	54	24	7	2.2	7.7

Sources: (col. 1) *Population Reference Bureau Data Sheet*. Washington, D.C., December 1965; (col. 2) United Nations *Demographic Yearbook, 1965*. New York, 1966; (cols. 3, 5) United Nations Food and Agricultural Organization, *Production Yearbook*, Vol. 23, 1969. Rome, 1969. Col. 4 calculated from cols. 1 and 2.

would have a very real effect in a market situation).

It is one thing to judge that things are "bad" and quite another to judge that they are "worse." As has been suggested, there is little evidence on the second, especially as one looks further and further back and is careful to add up the pluses and minuses. There is, on the other hand, widening and justified attention to how "bad" matters are in terms of quality.

Partial answers can be obtained by considering deterioration of specific *aspects* of life. Although good measurements still are scarce, air pollution, water pollution, urban density, overcrowding of recreation areas, etc., as evidenced in recent years, suggest a worsening. To the best of our knowledge, these conditions have not as yet become irreversible (except for vanished species); that is, they are, at a cost, amenable to treatment by both new technology and changes in incentives and institutions. It is perhaps worth noting, however, that the one area probably least amenable to such treatment is deterioration in the "space-solitude-privacy" complex due to sheer rise in numbers of people (from the subway rush to the crowded recreation spot), a phenomenon to which there is as yet no promising approach. This statement is not contradicted by the likelihood that life in a metropolis can provide more social privacy than in a small town. There are a few well-developed devices for dealing with the "overload" of environmental stress caused by numbers and proximity. But the intrusions, especially those of a physical kind, become harder to ward off, notwithstanding adaptive behavior. And they surely are a factor in the quality of life.

129. Future Shock

ALVIN TOFFLER. The Bodley Head Ltd., 9 Bow Street, London WC2E 7AL; (H) 1970; £2.50; or Pan Books Ltd., Cavaye Place, London SW10 9PG; (P) 1973; £0.50; 505 pp.

One of the few permanent concepts left is that of change. How much is enough? The multiplicity of futures proliferating in the overloaded present seems quite out of hand, quite unmanageable. Is it a question of difficulties in the "real future" or is the problem that of information overload in the present? Toffler, a former editor at *Fortune* and "underground" sociologist, has put together a readable book on the collision with tomorrow. JB

A strange new society is apparently erupting in our midst. Is there a way to understand it, to shape its development? How can we come to terms with it?

Much that now strikes us as incomprehensible would be far less so if we took a fresh look at the racing rate of change that makes reality seem, sometimes, like a kaleidoscope run wild. For the acceleration of change does not merely buffet industries or nations. It is a concrete force that reaches deep into our personal lives, compels us to act out new roles, and confronts us with the danger of a new and powerfully upsetting psychological disease. This new disease can be called "future shock," and a knowledge of its sources and symptoms helps explain many things that otherwise defy rational analysis.

How do we *know* that change is accelerating? There is, after all, no absolute way to measure change. In the awesome complexity of the universe, even within any given society, a virtually infinite number of streams of change occur simultaneously. All "things"—from the tiniest virus to the greatest galaxy—are, in reality, not things at all, but processes. There is no static point, no nirvanalike un-change, against which to measure change. Change is, therefore, necessarily relative.

That man-thing relationships are growing more and more temporary may be illustrated by examining the culture surrounding the little girl who trades in her doll. This child soon learns that Barbie dolls are by no means the only physical objects that pass into and out of her young life at a rapid clip. Diapers, bibs, paper napkins, Kleenex, towels, non-returnable soda bottles—all are used up quickly in her home and ruthlessly eliminated. Corn muffins come in baking tins that are thrown away after one use. Spinach is encased in plastic sacks that can be dropped into a pan of boiling water for heating, and then thrown away. TV dinners are cooked and often served on throw-away trays. Her home is a large processing machine through which objects flow, entering and leaving, at a faster and faster rate of speed. From birth on, she is inextricably embedded in a throw-away culture.

The increase in travel brings with it a sharp increase in the number of transient, casual relationships with fellow passengers, with hotel clerks, taxi drivers, airline reservation people, with porters, maids, waiters, with colleagues and friends of friends, with customs officials, travel agents and countless others. The greater the mobility of the individual, the greater the number of brief, face-to-face encounters, human contacts, each one a realtionship of sorts, fragmentary and, above all, compressed in time. (Such contacts appear natural and unimportant to us. We seldom stop to consider how few of the sixty-six billion human beings who preceded us on the planet ever experienced this high rate of transience in their human relationships.)

––––––––––––––

One of the more fantastic possibilities is that man will be able to make biological carbon copies of himself. Through a process known as "cloning" it will be possible to grow from the nucleus of an adult cell a new organism that has the same genetic characteristics of the person contributing the cell nucleus. The resultant human "copy" would start life with a genetic endowment identical to that of the donor, although cultural differences might thereafter alter the personality or physical development of the clone.

––––––––––––––

Communalism runs counter to the pressure for ever greater geographical and social mobility generated by the thrust toward super-industrialism. It presupposes groups of people who "stay put." For this reason, communal experiments will first proliferate among those in the society who are free from the industrial discipline—the retired population, the young, the dropouts, the students, as well as among self-employed professional and technical people. Later, when advanced technology and information systems make it possible for much of the work of society to be done at home via computer-telecommunication hookups, communalism will become feasible for larger numbers.

––––––––––––––

Every society faces not merely a succession of *probable* futures, but an array of *possible* futures, and a conflict over *preferable* futures. The management of change is the effort to convert certain possibles into probables, in pursuit of agreed-on preferables. Determining the probable calls for a science of futurism. Delineating the possible calls for an art of futurism. Defining the preferable calls for a politics of futurism.